60 0206808 3

AF845290

'Bath Librar

The Political Economy of European Employment

The Political Economy of European Employment focuses on the emergence of employment policy as a transnational political issue and examines unemployment in Europe in the context of globalization and the implementation of Economic and Monetary Union in the EU.

The authors address the transformation of the global economy over the past decades and consider the theoretical debates surrounding European integration. They analyse how various social and political forces, both national and transnational, have addressed the challenges facing the European economies and how this interplay has influenced the emerging EU social and employment policies. Finally, the focus turns to variations within the European Union and how to conceptualize the articulation of global, European and national dynamics.

The book will interest students and researchers of International Political Economy, Politics, Economics, European Studies, Public Policy and Industrial Sociology.

Henk Overbeek is Associate Professor of International Relations at the Vrije Universiteit, the Netherlands, and Adjunct Professor of International Relations at Webster University, also in the Netherlands.

RIPE Series in Global Political Economy

Series Editors: Louise Amoore *(University of Newcastle, UK)*, Randall Germain *(Carleton University, Canada)* and Rorden Wilkinson *(University of Manchester, UK)*

Formerly edited by Otto Holman, Marianne H. Marchand *(Research Centre for International Political Economy, University of Amsterdam)*, Henk Overbeek *(Free University, Amsterdam)* and Marianne Franklin *(University of Amsterdam)*

This series, published in association with the *Review of International Political Economy*, provides a forum for current debates in international political economy. The series aims to cover all the central topics in IPE and to present innovative analyses of emerging topics. The titles in the series seek to transcend a state-centred discourse and focus on three broad themes:

- the nature of the forces driving globalization forward
- resistance to globalization
- the transformation of the world order.

The series comprises two strands:

The *RIPE Series in Global Political Economy* aims to address the needs of students and teachers, and the titles will be published in hardback and paperback. Titles include:

Transnational Classes and International Relations
Kees van der Pijl

Gender and Global Restructuring:
Sightings, Sites and Resistances
Edited by Marianne H. Marchand and Anne Sisson Runyan

Global Political Economy
Contemporary Theories
Edited by Ronen Palan

Ideologies of Globalization
Contending Visions of a New World Order
Mark Rupert

The Clash within Civilisations
Coming to Terms with Cultural Conflicts
Dieter Senghaas

Global Unions?
Theory and Strategies of Organized Labour in the Global Political Economy
Edited by Jeffrey Harrod and Robert O'Brien

Political Economy of a Plural World
Critical Reflections on Power, Morals and Civilizations
Robert Cox with Michael Schechter

A Critical Rewriting of Global Political Economy
Integrating Reproductive, Productive and Virtual Economies
V. Spike Peterson

Contesting Globalization
Space and Place in the World Economy
André C. Drainville

Global Institutions and Development
Framing the World?
Edited by Morten Bøås and Desmond McNeill

Routledge/RIPE Studies in Global Political Economy is a forum for innovative new research intended for a high-level specialist readership, and the titles will be available in hardback only. Titles include:

1 Globalization and Governance*
Edited by Aseem Prakash and Jeffrey A. Hart

2 Nation-States and Money
The Past, Present and Future of National Currencies
Edited by Emily Gilbert and Eric Helleiner

3 The Global Political Economy of Intellectual Property Rights
The New Enclosures?
Christopher May

4 Integrating Central Europe
EU expansion and Poland, Hungary and the Czech Republic
Otto Holman

5 Capitalist Restructuring, Globalisation and the Third Way
Lessons from the Swedish Model
J. Magnus Ryner

6 Transnational Capitalism and the Struggle over European Integration
Bastiaan van Apeldoorn

7 World Financial Orders
An Historical International Political Economy
Paul Langley

8 The Changing Politics of Finance in Korea and Thailand
From Deregulation to Debacle
Xiaoke Zhang

9 Anti-Immigrantism in Western Democracies
Statecraft, Desire and the Politics of Exclusion
Roxanne Lynn Doty

10 The Political Economy of European Employment
European Integration and the Transnationalization of the (Un)Employment Question
Edited by Henk Overbeek

11 Rethinking International Political Economy
Edited by Mary Ann Tétreault, Robert A. Denemark, Kenneth P. Thomas and Kurt Burch

12 Rediscovering International Relations Theory
Matthew Davies and Michael Niemann

13 International Trade and Developing Countries
Bargaining and Coalitions in the GATT & WTO
Amrita Narlikar

* *Also available in paperback*

The Political Economy of European Employment

European integration and the transnationalization of the (un)employment question

Edited by Henk Overbeek

Routledge
Taylor & Francis Group
LONDON AND NEW YORK

UNIVERSITY OF BATH LIBRARY
18 MAR 2024
Withdrawn
20 17 JUL 2003 7
331.02(4)

First published 2003 by Routledge
11 New Fetter Lane, London EC4P 4EE

Simultaneously published in the USA and Canada
by Routledge
29 West 35th Street, New York, NY 10001

Routledge is an imprint of the Taylor & Francis Group

© 2003 Henk Overbeek for selection and editorial material; individual chapters the contributors

Typeset in Baskerville by Taylor & Francis Books Ltd
Printed and bound in Great Britain by MPG Books Ltd, Bodmin

All rights reserved. No part of this book may be reprinted or reproduced or utilized in any form or by any electronic, mechanical, or other means, now known or hereafter invented, including photocopying and recording, or in any information storage or retrieval system, without permission in writing from the publishers.

British Library Cataloguing in Publication Data
A catalogue record for this book is available from the British Library

Library of Congress Cataloging in Publication Data
The political economy of European employment: European integration and the transnationalization of the (un)employment question / edited by Henk Overbeek.
Includes bibliographical references and index.
1. Labour market–European Union countries. 2. Unemployment–European Union countries. 3. Labor policy–European Union countries. 4. Globalization–Economic aspects–European Union countries. 5. Europe–Economic integration. I. Overbeek, Henk.

HD5764.A6P635 2003
331.12'042'094–dc21 2002155136

ISBN 0–415–26872–9

Contents

List of illustrations

Tables

Figures

Notes on contributors

Uwe Becker is senior lecturer in political science at the University of Amsterdam; he received his PhD from the University of Amsterdam. His research interests include comparative politics in historical perspective, political economy and social theory. Recent publications include *Dutch Society and Politics in Historical Perspective* (editor, 1998, in Dutch); *European Democracies. Freedom, Equality and Sovereignty in Practice* (1999, in Dutch; German translation forthcoming); book chapters and articles on the Dutch political economy, among others in the *Journal of European Social Policy*, *New Political Economy* and *Industrial and Economic Democracy*.

Hans-Jürgen Bieling is Junior Professor (Hochschuldozent), Research Group on European Integration (FEG) at the Department of Political Science, Philipps-Universität Marburg (Germany), from where he received his PhD. Bieling's main fields of interest are European integration, social theory and political theory. His recent publications include *Flexibler Kapitalismus: Analysen, Kritik und Politische Praxis* (co-editor, 2001), *Die Konfiguration Europas: Dimensionen einer kritischen Integrationstheorie* (co-editor, 2000), *Dynamiken sozialer Spaltung und Ausgrenzung – Gesellschaftstheorien und Zeitdiagnosen* (2000) and *Wohlfahrtsstaat und Arbeitslosigkeit in Westeuropa. Neun Länder im Vergleich* (co-editor, 1997).

Emma Cerviño is a researcher, Centre for Advanced Study in the Social Sciences, Juan March Institute, Madrid; her research interest is the impact of changes in the labour market on trade union strategy.

Bob Jessop is Professor of Sociology, Lancaster University (Great Britain); he received his PhD from the University of Cambridge. Bob Jessop has written widely on state theory, social theory, political economy (especially the regulation approach, Fordism, and post-Fordism), post-war British politics, entrepreneurial cities and their governance, and welfare state restructuring. He is currently researching the restructuring of welfare regimes in Europe. His publications include *The Future of the Capitalist State* (2002), *Strategic Choice and Path-Dependency in Post-Socialism* (co-editor, 1996), *State Theory: Putting the Capitalist State in Its Place* (1990), *Thatcherism: A Tale of Two Nations* (1988), *Nicos Poulantzas: Marxist Theory and Political Strategy* (1985) and *The Capitalist State: Marxist Theories and Methods* (1982).

Henk Overbeek is Associate Professor in International Relations, Vrije Universiteit, Amsterdam (Netherlands); he received his PhD from the Universiteit van Amsterdam. Overbeek's interests are in international political economy and European integration. His publications include *Neo-liberal Hegemony and the Political Economy of European Restructuring* (co-editor, 1998), *Global Capitalism and National Decline* (1990) and *Restructuring Hegemony in the Global Political Economy* (editor, 1993). Henk Overbeek is co-editor of the RIPE Series in Global Political Economy (Routledge).

Magnus Ryner is Lecturer in Politics, University of Birmingham; he received his PhD from York University, Toronto. Ryner's research interest is on capitalist restructuring, transnationalization, and welfare capitalism in Europe. His publications include *Capitalist Restructuring, Globalisation and the Third Way: Lessons from the Swedish Model* (2002), *A Ruined Fortress? Neoliberal Hegemony and Transformation in Europe* (co-editor, 2003), *Neo-liberal Hegemony and the Political Economy of European Restructuring* (co-editor, 1998) and contributions to *Economic and Industrial Democracy*.

Thorsten Schulten is a Research Fellow at the Wirtschafts- und Sozialwissenschaftliches Institut (WSI) within the Hans Böckler Foundation, Düsseldorf (Germany). He is currently working on his PhD on Solidaristic Pay Policy in Europe. Schulten's research interest is on political economy of European integration and European industrial relations. He has been a frequent contributor to *Economic and Industrial Democracy*, *European Journal of Industrial Relations* and *WSI-Mitteilungen*, and he is co-editor of *Collective Bargaining under the Euro* (2001).

Leila Simona Talani is Lecturer in European Politics, University of Bath; she received her PhD from the European University Institute, Florence. Talani also teaches at the European Institute of the London School of Economics. Her research interests currently focus on globalization and illegal migration, with a special attention to Spanish and Italian public policy responses to illegal migration from the Middle East and Northern Africa area. Her publications include *Betting for and against EMU: Who Wins and Who Loses in Italy and in the UK from the Process of European Monetary Integration* (2000).

Stefan Tidow is a Research Fellow, Research Group on European Integration (FEG) at the Department of Political Science, Philipps-Universität Marburg (Germany); he received his PhD from the Philipps-Universität in Marburg. His main fields of interest are European integration, social policy and political theory. Tidow published the FEG Working Paper *Europäische Beschäftigungspolitik. Die Entstehung eines neuen Politikfeldes: Ursachen, Hintergründe und Verlauf des politischen Prozesses* (1998). He has published in the *Blätter für deutsche und internationale Politik* (1999), *Zeitschrift für Sozialreform* (1999) and has contributed to *Arbeitsmarkt- und Beschäftigungspolitik in der EU* (Platzer, 2000).

Brigitte Young is Professor of Political Economy and Gender Studies at the Wilhelms-Universität in Münster (Germany) and Advisor to the Commission of Enquiry of the German Parliament on 'Globalization of the World Economy – Challenges and Answers'; she received her PhD from University of Wisconsin (Madison). Her research interests include globalization, European integration, international political economy and feminist political economy. She is currently working on financial crises and human security. Her publications include *Gender, Globalization, and Democratization* (co-editor, 2001), *Triumph of the Fatherland. German Unification and the Marginalization of Women* (1999) and a special issue (as editor) of *PROKLA* on Globalization and Gender (no. 111).

Bastiaan van Apeldoorn is Lecturer in International Relations, Vrije Universiteit, Amsterdam; he received his PhD from European University Institute, Florence. Van Apeldoorn's research interests cover various aspects of the political economy of European integration, including processes of transnational class formation in Europe and the transformation of European capitalism. His publications include *Transnational Capitalism and the Struggle over European Integration* (2002), and articles in the *Journal of European Public Policy* (1998), *International Journal of Political Economy* (1998) and *New Political Economy* (2000).

Series editors' preface

This new volume in the *Routledge/RIPE Studies in Global Political Economy* appears at a time characterized by an atmosphere of intense insecurity. Aggressive US unilateralism, aimed at removing unfriendly regimes in so-called rogue states, is one cause of it; the partly related economic downturn is another. People all over the world face the (social and psychological) consequences of jittery stock markets, slackening output and rising unemployment. As this book goes to press, fears over a US attack on Iraq and its effect on oil prices reinforce business gloom and bring the prospect of global recession even closer.

It is a paradox of the age that the problem, and perception, of insecurity is tackled by further increasing it and/or shifting it to other people. The labour market is a case in point. The global economic crisis of restructuring which started in the 1970s has gone hand in hand with a re-commodification of labour, particularly in the European welfare states founded on the Fordist mode of production. In this sense, 'labour market restructuring' is synonymous with a less protected labour force and, thereby, a more insecure one. This increasing labour-market insecurity is euphemistically labelled 'labour-market flexibilization", a process that ranges from external (macroeconomic) flexibilization to internal (enterprise-level) flexibilization. The latter, *inter alia*, includes more lenient parameters for the 'hire-and-fire' conditions of the labour contract. In the European Union member states, this labour-market restructuring has been forced on welfare-state regimes under the terms of monetary unification. Under the criteria of Economic and Monetary Union (EMU), and in the absence of traditional instruments like interest and exchange rate policies, national governments have had to create 'flexible' labour markets in order to correct macroeconomic imbalances. In other words, they have used the workforce as a response to global recession. This policy has been legitimized by the 1997 European Employment Strategy of the European Union and is also at the heart of the more recent Lisbon strategy of economic, social and environmental renewal.

The Political Economy of European Employment. European integration and the transnationalization of the (un)employment question provides an excellent overview and discussion of these issues at the European level over the last two decades. Its focus is on the emergence of employment policy as a political issue; on the role of transnational forces in the making of national and European employment policies; and on the interconnection of the sub-national, national and supranational levels of decision-making in the European Union. As the editor, Henk Overbeek, argues, networks of transnational governance have come into existence which mediate the impact of global capital, commodity *and* labour markets on the national level. The contributions in the volume cover a wide range of topics: the global context of neo-liberal restructuring and the emergence of a European employment policy directed at more flexibility and employability; the role of transnational business in formulating the dominant competitiveness discourse at the European level; the decline of trade unions (e.g. in terms of union density rates) and the shift from demand- to supply-side corporatism; the gender dimension of labour-market restructuring; the impact of European monetary unification (i.e. the so-called convergence race) on national levels of unemployment. The volume also includes several country studies which underscore the (still existing) variations within the European Union. All the case studies discuss the importance of transnational patterns, forces of production and finance on the articulation of the global, the European and the national. An underlying question is how emerging networks of transnational governance, together with the concrete convergence obligations of EMU, are imposing labour-market policy convergence on the governments of Europe. Another – more implicit – issue being addressed here is on how different models of capitalism are converging. Or, to put it another way, how Rhineland capitalism is adjusting to the exigencies of Anglo-Saxon capitalism, *inter alia* as a result of the method of open co-ordination that is so central to the European Employment Strategy.

The editors strongly recommend *The Political Economy of European Employment* because it provides the reader with a wealth of theoretical insights and empirical information which can help make sense of the present crisis of neo-liberal restructuring and the concomitant transformation of labour in Europe. It is essential reading for those interested in the relation between global and European change in the 1980s and 1990s and the formulation and implementation of labour-market policies in a setting of transnational governance in the European Union.

Marianne Franklin
Otto Holman
Marianne H. Marchand

Acknowledgements

This book is the result of a long process. In the course of that process a number of people have contributed to its maturation and it is only right that I should attempt to name the most important ones.

The original idea to work on the theme of European employment issues was conceived by my long-time friend, colleague and conference roommate Otto Holman and myself. Maria Silvia Gatta, doctoral student at the University of Amsterdam, where we both worked at the time, contributed to our initial thinking on the topic. We have had to accept her decision that academic life was not for her, but we have always regretted our loss in that turn of events.

Together Otto and I convened a workshop on the political economy of European unemployment at the 1998 European Consortium for Political Research (ECPR) Joint Sessions at Warwick University, which turned out to be a memorable occasion. Unfortunately several of the participants were unable to participate in this book project, which followed from the workshop. Their contributions to the workshop sessions were nevertheless important for the conceptualization that we develop here. I am grateful to Klaus Armingeon, Janice Bell, Andreas Bieler and John Tomaney for their challenging input into the proceedings.

I am also grateful to Colin Crouch, who could not attend the workshop, and eventually also could not join the book project either, but supported the project in spirit and graciously sent me manuscripts of work he has recently done on the role of the Organization for Economic Co-operation and Development (OECD) in shaping employment policy.

A word of appreciation is also in order to two anonymous referees whose comments have been valuable in designing the final manuscript, and to the editors of this series, as well as to Heidi Bagtazo and Craig Fowley at Routledge, whose help and support have been priceless.

A special word of thanks is due to Otto Holman. After I moved from the University of Amsterdam to the Free University in 1999, our work rhythms gradually diverged. In the end, we agreed to a division of labour that implied that I would edit the unemployment book, while Otto would edit another book, a 'lovechild' of his he has been thinking about for a long time. Unfortunately, due to the pressures of work Otto had to abolish the plan to contribute to this book. Through no fault of his it took me much longer than expected to complete the work. The project of which this book is the product is nevertheless as much Otto's as it is that of the present authors or of myself, and for that contribution I am extraordinarily grateful.

Of course, I also need to thank my fellow authors. Some were in this project from the beginning, others joined at some later point in time, but all have had to endure the delays, for which they were mostly not responsible. For your professionalism, patience and, above all, collegial solidarity I am most thankful. Naturally, all remaining errors and deficiencies in the final composition of the book are solely my responsibility.

Finally, without the love and support of my family I would be unable to function. Thank you, Bart, David and Ingrid!

List of abbreviations

ABI	Acuerdo Básico Interconfederal
AMI	Acuerdo Marco Interconfederal
ANE	Acuerdo Nacional de Empleo
BDI	Bundesverband der Deutschen Industrie
BEPG	Broad Economic Policy Guidelines
BOE	Boletín Oficial del Estado
BP	British Petroleum
CAD	computer assisted design
CAG	Competitiveness Advisory Group
CAM	computer assisted manufacturing
CBI	Confederation of British Industry
CBS	Centraal Bureau voor de Statistiek
CCOO	Comisiones Obreras
CEC	Commission of the European Communities
CEEP	Centre of European Enterprises with Public Participation and of General Economic Interest
CEO	chief executive officer
CEOE	Confederación Española de Organizaciones Empresariales
CESOS	Centro Studi Economici Sociali e Sindacali
CGG	Commission on Global Governance
CGIL	Confederazione Generale Italiana del Lavoro
CGT	Confédération Générale du Travail
CISL	Confederazione Italiana Sindacati Lavoratori
CNV	Christelijk Nationaal Vakverbond
CoR	Committee of the Regions
CPB	Centraal Plan Bureau
DC	Democrazia Cristiana
DG	Directorate-General (of the European Commission)
DGB	Deutsche Gewerkschaftsbund
DTI	Department of Trade and Industry
EC	European Community; European Commission
ECB	European Central Bank
ECOFIN	Council of Economics and Finance Ministers

ECPR	European Consortium for Political Research
EEC	European Economic Community
EIB	European Investment Bank
EMF	European Metalworkers' Federation
EMS	European Monetary System
EMU	Economic and Monetary Union
EP	European Parliament
ERM	exchange-rate mechanism
ERT	European Round Table of Industrialists
ESC	Economic and Social Committee
ESF	European Social Fund
ETUC	European Trade Union Confederation
EU	European Union
FDI	foreign direct investment
FNV	Federatie Nederlandse Vakbeweging
FRG	Federal Republic of Germany
G7	Group of Seven (largest capitalist economies: USA, Japan, Germany, France, Italy, UK, Canada)
G8	G7 plus Russian Federation
GATT	General Agreement on Tariffs and Trade
GDP	gross domestic product
GDR	German Democratic Republic
GSP	Growth and Stability Pact
HRM	human resources management
ICT	information and communication technology
IGC	Inter-Governmental Conference
ILO	International Labour Organization
IMF	International Monetary Fund
IT	information technology
KWNS	Keynesian welfare national state
KWS	Keynesian welfare state
LO	Landsorganisationen i Sverige
M&A	mergers and acquisitions
NAFTA	North American Free Trade Agreement
NAIRU	non-accelerating inflation rate of unemployment
NAP	National Action Plan
NIDL	New International Division of Labour
OECD	Organization for Economic Co-operation and Development
PCE	Partido Comunista de España
PCI	Partito Comunista Italiano
PP	Partido Popular
PSI	Partito Socialista Italiano
PSOE	Partido Socialista Obrero Español
PSP	Propuesta Sindical Prioritaria
PvdA	Partij van de Arbeid

SAF	Sveriges Arbetsgivareförbund
SAP	Sveriges socialdemokratiska arbetarparti
SCP	Sociaal en Cultureel Planbureau
SER	Sociaal-Economische Raad
SEU	Social Exclusion Unit
SPD	Sozialdemokratische Partei Deutschlands
SSHRCC	Social Sciences and Humanities Research Council of Canada
SWPR	Schumpeterian workfare post-national regime
SWS	Schumpeterian workfare state
TEN	Trans-European Networks
TEU	Treaty on European Union
TNC	transnational corporation
UCD	Unión de Centro Democrático
UGT	Unión General de Trabajadores
UIL	Unione Italiana del Lavoro
UK	United Kingdom (of Great Britain and Northern Ireland)
UNCTAD	United Nations Conference on Trade and Development
UNHCR	United Nations High Commissioner for Refugees
UNICE	Union of Industrial and Employers' Confederations of Europe
US(A)	United States (of America)
WEF	World Economic Forum
WFTC	working families tax credit
WTO	World Trade Organization

1 Transnational political economy and the politics of European (un)employment

Introducing the themes

Henk Overbeek

Unemployment in Europe: why this book, and why now?

Long-term structural unemployment is one of the most serious social crises facing people around the world. In different parts of the world the problem has very different faces.

In Western Europe, the Great Depression of the 1930s with its mass unemployment culminated in the rise of fascism and national socialism and eventually the horrors of Holocaust and world war. The contours of more acceptable forms of full-employment policies were forged in the 1930s in the United States through the New Deal, and were elaborated in wartime Britain by leading Liberals such as Keynes and Beveridge. They laid the foundations for the full-employment policies that were pursued throughout the years 1945–70 by most, if not all, Western European governments, whichever composition the ruling coalition of the moment might have had. Until the early 1970s these policies were successful and basically uncontested. Only in the margins of the debate on the management of the *mixed economy* could one hear the occasional mutterings of diehard neoclassical economists such as Hayek and Friedman warning against the dangers of the inflation that was considered by Keynesians to be an acceptable and manageable price to pay for the maintenance of near-full employment.

And then the fairytale was shattered. Productivity growth stagnated, international competition stiffened, the Bretton Woods system collapsed, profits went down and prices and wages went up, and in 1973–4 the downswing was intensified in all respects by the inflationary and destabilizing effects of the oil crisis. Unemployment increased rapidly, and all of a sudden it became clear that Keynesian demand management might have been a successful instrument to deal with short cyclical movements of the economy, but it was unsuited to deal with a major structural crisis.

The new orthodoxy was defined by the 'village idiots' of earlier decades: monetarism restored unemployment to its earlier role of regulatory mechanism in the management of the economy. One government after another abandoned full employment as its top priority, instead arguing that price stability was the first condition for eventual recovery. Although right-wing parties such as the

British Tories embraced this new orthodoxy first and most enthusiastically, monetarism rapidly extended its ideological hegemony to the leadership (if not the rank and file) of Liberal, Christian Democratic and Social Democratic parties during the late 1970s and 1980s. By the early 1990s even most parties to the left of the Social Democrats had in practice abandoned their adherence to Keynesian demand management (for good analyses of the rise and fall of unemployment as a regulatory mechanism, see Clarke 1988 and Glyn 1995; for broader analyses, see also Layard *et al.* 1991; Layard 1998; Rifkin 1995; Summers 1990; Therborn 1986).

In Western Europe it took until the mid-1990s before unemployment (which had increased to double-digit figures in the recession of the early 1990s) was once again recognized as a social challenge which had the potential to undermine the legitimacy of the neo-liberal project, both in most countries domestically and at the level of the European Union. In the Netherlands the new 'Purple' coalition between Liberals and Social Democrats entered into office in 1994 with one simple slogan: *work, work, work!* Internationally, this renewed recognition of the need to address unemployment was reflected in the publication of the European Commission's White Paper on *Growth, Competitiveness, Employment* (1993) and the *OECD Jobs Study* (1994). The G8 Conference on Growth, Employability and Inclusion of February 1998 and the conclusion of the European Employment Pact by the European Council in Cologne in June 1999 confirmed the political centrality of the employment question in the global political economy.

For a brief period, early successes in a few cases (Ireland, Denmark, the Netherlands) seemed to lead to complacency: these success stories proved that it was possible to devise and implement supply-side strategies (tax advantages for capital, low interest rates, wage moderation, labour market flexibilization) aimed at the creation of new jobs. Employment in these countries expanded rapidly and unemployment was reduced markedly. The European employment strategy seemed designed to stimulate emulation of these policies in the big continental economies (France, and Germany in particular). Here, too, there were some successes in creating new employment, albeit not enough to reduce unemployment to the low levels of the 'miracle' countries.

Subsequent developments, however, have put the feasibility of this strategy into doubt. First, unemployment remained at unusually high levels even during the height of the boom of the late 1990s, most markedly in Germany, which is still struggling with the burdens of unification (see Chapter 10). Second, the nature of many of the new jobs is precarious. The flexibilization of the labour market, and especially the relaxation of redundancy regulations, has made a large segment of the new jobs extraordinarily vulnerable to conjunctural swings (see Chapters 8, 9 and 11). The collapses of the hi-tech sector and related industries and the bursting of the stock market bubble have already highlighted this precariousness of the new employment. Unemployment is once again rising in most European countries, and unrest about what will happen when the boom is over and recession sets in can already be noticed (e.g. European Commission

2001). With the reduction in unemployment benefits and other welfare entitlements of the past years, it is, further, quite possible that a new recession will be intensified by the accelerated drop in social demand associated with welfare state restructuring, even before the effects of the anti-cyclical policies of the European Central Bank are added to the equation. At the time of writing the prospects for the medium term in terms of the growth of employment are bleak at best.

A contribution to the literature on the political economy of (un)employment in Europe is therefore timely. This literature is large and diverse. There is in all cases a preponderance of analyses that approach the issues in question from a comparative perspective, analysing the performance of national systems relative to each other (good examples are Compston 1997; Bieling and Deppe 1997). There are also recent contributions that include at least attention to the employment strategies emerging at the EU level, such as the excellent collection by Nancy Bermeo (2001). There are, in addition, many books dealing with a broader set of issues of social policy and/or monetary union, but these usually do not focus directly or exclusively on the employment question; nor do they usually transcend the comparative framework. Examples of these include Brown and Compton (1994), Hantrais (1995), Iversen *et al.* (2000), Pierson (1995) and Frieden *et al.* (1998). There are, finally, quite a few studies by labour market specialists on aspects of the European labour market and labour market regulation, such as the excellent book by Addison and Siebert (1997).

What distinguishes the present book is, first, the focus on the emergence of employment policy as a political issue, rather than on the causes of and cures for unemployment as such. This book presents an analysis of how employment policy became politicized at the European level, and how this development articulates with the political struggle over employment policy at the national level. As such, this book further distinguishes itself by its attempt to develop a systematic *transnational* approach to the issues at stake. None of the approaches mentioned above shares with *The Political Economy of European Employment* a sustained and systematic effort to move beyond the limitations of the cross-national comparative approach.

These limitations are threefold. First, these approaches tend to succumb to the danger of what we might call 'statistics fetishism'. To develop a coherent comparative analytical framework, agreement is necessary on the relevant data. A particular problem that often tends to dominate discussions unduly is the incompatibility of national data. A second and related danger is the concentration on 'effective' policies, best practices, benchmarking, etc. Both of these tend to produce a technocratic and 'problem-solving' approach rather than a critical discourse (for clarification, see R.W. Cox 1981). Third, the approach that is based on the comparison of performance in a number of national polities assumes as given the ontological primacy of the national, and tends to treat national economies as closed and self-contained units. This may at first sight be justified if looking primarily at the main site of formal policy-making. However, in the era of foreign direct investment, transfer pricing, global financial markets and the rise of non-state actors and forms of private authority in the global economy this no longer suffices.

Transnational political economy

In this book we reject and aim to overcome these limitations. We depart from the conceptualization of capitalism as a *transnational* social system whose dynamic is not (or no longer) primarily determined by (sub)national factors and processes, but rather by transnational ones. We posit 'neo-liberal globalization' as the appropriate context in which to study the political economy[1] of unemployment in Europe. In this way we treat transnational processes and the dialectic between structural processes and the agency of social forces as central themes. This enables us to analyse how neo-liberal conceptions of labour market restructuring and employment policy became the guiding principles in post-Maastricht Europe and to show how ideology, agency and structure are dialectically interrelated.

Our book argues that the strategic discussions about European labour market restructuring and employment policy increasingly proceed transnationally. What do we mean by *transnational*? In current literature the term 'transnational' is used very frequently, but it is never defined properly: some use it as synonymous with 'international', others with 'supranational', and others again see it as coterminous with 'global'. For us, transnational processes are *constituted in a social space transcending national borders* (i.e. their dynamics are not fundamentally defined by the existence of national boundaries; in the words of Samuel Huntington (1991) they take place in relative disregard of national borders) and take place *simultaneously* in subnational, national *and* international arenas. Transnational does not negate the 'national' but subsumes it. Likewise, transnational actors are actors that are constituted in a social space 'beyond national boundaries' and operate at one and the same time in subnational, national and various international arenas.

Transnational processes are thus not juxtaposed with 'national' processes. Instead, we argue that subnational, national and international processes have become so intimately intertwined that national boundaries are no longer of decisive importance for an understanding of the dynamics of these processes, or of many of the actors involved in these processes.

This conceptualization does not deny that the 'national' continues to exist in many contexts, especially the political, institutional and cultural. Far from simply replacing 'national' with 'transnational' 'levels', a more thorough understanding of the 'transnational' compels us to undertake more and more complex and multileveled analyses. It is precisely one of the ambitions of this book to make this understanding come to life in our concrete studies of various related problem fields and different parts of Europe. We argue that it is no longer helpful to consider questions of labour market restructuring and (un)employment as though they could be understood in terms of national frameworks.

In taking this position we obviously refer to recent developments in the theoretical debate on European integration. An increasing number of authors argue that the EU is an emerging and new kind of polity, transcending the simple intergovernmentalist model of the EU as an (albeit special kind of) international regime that in no way threatens the sovereignty of its member states, but that at the same time is different from a supranational (federal) state (e.g. Schmitter 1991; Sandholtz and Stone Sweet 1998; see also Marks *et al.* 1996; Hix 1994,

1999). The basic point in this mode of thinking is that the notion of discrete political arenas no longer makes sense, since policy-initiation, decision-making and implementation and adjudication in the contemporary EU imply an *interconnection* of the subnational, national and supranational levels. In other words, the politics of the EU is not illuminated by identifying the 'level' ('supranational' or 'intergovernmental') to be privileged, but by accounting for exactly how 'levels' are connected in complex ways so as to constitute networks of governance (Marks *et al.* 1996). This is referred to as 'multilevel governance'. Elsewhere we have examined this approach in more detail. We raised three objections: the eclectic and mostly descriptive nature of the approach, its tendency to eliminate politics (i.e. the exercise of social power) from the analysis, and its neglect of the global embeddedness of the emerging EU mode of governance (for elaboration, see van Apeldoorn *et al.* 2003).

This book aims to transcend the limitations of both the comparativist and the multilevel governance approaches. What emerges clearly from our analyses, confirming the conclusions of theoretical analysis undertaken by several of us elsewhere (cf. van Apeldoorn 2002; Bieler and Morton 2001; Bieling and Steinhilber 2000; Cafruny and Ryner 2003; Ryner 2002), is that we must proceed from an integral understanding of the global capitalist system and recognize at least a three-layered structure of politics, economics and governance, in which the multilevel European polity is embedded within a global system. The distribution of relative weights of the various 'levels' cannot be established *ex cathedra* but is by definition fluid (in time, and over various issue areas).

Global dimensions of the political economy of employment

In Part I of the book we address the transformation at the level of the global economy of the past decades and consider how this transformation is dialectically related to the economic and ideological environment within which labour market restructuring in Europe takes place today.

In Chapter 2 Henk Overbeek elaborates on two developments at the global level that form the backdrop against which analysis of the European employment question must be made. Structural unemployment is causally linked to processes of restructuring in the world economy and the tendential emergence of a global labour market. The technological revolution of recent decades has made 'jobless growth' the norm rather than the exception. This structural transformation was paralleled by the emergence of global neo-liberalism as the hegemonic comprehensive concept of control permeating the ideological orientation not only of the traditional pro-market political forces, but also of European Christian Democrats and Social Democrats. 'Competitiveness' became the key imperative causing a massive shedding of labour, particularly during the recessions of the mid-1980s and the early 1990s. In the 1990s labour market reforms were declared one of the spearheads of capitalist restructuring, not only by national governments caught in a 'competitiveness race' and by international organizations reinforcing the destructive logic of this race by advocating even more far-reaching reforms (e.g. the Organization for Economic Co-operation and Development, OECD), but also by business pressure groups such as the European Round Table of Industrialists (ERT). This latter analysis is taken up in more detail by Jessop (Chapter 3) and by Bieling (Chapter 4).

Bob Jessop takes general changes in the European economies and their insertion into a wider social formation as a starting point to analyse the shift from a Keynesian welfare national state (KWNS) to a Schumpeterian workfare post-national regime (SWPR). He then relates both the general nature of the emerging SWPR and its variant forms to a concern with flexibility and employability as alternatives to the macro-economic pursuit of full employment associated with the KWNS. These themes are elaborated in relation to policy development and implementation around unemployment in the EU.

Hans-Jürgen Bieling (Chapter 4) analyses the adaptation over time of the hegemonic neo-liberal concept to changing circumstances. In a reflexive chapter Bieling deals with the social and political tensions within the regulative European framework, which stimulates 'competitive deregulation' and 'competitive austerity', on the one hand, and new forms of multilevel employment policy, on the other. He approaches these tensions by delineating the transformation of neo-liberal strategies over time from 'euphoric' to 'communitarian'. In view of the crisis of political legitimacy, Bieling argues, a communitarian rethinking of neo-liberalism fulfils at least three purposes: first, it delivers an effective critique of the devastating social effects of a disembedded economy; second, it leaves the prevailing social power structure intact; and, third, by stressing the importance and the productive potential of community networks it claims to provide a new perspective, which corrects and mitigates some of the painful social effects of neo-liberal restructuring without relapsing into old-fashioned Keynesian state intervention.

European dimensions of the political economy of employment

In Part II of the book we turn to the EU and analyse in detail how the challenges facing the European economies have been addressed by various (national and transnational) social and political forces, and how this interplay explains the particular shape and form of the emerging EU social and employment policies.

The chapters in this part analyse the interaction between structural transformation at the global level ('globalization') and the political and social struggles around employment, which take place within the European political space. In this force field different contending strategic conceptions of the course and direction of European integration emerged. The debates and processes of coalition building in this have coalesced around two (interrelated) axes:

- the institutional form of integration: 'Europeanization' versus intergovernmental co-operation;

- the relationship with the (world) market and the role of the state: market liberalization, deregulation and flexibilization versus (neo-Keynesian or neo-mercantilist) public steering and regulation.

Stefan Tidow (Chapter 5) first shows how employment policy has become an institutional concern of the EU by tracing its emergence in the early 1990s in the Maastricht Treaty on European Union and its further development via the White Paper, the Essen Summit, the Amsterdam Summit plus Treaty, the Luxembourg Employment Summit to the Cologne Summit and its aftermath. He then goes on to show that the political confrontations surrounding them represent a struggle over the (re)definition of the neo-liberal project. Employment policy in the EU was freed from the confines of 'social policy' to become a crucial ingredient of the current neo-liberal integration project. Essential in this project is the complex articulation of European and national policy arenas, which put national labour market regimes under strong competitive pressures. Supranational regulation within the European context is kept to the minimum, but the pressures of competitive restructuring permeate national systems and impose tendencies towards convergence.

Brigitte Young, too (Chapter 6), argues that the development of European employment and social policy has to be seen as part of a more comprehensive process of the rise of 'disciplinary neo-liberalism', with its focus on deregulation and political disengagement from the economy. She shows in detail how what may appear as a progressive step in the direction of gender, employment and equal opportunity policies fits quite well with the broader transnational 'market-making' efforts of the EU. The directives on sexual non-discrimination are foremost market-making instruments and only incidentally 'feminist'. The same can be said for most of the additions to the treaties and agreements on equal opportunity and employment since the Single European Act of 1986. These gender provisions in no way contradict the larger project of transforming the EU into a flexible transnational site of disciplinary neo-liberal governance.

The shift in the European context from a traditional vaguely Keynesian orientation firmly based on the primacy of the national framework for policy-making in the area of social and employment policy towards the neo-liberal hegemony structurally reinforced by the logic of the Single Market project and confirmed by the implications of Economic and Monetary Union (EMU) did not come about by coincidence or out of the blue. Bastiaan van Apeldoorn (Chapter 7) focuses on the agency of key players in this shift. More precisely, he examines the strategic role of the ERT in shaping the debate on European unemployment in the 1990s. He argues that the transnational class strategy of the ERT must be located within the structural transformation of (global and European) capitalism from a Fordist full-employment regime organized around the perspective of nationally embedded industrial capital towards a neo-liberal regime of flexible accumulation organized around the perspective of increasingly global industrial firms and, above all, financial capital. In this discourse, employment (creation) is articulated with (the need to improve) competitiveness, which in turn is articulated with labour market flexibility. The chapter documents how the ERT has been a key organization in promoting this neo-liberal competitiveness discourse. From the Delors White Paper onwards, Round Table ideas and concepts have shaped the policy discourse of the European Commission in the area of labour market, social and employment policies. The Commission documents were given an increasingly neo-liberal content: the unemployment crisis can only be solved if labour bears the burden of adjustment. Alternative solutions to or interpretations of the problem are marginalized as social-democratic and trade union forces are also successfully incorporated into the neo-liberal project for European order.

The articulation of global and EU tendencies with national politico-economic formations

In Part III, finally, we turn to the variations within the EU. Here the implicit question is continually how to conceptualize the articulation of the global, the European and the national. The starting point, the prism through which the national articulates with the European, in particular, must certainly be EMU. Its implementation in 1999 (which cast its shadow back as far as the Maastricht Summit of 1991) has fundamentally affected the parameters for national policy-making. On the one hand, the convergence requirements of EMU and the more general imperatives of 'competitiveness' impose a very strong de facto macro-economic policy convergence on the governments of Europe (irrespective of whether they are members of EMU or not). This process of policy convergence (towards liberalization and deregulation) is reinforced by the interventions of such international organizations as the OECD and the International Monetary Fund (IMF) and by the pressure of organized business at the transnational level (e.g. the ERT). On the other hand, in the absence of any *formal* policy harmonization the *transnational neo-liberal* pressures theoretically leave room for *national* initiatives to forge alliances backing what has sometimes been called *competitive corporatism* (Rhodes 2001). A parallel discussion here has been the one on the existence and significance of different 'models of capitalism' that was initiated by Albert (1993). Both of these notions serve as reference points for the discussion in the chapters making up Part III of the book.

Bob Jessop (Chapter 8) examines Britain's 'New Labour' government and Blair's role as architect of the 'Third Way'. He shows the continuity between the strategies of the Thatcher and Major governments for at least ten years and those of New Labour after 1997. At the European level (as well as in domestic policy-making) this is also reflected in British pressure for a minimalist Social Chapter, resistance to French and German proposals on job creation, and pleas for recognition of its 'New Deal' for the unemployed as a model policy for Europe. But there are discontinuities as well which illustrate that New Labour is developing its own distinctive version of neo-liberalism.

Uwe Becker (Chapter 9) looks at what counted for years as the most successful example of competitive corporatism, i.e. the Netherlands. The dominant explanation for what is popularly called the Dutch Miracle has been the one put forward by Visser and Hemerijck (1997): it accords primary significance to the consensual nature of the Dutch system of wage bargaining resulting in wage moderation. Becker argues that this analysis falls short – in terms of the truthfulness of the claims made on the expansion of Dutch employment (which he shows consisted in large part of substituting part-time work for full-time work), in terms of the explanation offered for the expansion of the jobs volume that did take place (which he shows depended on increasing income inequality and consumer spending driven by a real estate bubble), and in failing to uncover the power relations underpinning the so-called consensual nature of Dutch corporatism. Becker thus raises some serious questions regarding the possibility of national solutions to the unemployment crisis, without, however, dismissing that notion completely.

The same question regarding the remaining options for national strategies underlies the discussion by Magnus Ryner and Thorsten Schulten of developments in the heartland of continental social democracy (Chapter 10). They take up a theme of Robert Cox (1987), who argued that a counter-hegemonic project might arise from the 'state capitalist' development models on the European continent (or what later has been referred to as 'Rhineland capitalism' by Michel Albert (1993)). They start off by showing how EMU spearheads a 'transnational neo-liberal hegemonic project' in the EU. Against this background, the chapter analyses how Dutch, Swedish and German organized labour are strategically oriented, focusing on the issue of how to cope with unemployment. The chapter reaches a pessimistic conclusion, seeing as trade unions in the EMU core all function to integrate organized labour into the present neo-liberal EMU regime. This process is far advanced in the Netherlands but more tentative and contradictory in Sweden and Germany, where opposition is still strong. The chapter concludes that the defeat of the 'Lafontaine strategy' (although not without its own flaws) also represents a serious (maybe fatal) setback to attempts to construct an alternative at the European level (thus tying in perfectly with the conclusions reached by Stefan Tidow in his chapter).

The discussion of 'models of capitalism' is taken up in the final chapter by Emma Cerviño and Leila Simona Talani (Chapter 11), who raise the spectre of a 'Mediterranean' model of labour market regulation, characterized by the long endurance of rigid labour market regulation, embedded in a 'familial' form of capitalism. The authors show that the path to EMU, as defined by the Maastricht Treaty and by the subsequent agreement on the stability pact, directly and substantially affected the relations of power between various social forces, primarily those between organized labour and capital. Their chapter documents how in the case of Spain and Portugal national forces (employers, and transnational corporations in particular) instrumentalized the demands put on their governments by EMU to change the balance of forces domestically in their favour. In contrast, the trade unions have been forced to operate reactively and defensively. As elsewhere, they have proved unable to develop coherent autonomous positions that would enable them to mobilize support for an alternative politics of social protection.

In the brief concluding chapter (Chapter 12) an attempt is made to develop a typology of comprehensive orientations regarding social and employment policy. The objective is to provide some context against which it becomes possible to integrate the main conclusions of the various chapters into a coherent conceptualization of the trajectory of the discussions on European social and employment policy from the perspective of transnational political economy.

Notes

1 The term 'political economy' is used in different ways. In this book we situate ourselves in the tradition that goes back to the18th- and 19th-century European study of politics and the economy as forming a fundamentally integral social reality (Smith, Malthus, Ricardo, Marx). This view either pre-dates (Smith) or critiques (Marx) the separation between 'politics' and 'economics' that emerged in the course of the 19th century as a result of the spread and growth of industrial capitalism. Our conception of 'political economy' must therefore not be confused with the much more recent (new) political economy, which was primarily developed in the United States and refers to the application of methodology developed in the area of 'economic science' to the study of 'political' phenomena.

Part I

The changing political economy of employment

2 Globalization, neo-liberalism and the employment question

Henk Overbeek

Introduction

The return of widespread unemployment in the OECD in the 1970s is often attributed to processes of restructuring in the world economy. The technological revolution of recent decades has made 'jobless growth' the norm rather than the exception, and the imperatives of 'competitiveness' have caused a massive shedding of labour. In the current phase of the development of the global political economy, labour market flexibility is emphasized as one of the main determinants of 'competitiveness', which is (we are told) the ultimate goal of state economic policy. Both national governments caught in a 'competitiveness race' and international organizations have declared labour market reforms to be one of the spearheads of capitalist restructuring, which reinforces the destructive logic of this race by advocating even more far-reaching reforms (e.g. OECD 1994, 1995). Similarly, business pressure groups such as the ERT have taken the lead in propagating such reforms (see Chapter 7). The transnationalization of the global economy, i.e. the dissolution of the exclusive boundaries around the national economies so predominant from the 1930s until the end of the 1970s, has made employment a transnational concern beyond the confines of the OECD. Both 'globalization' and the extremely rapid growth of the labour force in many parts of the world have made policy-makers realize that unemployment is one of the most pressing social problems of today and tomorrow. The 1995 World Summit for Social Development in Copenhagen, at which the global employment crisis was one of the main themes discussed, highlighted this development (cf. Simai 1995a). No national government in today's globalizing conjuncture (with the possible exception of the US) can hope to be successful in developing an exclusively 'national' solution to the problem of employment, and academic circles increasingly recognize this.

In this chapter, we will do five things. First, we will define what we understand by globalization (in the next section). The third section briefly discusses the emergence of a global labour market as one important and often ignored dimension of the globalization process. The fourth section will briefly discuss the relationship (often seen as contradictory) between globalization and regionalization. In the penultimate section we turn to the emergence of neo-liberalism as the hegemonic concept. This section argues that globalization is not just about structural transformation, but is also a project pursued by concrete social forces for specific purposes. In the final section we briefly describe how neo-liberalism has redefined the problem of unemployment. Unemployment in the neo-liberal project has an important disciplinary role, and is seen as a problem of individual employability rather than as a structural property of a capitalist economy, or a temporary (because curable) disturbance in the way that Keynesianism has approached unemployment. This account will help the reader to make sense of the intricate and sometimes contradictory developments analysed in the chapters which follow.

Defining globalization

Few words have produced such a glut of interpretations as 'globalization'.[1] At least four issues have been central in this debate. The first of these is the nature of the phenomenon: what exactly is *global* about globalization, and is it primarily an economic 'thing' or is it also, or rather, political, cultural, ideological? A second theme is the question of uniqueness: is present-day globalization historically unprecedented, or is it simply a replay of earlier (and perhaps even more global) episodes in world history. Third, there is much debate about the causes of globalization, both in very general terms and in terms of the specific explanation of the current episode. Finally, of course, there is the debate as to whether globalization exists in any meaningful sense. This is not the place to review these debates in any detail, but we must clarify our understanding of the concept in rough strokes before we can move on to our more specific concerns.

As a start, a first approximation which will allow me to delineate my position in these debates, we can take a critical look at the widespread idea that globalization is about the intensification of trans-border transactions, primarily of an economic character.

A first important point to make, then, is that 'global' should not be understood as 'universal'. Early (and more recent) advocates have always maintained that the 'fruits of globalization' can be shared by all countries and peoples provided their governments follow the neo-liberal precepts of the IMF and the G7. Experience to date, however, has shown two things, both of which have been pointed out at length by most critics of the so-called globalization thesis (e.g. Hirst and Thompson 1996; Ruigrok and van Tulder 1995; also Krätke 1997). The first is that the great bulk of cross-border transactions that are key to this concept of globalization (trade, financial flows, direct investment) are concentrated within a limited number of core regions of the world economy (North America, Western Europe, Northeast and Southeast Asia). Second, and related, certain regions of the world economy seem to be largely bypassed by the quantum leap of internationalization: parts of Asia, South America and Eastern Europe, large parts of Central America and the Caribbean, as well as major parts of the former Soviet Union and most of Sub-Saharan Africa. These regions are said to be marginalized in terms of their dwindling shares in world trade and investment flows.

Unfortunately, these critiques of the globalization thesis often attempt to refute aspects of the globalization thesis with arguments that are quite similar in nature to the quantitative claims of the protagonists. The argument then becomes that the degree of internationalization is actually exaggerated and that earlier episodes in the history of the world economy were more global than the present one. However, 'globalization' is not 'internationalization'. This quantitative conceptualization negates the essentially qualitative nature of the process. The marginalization critique, in particular, ignores how the regions in question are affected by the globalization process. The fact that Sub-Saharan Africa's share in world trade is negligible says nothing about how the lives and existences of Africa's people have been intimately transformed by the impact of the changes in the global economy in terms of communication and culture, in terms of the transition from subsistence farming and state subsidies to cash-crop farming for the world market, in terms of the impact of the AIDS crisis etc. Africa may have become almost completely 'insignificant' from the point of view of the global economy, but the global economy permeates every aspect of the day-to-day lives of all Africans.

The essence of the transformation in the global economy that we are addressing with the term 'globalization' is qualitative. Elsewhere I have argued that globalization involves fundamental change in at least three key ways: a transformation of the dominant production and circulation relations ('economic' and 'social' globalization), a revolution in the role and significance of time and space ('technological' and 'cultural' globalization) and a radical change in the structures of governance and in the configuration of state power ('political' globalization) (Overbeek 1998: 57ff.). All these fundamental changes relate somehow to the transcendence of 'the national' as the primary constitutive dimension. Local, national, international and regional structures, dynamics, realities are encapsulated by an overarching and increasingly dominant globe-spanning network of social relations.

But if these are observations on the meaning of 'global' in globalization, what exactly is effecting this process? Revolutionary technological innovations, inter-firm competition, purposive policy decisions, American imperialism – these have all been identified, separately or in combination, as the causes of globalization. These factors are all important, certainly, either as facilitators (e.g. technology) or as epiphenomena (e.g. the much abused MacDonaldization). But when one summarizes the literature the conclusion is inescapable that at a deeper (or, rather, more abstract) level 'globalization' is about *commodification*. We have witnessed in the decades since the late 1970s a sudden and unprecedented process of deepening commodification; not just the quantitative growth of existing forms of commodification (the growth of international trade and finance), and not just the incorporation of new politico-geographic regions into the capitalist world market and its networks of commodified interaction (the demise of the planned socialist economies), but also the subordination to market forces of areas of human activity and indeed existence that were hitherto not commodified in any real sense of the word at all (human reproduction, intellectual property, traditional medicine, etc.). After decades of privatization and marketization, very few spheres of life remain that are shielded from the pursuit of private profit. Thus, globalization is about the spread of market civilization, as Stephen Gill has named it (Gill 1995).

Identifying commodification as the hard core of globalization enables us to transcend a debilitating impasse in the globalization debate: the futile discussion about whether globalization is new or, on the other hand, is the 19th century revisited. The phenomenon of commodification is not new to the world. Some have recently argued that the global economy, trade, commercial enterprise and even capital accumulation have an uninterrupted history of at least 5,000 years (e.g. Frank and Gills 1993; Frank 1998). More familiar is the claim that the start of the epoch of generalized commodity production can be traced back to the crisis of feudalism in Europe and the creation of the capitalist world market after the so-called discovery of the Americas at the end of the 15th century (e.g. Frank 1975; Wallerstein 1974).[2] The subsequent expansion of the capitalist world market was an uneven process characterized by fits and starts, by periods of rapid intensification alternating with periods of stagnation and even reversal, wrought with contradictions and deflected by obstacles often of its own making. In those 500 years we can identify three episodes of intensified market expansion and deepening commodification, namely the episode of the original creation of the world market ('world-economy' in Wallerstein's (1974) terminology) and the expansion of *mercantile capital* in the period 1492–1648; the expansion of *industrial capital* and the rise of imperialism in the second half of the 19th century; and, finally, the present episode of globalization characterized by the global expansion of *transnational capital*. The best way to look at these episodes[3] is as distinct periods characterized by intensified change in a historical process of much longer duration, namely the process of capitalist development that has engulfed the globe since the 15th century.

Given that in all definitions of 'capitalism' the commodification of labour power takes centre stage, it is remarkable that more theorists have not identified the development of the global labour market as one of the essential dimensions of globalization.

Towards a global labour market

In their path-breaking study of the so-called New International Division of Labour (NIDL) of the 1970s, the German researchers Fröbel, Heinrichs and Kreye observed an accelerating relocation of labour-intensive production processes from the older industrial economies to low-wage countries in Asia and Latin America. Three preconditions made this relocation drive possible: the existence of a sheer inexhaustible reservoir of cheap labour in large parts of the Third World; new production technologies making it possible to separate spatially the labour-intensive parts of the production process from the capital-intensive parts; and new transport and communication technologies facilitating the co-ordination of dispersed production and assembly establishments. The authors concluded that 'the coincidence of these three preconditions...has brought into existence a world market for labour and a real world industrial reserve army of workers, together with a world market for production sites' (Fröbel *et al.* 1980: 13).

Now, there have been many critical reactions to this work, both on theoretical grounds and on empirical grounds (for a good critique, see R. Cohen 1987). Nevertheless, their emphasis on the emergence of a global labour market (not as a full-blown reality but certainly as a tendency) has remained important and insightful. One important implication is that, contrary to much popular imagery, migration is not the only, and numerically not the most important, way in which labour forces throughout the world increasingly compete directly with labour forces elsewhere. Crucial for this argument is that because of the rapid development of new communication and information technology foreign direct investment (FDI) has become a functional alternative not only to trade but also to labour migration. In other words, mobility of capital can substitute for the mobility of goods and labour power. The concept of a global labour market has in this sense become at least a possible reality (cf. Harris 1995: 21–84; Suda 1994). The implications for employment worldwide are obviously far-reaching (Lonnroth 1994; Simai 1995b).

What are the mechanisms that integrate an increasing proportion of the world population directly into capitalist labour markets and lock national and regional labour markets into an integrated global labour market? They are principally of three kinds: first, there are those connected to the spread of transnational trade and production; second, there are the effects of new (both in the sense of the most recent and in the sense of novel) forms of the commodification of labour power globally; and, third, there are the various forms of labour migration that enhance the overall tendential integration of labour markets globally. Let us take a brief look at each of these three sets of mechanisms.

Transnational production

Nationally or regionally bounded labour markets are increasingly integrated by the internationalization of trade and, especially, of production. The importance of the new form of transnationalization as contrasted with the earlier phases of globalization in which commercial capital and money capital moved across borders cannot be overstated. Whereas mercantile and money capital impose an abstract and indirect discipline on labour, FDI directly reproduces capitalist relations of production *within* the host countries (Poulantzas 1974). Transnational corporations thus have a strong impact on the shape of the world economy. This was grasped eloquently in the following quote from the 1994 *World Investment Report*:

> they organize the production process internationally: by placing their affiliates world-wide under common governance systems, they interweave production activities located in different countries, create an international intra-firm division of labour and, in the process, internalize a range of international transactions that would otherwise have taken place in the market.
>
> (UNCTAD 1994: 9)

A few key statistics confirm that transnational production has indeed become by far the most important engine of accumulation in the global economy:

- After a slowdown in the early 1990s, direct investments were growing explosively in the closing years of the century. As a consequence, the share of foreign investment inflows in world gross fixed capital formation has grown rapidly, from 1.1 per cent in 1960, via 2.0 per cent in 1980, to 7.4 per cent in 1997 and around 12 per cent in 2000 (UNCTAD 1994, 1998, 2001).
- By 2000 total assets of foreign affiliates of transnational corporations (TNCs) stood at $21 trillion. Sales by foreign subsidiaries reached $15.7 trillion (UNCTAD 2001, ch. 1: 10). In addition to FDI, through strategic alliances and other non-equity arrangements TNCs gain control over great assets and huge markets that are not measured in these statistics.
- In 1960 worldwide sales by foreign affiliates of TNCs were smaller than world exports, but in 2000 they stood at 247 per cent of world exports: $15.68 trillion versus $6.35 trillion (UNCTAD 1998, 2001; World Bank 2002).
- More than half of world exports in 2002 were exports of foreign affiliates, against only one-third in 1997 (*ibid.*).
- The rapid expansion of FDI is increasingly tied up with the explosive increase in mergers and acquisitions (M&A) in the world. The total value of cross-border M&As in 1997 was approximately $342 billion (up from less than $100 billion in 1992), representing 58 per cent of FDI flows (UNCTAD 1998: 19–20). In 2000 these figures were $1,144 billion and 90 per cent, respectively (UNCTAD 2002, ch. 1: 10).
- Both FDI and cross-border M&As are mostly concentrated within the developed world, thus reinforcing tremendously the process of *transnationalization* within the OECD area, i.e. the rapidly intensifying interpenetration of the OECD economies (capital markets but also labour markets).
- *Direct* employment by foreign affiliates of transnational corporations increased from 17.5 million in 1982 and 23.7 million in 1990, to 45.6 million in 2000, growing at an annual rate in the years 1997–2000 of nearly 8 per cent. Of course, the size and growth of *indirect* employment through subcontracting and licensing is also very significant (UNCTAD 2002, ch. 1: 10; see also Bailey *et al.* 1993).

The conclusion is clear: the growth of transnational production plays a significant role in the linkage of national and regional labour markets, especially in the OECD area, which accounts for some three-quarters of the global economy.

Commodification of labour power

Labour power not previously bought and sold on 'free' labour markets is commodified in various ways. In the view of Immanuel Wallerstein, world capitalism has always employed the incorporation of non-capitalist areas and spheres as one of the ways in which it could combat its innate periodic crises. This is partly because of the new markets opened up and the new sources of cheap raw materials to be exploited, but also because in times of crisis capital will search for cheap labour power. And labour power will be cheapest in areas where people have not yet been proletarianized. In his view, capitalist expansion is about semi-proletarianization: tapping labour power that is, as it were, subsidized by non-capitalist activity (e.g. subsistence farming) (see Wallerstein 1983). It is, of course, the dialectic of unintended outcomes that this search for semi-proletarian labour power tendentially leads to the full proletarianization of human labour across the globe.

First, there is the incorporation of previously disconnected areas into the capitalist world market. In the past 25 years the world has witnessed an unprecedented offensive to break down the barriers that had shielded large portions of the world's population from direct participation in the world market, primarily in the former 'socialist' economies but also in the remaining pre-capitalist societies on the fringes of the modern world. With the incorporation after 1978 into the world market of China, the Soviet Union, Eastern Europe and Indochina (soon to be followed, it seems, by Cuba and North Korea) the existence of a separate social and economic system organized on non-capitalist principles has come to an end. In much of the Third World, the effects of the debt crisis of the early 1980s and the subsequent imposition of IMF conditionality intensified the ongoing process of proletarianization of the population through urbanization and the disintegration of subsistence economies. The incorporation of distant regions continued with the deeper and deeper penetration of a range of arctic and tropical forest regions, to such an extent that the proportion both of the territory and of the population of the globe exposed to the penetration of capital is now approaching 100 per cent.

A second means of further proletarianization of labour consists in the commodification of economic activities within capitalist societies that were previously organized outside the market. Since the advent of neo-liberal restructuring this process has progressed rapidly through liberalization and privatization, both in the economies of the developed industrial welfare states and in the semi-peripheral and peripheral developmentalist states that have been subjected to various forms of structural adjustment programmes (cf. several of the contributions to Suda 1994). This has led to a growth of 'informal sectors' in the Third World but also in many OECD countries, as well as to increasing official labour market participation rates in the industrial economies and to what has been termed the 're-commodification' of the workforce in the OECD countries (cf. Seeleib-Kaiser n.d.).[4]

One of the contested claims by Fröbel, Heinrichs and Kreye was that the NIDL was creating structural unemployment in the industrial countries. The combined effects of the relocation of labour-intensive production processes to low-wage countries and the rationalization efforts leading to heavy investment in labour-saving technology in the industrial economies themselves (producing the much debated phenomenon of 'jobless growth') would inevitably produce a structural labour surplus (Fröbel *et al.* 1980; see also Mishra 1999). Indeed, the share of industrial production in gross domestic product and industrial employment has consistently fallen in the industrial countries.[5]

However, there have been counteracting tendencies. There has been a sharp growth in tertiary-sector output and employment, giving rise to the notion of a service economy. These developments have transformed the economy from a Fordist model (with mass production and mass consumption sustained by one or another form of welfare state) into a model of flexible accumulation (with lean production and just-in-time delivery supported by a competition state) (see Chapter 3). The labour market *within* the advanced capitalist economies is in fact increasingly characterized by a 'core–periphery' structure (R.W. Cox 1987). On the one hand, service employment has grown at the higher ends of the labour market hierarchy. This is, of course, as is often observed, related to the information and communication technology (ICT) revolution, but it is also caused by another phenomenon. The tendency of industrial conglomerates to outsource for non-core services has been responsible for a significant 'cosmetic' shift from industrial to service output and employment without any underlying shift in the types of concrete labour performed: an industrial company can employ its own cleaners or advertising experts, in which case they show up in the statistics as industrially employed, or it can contract an external cleaning or advertising firm, in which case their employees are registered as service workers.

There is of course a limit to the degree to which services can absorb labour from industry, as Mishra rightly remarks (Mishra 1999: 23). Commercial service industries such as retail banking have themselves been subjected in recent years to several waves of rationalization leading to mass redundancies. Many of these types of labour are themselves, furthermore, subject to the effects of the internationalization of labour markets. However, in the area of personal services this is not the case. With the abolition of the 'family wage' and the intensification of exploitation, as well as for demographic reasons, the demand for personal services has increased tremendously. In areas such as childcare, healthcare and care for the elderly it is unquestionable that the coming decades will see a steep rise in the demand for qualified workers. At present the neo-liberal dogma seems to prescribe that these services will mostly have to be financed privately. Whether this will continue to be the case is debatable: the 'market' at present seems to be unable to guarantee a steady supply of sufficiently qualified workers in these areas. The intensification of the conditions of work has also, particularly in the so-called *global cities*, led to the re-emergence of domestic labour and the reappearance of sweatshop production and repair. This has led to a rising demand for unskilled and low-skilled service workers and to a 'peripheralization' of labour (Harris 1995; Navarro 1998; Sassen 1991, 1996; Stalker 2000). This development is in many cases linked to the rise of undocumented immigration.

Global labour mobility

Nationally or regionally bounded labour markets are also further integrated by increased international labour mobility in its various forms. First, the spread of TNCs brings with it increased international mobility of top- and intermediate-level managers and executives. Simultaneously, the internationalization of services (engineering, advertising, software development) creates increased international mobility of technical and commercial experts. A lack of certain categories of highly skilled personnel has over the years resulted in a steady brain drain from the Third World. This demand, combined with their own need for foreign-exchange earnings, has induced governments of Third World countries to actively promote outward migration of skilled workers and professionals. Through workers' remittances the inflow of hard currency is thus increased. Worldwide, remittances have surpassed development aid as a source of foreign exchange. In 1995 worldwide remittances ran to $70 billion; in the same year development aid totalled $66 billion (World Bank 1997).[6]

Second, the combination of more restrictive immigration policies and labour market flexibilization and deregulation in the OECD countries creates increased opportunities for illegal immigration (increasingly through the intervention of organized crime). Indeed, the employment of undocumented foreign labour has in many cases become a condition for the continued existence of small and medium-sized firms, creating a substantial economic interest in continued (illegal) immigration (Brochmann 1993: 119–120; also Papademetriou 1994: 27).

Finally, the economic and political crisis of the state in many Third World countries and the resulting intensification of social and ethnic conflicts swell the ranks of international refugee movements and drive up the outward flow of migrant workers. In peripheral areas of the world (e.g. Africa, Eastern Europe, Central America) the two most important changes since the mid-1970s (often interacting) have been the debt crisis and the ensuing imposition of structural adjustment policies, and the end of the Cold War. The Structural Adjustment Programs of the IMF and the World Bank and the withdrawal of military and economic assistance by the superpowers both resulted in a substantial reduction in external financial resources available for redistribution by the state. In many cases this seriously affected the ability of governments to co-opt rivalling elites into the power structure, resulting in serious social and political crises, economic disasters, and regime change or state collapse. These complex processes largely explain the surge in forced movements of people since the mid-1970s across the globe, in search of protection and in search of a new and better life (cf. R. Cohen and Deng 1998; Loescher 1993; UNHCR 1997; Zolberg *et al.* 1989).

Globalization and regionalization

These data on the concentration of capital within the core area of the world economy and on the rise of a global labour market do not bring out fully that in fact this process is one of *regionalization*. The largest TNCs increasingly build complete integrated production networks within each of the three most important regions, i.e. North America, Western Europe and East Asia/Pacific, the so-called Triad (cf. UNCTAD 1993). The reasons for this are both general and specific. In general, productive capital is not 'footloose': the relative fixity of productive assets, the skill requirements for the workforce, and the social and political embeddedness of productive capital explain its limited mobility. More specifically, the particular pattern of Triadic concentration is explained by the exigencies of 'flexible accumulation' (just-in-time delivery, small-batch production, cultural diversity) and by the desire on the part of TNCs to seek insulation from exchange-rate volatility. Politically, 'regionalization' is manifested in the formation of regional blocs: in response to globalization, states initiate regional integration schemes (such as the EU or the larger European Economic Area, the North American Free Trade Agreement (NAFTA), Mercosur), which themselves in turn reinforce the incentives for TNCs to establish regionally integrated production networks.

The patterns of regional concentration in the globalization process simultaneously create a framework for the consolidation and intensification of regional migration networks. Movements of people are partly occurring in regional contexts as well, not just as a reflection of the emerging new production and labour market structures, but also because of a series of factors that are migration specific, such as geographic proximity, cultural affinity, historical linkages and migration chains.

In Western Europe (1995) 35 per cent of foreign residents come from other Western European countries, and some 36 per cent come from the Mediterranean countries that were the traditional suppliers of 'guest workers' during the post-war decades. Some 5 per cent come from Central and Eastern Europe, leaving less than 1 in 4 who come from further away (Eurostat 1997: 48–9).

This relative regional concentration of migration patterns – in line with the regionalization of trade, investment and political relations – suggests that the regional context is extremely important in shaping transnational labour markets. Not only does it provide the material basis for migration and labour market policies, but, given the correlation between the different forms of 'regionalization', it is also much more likely that states will be able to reach agreement regionally on such policies given the multitude of possible compensatory concessions in other fields. The scope for bargaining on a global scale is much more limited.

In Europe, regionalism in the sphere of the regulation of migration and labour mobility has taken the form of a sharply restrictive yet selective immigration regime. On the one hand, there is the relaxation of visa requirements for the countries in Central and Eastern Europe foreseen in the accession agreements. There are also provisions (in place since shortly after the collapse of the communist regimes in the early 1990s) for the granting of temporary work permits (sometimes in the guise of training programmes). On the other hand, unwanted would-be immigrants travelling through states sharing borders with the EU are increasingly faced with a *cordon sanitaire* erected along the outer limits of the Union. To the east, the Central and East European countries (Poland, the Czech Republic, Slovakia, Hungary and Slovenia, as well as Romania, Bulgaria and the Baltic states) have signed readmission agreements with the EU, incorporated into the Europe Agreements and later the Accession Partnerships. In exchange, the EU provides technical and financial assistance to strengthen the eastern border controls. The result of this policy is rapidly becoming visible: the countries in Central Europe have now themselves become attractive to tens of thousands of labour migrants from the Ukraine, Belarus and beyond. To the south, the EU is constructing a similar fence via the Euro-Mediterranean Partnership agreements concluded in Barcelona in late 1995, which include readmission agreements, border-control co-operation and aid. Eventually, this Partnership with all states on the southern and eastern shores of the Mediterranean Sea will evolve into a free-trade zone. If this trend continues, we may assume that once the Mediterranean countries have improved their border controls and proven reliable partners in the readmission agreements the EU might ultimately agree to a relaxation of the immigration controls on Mediterranean workers as well (but at this point in time the realization of such a development is still far off and therefore quite uncertain).

In any case, these brief references to the development of a more open regional labour market indicate that globalization is an ambiguous and contradictory process: it produces universalizing as well as localizing tendencies, and in a sense assumes the form of 'regionalization' – the restructuring of the global political economy into macro-regions.

Globalization as neo-liberal agency

Structure and agency in the rise of a global labour market

In the previous section we analysed the transformation of labour markets in the global political economy over past decades. We argued that the process of global restructuring has involved the tendential creation of globally connected, regionally nested labour markets in which national labour forces compete through a number of mechanisms involving increasing mobility of capital, goods and labour power. This internationalization of labour markets has often been considered a major factor in the rise of mass unemployment since the 1970s. In the previous sections we indicated that we see no inevitable reason why this would be so: the rise of unemployment in the 1970s is not the direct and inescapable result of the structural transformation of the global economy. The real question is under what conditions the available labour supply will be employed to perform the socially useful work for which there is ample demand: will these conditions be dictated exclusively by the dynamic of the capitalist market, or will considerations of social need and equity be somehow applied? To consider this question, we must now also briefly look at the role that agency and ideology have played in the transformation of the global economy and in the return of mass unemployment.

The rise of neo-liberalism

The role of ideas in the configuration of politics is a problematic issue. It is widely recognized that private interests (individual or collective) do not translate directly into political convictions; nor do political convictions translate directly into policy output. As Robert Cox has elegantly explained, there is an intimate reciprocal relationship between objective factors (technology, political structure, social power hierarchy), subjective factors (ethical convictions, diverging conceptions of rationality, class bias) and institutional forms (dominant modes of labour relations, for instance) (R.W. Cox 1987: 29). Every social formation is defined by a particular combination of objective, subjective and institutional factors. Such a combination, to follow Cox's Gramsci-inspired conceptualization, is expressed in a *historic bloc*, i.e. the 'particular configuration of social classes and ideology that gives content to a historical state' (*ibid.*: 409n.), the concept that Gramsci used to analyse the class nature of the state in capitalism. The ideational plays a particularly strong role in cementing the subjective unity of the historic bloc through the articulation of political convictions and programmes. Does this mean that there is no relation at all between the sphere of politics and the sphere of 'economics', as it is usually but mistakenly called? By no means. In modern politics in capitalist societies, private and fractional interests tend to coagulate around

> largely implicit, but no less definite, common programs, or *comprehensive concepts of control.* Such concepts are political formulas that lend cohesion and cogency to the rule of particular classes and fractions of classes by translating idealized class and fractional viewpoints into a strategic orientation for society as a whole. Their capacity to be presented as a necessary and/or legitimate expression of the general interest derives from their basis in pivotal positions in the economy, which at particular junctures in the process of capital accumulation and social development acquire a relevance beyond this mere 'function'.
>
> (van der Pijl 1989: 7–8)

Through this notion we can understand how politics is structured by the dynamics of the accumulation process: not directly, but mediated by the ideational level.

The crisis of the latter half of the 1970s was not a simple conjunctural disturbance, but affected all aspects of the post-war order: social relations of production, the composition of the historic bloc and its concept of control, the role of the state, and the international order. Change in such a complex set of relationships, such as the rise of neo-liberalism in the 1980s and 1990s, cannot be reduced to one single factor (technology, for instance), but can only be grasped by considering how objective, subjective and institutional changes have dialectically interacted to produce a new socio-political reality. In the previous sections we concentrated on the objective and the institutional factors involved. This section pays attention to the role of ideology in the process.

The comprehensive concept of control emerging as a response to the organic crisis of the 1970s has become known as *neo-liberalism.*[7] Neo-liberalism elevates identifiable fractional interests to the level of a claimed 'general' interest: it expresses the outlook of *transnational circulating capital* – primarily international money capital, but also an increasing proportion of the capital embodied by transnational industrial corporations as these became more and more dominated internally by financial managers rather than production engineers. The key to understanding the 'solution' to the crisis offered by neo-liberalism lies in the role that *money capital* as capital-in-general plays in the restructuring of both the spatial and technical aspects of production and the social relations of production, in order to adjust production to consumption and restore profitability by raising the rate of exploitation and the mass of surplus value. Capital must be liberated from all unnecessary constraints on its mobility before this restructuring can be undertaken. This 'general' capitalist interest was reasserted through the adoption of monetarism. Monetarism holds that by making money scarce, inflation can be combated effectively and sound micro-economic reasoning can be forced upon the state and society as a whole. Although unpopular since the 1920s, it had always continued to attract the support of economists, journalists and government officials, particularly in the USA and Britain. After 1945 it was propagated by a number of private transnational groups such as the Mont Pèlerin Society (inspired by Friedrich Hayek and Milton Friedman), and, as the crisis of the 1970s deepened, its voice grew louder and succeeded in winning over more and more influential bodies. The monetarists scored important victories in Chile (with the rise to prominence of the 'Chicago boys' in 1975) and Britain (with Margaret Thatcher's emergence as the country's leader in 1979). The decisive turning point came when, also in 1979, Paul Volcker was appointed chairman of the US Federal Reserve Board and initiated a strict monetarist regime that drove up real interest rates in the US and the world economy. This rise of monetarism as the doctrine directing monetary policy resulted in a rapid shift in the class structure away from the corporate-liberal pattern to an individualist one in which the interests of the rentier and the 'venture capitalist' were predominant. Rentier incomes rose, stock ownership was popularized through privatization, and bank profits increased relative to those of industry. Investment banking and financial services became the hottest industries.

In reaction to the tenets of the disintegrating corporate-liberal or Keynesian consensus of the years 1945–71, neo-liberalism extolled the virtues of the free market and the withdrawal of the state from the management of the economy. Its core concepts and precepts (liberalization, privatization, deregulation and internationalization), as well as its new acquisitive individualist ethic, gradually became hegemonic and have apparently eclipsed traditional social democracy. The victory of neo-liberalism was even interpreted as the 'End of the Social-Democratic Century' (Dahrendorf 1990).

This process is not as straightforward as it might seem from this account. In fact, there is a complex and dialectical relationship between neo-liberalism as *process* and neo-liberalism as *project*. Certainly, there is such a thing as a neo-liberal project that is pushed consciously and purposefully by its protagonists (organic intellectuals, entrepreneurs and politicians, organizational representatives, etc.). This is where the agency of individuals such as Milton Friedman and organizations such as the Mont Pèlerin Society, were crucial during the 1970s and 1980s, and this is where agents such as the World Economic Forum and others carried forward the neo-liberal onslaught in the 1990s (cf. van der Pijl 1998). But of course, as critics of this approach will quickly point out, these programmes have never been simply put into practice. A hegemonic project or comprehensive concept of control is shaped, and continuously reshaped, in the process of struggle, compromise and readjustment, resulting in 'a succession of negotiated settlements, of concessions to the rigidities and dynamics of structures as well as the political possibilities of the moment' (Drainville 1994: 116).[8]

In the early days of the trajectory of neo-liberalism, it is primarily a *deconstructive* project. In general terms neo-liberalism emerged first as the concept with the most convincing analysis of the crisis of Keynesianism and so defeated corporate liberalism and social democracy in one country after another. Gradually, neo-liberalism acquired *constructive* traits through the policies of structural adjustment, liberalization, deregulation, privatization; corporate liberalism was discredited, no new alternative could be articulated, and the tenets of neo-liberalism became increasingly accepted as valid and legitimate. Eventually we have seen a form of *consolidation*, internationally as well as within the advanced industrial countries. Any notion of an alternative to the global rule of capital became utterly 'unrealistic' and discredited, and neo-liberal reforms were 'locked in' and 'normalized'. The significance of the demise of real socialism in this respect cannot be overstated (Mishra 1999: 111–12): until its definitive discomfiture and disintegration, the mere existence of an alternative economic and social system provided an incentive for the capitalist class in the West to accommodate the working class. With the demise of really existing socialism this incentive lost its force, opening up political space for a more radical overhaul of the structures of corporate liberalism.

The precise mix of elements (free market ideology and neo-conservatism, destructive and constructive) and the duration of the various phases vary from country to country depending on the political conjuncture, historical factors and the country's particular place in the global order. Elements that are alien to the hegemonic neo-liberal concept will persist due to particular historical circumstances, as with the tenacity of corporate-liberal structures in the Germany of the neo-liberal 1980s and 1990s (van der Wurff 1993). Nevertheless, there can be no doubt regarding the general direction of affairs throughout the OECD world.

This ideal-typical trajectory of the rise of neo-liberalism is perfectly illustrated by the neo-liberal redefinition of the unemployment problem.

Return to unemployment as regulatory mechanism

Mass unemployment and the concomitant social and political crisis of the 1930s provided the main inspiration for the 'Keynesian consensus' of the post-war decades. Mass unemployment was considered a politically dangerous and ethically unacceptable by-product of capitalist development. Keynes was believed to have provided governments with the instruments that would make it possible to pursue full employment without compromising the capacity of capital to accumulate. Counter-cyclical demand management could counter conjunctural unemployment, while structural unemployment could be kept to a minimum through government industrial policy and public investment, as well as through a general improvement in the educational levels of the labour force. However, as Kalecki pointed out in his famous 1943 article, maintaining full employment is possible technically, but it is politically and ideologically contested because a rigorous full-employment policy undermines the disciplinary effects of 'the sack' on the workforce (Kalecki 1990). Unemployment, or rather the threat of it, is crucially important in keeping wages down and in otherwise mitigating worker radicalism.

The neo-liberal assault on corporate liberalism in the area of labour market restructuring picked up precisely on this point. The Thatcher government, for instance, quite deliberately precipitated a serious recession upon coming into office and allowed unemployment to rise sharply before continuing to confront the trade union movement politically. Looking back, we can see that the neo-liberal offensive proceeded in two distinct (but not necessarily consecutive) ways.

The first offensive was directed in a negative way against the very institutions that had come to characterize labour relations throughout the advanced industrial world: collective bargaining, job protection, recognition of union rights and (especially in continental Europe) the practices of tripartite corporatism. *Flexibility* became the catchword to express the thrust of this drive: flexible wage rates (upward and downward), flexible labour markets (simplified rules for hiring and firing, lower benefits to increase the willingness to work under deteriorated conditions) (see Chapters by 3, 5 and 7 for more detail).

The second offensive, in line with the general individualism of economic liberalism, entailed the redefinition of the causes of unemployment. In the postwar episode unemployment was seen as a structural problem of the capitalist economy: it could be caused by underconsumption (to be rectified by redistribution of income), by underinvestment (to be addressed by public investment programmes) or by industrial restructuring (to be addressed by state industrial policies), but in each case unemployment was essentially something external to the unemployed worker. Neo-liberalism has redefined unemployment as a personal defect of the unemployed, who is incapable (or unwilling at the prevailing wage rate) to avail him- or herself of the opportunities in the labour market. *Employability* has become the label for these views: it is the personal responsibility of individuals to make sure that they qualify for employment (whatever the changes in the structure of the labour market). The role of the state in this view is to engage in an *active labour market policy* that encourages and facilitates workers to upgrade their skills and qualifications (again, for more details refer to Chapters 3–8 of this volume).

The remaining chapters in Part I will address in more detail the transition from the Keynesian to the neo-liberal paradigm in fairly general terms. Part II details how this transition took place at the level of the EU, and how and under whose auspices employment and labour market policy developed into a major political arena in the EU. Finally, in Part III the complex dialectical interaction between the national and the European levels is detailed.

Notes

1 To the extent that the term 'globalization' is contaminated with the unfounded and often apologetic connotations of universality and homogeneity (see the paragraph which follows in the main text) it might be preferable to reject the term altogether and replace it with the concept of *transnationalization*. This seems a strategy, however, that is bound to fail: globalization has simply become too deeply entrenched for us to be able to replace it. We will therefore insist wherever appropriate on our specific understanding of the term.

2 In general terms I tend to agree with Wallerstein's position in his debate with Frank and Gills, namely that what distinguishes the post-15th-century world-economy from the preceding world economy (without hyphen) is the international division of labour which came to concern the trade in essentials (such as timber, grain, etc.) rather than the trade in luxury products (silk, spices) characteristic of earlier ages (Wallerstein 1993). This position does not imply (at least not for me) that *capitalism* as a mode of production can be said to have been firmly established within all social formations that were part of this world-economy. Mandel's position, distinguishing between 'capitalist world market' and 'capitalist mode of production', enables us to evade many of the futile discussions into which Frank and Wallerstein have allowed themselves to be drawn (see Mandel 1972).

3 I try to avoid using terms like 'cycles', 'stages' or 'phases', which have all been tainted with quite specific connotations that would lead us into debates that are not pertinent to our present purposes.

4 In the US the labour force participation rate increased from an average of 67.5 per cent in the 1970s to 75.8 per cent in 1989 and 77.6 per cent in 1998 (estimate); in Japan the comparable figures are 71.3, 73.3 and 79.0 per cent; For the EU as a whole they are less outspoken, namely 66.0, 66.2 and 66.6 per cent (cf. OECD 1996a: A22).

5 In the EU the share of industry in total employment fell from 39.5 per cent in 1975 to 33.3 per cent in 1990 and 29.3 per cent in 1999; for services these figures were 49.5, 60.1 and 66.3 per cent, respectively; for agriculture they were 11.1, 6.7 and 4.4 per cent (data from European Commission 2000e: 85).

6 In India, for example, the government has taken an active role in this trade. It recently announced plans to spend $650 million to double India's current annual output of 100,000 IT graduates by 2002, and to reach 500,000 by 2005 (Chanda 2000). Indeed, remittances in India cover more than half of the negative balance of international trade. At the same time, India has illiteracy rates of some 35 per cent for men and over 60 per cent for women (World Bank 1997).

7 For more elaborate accounts of the rise of neo-liberalism, see Overbeek (1993), van der Pijl (1984, 1989, 1998); see also my study of Thatcherism (Overbeek 1990).

8 In his study of the 'Swedish model', Magnus Ryner presents us with an exemplary study of how the rise of neo-liberalism resulted from a sustained ideological offensive carried out by representatives of Swedish transnational capital who fully understood the nature of the *war of manoeuvre* they were engaged in (Ryner 2002: ch. 6).

3 Changes in welfare regimes and the search for flexibility and employability

Bob Jessop

This chapter argues that recent changes in labour market policies in the European Union are closely related to the more general restructuring, strategic reorientation and rescaling of welfare regimes and that this latter transformation is related in turn to fundamental changes in the form and dynamic of capitalism. Distinguishing cause and effect in these interrelations is difficult, however, because so many features of our once taken-for-granted economic, political, social and cultural landscape are changing at the same time. My discussion of these issues will focus initially on the *structural coupling* of economic and political transformations without attempting to judge the relative causal weight of economic and political factors. Thus I first present a four-dimensional framework for analysing changes in welfare regimes and then identify a tendential transformation in these regimes along all four dimensions. This sort of transformation can be discerned well beyond the member states of the European Union, which suggests that any explanation couched purely in terms of specific features of the emerging European economy and/or polity will be limited. Accordingly, I will argue that these changes can be explained in part through the more general restructuring, reorientation and rescaling of the capitalist economy and in part through the more general restructuring, reorientation and rescaling of the principles of statehood. Within this general context we can consider the distinctive features of these changes in the European Union and how they are mediated and overdetermined by its distinctive institutional features and balance of forces.

Four dimensions of welfare regimes

As a basis for considering how unemployment policies (and labour market policies more generally) have been undergoing reorganization in the wider context of contemporary capitalist restructuring, I suggest that there are four basic dimensions to the state's involvement in securing the conditions for capitalist reproduction. These are: the state's distinctive economic contribution to securing the conditions for profitable accumulation of private capital; its distinctive social contribution to the reproduction of labour power as a fictitious commodity; the primary scale (if any) on which policy-making (as opposed to policy implementation) in the fields of economic and social policy is determined; and the primary means of supplementing the always more or less inadequate role of market forces in capital accumulation and social reproduction. Seen in these terms, recent changes in welfare regimes in advanced capitalist societies in Western Europe, North America and the Antipodes can be summarized in terms of a tendential and uneven movement from some version of the Keynesian welfare national state (KWNS) to some version of a Schumpeterian workfare post-national regime (SWPR). Although the reasons for this shift are primarily grounded in responses to specific economic and social problems, such responses are always politically mediated. Thus national variations in the pace, direction and emerging patterns of the SWPR are often rooted in their respective initial starting points, differences in modes of growth and insertion into the global economy, and the institutional specificities and distinctive balance of forces. This means that, even if certain general tendencies can be identified and grounded in the logic of contemporary capitalism, this does not justify a simple 'one-size-fits-all' account of welfare restructuring. Instead, proper comparative analyses are required to comprehend and explain variations as well as similarities across the advanced capitalist economies.

The four criteria proposed here derive from basic features of capitalism. The first criterion is the state's distinctive role in securing conditions for profitable private business. This is the broad field of economic policy. It is important because market forces alone cannot secure the conditions for capital accumulation and are always supplemented by non-market mechanisms. This insufficiency is grounded in generic tendencies towards market failure and in specific contradictions and dilemmas associated with capitalism. The second dimension refers to the state's distinctive roles in reproducing labour power individually and collectively over various time-spans, from everyday routines through individual lifecycles to intergenerational reproduction. This is the broad field of social policy. It matters because labour power is a fictitious commodity (Polanyi 1957; de Brunhoff 1968). In other words, although it is bought and sold in labour markets and may add value in production, it is not itself directly (re)produced in and by capitalist firms with a view to private profit. Instead, labour power enters the market economy from outside and is embodied in individuals who have other identities than that of bearers of labour power. This poses economic problems as regards its individual and collective suitability to capital's needs and its own survival in the absence of a secure income or other assets; social problems regarding social inclusion and cohesion; and political problems regarding the legitimacy of state intervention in this area and its relation to other identities that workers may have. The third dimension refers to the main scale – assuming there is a main scale – on which economic and social policies are decided – even if underpinned or implemented on other scales. This is important, as economic and social policies are politically mediated and the scales of political organization may not coincide with those of economic and social life. The fourth dimension concerns the relative weight of the mechanisms deployed in the effort to maintain capitalist profitability and reproduce labour power by compensating for market failures and inadequacies. Top-down state intervention is just one of these mechanisms; and, as is well known, states as well as markets can fail. This suggests the need for other supplementary mechanisms and, insofar as these also tend to fail, for attention to be paid to the balance among them (Dunsire 1996; Bochel and Bochel 1998).

The ideal-typical post-war welfare regime in advanced capitalist economies (apart from Japan) can be defined in these terms as a Keynesian welfare national state on the following grounds. First, in promoting the conditions for profitable accumulation, it was distinctively *Keynesian* insofar as it aimed to secure full employment in a relatively closed national economy and pursued this goal mainly through demand-side management. Second, in reproducing labour power as a fictitious commodity, social policy had a distinctive *welfare* orientation insofar as it tried:

- to generalize norms of mass consumption beyond male workers in Fordist economic sectors earning a family wage with the declared aim of ensuring that all national citizens and their dependants might share the fruits of economic growth (and thereby also contribute to effective domestic demand); and
- to promote forms of collective consumption favourable to the Fordist growth dynamic, with its base in a virtuous national circle of mass production and mass consumption.

Thus economic and social policies were linked to economic and social rights attached directly or indirectly to citizenship of a national territorial state – whether this citizenship was based on descent, acculturation, naturalization, political tests or some other criterion (on types of national state, see Jessop 1999). Third, the KWNS was *national* insofar as economic and social policies were pursued within the historically specific (and socially constructed) matrix of a national economy, a national state and a society seen as comprising national citizens. Within this matrix it was the national territorial state that was mainly held responsible for developing and guiding Keynesian full-employment and welfare policies (Hoffman and Hoffman 1997; de Swaan 1992). Local and regional states acted mainly as relays for policies framed at the national level; and the various international regimes established after World War II were mainly intended to restore stability to national economies and national states. In this sense, the dependence of the post-war expansion of the international economy on the presence of nationally 'embedded liberalism' (Ruggie 1982) can be contrasted with its subsequent disembedding through globalization. And, fourth, the KWNS can be seen as *statist* insofar as state institutions (on different levels) were the chief supplement to market forces in securing the conditions for economic growth and social cohesion. It was the combination of market and state on different levels that prompted the use of the term 'mixed economy' to describe the post-war system (classically, Shonfield 1965). Alongside its role in facilitating and correcting the operation of market forces, the state also significantly shaped civil society and thus its citizens' identities.

There was never a pure form of KWNS. At best, one finds particular welfare regimes that combine features of several possible variants or sub-types of KWNS with other economic and social policy functions, scales of action or modes of governance. There are four commonly cited forms of welfare regime – market liberal (sometimes subdivided, and justifiably so, into North Atlantic and Antipodean variants), social democratic, conservative corporativist (or Christian democratic)[1] and Mediterranean (or Southern European). This schema builds on the well-known threefold typology of liberal, social-democratic and conservative welfare regimes that was first proposed by Esping-Andersen (1985). His typology was mainly based on just one aspect of just one of the four dimensions presented above, namely the state's role in decommodifying men's waged labour. He did not consider the state's roles in relation to women's waged and unwaged labour; nor did he examine other dimensions of the state's involvement in social reproduction (e.g. education, health or housing). But he did give a secondary role to a related aspect of the fourth dimension, i.e. the governance mechanisms used in the social reproduction of labour power. In particular, in addition to liberal market forces he referred to corporativist insurance schemes, formally rational state redistribution, and, in later work, clientelism and the family. We should also note that his typology was initially developed to explore how the balance of social forces at the founding moments of welfare regimes in different societies led to different types of welfare regime, and then continued through its path-dependent effects to shape, in large measure, their subsequent development. Esping-Andersen and others have since deployed the resulting taxonomy for many other purposes, but it still bears the path-dependent imprint of his initial research question. This makes it less relevant for showing how different welfare regimes have come to be integrated into broader modes of economic regulation and/or distinctive 'historical blocs' (i.e. mutually implicated, structurally coupled and historically co-evolving ensembles of economic, political and socio-cultural relations). It is also said to be less useful for analysing the quite distinctive features of the recent politics of welfare *retrenchment* (as opposed to expansion) in response to the emerging crisis of welfare regimes (cf. Pierson 1995).

This suggests that one could usefully extend Esping-Andersen's typology to take account of cases excluded from his original study, to reflect the most incisive criticisms of its theoretical and empirical foundations,[2] and to integrate the other dimensions of welfare regimes noted above. In particular, the typology should be modified to include modes of economic intervention (previously ignored) and modes of governance (previously treated rather perfunctorily). This should permit a more sophisticated analysis of the path-dependent structural coupling among modes of economic growth, modes of regulation and the nature of welfare regimes. The political economy of scale is less germane to Esping-Andersen's typology because during the relevant time period his cases were all marked by the primacy of the national scale. Nonetheless, the issue of scale should still be incorporated in the revised typology in order to facilitate comparisons with earlier and later periods. The earlier period is particularly relevant to the origins and development of welfare regimes because local state capacities and the forms of domestic politics affected the balance of economic and political forces during the formative period of welfare regimes. For example, strong localist and/or regionalist tendencies tend to be associated with corporativist or Southern European regimes rather than with liberal or universalist social-democratic regimes. The later period is significant because the diversity of contemporary welfare regimes at the national scale has affected (and still does) attempts to promote economic integration and build a Social Europe.

Regarding the relations among modes of economic growth, modes of regulation and welfare regimes, there seems to be a close relationship between the liberal welfare regime and finance-based, market-regulated capitalist regimes; between social democratic welfare regimes and small open economies with strong, niche-market oriented, high-skill, high-productivity, high-wage, flexibly specialized export sectors; between more conservative, corporativist welfare regimes and larger economies, open or closed, with close co-ordination between industry and finance as well as close co-ordination between large industrial concerns and small and medium-sized enterprises; and, finally, between the Southern European welfare model and late-developing, peripheral Fordist economies with large agrarian sectors, traditional social structures and family capitalism. Such correlations need to be explained, of course, rather than merely posited. Fortunately there is a growing body of work that is concerned with this question from various institutionalist perspectives (e.g. P.A. Hall and Soskice 2001; Huber and Stephens 2001; Ebbinghaus and Manow 2001). The approach adopted here is premised on the heuristic and explanatory power to be expected from combining a regulationist approach to modes of growth and their regulation with a state-theoretical approach to the political mediation of pressures for economic and social policy intervention.

An explanation in regulationist terms would examine at least three variables. First, it would examine how different patterns of finance–industry relations are connected to the relative dominance of a 'money-capital' or a 'productive-capital' concept of the economic process on the part of the leading fraction(s) of capital. The former concept is more liberal (and, often, internationalist) in its concern with formally free circulation and exchange; the latter is more sensitive to the substantive interdependence (or socialization) of the productive forces, and more interventionist (and, perhaps, protectionist) in its concern with securing the substantive conditions for the production of surplus value (van der Pijl 1984: 8–34; Overbeek 1990: 25–9). This has obvious implications not only for economic policy, including modes of intervention, capacities for state planning or economic guidance, the levels and incidence of taxation, and education and training policy, but also for the relative weight of market forces and state provision in social policy (cf. Polanyi 1957; Boyer 1997; P.A. Hall and Soskice 2001; Soskice 1999a; Huber and Stephens 1999, 2001). Second, it would consider the timing of the emergence of formally free labour markets in relation to the onset and development of industrialization, the timing of the breakdown of guild supervision of urban labour and the timing of the abolition of feudal labour dues (Crouch 1993; Biernacki 1995). For, as Biernacki has shown, these affect the prevailing cultural conceptions of labour power, especially whether it is regarded primarily as one substitutable factor of production among others or as a distinctive set of creative capacities with attached rights and duties. These cultural perceptions not only affect the organization of production, labour market institutions, industrial relations and the propensity for corporatist co-operation, but also influence the more general economic and political demands raised by the labour movement (Biernacki 1995).[3] The coupling between labour market organization and welfare regimes has also recently been explored in work on unemployment policies by Visser (2000) and on production regimes and welfare by Huber and Stephens (1999, 2001). Third, it would examine how different modes of inter-firm competition and/or co-operation lead to the relative dominance of formal market exchange or networking in securing the conditions of valorization, innovation, etc.[4] These sets of factors operate initially at the level of branches and sectors (e.g. the organization of the labour process, the structure of labour markets, training regimes or the differential development of paternalism and occupational welfare) but, depending on the relative structural dominance and hegemonic capacities of specific economic sectors and fractions of capital, their specific effects can become more general (or even universal) within particular regional or national formations. This dominance is typically mediated through the strategic selectivity of state forms, which make it harder or easier to promote universal welfare, and the changing balance of political forces. The relative weight of different factors also varies with stages of capitalism. Thus, to take one highly topical example, the money concept of capital had a reduced significance during the period of Atlantic Fordism compared with the current period of neo-liberal globalization (van der Pijl 1984; van Apeldoorn 1998).

An explanation in terms of the strategic selectivity of the state would focus on various factors. These include modes of representation, the articulation of the state apparatus across different branches, functional domains, territorial scales and modes of intervention; and, for the wider political system, the way in which party systems and patterns of industrial relations have been shaped by extra-economic as well as economic factors (e.g. Rokkan 1978, 1999; Crouch 1993; C.J. Martin 1995). What is interesting here is how the strategic selectivity of the state system on different scales, but especially at the national level, involves a more or less systematic configuration of constraints and opportunities on corporate strategies, regarding not only their immediate market situation but also many other aspects of production and welfare regimes (for recent analyses of these configurations and their implications for institutional complementarities, see the various contributions to P.A. Hall and Soskice 2001; on the link between state traditions, trade unionism and industrial relations, see Crouch 1993).

Just as there is no pure KWNS, so there is no pure crisis of the KWNS – only specific, path-dependent, nationally variable crises. In some cases there has been greater continuity, linked to the dominance of the view that there was a crisis *in* the welfare state, with largely incremental shifts towards the new welfare regime (e.g. Denmark); in others there has been greater discontinuity – admittedly more marked in declared policy changes than actual policy outcomes – linked to a discursively constructed crisis *of* the welfare state (e.g. Britain). There are two complicating factors in this regard, especially in distinguishing the North American and Antipodean cases from those in continental Europe. The first such factor is, of course, the development and intervention of the European Union as a strongly institutionalized form of supranational co-ordination of responses to the economic and social problems associated with the crisis of Atlantic Fordism. And the second is the more recent movement towards a globalizing, knowledge-based economy (on these issues, see Jessop 2000a, 2000b).

Crisis in the KWNS

The KWNS began to fail as a mode of securing the reproduction-regulation of Atlantic Fordism when its institutional coherence became inconsistent with the objects it was governing, the practices being deployed to govern them, and the identities and interests of the active agents and/or 'passive' subjects of the KWNS regime. Thus, taking its four dimensions in turn, I would identify the following crisis tendencies. First, the primary object of economic governance in the KWNS was the national economy. The emergence and consolidation of Keynesian practices had helped to delimit and reproduce the national economy (Tomlinson 1985). They provided the means of measuring national economic performance, controlling economic flows across national borders, setting economic aggregates such as inflation, employment and growth as goals of national economic management, and creating the infrastructure for national economic development. But Keynesian economic management became increasingly problematic and generated stagflationary tendencies (stagnation plus inflation) that fuelled the emerging crisis of the Atlantic Fordist economy that the KWNS was supposed to manage (Boyer 1991). Economic internationalization exacerbated these problems. It undermined the national economy as an object of economic management and led to quite different conceptions of the economy and, a fortiori, its mechanisms of economic and social governance. States could no longer act as if national economies were more or less closed and their growth dynamics were primarily domestic (Teeple 1995). Replacing the national economy as the primary object of economic governance is the knowledge-driven economy in an era of globalization (Castells 1996). Its growth dynamic depends on how effectively a given economic space – not necessarily a national economy – is inserted into the changing global division of labour. This in turn has prompted concern with international economic competitiveness and supply-side intervention – initially to supplement national demand management, later as the primary objective and means of economic intervention.

The imagined scope and inclusiveness of the economy that needs governing have also expanded. This is no longer interpreted in narrow terms but has been extended to include many additional factors, deemed 'non-economic' under the KWNS regime, that affect economic performance. This expansion is reflected in concepts such as 'structural competitiveness' (Chesnais 1986) or 'systemic competitiveness' (Messner 1997) – concepts that highlight the combined impact of diverse societal factors on competitiveness. State managers therefore intervene in a growing range of economically relevant practices, institutions, functional systems and domains of the life-world to enhance competitiveness. This has two interesting and paradoxical effects on the state. First, whilst it expands the potential scope of state intervention for economic purposes, the resulting complexity renders post-war top-down intervention less effective – requiring that the state retreat from some areas of intervention and reinvent itself as a condition for more effective intervention in others (Messner 1997). And, second, whilst it increases the range of stakeholders whose co-operation is required for successful state intervention, it also increases pressures within the state to create new subjects to act as its partners. Thus states are now trying to transform the identities, interests, capacities, rights and responsibilities of economic and social forces so that they become more flexible, capable and reliable agents of the state's new economic strategies – whether in partnership with the state and/or each other or as autonomous entrepreneurial subjects in the new knowledge-driven economy (Barry *et al.* 1996; Deakin and Edwards 1993; Finer 1997; Jones 1999).

Second, the generic object of social governance in the KWNS (as in other forms of national state) was a national population divided, in the first instance, into citizens of the national state and resident aliens. But this population was categorized and governed in distinctive ways suited to Atlantic Fordism and its mode of regulation. Above all, social policy was premised on conditions of full or near-full employment, on lifelong employment – albeit not necessarily with the same employer – with a family wage for male workers, and on the patriarchal nuclear family as the basic unit of civil society (Esping-Andersen 1994). The KWNS was also premised on a class compromise between organized labour and organized business in which responsible unionism and collective bargaining permitted managers to manage and workers to benefit from rising productivity as wage earners and welfare recipients. There were nonetheless some marginalized or overburdened social groups. The most notable of these groups were women as housewives, mothers and secondary participants in the labour force, and immigrants or other workers (and their families) who worked in disadvantaged segments of the labour market (Lewis 1998). This pattern was undermined both economically and socially. The crisis of Atlantic Fordism undermined the assumptions of full employment, the family wage and the gendered division of labour, and also led state managers to see the social wage increasingly as a cost of international production rather than as a source of domestic demand. There was also a growing contradiction in the field of social reproduction, with encouragement to immigration for economic purposes being accompanied by increasing concern to police the boundaries of national citizenship and its associated welfare rights. In particular, whereas the European states of Atlantic Fordism had previously been seen largely as countries of *emigration* and/or, in the wake of post-war decolonization, *return* of nationals to their homelands, the 1970s witnessed the construction of immigration as a threat to national cohesion, full employment, and the welfare state (cf. Kofman 1995; also Bieling 1993). More generally, KWNS in Europe was also affected (admittedly to different degrees) by a weakening of the national identity and solidarity that shaped it in its formative period and helped sustain the coalition behind it. This is reflected in changes in the values, social identities and interests associated with the welfare state. Indicators of this included rejection of the social-democratic and/or Atlantic Fordist commitment to a class-based redistributive politics; a pluralistic identity politics and 'politics of difference' that emphasizes mutual respect, authenticity and autonomy; increased concern for personal empowerment rather than for the bureaucratic administration of legal rights, monetized entitlements and uniform public services; and expansion of the so-called 'third' sector, which supposedly operates flexibly outside the framework of pure markets and the bureaucratic state (but often in close conjunction with them as a 'shadow market' and 'shadow state'). These shifts have fragmented the KWNS coalition of forces, led to demands for more differentiated and flexible forms of economic and social policy, and led to concern with problems of social exclusion and ensuring lifetime access to the benefits of a restructured welfare regime (e.g. lifelong learning).

Third, the primacy of the national scale of economic and social governance depended on the coincidence of national economy, national state, national society and the survival of the national state as a sovereign body. This structured coherence has also been weakened. The national economy has been undermined by internationalization, the growth of multi-tiered global city networks, the formation of triad economies (such as the European Union), and the re-emergence of regional and local economies in national states. This complex articulation of global–regional–national–local economies is related to the 'hollowing-out' of the national state as its powers are delegated upwards to supra-regional or international bodies, downwards to regional or local states, or outwards to relatively autonomous cross-national alliances among local metropolitan or regional states with complementary interests. There are also growing attempts to internationalize (or at least, in the case of the EU, to Europeanize) social policy. And, third, the unity of the nation-state has been weakened by the (admittedly uneven) growth of multiethnic and multicultural societies and of divided political loyalties (with the resurgence of regionalism and nationalism as the rise of European identities, diasporic networks, cosmopolitan patriotism, etc.) (Jessop 1999). Thus we see a proliferation of scales on which economic and social policy is pursued as well as of competing projects to reunify inter-scalar articulation around a new primary level – whether this be the industrial district, the city-region, wider subnational regions, cross-border regions, the triads or the global level. In this context, the European Union is only one among many such projects to find a new scale on which the conditions for economic expansion can be secured once again.

Finally, the state's role in the mixed economy was undermined by several factors. These include: growing political resistance to taxation and an emerging pattern of stagnation-inflation (or 'stagflation'); crisis in post-war compromises between industrial capital and organized labour; new economic and social conditions and attendant problems that could not be managed or resolved readily, if at all, through continuing reliance on top down state planning and/or simple market forces; growing resentment about the bureaucratism, inflexibility and cost of the welfare state as it continued to expand during the late 1960s and 1970s; and the rise of new social movements which did not fit easily into the post-war compromise. Moreover, as society became more complex, and as new economic and social conditions emerged that could not be managed or resolved readily, if at all, through the market and state as modes of governance, increasing reliance came to be placed on networks and partnerships as modes of co-ordination. Organizationally, the Fordist period was one of large scale, top-down hierarchical structures, and this model spread to the state's economic and welfare roles. This paradigm has since been challenged by a new 'network paradigm' that emphasizes partnership, regulated self-regulation, the informal sector, the facilitation of self-organization and decentralized context-steering (Messner 1997). Overall this involves a tendential shift from imperative co-ordination by the sovereign state to an emphasis on interdependence, divisions of knowledge, reflexive negotiation and mutual learning. In short, there is a shift from govern*ment* to govern*ance* in the narrow sense.

The Schumpeterian workfare post-national regime

These changes are reflected in four general trends in the restructuring of the KWNS. The first is a shift from Keynesian aims and modes of intervention to Schumpeterian ones; the second is a shift from a welfarist mode of reproduction of labour power to a workfarist mode; the third is a shift from the primacy of the national scale to a post-national framework in which no scale is predominant; the fourth is a shift from the primacy of the state in compensating for market failures to an emphasis on networked, partnership-based economic, political and social governance mechanisms. These trends can be considered separately. Indeed, both severally and in combination, they have developed in quite different ways in the various Atlantic Fordist economies. They can nonetheless be summarized in terms of the suggestion that the KWNS is giving way to an SWPR. Moreover, whether viewed individually or in aggregate, these four changes are closely connected to the search for solutions to the Atlantic Fordist crisis.

The ideal-typical SWPR can be described as follows. First, regarding its functions for private capital, it is *Schumpeterian* insofar as it tries to promote permanent innovation and flexibility in relatively open economies by intervening on the supply side and to strengthen as far as possible their structural and/or systemic competitiveness. The Schumpeterian moment is sometimes termed the 'competition state' (Cerny 1990; Hirsch 1995a). This correctly identifies the increased importance of competition in the state's economic policy role, but since there are many forms of competition it fails to specify what is distinctive about the state's contribution in promoting new forms of competition. Of particular importance here is the emphasis on innovation and enterprise linked with the widespread belief that a new long wave of technological change is occurring. Thus, just as Keynes was the emblematic economist for the post-war welfare state, Schumpeter has been posthumously invoked as the emblematic economist for today's restructuring. This is reflected in a broadening of the scope of economics, economic calculation and economic intervention to include a whole range of activities previously regarded as extra-economic. This is partly related to the growing importance attached to international competition and the way in which this turns the general institutional features of societies into stakes in the new competitive race. Previous discussions of the 'competition state' have also tended to confine it to the level of the local or national state and thus to ignore the rescaling of state intervention upwards as well.

Second, regarding social reproduction, the SWPR can be described (at the risk of some misunderstanding) as a *workfare* regime insofar as it subordinates social policy to the demands of labour market flexibility and employability and to the demands of structural or systemic competitiveness. In this sense, social policy is now modelled on human capital theory and becomes a form of human resource management. Complementing these new strategic concerns in economic and social policy has been the demotion or rejection of other, earlier policy objectives. Thus, whilst the KWNS established full employment as one of the main goals of state action, in the SWPR it is regarded more as a desirable by-product of the successful promotion of structural or systemic competitiveness. Likewise, whereas the KWNS had a qualified commitment to redistributive politics to promote social equality and to even out regional development, the SWPR accepts increasing economic, social and regional inequalities and compensates for these through more limited policies aimed at combating social exclusion. Similarly, whilst the KWNS tried to extend the social rights of its national citizens, the SWPR is more concerned to provide welfare services that benefit business and thus tends to demote individual needs to second place. This includes putting downward pressure on the social wage qua cost of international production. Even where there appear to be strong continuities with the KWNS, the SWPR gives the inherited features a new inflection. Thus, although concern with training and labour market functioning has long been a feature of state involvement in the social reproduction of labour power, the SWPR puts more weight on flexibility and gives it new connotations (Ainley 1997). This is also why there is a major reorientation on the part of the state to the making and remaking of the subjects who are expected to serve as partners in the innovative, knowledge-driven, entrepreneurial, flexible economy and its accompanying self-reliant, autonomous, empowered workfare regime (for a recent illustration, see Blair and Schröder 1999).

Third, compared with the earlier primacy of the national scale, the SWPR is '*post-national*' insofar as the increased significance of other spatial scales and horizons of action (or 'relativization of scale'; see Collinge 1996) makes the national territory less important as a 'power container'. This is associated with a transfer of economic and social policy-making functions upwards, downwards and sideways. On a global level, this can be seen in the growing concern of a growing number of international agencies (such as the IMF, World Bank, OECD and International Labour Organization, ILO) and intergovernmental forums (such as the G8) with the shaping of current social as well as economic policy agendas. In part, the European Union acts as a relay for these agenda-shaping efforts and in part it has itself played an active role in developing its own agenda for countries outside its borders. This is most clear in the case of the post-socialist economies, especially those in the front ranks of new candidate member states; but can also be seen in its interest in social as well as economic policy in associate member states and North Africa (cf. de Swaan 1992; Deacon 1995, 1996; Leibfried 1993; Wilding 1997). The EU level is also imposing more numerous and tighter restrictions on national economic and social governance, especially through the norms of the Single Market, the Maastricht criteria for economic convergence and the requirements of EMU. This is reflected in the tendential Europeanization of labour market policies, in the transformation of national corporatist and bargaining arrangements, and in the development of 'social pacts'. What is emerging in this context is a series of multilevel government and/or governance regimes oriented to issues of the inter-scalar re-articulation of the economic and political – with the European Union just one among many such emerging regimes (Poulantzas 1978; Jessop 2000b). At the same time there are tendencies to devolve some economic and social policy-making to the regional, urban and local levels on the grounds that policies intended to influence the micro-economic supply-side and social regeneration are best designed close to their sites of implementation. In some cases this also involves cross-border co-operation among regional, urban or local spaces. In all three regards welfare regimes have become more post-national. Yet paradoxically, as we will see below, this often leads to an enhanced role for national states in controlling the inter-scalar transfer of these powers – suggesting a shift from sovereignty to a *primus inter pares* role in intergovernmental relations.

The post-national moment of economic and social policy restructuring is complex because of the proliferation of scales and the relativization of scale with which it is associated. There are clear differences among the triads here. NAFTA is primarily a continental trading system based on America's dominance as a quasi-continental economy (itself comprising many different regional economies with different levels of economic performance), with Canada and Mexico being increasingly obliged to internalize US production and consumption norms as well as to find their place as best they can within an emerging continental division of labour. The East Asian triad has developed an increasingly important regional division of labour organized primarily under Japanese regional hegemony, but it has no coherent institutional mechanisms to ensure effective co-ordination and is weakened by Japan's continuing inability to break out of its political impasse, as well as by the residual bitterness felt by significant social forces in countries occupied by Japan in the 1930s and 1940s. The European Union provides the only example among the three triad regions of a clear commitment to economic, political and social integration and, more ambivalently, to the development of supranational state structures. Nonetheless, all three regions/triads are linked to internationalization of policy regimes not only in economic but also in juridical, political and social fields, etc. This excludes any easy generalization from the EU case to the other two triads – or vice versa; this is itself a sign that one should not push globalization too far as a general explanatory framework of recent changes.

Finally, regarding the mode of delivery of economic and social policies, the SWPR has become more regime-like relative to the statism of the KWNS. This is reflected in the increased importance of non-state mechanisms in compensating for market failures and inadequacies and the delivery of state-sponsored economic and social policies. One aspect of this is the increased importance of private–public networks to state activities on all levels – from local partnerships to supranational neo-corporatist arrangements (e.g. Clarke and Gaile 1998; Falkner 1998). The often remarked shift from government towards 'governance' (from imperative co-ordination to networking and other forms of self-organization) means that traditional forms of intervention now play a lesser role in economic and social policy. This does not mean that law and money have disappeared, of course; instead, active economic and social steering now tends to run more through soft regulation and reflexive law, additionality and private–public partnerships, organizational intelligence and information-sharing, etc.. A key role is also played by 'meta-steering' (which I have described elsewhere as 'meta-governance'), i.e. the organization of the institutional framework and rules for individual modes of governance and the 'collibration' (or rebalancing) of different modes of governance (see Dunsire 1996; Jessop 1998a). This can be seen at the European level, where EU institutions typically operate less in the manner of a rescaled, supranational sovereign state apparatus than as a nodal point in an extensive web of meta-governance operations. Thus they have a central role in orchestrating economic and social policy in and across many different scales of action involving a wide range of official, quasi-official, private economic and civil interests (i.e. a supranational sovereign state) (Tömmel 1994, 1998; Ekengreen 1997; Willke 1992, 1996; Sbragia 2000).

How does this relate to the European Union?

I now argue that each of the four shifts identified above is evident in the development of economic and social policy in Europe. This is hardly surprising because the hypothesized transition from the KWNS to the SWPR derives from theoretical analysis of developmental tendencies in capitalism combined with careful empirical observation of national economies within the circuits of Atlantic Fordism. But, since the account presented above derives from the North American and Antipodean cases as well as from Northwest Europe, and also took the national economy and national state in Atlantic Fordism as its theoretical and historical starting point, it will be worth re-examining the argument from the perspective of the EU to see whether tendencies at the national level are also reflected at the level of the European Union. It is also a key part of my argument that shifts in labour market policy are related to the more general restructuring, reorientation and rescaling of state involvement in securing the reproduction-regulation of contemporary capitalism. Thus it is important to show how shifts in the EU's involvement in employment policy are connected to other changes in the European Union. Accordingly, I will briefly summarize the ways in which these changes are reflected in the development of Social Europe.

First, it is quite clear that the EU's overall economic policy has been reoriented in the direction of a Schumpeterian strategy from an earlier period when it was more suited to Atlantic Fordism. The origins of European integration can be found in post-war reconstruction, which prepared the ground for Atlantic Fordism in Europe (for details, see van der Pijl 1984). Thus, in addition to their initial post-war role in restructuring iron, steel and coal in this context, the European communities also emphasized the creation of an integrated market so that industrial enterprises could realize optimal economies of scale. This involved an essentially liberal *Ordnungspolitik* to create a single market and was an important supplement to the pursuit of national Keynesian policies – especially as the Treaty of Rome left official responsibility for employment policy at the national level. Indeed, as Sbragia notes, the EU's basic constitutional framework structurally privileges liberal economic strategies: 'the norm of economic liberalization, embedded in the Treaty of Rome, was reinforced and elaborated in the Single European Act and the Treaty of Maastricht' (Sbragia 2000: 224). Thus even when the EU, under Delors' presidency (1985–95), began to develop a more active employment policy and to plan for a Social Europe, and then attempted to institutionalize these twin responsibilities for the first time in the Maastricht Treaty (1991), this occurred in an institutional context that was already biased in favour of liberalism and in an ideological climate that was dominated by neo-liberalism. On the latter point, we should note that the collapse of Soviet bloc communism had led to a Western-orchestrated *neo-liberal system transformation*; that neo-liberalism became hegemonic in the West with the *neo-liberal regime shift* in Reagan's America and Thatcher's Britain and with a resurgent American influence on many international institutions; and that even the more regulated national variants of capitalism began undertaking *neo-liberal policy adjustments* within their traditional modes of economic and social regulation.

It is worth noting here that the six initial members of the European Economic Community (EEC) had modes of growth and modes of regulation belonging to one or other of the regulated varieties of capitalism, and had either one or other form of conservative-corporativist welfare regime or, in Italy's case, a clientelist Mediterranean welfare regime (cf. Ruigrok and van Tulder 1996; Hantrais 1995). This suggests that the institutionalized commitment to economic liberalism might initially have provided the basis for the integration and consolidation of regulated capitalism on a wider scale rather than the means to push through a far-reaching liberal programme. The situation changed, however, as new members with different modes of growth, modes of regulation and welfare regimes joined the European Community. This introduced greater economic and social heterogeneity into the European economy and helped to shift the balance of forces in a neo-liberal direction. It has been correspondingly more difficult to establish the conditions for rescaling state planning from the national to the European level or to establish Euro-corporatism (on Euro-corporatism, see Falkner 1998 and Vobruba 1995; on its limits, see Streeck 1995a). Likewise, rather than seeing a rescaling of the welfare state upwards to the European Union, EU social policy largely takes the form of social regulation. For, as Majone notes,

> measures proposed by the Commission in the social field must be compatible with the 'economic constitution' of the Community, that is, with the principle of a liberal economic order. This requirement creates an ideological climate quite unlike that which made possible the development of the welfare state in the Member States.... The economic liberalism that pervades the Founding Treaty and its subsequent revisions gives priority to the allocation of public policy over distributional objectives. Hence the best rationale for social initiatives at Community level is one which stresses the efficiency-improving aspects of the proposed measures.
>
> (Majone 1993: 156)

These difficulties have been reinforced by the manner in which the EMU has been instituted. The convergence criteria established under the Maastricht Treaty have made it more difficult for member states to break out of the neo-liberal framework, and the limited EU budget prevents it from financing a major expansion of a European welfare regime. Indeed, in certain respects the EMU serves as a new 'gold standard', requiring conformity to relatively rigid norms of economic and political conduct favourable to a liberal (money) conception of economic stability and growth. In particular, compliance with the Maastricht criteria have required public spending cuts or constraints, social security and welfare reforms, and more or less significant privatization of state-owned enterprises and commercialization of public services. Nonetheless, even in this context we can discern a growing concern with active involvement in promoting competitiveness, innovation and enterprise in line with Schumpeterian perspectives. Although the main thrust of this involvement accords well with neo-liberal strategy, it is nonetheless flanked by neo-statist and neo-corporatist strategies, illustrated by key features of EU technology policies and social policy, respectively (for a brief summary of the distinctions between neo-liberal, neo-statist and neo-corporatist variants of the SWPR, see Figure 3.1; for some elaboration, see Jessop 2000c; see also Gottfried 1995). A very interesting development in this area is, of course, the resurgence of corporatism in a new guise – social pacts oriented to wage restraint, social security reform, supply-side competitiveness and general conformity to the logic of the new monetary system (see Deppe *et al.* 2000; Regini 2000; Grote and Schmitter 1999; Rhodes 1998).

Second, welfare and social policy was retained as a national competence in the founding treaties of the European Community, and policy-making at the European level in these fields has systematically lagged behind macro-economic, industrial and technology policies. Thus, as Kuhnle notes:

> There exists as of today no European social law on the basis of which individual citizens can claim benefits from Brussels; no direct taxation or social

Neo-liberalism

1 Liberalization - promote free competition
2 Deregulation - reduce role of law and state
3 Privatization - sell off public sector
4 Market proxies in residual public sector
5 Internationalization - free inward and outward flows
6 Lower direct taxes - increase consumer choice

Neo-statism

1 Government as agenda-setter rather than planner
2 Guidance of national economic strategy
3 Auditing performance of private and public sectors
4 Public–private partnerships under state guidance
5 Neo-mercantilist protection of core economy
6 Expanding role for new collective resources

Neo-corporatism

1 Rebalance competition and co-operation
2 Decentralized 'regulated self-regulation'
3 Widen range of private, public and other 'stakeholders'
4 Expand role of public–private partnerships
5 Protect core economic sectors in open economy
6 High taxation to finance social investment

Neo-communitarianism

1 De-liberalization - limit free competition
2 Empowerment - enhance role of third sector
3 Socialization - expand the social economy
4 Emphasis on social use-value and social cohesion
5 Fair trade not free trade, think global, act local
6 Redirect taxes - citizens' wage, carers' allowances

Figure 3.1 Variant forms of the Schumpeterian workfare post-national regime

> contributions to EU which can finance social welfare; and there hardly exists any welfare bureaucracy in the EU.
>
> (Kuhnle 1999: 6)

Nonetheless, there is increasing evidence of a complex and complicated reorientation of welfare policy at the European level. This involves two apparently contradictory tendencies. On the one hand, some welfare policies (such as equal pay, equal opportunities, portable welfare benefits, minimum standards for health and security at work, and rules on working hours) have been gradually rescaled to the EU level to supplement the more traditional nationally scaled welfare measures; and some structural policies have also been rescaled at a European level to facilitate industrial restructuring, compensate for uneven regional development, support agriculture and help to regenerate declining communities. On the other hand, the emergence of social policy at the European level tends to assume a workfare rather than welfare orientation. Thus, 'the political point of reference [of such economic and social policy initiatives] is not so much social integration but rather the instrumentalization of policy as a resource for competition oriented structural change' (Deppe *et al.* 2000: 20). In short, there is a growing mix of welfare and workfare strategies at the European level, but they are unified around the concern to create the conditions for an effective single market in post-Fordist rather than Fordist conditions.

One of the earliest signs of this reorientation can be found in the European Commission's White Paper on *Growth, Competitiveness, Employment* (1993). This reviewed a wide range of factors affecting the competitiveness of the European economy and its capacity to generate good jobs and sustainable economic growth; and it recommended an equally wide range of trans-European macroeconomic, environmental, infrastructural, technological, educational, vocational and social policy initiatives that might address – rhetorically at least – the challenges of the coming century. In the field of labour market policy, for example, the Commission called for a broad 'advanced training offensive' and other measures to enhance labour market flexibility. This reorientation was taken further at the 1994 EU Summit in Essen, when it was finally recognized that effective employment policies conducted exclusively at the national level can no longer be successfully managed under the conditions of globalization and European integration (Hoffman and Hoffman 1997: 22). The Treaty of Amsterdam finally embedded a commitment to full employment as a 'matter of common concern' for the EU, translated this into the goal of reaching a 'high level of employment' without undermining competitiveness, and established an Employment Committee to discuss appropriate policy in this area and to monitor progress. In line with the European Union penchant for 'meta-governance' rather than direct top-down intervention, however, the Community's responsibility in this area is to complement the activities of member states by developing a 'co-ordinated strategy', to formulate common guidelines, to establish benchmarks and 'best practice', and to monitor the pursuit of national action plans for employment.

An examination of the emerging practice in this area over the last three years (up to the time of writing, namely the end of 2001) reveals both the extent to which the workfarist reorientation of social policy has penetrated to the EU level and also how far it is linked with expansion of the domain of the 'economic' into areas previously regarded as non-economic. One aspect of this, as noted by Deppe, Felder, and Tidow (2000: 15–16), is that, for the first time, the breadth of the EU labour market guidelines has forced the ministries of economy, culture, finance, welfare and labour to present a joint plan and to relate the separate policies to each other. This can be interpreted as the extension of the logic of commodification or, at least, of capitalist economic calculation into the wider society. Such pressures are also incremental, building up ratchet fashion with each successive cycle of national employment pacts.

Third, almost by definition European economic and social policy illustrates the post-national nature of the emerging welfare regimes. Before considering the EU's role, however, we should note that it is itself part of a more complex internationalization of economic and social policy. Its policies are evolving within a broader framework of growing involvement in agenda-setting and policy-making by international institutions, supranational apparatuses, intergovernmental organizations and forums, transnational think tanks, and transnational interest groups and social movements (cf. Deacon and Hulse 1997; on policy transfer, see Dolowitz and Marsh 1996; Peck and Theodore 2001; and Stella 2000). It is important to recognize, with Deacon and Hulse, that there is some real disagreement among these different bodies on policy recommendations; but this should not be exaggerated, since the bodies aligned with the 'Washington consensus' have tended to be the most influential in the internationalization of economic and social policy. In particular, Deacon and Hulse note some convergence between EU and OECD policies as the EU has discovered the adverse impact on competitiveness of KWNS social policy and the OECD's Directorate of Education, Employment, Labour and Social Affairs has come to recognize the economic benefits of expanded income-support programmes (Deacon and Hulse 1997: 45–58). This development, mediated through an increasingly dense web of parallel power networks, reflects the increased formation of a transnational capitalist class concerned to secure the conditions for capital accumulation on a global scale. This is associated with a 'new constitutionalism' (Gill 1995, 2001), i.e. an attempt to establish a new articulation between the economic and the political on a global rather than merely national scale. But it is also associated, as noted above, with attempts to re-articulate the relationship between the economic and the extra-economic conditions for capital accumulation in a globalizing, post-Fordist, knowledge-based economy.

The European Union has a key role in this new constitutional settlement. Unsurprisingly, therefore, its still emerging character as a political-arena entity is subject to pressures from well beyond its borders (especially from the USA); and it is also becoming involved in international forums on various scales to restabilize the conditions for economic growth and stability in the wake of the crisis of the primacy of the national scale in the post-war 'embedded liberal' international settlement. At the same time, the tendential Europeanization of economic and social policy is also closely linked, in accordance with the principle of subsidiarity, to the increased role of subnational and cross-national agencies, territorial and/or functional in form, in its formulation and implementation. In this regard there is an interesting scalar division of labour between the EU, national states and subnational tiers of government. For, whereas national states retain significant powers in the traditional spheres of the sovereign state (military, police) and in welfare policy (where the limited EU budget blocks a major role in general social redistribution even if it acquired this competence), the EU has acquired increasing influence over economic policy.

Fourth, although the EU has never acquired the characteristics of a supranational sovereign state or even a confederation of states and so cannot be said to have undergone a shift from supranational govern*ment* to supranational gover*nance*, it has developed an increasingly wide and deep array of both governance and meta-governance capacities that enable it to influence economic and social policy in most areas and on most scales. Four specific features of the EU give it special influence here: the role of judges and litigation (which enables the EU to override national laws and to 'constitutionalize' the treaties); its location at the heart of information flows (which gives it a relative monopoly in organizational intelligence); fiscal poverty (which limits its vulnerability to claims on public spending and thereby circumscribes the political agenda) (Sbragia 2000); and the increasing adoption of European projects and guidelines which entitle the EU to monitor national and regional state activities and partnerships across an increasingly interconnected set of policy areas – thereby giving a means to steer national policy and endow it with greater coherence (Deppe *et al.* 2000; Majone 1993; Wallace 2000). The distinctive form of meta-governance in the EU, which invalidates attempts to judge its role in terms of traditional criteria associated with the sovereign national state, is well expressed by Sbragia, as follows:

> The European Union governs in the sense of 'steering' because it is structurally designed [to keep] certain questions off the table while insisting that others be kept on the table. The use of treaties rather than a constitution, the institutionalization of the norm of economic liberalization in those treaties, the creation of a powerful court, its unusual access to information, and the lack of public funds all help the Union steer.
>
> (Sbragia 2000: 236)

Likewise, Tömmel, having noted the key role of regional and local authorities and various public–private partnerships in performing governmental roles in a complex web of co-operative networks organized in tangled (or, more paradoxically yet, de-hierarchized) hierarchies, suggests that the Europe of Regions is becoming

> an indispensable element of an emergent, new open and flexible system, in which the EC – or the Union as a whole – will stimulate competitive and

> co-operative behaviour and performance of decentralized – public and private – agents and institutions, by using open, market-oriented steering mechanisms and by institutionalizing more complex procedures in decision-making and consensus-building.
>
> (Tömmel 1998: 75)

In short, meta-steering is one of the most significant areas in which the EU is involved in restructuring, reorienting and rescaling welfare. The very fact that these activities do not conform to the traditional notion of the exercise of state power has made it hard to see their significance for the overall dynamic of state formation at the European level. But they have nonetheless played a key role in the gradual rise of an EU workfare programme to promote full employment via enhancing the flexibility and employability of workers in the interests of greater competitiveness and enterprise in the transition to post-Fordism. This still leaves scope for different national or regional interpretations of flexibility and employability – ranging from the neo-liberal model promoted by Thatcherism and retained under New Labour (see Chapter 8), through the neo-statist model found in France, to more neo-corporatist patterns associated with the Scandinavian and other Rhenish economies. The European Employment Strategy is a particularly good example of this situation and, in this regard, as Leibfried and Pierson note, it is a key element in 'Europe's emerging multi-tiered system of social policy' (2000: 288).

Conclusions

I have tried to develop five main points in this chapter. First, the changing nature of economic and social policies in the European Union cannot be regarded as a unique product of the specific dynamic of the emerging Europolity, whatever form this might eventually take. For similar changes can be found in other economies and regions that were once dominated by Atlantic Fordism and one or another form of Keynesian welfare national state. Second, there is a close connection between changes in economic and social policies in the European Union insofar as both sets of policy changes represent emerging responses to the crisis of the Atlantic Fordist mode of growth (and its specific instantiations in different national and regional models of post-war capitalism within the overall circuit of Atlantic Fordism) and/or to the associated crisis of the KWNS (again in one or other of its variant forms). This means that, whilst there are historically specific institutional dynamics and specific configurations of social forces in the different areas of economic and social policy (and, indeed, their nationally specific demarcations and subdivisions), there are also material, social and spatio-temporal linkages between them that require increasing attention in a post-Fordist period to the overall coherence and co-ordination of these different policy areas. Third, the reorientation of economic and social policy is also closely related to their rescaling and their modes of governance and delivery. This is partly due to the changing nature of capital accumulation and partly due to the crisis of the national state as the primary scale on which the Fordist mode of regulation was organized. This requires increasing attention to activities above, below and beyond national borders and to their co-ordination in tangled hierarchies of networked institutions, organizations and individuals. Moreover, even when one is primarily concerned with the redesign of economic and social policy at the level of the European Union, it is still essential to look at the broader international context within which this redesign is occurring, as well as its implications for economies and states on its borders.

Fourth, in thinking about the Europeanization of economic and social policy as part of the general emergence of the SWPR, we must be careful not to make two common mistakes. We should not mistake Europeanization for the rise of a supranational European state when what is actually emerging (at least until now) is a complex, multi-tiered, multi-sphered, and multi-centric political space that serves to condense a changing balance of forces rather than to consolidate a new state form for its own sake. In this sense, many of the ambiguities surrounding the emerging Europolity have important political functions and the tensions involved in its construction represent clear differences in economic and political strategy. Nor should we mistake the process of Europeanization for a withering away of national states. Even if the national economy–national state–national society spatio-temporal fix is no longer primary, this does not mean that the national state has ceased to be a central nodal point in the overall articulation of economic, social and political spaces and activities. For this reason we can expect to see continuing divergences in the nature of economic and social policy regimes, reflecting the continuing path-dependent legacies of different models of capitalism, different state traditions, different balances of forces, and different accumulation strategies and hegemonic projects. But these divergences will develop within the framework of struggles over the future shape of the global division of labour, the relation between the three main triad powers and, especially, the relation between the USA and Europe.

Fifth, and finally, I have tried to indicate that the specific shape of the emerging European SWPR was not pre-given or pre-scripted by the logic of the transition from Atlantic Fordism to a globalizing, knowledge-driven economy, but has been moulded by the struggle for hegemony between different accumulation strategies and hegemonic projects. It is the neo-liberal project of a transnational class that has come to dominate for the moment. Whether or not this dominance continues depends on the capacity of the forces arrayed against it to develop their own counter-hegemonic project and to conduct a war of position against the entrenched positions of the dominant neo-liberal forces.

Notes

1 Pitruzello (1999) subjected Esping-Andersen's typology to cluster analysis and, on this basis, developed a new fivefold typology. This not only distinguishes between Antipodean and the Anglo-American liberal market regimes but reclassifies the other cases into three groups: universalistic (Belgium, Denmark, Norway, Sweden), Bismarckian (Germany, Swizerland and the Netherlands) and a new subdivision of the conservative-corporatist model (Austria, Finland, France, Italy and Japan).

2 Pitruzello (1999) provides a good overview of mainstream critiques; see also Abrahamson (1999) and, for feminist critiques, Daly (1994) and Bussemaker and van Kersbergen (1994).

3 On Germany, Britain, France and northern Italy in this regard, see Biernacki (1995).

4 Soskice includes the following elements in his notion of the production regime: the financial system, industrial relations system, education and training system, and the intercompany system (Soskice 1999a: 102).

4 European employment policy between neo-liberal rationalism and communitarianism

Hans-Jürgen Bieling

Introduction

In spite of recent economic growth and the chances of a 'new economy' in Western Europe (CEC 2000), the employment issue is still a core problem of the current socio-economic situation. For, on the one hand, the overall rate of unemployment is still very high in the European Union (EU), not to speak of the precarious situation for particular regions or social groups. And, on the other hand, the rather modest process of job creation is based to a large degree on the expansion of atypical – i.e. part-time, fixed-term and precarious – forms of employment, mainly in the service sector. Nevertheless, public debates tend to ignore such social problems related to the employment issue. Instead, there seems to be an emerging awareness, against the background of economic recovery and the new European framework for co-ordinating national employment strategies via 'benchmarking' and 'regime competition', that mass unemployment is more or less a problem of the past.

This contribution is more cautious and hesitates to adopt the over-optimistic message of a new era of prosperity and full employment. It puts some question marks on many rather superficial observations by outlining the broader socio-economic and politico-ideological context, in which the (un-)employment issue must be placed. For both the roots and causes of unemployment as well as the recent strategies and forms of employment regulation are related to the deep crisis and fundamental restructuring of global capitalism from the mid-1970s onwards.

In this context, three dimensions of radical change are particularly relevant. First, after high economic growth rates during the 'Golden Age' period (Marglin and Schor 1990) and a short period of full employment, capitalism changed its *mode of economic reproduction*. As the world economic crises of the years 1974–5, 1980–2 and 1991–3 have shown, business cycles have become synchronized, average growth rates slowed down and the job-performance of economic growth was rather poor. The old constellation of Fordist prosperity dissolved. Instead, on the basis of new technologies, i.e. biotechnologies, genetic engineering, new materials, robot technologies, and in particular microelectronics – often summarized as the 'third industrial revolution' – corporations introduced more flexible forms of work and production. These changes also fostered strategies of rationalization, not only in industrial production, but also in the service sector.

The second dimension of radical change concerns the *regimes of international economic regulation*. After the collapse of the Bretton Woods system, capital and financial markets became more and more deregulated (Helleiner 1994; Huffschmid 1999). The results are well known. Global increases in foreign direct investment and an explosion of monetary transactions undermine the capacity of the nation-state to exert its sovereignty in the field of monetary and fiscal policy. The constraints of a politically uncontrolled monetary system favouring transnational banks and corporations make it difficult if not impossible to pursue a Keynesian economic and employment policy. Moreover, intensified economic competition exerts pressure on social rights provided by national welfare states, i.e. workers' rights and payrolls (guaranteed before by strong trade unions) and the right of the unemployed and disadvantaged to social benefits. In the era of globalization the tensions between the imperatives of finance capital on the one hand and labour interests on the other become sharper and more problematic (Altvater and Mahnkopf 1996).

Third, neither the changes in work and production nor those in the regulation of the global political economy stand alone. Both not only are results of systemic processes, but are supported by *neo-liberal social and political forces*. This is evident also in the new dynamic of European integration during the 1980s and early 1990s, when these forces established an autonomous political system of transnational governance, which Stephen Gill (1992, 1998) has called 'new constitutionalism'. The pivotal projects of this period have been the European Single Market on the one hand and the European Monetary System (EMS) and Economic and Monetary Union (EMU) on the other hand. The Single Market programme was committed to the neo-liberal philosophy of intensified competition via deregulated and more flexible markets for goods, capital, services and labour. Its inherent logic of 'competitive deregulation' affected above all the modes of (national) social regulation, since it intensified the pressures to deregulate industrial relations systems and the welfare state. At the same time, this development has been accompanied by monetarist objectives. These objectives were first strengthened by the EMS under the direction of the German Bundesbank, and then, from the early 1990s, by the project of the EMU and the 'Maastricht' criteria of fiscal and monetary convergence (McNamara 1998). As a result, the logic of 'competitive' or, later, 'decreed' austerity which was established by these institutional arrangements deeply affects the capacity of the state to provide social security and to fight the unemployment problem by means of Keynesian deficit spending and demand management.

There is little doubt that this neo-liberal and monetarist framework determines economic and monetary policies as well as strategies of employment creation. In spite of continuing tensions and conflicts between European governments about how to shape the EMU, the consensus on the basic objectives and priorities of economic and monetary unification – intensified competition, economic modernization, sound budgetary policies and low inflation – is not really contested. However, to understand the conceptual foundations of the emerging multi-level structure of employment regulation it is not sufficient to look only at the neo-liberal constraints for more socially motivated strategies. Current employment strategies are not simply neo-liberal, but are based on the idea of an 'activating state'. In general, this idea is combined with a stronger involvement and greater responsibility for the so-called 'social partners' (Falkner 1998; Hümer *et al.* 1999; Teague 1999a). It came into play after the difficulties in ratifying the Treaty of Maastricht. As these problems surfaced in some member states, political leaders – most of them Social Democrats – and EU representatives showed an increased awareness of the social and employment problems within each society. Most of them draw an explicit link between the crisis of political legitimacy of the EU and the continuing social crisis, with its roots mainly in persistently high unemployment. To solve, or at least relieve, the legitimacy problem, the Commission endeavoured to extend the competencies of the EU in the area of employment policy (Tidow 1998; Goetschy 1999; Johansson 1999). It was successful insofar as the member states finally agreed on concrete guidelines and measures in order to co-ordinate national labour market policies (see Chapter 5 for detailed elaboration).

This tension between the neo-liberal and monetarist framework, on the one hand, and the emerging forms of European multi-level employment policy, on the other hand, defines the central argument of this chapter. Neo-liberal strategies have over the past few years been transformed and modified into something that, for want of a better term, should be characterized as (practical) '*communitarian neo-liberalism*'. This assessment will be made more understandable by distinguishing the current phase of hegemonic neo-liberalism from its previous phases (in the subsequent two sections, pp. 54–61). First, the rise of neo-liberalism during the 1980s, in particular in the form of the Single Market project, has been largely 'euphoric'. In the context of the EMU project, however, the pressure of competitive austerity and the 'disciplinary' aspects of neo-liberal restructuring became more evident. This not only fostered the crisis of political legitimacy but also stimulated a communitarian rethinking of neo-liberalism (pp. 61–69). Such an ideological shift fulfilled at least three purposes. First, it provided a modest but very popular criticism of the devastating social effects of a disembedded economy. Second, its criticism of excessively deregulated markets had no profound impact on the prevailing socio-economic order. Third, by stressing the importance and the productive potential of community networks, it allegedly opened up a new perspective in order to correct and mitigate some of the most painful social effects of neo-liberal restructuring without relapsing into an allegedly old-fashioned style of Keynesian state intervention. Obviously, the new employment approach is, rather, inspired by an improved co-ordination and fine-tuning of monetary, financial and wage policies, as well as of socio-economic reforms. Nevertheless, national institutions and political settings remain crucial, particularly where labour markets and social regulation systems are concerned. Thus, from time to time tensions between the European-defined macro-economic framework and national paths of adjustment – more or less mediated on the basis of communitarian ideas – will come to the fore (pp. 69–71).

European integration and neo-liberal restructuring

At first glance, neo-liberalism seems to be a very vague concept. There have been, and still are, of course, various kinds of neo-liberal policies, for example Reaganomics in the US, monetarist policies in Chile under Pinochet and various radical free-market strategies in Eastern Europe after 1989. Even within the European Community (EC) there have been huge differences, between Thatcherite policies in the UK and fairly modest deregulation in Germany and other countries in continental Europe. In short, neo-liberal restructuring is strongly mediated by social and economic conditions, institutional inheritances and political cultures and traditions. In this sense neo-liberalism is not simply tantamount to the ideological concepts developed by the Mont Pèlerin Society. It should be understood, rather, as a fairly broad process, as 'a succession of negotiated settlements' involving many 'concessions to the rigidities and dynamics of structures as well as the political possibilities of the moment' (Drainville 1994: 116).

However, in terms of economic and social policy there are at least two features which are common to all variants of neo-liberalism. First, with regard to macro-economic conditions it implies a fiscal policy that corresponds to the *monetarist doctrine of low inflation*. This aim takes absolute priority over all other, rather socially defined, criteria such as social security and full employment. The latter are commonly seen by neo-liberals as necessarily leading to increasing rates of inflation. Most argue that a balanced economic development requires a minimum level of unemployment. For this, they refer to the NAIRU, the so-called non-accelerating inflation rate of unemployment, i.e. a variation on the natural rate of unemployment theorem originally invented by Milton Friedman (Michie 1995: 84–5).[1] Second, from a micro-economic perspective neo-liberalism implies *policies of deregulation, flexibilization and privatization*. The main objective of this second dimension is to extend the influence of the market and to promote cross-border exchange of commodities and capital, the circulation of financial assets and labour mobility. This should further enhance competition, investment, productivity gains and, as an effect of trickledown, also more jobs and employment. In addition to this, the expansion of the market has an impact on social power relations. While strategies of deregulation and flexibilization tend to restrain the power of solidaristic forces and organizations – from trade unions to new social movements – they expand the scope and power of transnational capital.

In comparison with neo-liberal restructuring in other areas of the world there are two peculiarities of Western Europe. First, most West European countries can be described as *highly regulated and institutionalized*. It is not only the welfare state but also the dense network of labour and industrial regulations which – to a certain degree – keep the mechanism of the market under political control. In this sense there still remain many political targets for neo-liberal attacks, all aimed at weakening trade unions, loosening the restrictions of security standards and abandoning positive labour-market regulation. Second, the regulation of economic and political affairs could not be adequately understood by looking only at either the national or the European level. In contrast to a simple free-trade association, the EC and now the EU is characterized by a *system of multi-level-governance* (Marks *et al.* 1996; Kohler-Koch and Eising 1999). With regard to most policy issues there is a complementary structure between the different levels. Hence it is always necessary to consider the national level when analysing supranational policies, and vice versa. This mutually reinforcing and complementary structure not only is relevant to the processes of institution building and political regulation, but should be assumed also with regard to the strategies of national and transnational social forces.

The transnational interplay of political and social forces can be analysed within the concept of *hegemonic structures in transnational relations*, which, inspired by the writings of Antonio Gramsci, was developed by Robert W. Cox (1981, 1983, 1987). This is a very instructive concept in examining West European affairs too (Bieling and Steinhilber 2000) because it offers a perspective which regards the economic, social and institutional elements of coercion as well as those of consensus. Besides, the concept is not restricted to any single aspect of radical change, but strives to encompass all – even the cultural and ideological – dimensions. Paraphrasing Cox's concept of world hegemony and applying it to Western Europe, one can understand hegemony within the EU as 'a complex of international social relationships which connect the social classes of the different countries'. Accordingly, it 'is describable as a social structure, an economic structure, and a political structure; and it cannot be simply one of these things but must be all three'. Furthermore, European hegemony 'is expressed in universal norms, institutions and mechanisms which lay down general rules of behaviour for states and for those forces of civil society that act across national boundaries' (R. W. Cox 1983: 171–2).[2]

However, it is necessary to refer to some modifications of the concept of hegemony. First, in Western Europe there is no unambiguous single dominant mode of production that ascends from one dominant national economy and penetrates the others. Instead, there are selective and asymmetrically structured modes of economic interdependence which fall short of giving any single national economy the status and the capacity of a European superpower. Besides this, Cox recognizes the relevance of transnational organizations – their rules, norms, ideologies and co-opting capacities – for reproducing hegemonic structures. Unlike the mechanisms of global governance, the European agreements and institutions have more regulative, conditional and obligatory capacities at their disposal. And, finally, hegemonic structures in the EU seem to be more dynamic than those within global orders, so that it is probably useful to pay particular attention to the political projects shaping the process of hegemonic reproduction and transformation. To understand the dynamics of neo-liberal restructuring in the EC we should therefore look at those successive steps or *specific projects* that gave the EU its present shape.

After a period of economic recession and political stagnation, the so-called era of 'Eurosclerosis', the inauguration of the *EMS* in 1979 was a first important step in preparing the neo-liberal agenda. Though the EMS was rather a defensive reaction against the risks of highly volatile exchange rates, it had a major impact on the content of West European fiscal and monetary policies in general.

This was mainly due to its inherent asymmetrical burden of adjustment (Tsoukalis 1997: 152–62). To avoid devaluation and a loss of confidence in the currency, most countries, notably those with high budget deficits, had to accept anti-inflationary policies, i.e. policies of austerity, tight money, high interest rates and moderate wage increases. This shift towards the priorities of monetarism was strongly supported by the German Bundesbank. Since the Deutschmark was the anchor currency of the EMS the Bundesbank was in charge of disciplinary power, which left other countries little scope to reject deflationary instructions. The spread and success of monetarist objectives was, however, not due to external pressures alone. Throughout the EC there was a remarkable shift of political orientations among political and economic elites, as well as among most officials of central banks. Most of them committed themselves deliberately to the objective of monetary stability (McNamara 1998).

The EMS was only the first step in preparing the EC for more far-reaching projects of neo-liberal restructuring. By stimulating a new hegemonic discourse on budget discipline, tight money, efficiency and competitiveness, neo-liberals provided their own interpretation of the coming challenges and obvious strategic solutions. At the latest, this became feasible after the defeat of the left-wing government in France in 1983 (Helleiner 1994: 140–5; J. Smith 1997: 70–88). Its failure to boost the domestic economy by a set of demand-side policies contributed to a common awareness that there was no alternative to adjusting to the globalizing economic environment. Hence it was not really a surprise that in the mid-1980s the then president of the European Commission, Jacques Delors, announced the project of the *Single Market* (see also Chapter 7). The removal of non-tariff barriers for commodities, services, investment and the workforce gave both neo-liberal thinking and European integration a decisive push. While neo-liberals won new opportunities to extend the influence of market competition, the integration process got a new attractive and feasible objective: its attraction was based on the proclaimed gains of the Single Market in terms of industrial modernization, increasing productivity, economic growth and additional employment (Cecchini 1988).

Without doubt, the Single Market was the heyday of neo-liberal restructuring. It created widespread support by proposing a simple message on how to overcome the predicament of European industry. Although it was welcomed by almost everybody, it already had a disciplinary impact. Most evident have been the indirect consequences of enhanced competitive pressures, for instance redundancies as a result of accelerated rationalization or lower social standards in order to adjust to changing market conditions. Nevertheless, these aspects were not regarded as problems which caused serious trouble, since economic growth and working-time reductions provided a lot of new jobs in the second half of the 1980s (Symes 1997). The situation did not change until the 1990s, when economic recession caused rising levels of unemployment. Since then, discontent with the economic and social conditions in Western Europe in general and with the guiding neo-liberal principles and political strategies in particular have gradually emerged.

The discontent was not primarily directed against the Single Market but, rather, tackled the project of the EMU. Unlike the Single Market, *Monetary Union* was not considered to be a project that would only generate winners in a positive-sum game. This was hardly surprising, since in a situation of economic crisis, with monetarist instructions even strengthened as a consequence of German unification, political debates focused mainly on social cutbacks and an intensified dismantling of the welfare state.[3] Moreover, in a number of countries people feared a mere remodelling of the EC after the German example. These two aspects, the fear of even stronger leadership by Germany and the uncertain but probably devastating social impact of austerity measures, generated the 'post-Maastricht crisis' (Deppe and Felder 1993). This became particularly evident when almost half (France) or even the majority of voters (Denmark) rejected the Treaty on European Union. Sceptical views have by no means been limited to these two countries. Opinion polls revealed an increasing pessimism throughout the EU. Obviously, in the context of intensified public discussions about EMU people had become more aware of the costs of neo-liberal restructuring.

Contradictions of neo-liberal restructuring

Neo-liberal restructuring has led to a situation in which economic and political elites support further economic and monetary integration, while large parts of the population are in doubt about any positive impact of the EMU. Since the end of the 1980s it is not exaggerated to speak of a dissolution of the previous '*permissive consensus*' (Obradović 1996). The generally approved attitudes towards European integration were replaced by a pessimistic awareness which equated the EMU with only modest growth, increasing unemployment, public budget problems and social benefits cuts; in short, with the spread of social insecurity. In a way, based on strict economic adjustment and accompanied by various forms of social scaling-back EMU became the symbol of a disciplinary mode of European governance. In many member states it has been criticized by large parts of the population, trade unions and left-wing parties on grounds of its overly monetarist orientation. This criticism gained momentum when in the mid-1990s social protest against austerity measures entered the scene. In France the wave of resistance was most manifest due to mass strikes in the public sector (Steinhilber 2000: 87–103). However, there have been many other examples, as well as mainly female resistance against the retrenchment of the welfare state in Scandinavia, protest and roadblocks by farmers in Greece and Spain, and many union strikes and demonstrations in Belgium, Italy and other member states. Of course, these political campaigns and manifestations have been highly fragmented and defensive in character. And even the activists only sometimes regard themselves as part of a new kind of European protest or even a new transnational social movement. Nevertheless, all the various forms and contents of social resistance seem to be an expression of a deeper logic of capitalist development.

The new politics of 'austerity': social exhaustion and public resistance

In the course of recent decades, according to Kees van der Pijl (1998: 31–63), European societies have entered a new stage of capitalist development. They are increasingly subjected to the discipline of the market and the process of capital accumulation. Of course, market competition and the ravenous appetite of capital for expanding its spheres of investment, i.e. continuous subordination of society and nature to the reproduction of capital, have always been a central feature since capitalist society came into being. Some recent changes in capitalist development are, however, remarkable. To analyse these changes, van der Pijl picks up Marx's differentiation between formal and real subordination of labour to capital. Whereas formal subordination was the main feature of the period of original accumulation, real subordination is characterized by the intensified exploitation of the labour force. Hence the latter is a result of ongoing transformations within the production process itself. Both aspects of capitalist modernization continue to be relevant today. But in addition to them a third focus of accumulation, the capitalist penetration of spheres of reproduction, becomes increasingly important. Following Rosa Luxemburg, Burkard Lutz (1984) has termed this process 'internal conquest' ('innere Landnahme'), which in the age of Fordism, however, has been hampered, or at least moderated, by relatively encompassing social regulation and state intervention. In the meantime, the general economic environment and the mode of political regulation have changed profoundly. Whereas the Fordist welfare state moderated the capitalist penetration of the sphere of reproduction and eased any major social trouble, the new '*national competitive state*' (Hirsch 1995b) tries to enforce rather than to limit the economic pressures of market competition.

Eventually this encourages an intensified exhaustion of society, as many changes in the overall mode of capitalist reproduction already underline. Let me list only a few. First, there is the privatization and reorganization of the public sector. In search of greater economic efficiency many social tasks and services are delegated either to families or to private service enterprises. This affects, above all, the public infrastructure, in particular those areas which are not immediately relevant to economic competitiveness (public leisure centres, parts of the education system, advice centres, medical prophylactics, etc.). Another example refers to more flexible industrial relations (Ferner and Hyman 1998). In general, this implies a decrease in trade union power and a limited scope for wage regulation, which in turn fosters the spread of low-paid atypical and precarious employment with low social and security standards. A third example is the dismantling of the systems of social insurance, i.e. the reduction or abolition of social entitlements (Bieling and Deppe 1997). Lower social standards (restricted access to and reduced volumes of social benefits) tend to reverse the political de-commodification of the Golden Age period, and indicate a new re-commodification of the workforce. Fairly often welfare reforms are an element of new workfare strategies, since they force the unemployed to accept any work which is available.

It would be no problem to extend this list. Socially painful and repressive effects of intensified subordination are better understood if the generally changed conditions of reproduction of the labour force are considered. The key is in the extension of micro-economic rationality criteria to social regulation and the labour market ('microeconomic imperialism'). This implies that for an increasing number of people the social reproduction of labour – wages, social benefits, public services – and the organization of 'daily life' become insecure and increasingly difficult. Since large parts of the population have only scarce cultural and regenerative capacities at their disposal there are new forms of *social struggle*, which mainly focus on *survival* and against the tendencies of *social exhaustion* (van der Pijl 1998: 43–9). Most forms of protest against strategies of 'competitive deregulation' and competitive or decreed 'austerity' should be understood as a new kind of resistance which is typical of the new 'post-Fordist' era of capital accumulation. However, by generating the complementary features of globalization and social fragmentation, neo-liberal restructuring hinders the process of class formation along the old, relatively clear-cut lines of capital and labour (Bieling 2000a). This by no means implies an overall dissolution of class struggle. Instead, class struggles become more dispersed and not only in the sphere of production: contested issues increasingly concern the organization of *reproduction* too, i.e. education, relaxation, recovery, leisure, etc.

In this context, neo-liberals presented their political strategies of transformation as painful but necessary means to improve the conditions of industrial modernization and competitiveness. Until the end of the 1980s, most of the disciplinary effects – unemployment, impoverishment and social control – were generally endured in anticipation of economic and social recovery. At least for a short while the prevailing 'deregulation' initiatives, condensed in the project of the Single Market, gathered strong public support. This was the political expression of the formation of a transnational *historical bloc* of hegemonic neo-liberal forces based on a market-oriented consensus. As already outlined before, its overwhelming attractiveness was subsequently weakened in the course of the 1990s. The exhaustive impact of these policies, in particular of 'austerity' measures, was increasingly recognized. Due to the reinforcement of its disciplinary effects, European integration became less hegemonic and more supremacist (Gill 2000a).

Unemployment and the crisis of political legitimacy

Social and employment prospects within the EU have generally deteriorated due to the 'new constitutionalism' represented by EMU. Adjustment pressures became most evident for those who were unemployed or received some other social benefit, but also for those who had to pay for this, who had to work harder because of intensified competition, who felt insecure about their future employment perspectives, and who were afraid of an impaired quality of life. All this indicated a remarkable shift in the social climate in Western Europe. After a short optimistic period, new forms of social apathy, political scepticism or even pessimism could be observed. Following the difficulties in the ratification process of the new EU treaty, there was an obvious lack of solidaristic ideas and incentives. Although the post-Maastricht crisis was not characterized only by social problems such as persistent unemployment, in view of the economic recession and the impact of globalization social issues became increasingly important (Lipietz 1996). First of all, however, the post-Maastricht crisis was regarded as a crisis of fading political legitimacy in the broad sense of the word. On the basis of partly contrary interests, academics and politicians suggested different solutions. Some tried to reduce the problem of legitimacy to the *institutional aspects* of European integration, i.e. to a lack of transparency within the decision-making process, unclear competencies, the loss of national sovereignty and so on. Others put more emphasis on *social problems*. From this point of view, problems of unemployment, social exclusion and social insecurity have undermined confidence in the prevailing technocratic style of European integration. Though there have been some further aspects of the legitimacy crisis – ecological issues, foreign and peace policies, etc. – one consequence of the debate was a new and palpable common focus: the creation of something paraphrased by the term 'Citizens' Europe'.

The link between issues of unemployment and social exclusion, on the one hand, and the incessant crisis of political legitimacy, on the other hand, was often stressed, even by the Commission itself. Of course, many declarations were no more than non-binding lip-service without any consequence. For a while it seemed as if symbolic gestures were a cheap but very effective means of fostering public support. This was not wrong at all. Besides this, however, there have also been a few signs that symbolic politics stimulated a dynamic of its own which was receptive to public pressure. Even if the development of a European employment strategy made progress only gradually, it gave more scope for action to all those initiatives and forms of protest which were directed against straightforward neo-liberal and monetarist strategies. It could be seen as the doubt of political representatives as to whether the crude neo-liberal and monetarist framework was still sufficient. For policies of deregulation and austerity did not improve employment perspectives; nor did they mitigate the *twofold crisis of social disintegration and political legitimacy*.

This was recognized fairly soon by the European Commission, particularly by Jacques Delors (Ross 1995a). In order to cushion the devastating consequences of neo-liberal policies, it often took the initiative for more social co-operation and regulation at the Community level. The best-known examples of the social engagement of the European Commission (A. Martin and Ross 1999) are a range of directives concerning safety, health and gender equality in the workplace, the directive on European Works Councils, the social dialogue between UNICE, CEEP and ETUC, a couple of framework agreements on part-time, fixed-term jobs and parental leave, and the new employment title, which after many conceptual debates (CEC 1993) and EU summits was eventually incorporated into the EU Treaty (Tidow 1998; see also Chapter 5). Whereas all these initiatives on the supranational level remained rather weak, more promising developments took place at the national level. Here, there was a change in the composition of governments in a range of EU countries after the electoral defeat of neo-liberal parties. Whereas conservative parties had taken office in the late 1970s and early 1980s, renewed social-democratic and socialist parties succeeded in the mid-1990s. Currently, the latter participate in most member-state governments, with the exception of few countries – e.g. Spain and Austria. This does not mean that old variants of Keynesian state intervention and the policies of the Golden Age period are back on the political agenda, for in the meantime almost all social-democratic parties have fundamentally altered their image and changed the priority of their objectives (Sassoon 1996: 730–45; Giddens 1998; Unger *et al.* 1998; Bieling 2000b). As official programmes, proclamations and, even more so, the political praxis have revealed so far, new social democrats have largely accepted the profound philosophy of neo-liberal restructuring, i.e. the extension of market-driven modernization and the retrenchment of the welfare state (see Ryner 2002; also Chapter 8 of this volume).

One may even be tempted to judge that only the name of governments changed, and not the political objectives pursued by them. This impression is not wrong at all, for the dismantling of the welfare state, market deregulation and workfare strategies are still at the top of the political agenda. However, apart from the adoption of neo-liberal aims and measures there are still some significant differences. For instance, most socialist or social-democratic parties regard the unfettered market and public budget cuts as a means of sound economic, social and employment policies rather than as an end in itself. In this sense, they stress the importance of accompanying forms of social and ecological re-regulation. Besides, they avoid measures of shock therapy, and propose that further steps towards the expansion of market pressures can best be taken gradually. This more cautious assessment of the market corresponds with an at least rhetorical, but often even trustworthy, proclamation that the top priority of political regulation must be improved *infrastructure, education and new initiatives for social cohesion.*

Since the mid-1990s the necessities of social cohesion have been stressed by many other political forces too. Thus, the notion of common values and identities, the need for solidarity and some other characteristic features of the communitarian discourse became the focus of political debates and strategies.[4] Its attractiveness was partly due to the fact that *communitarian thinking* did not offer clear-cut solutions but was open to a wide range of interpretations. In a way, communitarian thinking is found among more left-wing politicians as well as among rather liberal and even conservative proponents. Despite this variety, communitarian solutions do share a common feature: they all remain in a subordinated relationship to the basic neo-liberal framework.

Neo-liberalism and the power of communitarian ideas

The spread and success of practical communitarianism can be explained by two peculiarities of the communitarian discourse. First, communitarian writings seem to present a *commonly accepted view of the new social question.* They sketch its different forms of appearance, its content and some of its reasons as moments in an ongoing process of social disintegration. This perspective is often expressed by terms like 'anomie', 'problems of social cohesion', '*fracture sociale*', 'social exclusion' and so on. Second, communitarians offer a 'solution' to the social and political crisis that is directed against both the neo-liberal fetishism of the market and the old-fashioned support of 'big government'. In preferring a largely neglected third dimension, namely the *virtues and advantages of the community*, they stress the meaning of families, schools, public infrastructure, different forms of – locally organized – social networks, neighbourhoods, etc. This new perspective claims to overcome the impasses of extended state intervention and traditional Keynesian demand management as well as the shortcomings of market-oriented neo-liberal strategies.

The 'new social question' and the proposals of practical communitarianism

Most social scientists inspired by communitarian ideas would largely agree with the changes in capitalist societies outlined above. Take, for instance, the very influential writings of Robert Reich (1992) and of Jeremy Rifkin (1995), both of whom – albeit with some significant analytical differences – assume a new era of capitalist development. The roots of this radical change are located in the dynamics of globalization as well as in new forms of work and production. Like other popular authors,[5] they consider these developments, including their effects of social disintegration, as mainly caused by a socially disembedded world economy that runs out of political control. They hold that social relations, forms of communication, patterns of culture, common values – in short, social bonds – are deeply affected by the structural changes of economic reproduction. Superficially, the communitarian view acknowledges the dynamic of 'social exhaustion' outlined above. Nevertheless, there are two modifications that give the communitarian diagnosis a rather different meaning.

First, the charge of capitalism is less sharp and radical than it appears to be. The shifts in the spheres of economy, policy, culture and ideology are rarely analysed in terms of *social interest and social conflict*. Mostly they are described as the result of an abstract logic of modernization or of a low sensitivity of elites to the needs of the rest of society. Though communitarians regard the public sphere and civil society as very important areas, they do not connect them to the struggle between different forces or social blocs proposing alternative political projects. From this perspective, modern society is primarily a network of different social groups whose relations are organized foremost on a horizontal level. Structures of dominance and more contradictory power relations are either ignored or simply accepted. This relates also to the diagnosis of the contemporary social crisis. Thus, communitarians complain, above all, about processes of social fragmentation and disintegration induced by a dissolution of previously given community ties, common values, public infrastructures, etc.; and, against this, they emphasize the necessity of social integration by a renewed normative sense of social obligation, responsibility, education, learning and so on.

Second, this rather harmonious perspective of social reintegration is even stronger in the writings of those communitarians who ignore issues of exploitation, alienation, power and dominance – in short, the *material conditions of social reproduction* – almost completely. This is the case with influential communitarians like the group of Robert Bellah *et al.* (1985, 1992) or, in particular, Amitai Etzioni (1988, 1993, 1996). Unlike more critical authors who are concerned about the socially devastating effects of an unbridled global capitalism, these communitarians direct their attention towards cultural transformations. Etzioni, for instance, regards the contemporary social crisis primarily as resulting from an eroded community consensus, weakened social bonds, a rotten common infrastructure and moral decay. From his point of view, the relation between individual rights and responsibilities was thrown out of balance from the late 1960s onwards. This means that only a minority is concerned about community life, and increasingly people just care about their own career and cultural emancipation. According to Etzioni, the loss of common values and commitments is mainly produced by the dynamics of rampant individualism, propelled by utilitarian or hedonistic attitudes.

Both modifications, in particular the latter, have far-reaching consequences. First, they weaken the criticism of neo-liberalism by regarding the new social question as primarily caused by cultural processes. Hence their overall endeavour for a socially sustainable economy is not based on economic principles and they do not really question the measures of monetarist and neo-liberal restructuring. On the contrary, in the name of subsidiarity most of them accept or even support the dismantling of the welfare state through deregulation and tight monetary policies. Thus the proposals suggested by communitarians should not be regarded as fundamental corrections but, rather, as *soft modifications* – a moral amplification and completion – of the given neo-liberal framework. To put it more positively, communitarian thinking can be seen as a more liberal and modernized variation of neo-conservatism. Compared to neo-conservative ideas it puts more emphasis on democratic structures, open-minded public communication and new forms of social participation. As an ideology, it obviously corresponds much better with the required adjustments to global competition, for it engenders stronger support among the upper working class and the new middle classes (Blackburn 1997: 4–5).

The complementary relationship between neo-liberalism and communitarianism provides the key to understanding why a range of communitarian reflections, including a culturally biased interpretation of the new social question, have become so familiar in public debates. Even many writers and politicians who would not regard themselves as communitarians have picked up the normative orientation of the community topic. The pivotal dimensions of a well-organized society are summarized in the Manifest of American Communitarians (Etzioni 1993). In looking for the moral foundations of a liberal and democratic way of life, the manifest stresses the generative potential of the family, institutions of training and education (schools, universities, etc.), and communities grounded in the *principle of mutual responsibility*. The various networks of reproduction are regarded as crucial for the cohesion of society, because of their specific social and moral performance. They facilitate a deeper meaning to life, provide values and norms to build up individual identities, and uphold the importance of virtues and responsibilities. All in all, they stimulate a new common spirit which enhances the cultural potential for improved social cohesion.

These general objectives mean that advanced capitalist societies must follow the path towards a 'sustainable market economy' which is able to regenerate its basic ecological and – in this context more important – social sources. If this is not the case due to mass unemployment, communitarians complain about wasted skills and unused capacities of work. From their point of view this has at least two major negative consequences. On the one hand, societies with high unemployment foster social inequality, poverty, loneliness and the decay of integrated communities. In the long run, therefore, they will turn out to be *not socially sustainable*. On the other hand, high unemployment generates increasing welfare expenditure, passive individuals and diminishing capacities to work. For the affected economies these outcomes mean *decreasing global competitiveness* and a further deterioration in the perspectives for sustainability. To avoid such a vicious circle, communitarians propose, with more or less emphasis, three objectives. First, they propose to re-embed the global economy by establishing a new international institutional settlement. Second, they plead for an overall improvement in the conditions of community life. Intact communities are seen as a substitute for the centralized welfare state and as a source of the encouragement of individual commitment. And, third, related to this, they stress the urgent need for better-equipped public institutions, particularly where education and vocational training are concerned, i.e. family ties, neighbourhood networks, schools, enterprise training centres, etc.

Social democracy and the enticing charm of successful communitarian politicians

Communitarians proclaim the vision of a socially cohesive society. For this, they propose a new third way beyond 'laissez-faire' and 'big government' (Giddens 1998; for a critique, see Ryner 2000, 2002). This is related not only to the defeat of the former social-democratic projects of full employment, Keynesian state intervention and welfare-state expansion (Anderson 1994), but also to more recent troubles of successive neo-liberal projects. In view of the lack of other appealing ideas and political orientations, it is no accident that political parties' programmes and proclamations are increasingly inspired by communitarian arguments. Their vagueness makes it possible to pick them up from very different perspectives. There are communitarians in almost every political party, but apparently above all within social-democratic and socialist parties. The adaptation of the community issue was typical of Bill Clinton and the New Democrats, but also of Tony Blair and New Labour.[6] And after that it has become even more popular with many other social democrats in Western Europe as well (Meyer 1999).

This popularity across Western Europe is not difficult to explain. There are many reasons, but the most important refers to the general internal conditions of socialist and social-democratic parties. Sassoon (1996: 730–54) points out that almost all 'new revisionist' socialist parties are confronted with a *structural dilemma* after having lost their historical dimension and accepted capitalism as a permanent feature of modernity which should be subjected to political control rather than overthrown. Socialists can still pursue their traditional values of freedom, equality, justice and solidarity, but only insofar as the viability of capitalism is not seriously impaired. In case of doubt, however – particularly if socialists are in government –, this tension tends to be dissolved to the detriment of the values proclaimed. The European projects of the Single Market and Monetary Union[7] have clearly confirmed this dilemma. Hence, socialists are repeatedly forced to deny their original intention, since they are pushed – again and again – to adjust to the given economic necessities and to revise and reassert their political and ideological position.

In this context Tony Blair and the Labour Party are obviously the most striking example. Without doubt they offered a very radical revision of socialist objectives. By turning necessity into a virtue, they announced a reconciliation of socialist values with the changed economic climate. For this, they still argued in favour of 'constructing a community in which "power, wealth and opportunity" would be "in the hands of many not the few" '. And, in order to achieve these ends, they now speak of a ' "dynamic economy", with "a thriving private sector" and "high quality public services", a "just society", an "open democracy" and "a healthy environment" ' (Sassoon 1996: 739–40). These few terms give an impression of the kind of argument presented by Blair (1997). First, there are the *requirements of global competitiveness*. With regard to this issue, the pivotal points are an improved infrastructure, provided by better human capital resources, an intensified promotion of education and training, research and technological progress, modern transport and energy policies and – not forgetting – anti-inflation policies and policies of budget consolidation. Besides these largely economic issues, the other part of his vision deals with the question of social welfare and security. Here again, Blair pleads for an improvement of education, training and vocational schemes. But he also mentions more flexible labour markets, flexible working conditions and, moreover, cohesive civil societies in which people are willing to *accept more public duties and social responsibilities*. Strikingly, Blair steadily invokes the community issue, including its typical dimensions of co-operation, solidarity, responsibility, obligation, mutual trust, sense of belonging, common work, etc. All these terms correspond very well to the old term 'subsidiarity', now given a new meaning.

Subsidiarity not only became prominent again in the debates on reform of the EU, but was already present in right-wing criticism of the welfare state. It was a common feature of neo-liberal and neo-conservative attacks emphasizing the responsibilities of individuals, families and community networks in order to reduce social entitlements guaranteed by the state. Obviously the new centre-left became more familiar with these right-wing debates through the adoption of communitarian ideas. This is particularly evident in the abandonment of the rhetoric of class and its being supplanted by the rhetoric of community bonds. Moreover, there is another remarkable shift of orientation. The prime focus of political concern is no longer the firm – i.e. conditions of work, income and so on – but the family. The latter are seen as crucial for education and training, for generating moral virtues and social commitment, and for the prevention of crime. In this regard, both shifts of orientation suggest a new, more progressive meaning of conservatism, namely the endeavour to preserve reliable social relations in a non-traditional way (Giddens 1995).

The adoption of conservative themes is accompanied by a turn towards neo-liberal arguments. In fact, Joan Smith (1997) reveals that the underlying assumptions of neo-liberal and communitarian thinking are *complementary rather than contradictory*. The social-democratic proposals for a 'New Settlement' in tax, welfare and employment regimes largely support this conclusion. For example, New Labour first accepted the perspective of the New Right that the contemporary social crisis is a crisis of welfare more than of capitalism. Hence, budget deficits are not seen as 'created through unemployment, the under-taxation of companies and the redistribution of the tax burden away from the rich', but, instead, 'by scroungers and an "underclass" of welfare dependants' (*ibid.*: 177). In a second step, this view is reinforced by highlighting the socially devastating effects of persistent unemployment (Bowring 1997). This means poverty, crime, social disorder, the destruction of inner cities and, more generally, the disintegration of families and communities. A further aspect is the need for the dissipation of competitive capacities like skills, personal engagement, innovation and creativity. There is scarcely a critical remark about the process of neo-liberal restructuring. Practical communitarians direct their attention almost exclusively towards suffering communities and wasted competitive potentials. Thus, in a third step, they develop a twofold approach for rebuilding a good society on the basis of a constitutional neo-liberal order. First, they suggest tapping new economic capacities and exploiting them by measures of deregulation and flexibilization, by improved education and training systems and by more active labour-market policies. Second, they simultaneously provide an appropriate ideology, i.e. a set of normative and cultural orientations, to make people more willing to accept and support the socio-economic adjustment efforts in the name of global competitiveness. At least in this regard the discourse of regenerated community structures is very suitable.

Communitarianism and the formation of 'competitive communities'

Blairism is only one, but a very impressive, example of how to redefine old socialist values in the era of global competition. Other forms of political reorientation inspired by communitarian ideas can be found in most of the other member states of the EU as well. What seems to be common to all paths of socio-economic reform and adjustment is a radically *changed interpretation of social problems*. They are nowhere seen as an injury caused by structures of power, exploitation and dominance which ultimately have their roots in capitalist class structures, but primarily as an obstacle to global competitiveness. A similar shift of meaning concerns the word 'solidarity'. After it had become a central issue on the political agenda it lost its original content. From a communitarian point of view, solidarity is no longer seen as the resource of the oppressed to organize themselves against those who are in positions of dominance. Detached from the fight for social rights, better working conditions, higher wages, etc., solidarity instead represents above all the reference point of a new kind of – local, regional, national or even European – community building, which takes place within the given socio-economic structures and power relations for the sake of improved global competitiveness (Streeck 2000).

So eventually 'sustainable competitiveness' does not imply a strengthening of communities against the dynamics of deregulated and flexible markets. More important is the assault upon the bureaucratized institutions of the welfare state. The financial pressures already exerted on the latter are complemented ideologically by the renewed spirit of communities. Various communities offer hitherto hidden competitive capacities and the potential for mutual responsibility. In this way, projects of 'communitarian neo-liberalism' are becoming more influential across Western Europe. This can even be shown in the formation of '*competition communities*', a recently accentuated feature of the European multi-level-system. Of course, at the *European level* it would be exaggerated to speak of a cohesive competition community. There are only rudimentary structures of an identity-based European civil society. A common awareness is limited to the organization of economic relations, i.e. to the common market and close co-operation in economic affairs, because of the triadic structure of global competition. In the past, it was mainly the Commission which tried to extend and strengthen this European economic identity in the transition to the 'information society'. Inspired by the project of the 'information highway' in the US, this paradigm was considered as adequate to supplement the main economic objectives, because it emphasized the communicative and social dimensions of a sustainable model of development – often labelled the 'European Model of Society' or 'Rhenish Capitalism'.[8] The Commission's reflections are most explicitly outlined in the White Papers on *European Social Policy* (CEC 1994) and *Growth, Competitiveness, Employment* (CEC 1993). The proposals of the latter are based on a compromise: neo-liberal labour-market policies and the acceptance of the existing monetarist criteria are combined with more active employment measures and new interventionist proposals concerning the creation of trans-European networks (for more detail, see Chapters 5 and 7).[9]

The meaning of a competition community is more obvious at the *national level*, for most national strategies seek to overcome the internal problems of social fragmentation and exclusion by enhancing the conditions of economic investment. Different measures for improved productivity are thereby condensed within the transformation of the nation-state. In view of the process of neo-liberal restructuring, social scientists argue that the 'Keynesian welfare state' is supplanted by an emerging 'national competitive state' (Hirsch 1995b) or, as Jessop (1993; also Chapter 2 in this volume) has labelled it, a 'Schumpeterian workfare state'. This transition is due not only to fundamental changes in the material conditions of life – the so-called 'post-Fordist society' – but also to the general framework of the Single Market and EMU and its inherent policies of socio-economic restructuring. In many countries this process is mediated via new corporatist arrangements, which in contrast to the older forms of 'social corporatism' can perhaps be termed 'competitive corporatism' (Rhodes 1998; for a critical appraisal of this concept, see Chapter 9). Basically, this includes a different social compromise, a new 'peace formula' between the so-called 'social partners'. In the words of Wolfgang Streeck:

> While in the past industrial relations were about negotiating a secure status for workers and unions, insulating these from economic fluctuations, in the national industrial relations systems of today – deeply enmeshed in competitive international markets as they are – it is about adjusting the governance of the employment relationship to the imperatives of joint competitive success.
> (Streeck 1998b: 15)

This new kind of corporatism rests, above all, on two ambiguous but typical elements. On the one hand, it tends to reinforce neo-liberal restructuring as a process of regulatory competition. In a medium- to long-term perspective many contradictions and problems of social exhaustion are therefore intensified. On the other hand, however, it claims to avoid these negative impacts insofar as they are a burden on improved 'national' competitiveness. Therefore the new competitive arrangements also include some accompanying regulative measures – concerning infrastructure and skills – which are seen as necessary accompaniments to stabilize the process of restructuring. And in this context communitarians offer a suitable ideological means by stressing the capacities and virtues of the national community.

Similar processes can be observed on the *regional* and on the *firm level*. Some extreme neo-liberal positions exaggerate the regional competition of an allegedly rising 'regional state' (Ohmae 1993). But even more cautious observations refer to regional changes in social relations, identities, political co-operation and forms of economic reproduction (Dörre 1999). Most of these changes are part of new strategies of competitive modernization. Taking into account the specific regional conditions, it is the purpose of public–private partnerships to develop new or mobilize hitherto hidden capacities for economic progress. Economic regionalism receives the support not only of regional movements but also of the European Commission, which seeks to use its means very effectively by pursuing a market-oriented approach (Tömmel 1995). On the firm level the creation of competitive communities means basically (re-)establishing an enterprise corporatism (Crouch 1998) – e.g. via 'corporate investment bargaining' (Mueller 1996) – which corresponds with the conditions of reinforced rationalization and global competition. Such a tendency is expressed, among other things, in new management strategies,[10] a growing influence on shareholder value, the overall decentralization of industrial relations, thereby intensified pressures of competition and the fear of redundancies (Dörre 2000). Besides this, there is the endeavour to utilize the various forms of works councils to initiate the ideology of value-creating communities (Schulten 1996).

Whatever the concrete mode and specific content of reorganization may be, it should have become evident that there are some developments which complement and modify the market-radical neo-liberal ideology. More modest forces within the hegemonic bloc try to confront and overcome social and political troubles without leaving the path of neo-liberal integration in principle. In this regard the political philosophy of 'communitarian neo-liberalism' provides a new common view. It accommodates the vision of a socially balanced and cohesive society to the aim of improved economic performance and competitiveness. Its major contributions and advantages are threefold. First, the mobilizing and productive power of communitarian strategies might help to overcome the social contradictions of rigorous neo-liberalism by emphasizing the cultural dimensions of social regulation, i.e. values, social bonds, responsibilities, obligations, etc. Second, communitarian ideas are very appealing within the public sphere. They provide an effective rhetoric to transform the relations of civil society and to assure public support for the necessities of neo-liberal competition. And, finally, communitarian arguments are not only symbolic in character. On the contrary, they suggest a high-quality path of economic modernization, or what some call a strategy of 'progressive competitiveness'.[11] At the same time, however, this is often combined with stronger 'incentives to work' and the promotion of workfare programmes.

Towards a new mode of employment regulation: national models and state strategies

Since the mid-1990s all the different aspects of communitarianism have become more or less evident in the new European employment strategy. The new approach is, in principle, the outcome of three major summits. Observers speak of a three-pillar strategy, which is based in the Luxembourg, the Cardiff and the Cologne processes (Platzer 1999). Whereas Cardiff was mainly concerned with an improvement of the Single Market, particularly in the area of financial services, and Cologne introduced the macro-economic dialogue between the European Central Bank (ECB) and the social partners, in order to create a – symbolically negotiated – more balanced monetary policy approach, Luxembourg already defined the general framework and the core objectives of the new European employment approach. The objectives were expressed above all in some common employment guidelines (CEC 1998), which mainly suggested reducing non-wage labour costs. The first guideline emphasized facilitating company start-ups. *New spheres of investment and employment* should be tapped by tax reductions, European Investment Bank (EIB) credits, or non-profit activities in a 'third sector', i.e. within an area that is dominated neither by the market nor by the state. The second one, which proclaimed the need for a *new culture of 'employability'*, was directed at the reduction of mismatch unemployment. For this, it demanded a generally improved vocational infrastructure and a facilitated transition from school to work. Besides, it suggested a shift from passive to active employment measures, in particular an extension of training programmes to youth and long-term unemployed. The third objective was directed towards the *improved adaptability of business and the workforce.* This meant, for instance, more flexible forms of work organization, more investment in human resources and technology, continuous vocational training measures and so on. And, finally, the fourth guideline recommended *more equal opportunities for women and men.* Apart from this last guideline, a concession to Scandinavian equality regulations, other objectives are largely in accordance with the neo-liberal approach of labour-market deregulation and flexibilization. Besides these, however, it contains some other vague but ideologically important elements which aim (or so it would seem) to establish a *changed political culture* as a precondition for innovation, investment and employment. In accordance with the objectives proclaimed by the Commission's 'pact of confidence' (CEC 1996) – a report suggesting a co-operative approach to socio-economic modernization – they breathe the spirit of communitarian ideas (for more elaboration, see Chapters 5 and 6).

In addition to this narrow labour-market-centred employment approach, minor modifications to the operation of EMU, such as the regrouping of funds or new modes of economic co-operation, allowed at best a gradual shift within the general macro-economic framework. Whether a more growth- and employment-friendly approach will be realized is completely dependent on the willingness of the ECB to loosen its monetarist stance. In turn, this implies that European employment policy virtually boils down to adjustment measures within the existing national frameworks of labour-market and social-security regulation. In this context, as already seen, communitarian ideas might develop some influence. The way they become relevant is, however, subject to a fairly complex set of different factors. One is, indeed, the concrete unfolding of communitarian ideas within epistemic communities, political debates and public discussions at large. Even more important are the existing national power configurations, cultural inheritances and the structures and institutional settings of existing labour-market and welfare regimes. In this sense, Gøsta Esping-Andersen (1990) developed a convincing conceptualization of the different types of welfare states, i.e. the specific institutional arrangements of social and labour-market regulation. Since then, of course, many aspects of these arrangements have changed. This was due not only to particular national difficulties, but also to the overall transformation within the capitalist mode of reproduction. In this process, next to the deep socio-economic crisis and reorganization of global capitalism *European integration* itself emerged as a very influential factor in terms of competition-oriented national social reforms (Bieling and Deppe 1997).

Until the mid-1990s the influence of European integration was mainly *external*, defining structural constraints – economic and regulatory competition and austerity requirements – to limit the national scope of social regulation. Recently this has changed, as a consequence of the new European employment approach, essentially based on political 'benchmarking' procedures and commonly praised national 'best practices' (Tidow 1999), which partly also internalize, and thus *transnationalize*, the criteria for 'good socio-economic governance'. These criteria are at best vaguely defined. They include, above all, economic performance and productivity, economic growth and its employment intensity. It is rather arbitrary which national strategy or national model is called out as a new best practice. Whereas from the mid-1990s onwards many observers and commentators first referred to the Dutch model (see Chapter 9), more recently the focus has shifted, first, to the Danish and now to the Irish model. All these countries are characterized either by a strong tradition of welfare-state regulation or state intervention or at least by a revival of corporatist arrangements.[12] This indicates, first, that, to a certain extent, neo-Keynesian, i.e. more activist and interventionist, state strategies (Teague 1999a: 106–35) become more important again on the national level, even if they primarily aim to improve the flexibility and competitiveness of social and labour-market regulation. And, second, most discussions reflect an increasing awareness that markets alone operate sub-optimally and that stimulation of economic growth and job creation should be based on better co-ordination of monetary, financial and wage policies.

Within the existing socio-economic order, however, financial and wage policies are still politically subordinated and therefore secondary to the primary goals of market competition and public budget consolidation. Hence there is no reason so far to believe that the *exhaustion of society* as a consequence of intensified capital accumulation is a thing of the past. On the contrary, the more sophisticated social-democratic strategies of social reform and the corporatist involvement of the social partners provide an even more appropriate lever to rearrange the social regulation of labour markets for the sake of enterprise and national and European competitiveness. This implies persistent and even harsher adjustment pressures in terms of social and regulatory working and living conditions, so that the employment issue will still represent an important and contested policy area even if the official rate of unemployment continues to decline. At the moment, most difficulties related to (re-)commodified workplace and living conditions – economically defined flexibility, permanent stress, social insecurity – are only concealed by a general upward economic trend. Therefore, in a longer-term perspective it is to be expected that, irrespective of all communitarian cheap talk, the more disciplinary aspects of socio-economic restructuring will surface again.

Notes

1 As Paul Teague (1994) argues, Richard Layard and Stephen Nickell, who developed the NAIRU theorem, should not be regarded as neo-liberals in the narrow sense of the word, but, rather, as representatives of a new Keynesianism. However, the content and the strategic conclusions correspond very well with the neo-liberal or, more precisely, monetarist objective of low inflation. Despite the static perspective of economic development which is expressed in NAIRU's search for a unique equilibrium between the rates of unemployment and inflation, this way of thinking seems to

be very influential, at least insofar as its strategic proposals, i.e. low wages and budget consolidation, are at the top of the political agenda.

2 One should add that the modes of regulation and the set of institutions are crucial for hegemonic reproduction:

> Indeed, international organization functions as the process through which the institutions of hegemony and its ideology are developed. Among the features of international organizations which express its hegemonic role are the following: (1) they embody the rules which facilitate the expansion of hegemonic world orders; (2) they are themselves the product of the hegemonic world order; (3) they ideologically legitimate the norms of the world order; (4) they co-opt the elites from the peripheral countries and (5) they absorb counter-hegemonic ideas.
>
> (R.W. Cox 1983: 172)

3 Anderson puts this as follows:

> In a system of the kind envisaged at Maastricht, national macro-economic policy becomes a thing of the past: all that remains to member states are distributive options on – necessarily reduced – expenditures within balanced budgets, at competitive levels of taxation. The historic commitments of both Social and Christian Democracy to full employment and traditional welfare services, already scaled down or cut back, would cease to have any further institutional purchase.
>
> (Anderson 1997: 130)

4 In the context of this paper, 'communitarianism' refers to the philosophical debates (e.g. of Michael Sandel, Charles Taylor, Michael Walzer, Alaisdair MacIntyre) only insofar as philosophical and sociological writings have some influence on public interpretations, perspectives and political strategies. The focus is more on those practically oriented communitarians such as Etzioni, Giddens and other intellectuals affiliated to the 'Communitarian Network' and its periodical *The Responsive Community*.

5 Christopher Lasch (1996), Benjamin Barber (1996) and, in France, Viviane Forrester (1998) published influential books which adopt a similar perspective. Like Reich and Rifkin they have, however, an important advantage in comparison to mainstream communitarianism: they refer to theoretical questions and arguments which are profoundly rooted in the area of political economy.

6 Blair and Clinton are very alike. They represent themselves well in the media, had hard neo-liberal predecessors in government and were confronted with immense social problems, a rotten public infrastructure and a substantially weakened welfare state. The impact of the social crisis had run so deep that both had electoral success even in countries with a long individualistic culture and tradition.

7 Sassoon says:

> The Maastricht Treaty had decreed that inflation, and not unemployment, was the main enemy. This was now fully accepted by the Labour Party and by all other European socialist parties. A national road to social democracy – or even modernization – was no longer possible. Here lies the authentic neo-revisionism of the 1990s.
>
> (Sassoon 1996: 739)

8 The main elements of the 'Rhenish' (or Rhineland) model are described by Albert and Gonenc (1997): joint decision-making (co-decision rights), a consensus-based 'social market economy', high-skill and high-productivity production which guarantees wages, risk- and benefit-sharing within the enterprise and relatively high social standards at the expense of a rather narrow consumer choice.

9 Keynesian elements which mainly concerned the financing of trans-European networks were kicked out very early in the bargaining process by the German and British ministers of finance.

10 According to Teague (1994), the new management strategies are inspired by a new Keynesianism supportive of flexible but high-quality work and production. Insofar as they concern the regulation of internal labour markets, they are susceptible to those new concepts – human resource management (HRM) and security, training, and employee involvement (SET) – which strengthen the social bonds within companies.

11 The concept of 'progressive competitiveness' can be traced back to several debates of and suggestions made in the early 1990s. In a way, it is a mixture compounded of different points of reference: the former success of the 'German model' (Albo 1997: 6–7); a misreading of the 'Swedish model' (Ryner 2000, 2002); and the last ambitious project of Jacques Delors, i.e. the construction of a transnational European information society (CEC 1993). In the meantime, however, all variants of the concept of 'progressive competitiveness' have suffered a defeat of some sort. This might be one reason why nowadays its progressive features have been diluted in the concept of 'competitive corporatism'.

12 All these countries are, however, small and highly export dependent, so that it is difficult to generalize their economically successful strategies to the larger European states without discussing the far-reaching consequences for the European economy. Obviously, the new benchmarking discourse is full of ideologically motivated arguments. This is underlined, for example, by the fact that virtually no one referred to the Austrian model, despite Austria's continually low rates of unemployment.

Part II

Europeanizing employment policy

5 The emergence of European employment policy as a transnational political arena

Stefan Tidow

Introduction

The establishment of a European employment policy was the object of intense political debate at the European level throughout the 1990s. The recession at the start of the decade pushed the struggle against mass unemployment, which reached a dismal record of 11 per cent by 1992, forcefully on to the European Union (EU) agenda (EC 1993). Since then no European Summit has gone by at which the struggle against unemployment was not declared to be a top priority. Momentarily, this almost ritually repeated battle cry seemed to be mostly of a symbolic nature. Towards the latter part of the decade, however, the debate intensified and the struggle over the approach to take became sharper. The emerging dynamic with which a European employment policy began to take shape surprised political and academic observers in equal measure.

The shaping of the new policy and its institutional grounding involved a repeated oscillation between the creation of political openings and the subsequent emergence of new political limitations. Even the 1997 Amsterdam Summit, at which a so-called Employment Chapter was added to the Treaty, did not represent the end of the political struggle, which had begun with the European Commission White Paper on *Growth, Competitiveness and Employment* (EC 1993). Following the 1997 Treaty revisions the debate over the further development and institutional strengthening of European employment policy was carried forward at the subsequent European Council summits in Luxemburg, Cardiff, Cologne and Lisbon.

A European employment policy does not easily fit with the image of European integration as essentially a neo-liberal project as it has emerged since the enactment of the Single European Act (1986). The implicit recognition that the problem of mass unemployment requires a common policy approach evidently contradicts the original philosophy of the Single Market. Enhanced competitiveness alone, resulting from systematic deregulation, would guarantee sufficient economic growth in the European economies to eradicate unemployment almost automatically. The political process which led to the formation of the new policy arena can be interpreted as a political struggle over the modification of this neo-liberal character itself to the extent that the original optimism accompanying the arrival of the Single Market faded, the member states of the

EU were facing new challenges after the agreement on monetary union and the legitimacy of the European enterprise fell to new depths.

We must nevertheless be careful with overstated interpretations. Undoubtedly, the political changes of the 1990s – above all the government changes in France, Great Britain and Germany – have had an impact on the shaping of the employment agenda. It would, however, be premature to conclude from the existence of a formal Employment Chapter and from an apparent social-democratic predominance in Europe the contours of an emerging 'regulated capitalism' (cf. Pollack 1998).

In this contribution I will attempt to demonstrate two things. First, the formation of a European employment policy can be interpreted as an attempt to react to the deep economic and political crisis of the early 1990s by modifying the direction of the European integration project. This integration project is constituted by a synthesis of the interests of member states and their respective concrete state projects. It guarantees the coherence of national state projects, international system and world market, and it takes on concrete form in an intergovernmentally shaped political process which fixes the dominance of economic integration legally. Second, this attempt to use employment policy to achieve a new purpose for the integration project has failed. On the contrary, it can be argued that the restrictive framework of the Single Market-cum-monetary union has been written into the formulation and institutionalization of the new policy. European employment policy was made to fit the existing integration project and thus became one of the pillars of supply-side-oriented neo-liberal restructuring.

failed though

This is not to say that nothing has changed. In fact, some form of partial modification was eventually achieved. To understand European integration exclusively as a deregulation project would be to overlook its actively structuring elements. We can observe a changed division of labour between European and national institutions and the introduction of new forms of governance actively pushing the Schumpeterian transformation of the state forward (cf. Chapter 3; see also Felder 2001). This contradictory process of continuity and discontinuity can be characterized as a 'passive revolution' (cf. Gramsci 1971). The core proposition of this contribution is as follows. The European and the national levels in the field of employment policy have become intimately intertwined, but the political profile of this mode of multi-level governance does not represent a true rupture with neo-liberal philosophy. Rather, it unveils the contours of a politically mediated transformation toward what one might call 'best-practice capitalism', which is compatible with the philosophy of the new ('Third Way') social democracy as much as with the continuities of the Schumpeterian workfare state.

The post-Maastricht crisis

Labour market and employment concerns have been in some respect elements of the integration process from the earliest phases, not just because they are difficult to separate from broader macro-economic policy concerns, but above all because the free movement of workers is one of the core freedoms of a common market. With the European Social Fund (ESF) the Community had a financial instrument at its disposal to further the vocational and geographic mobility of workers. The Treaty of Rome, moreover, provided for co-ordination of economic policies. One must, however, not attach too much weight to these provisions. The ESF was not only sparingly funded, it was also primarily developed as an instrument for regional redistribution (Kaluza 1998). And economic policy co-ordination habitually foundered on the existence of different national state projects. Nor was co-ordination absolutely necessary under the conditions of 'embedded liberalism' (Ruggie 1982). An external free-trade orientation was quite compatible with various specific – more or less protectionist and interventionist – internal macro-economic strategies.

The rise in unemployment at the start of the 1970s did give rise to more intensive debates about Euro-wide strategies, but these only produced declaratory politics, no concrete policy initiatives (Berié 1993). On the contrary, a way out of the crisis of the Fordist welfare constellation (cf. Chapter 3) was not pursued through European policy co-ordination but first of all through the strengthening of national strategies and of the national Keynesian welfare state (Ambrosius 1996). In a narrower sense, therefore, when referring to the early decades of European integration we can at best speak of fragmented and partial initiatives towards a European employment policy (Tidow 2000).

When towards the end of the 1970s the road to neo-liberal restructuring was taken with the establishment of the European Monetary System, and when a few years later the Single Market project was launched, this represented not only an explicit rejection of any 'social dimension' (Streeck 1998a) but also the conscious exclusion of employment policy concerns. Unemployment would have to be countered only through an intensification of market competition. The Cecchini Report (Cecchini 1985) expressed this new philosophy clearly: flexibilization, deregulation and privatization were presented as the guarantors of a new dynamic of competition and growth in the Single Market. Unemployment would then automatically sink to its 'natural rate'.

This expectation was not realized. During the early 1990s mass unemployment reached record highs and the issue jumped on to the European political agenda. This is explained not only by the pressing problems involved, but also, and more fundamentally, by the deep legitimation crisis of the EU in the wake of the difficulties experienced in the ratification in various countries of the draft Treaty on European Union (TEU) agreed in Maastricht. This 'post-Maastricht crisis' (Deppe and Felder 1993) differs in essential respects from all earlier crises in the European integration process. It reflects a far-reaching transformation of statehood and a new political reality resulting from the realization of the Single Market and the transition to monetary union. This process can be seen as a concrete 're-territorialization' of European politics in the context of abstract globalizing tendencies. In contrast with earlier conflicts, it was not a crisis in the relations between European governments and their national political projects, but a profound conflict between governing and governed throughout Europe which found a political expression simultaneously in various national contexts as well as in the European political arena (see also Jessop 1995). The national state had to

> protect its society from the considerable negative consequences of globalisation, but at the same time to open it up for this process and to make it fit in order to guarantee its survival in the intensifying competitive struggle, because retreat or closure are synonymous with decline.
>
> (Ziebura 1992: 469)

Governments were visibly overextended. They were caught up in the dynamic of their national modernization offensives, the concomitant social fragmentation and disintegration and the resulting increased societal resistance (Bieling and Deppe 1997). Externally, increased global competition for capital, economic interdependence and the shackles of the Maastricht convergence criteria put on the thumbscrews and in turn blocked the elaboration of the internal compromises that would have been necessary to achieve a new accumulation dynamic. Internal crisis and the crisis of the integration process thus mutually reinforced each other. In response, the European Commission undertook cautious attempts to modify the integration project in order to enhance its public legitimacy. The reduction of mass unemployment seemed the most promising route. What made a European employment policy particularly relevant in political terms was the fact that it implicitly addressed the two dimensions of the perceived crisis simultaneously. It provided an answer to the diminishing capacity to act on the part of the national state and it addressed the legitimacy crisis of the European project, which threatened only to reinforce the problems.

The White Paper strategy

With the White Paper *Growth, Competitiveness, Employment* (EC 1993) the European Commission, at the request of the European Council, presented for the first time a comprehensive strategic plan to respond to these challenges. During the late 1980s the Commission had already recognized that the Single Market project required a 'social dimension' to make it socially acceptable (Ross 1995a).[1] The White Paper was an attempt to modify the integration project from above. It identified (without explicitly naming it) as a fundamental dilemma for the member states deriving from the TEU the need to ensure macro-economic stability without being able to compensate for the employment effects. The solution to this dilemma was to attempt to let monetary, fiscal and wage-determination policies function as stabilizing factors, and to achieve growth and employment through labour-market and structural policy reforms (W. Schröder 1994). The various elements of the strategy were not novel in themselves, but the specific combination of policies did represent a qualitative innovation. In the eyes of the Commission this meant 'significant changes, but it does not simply mean a deregulation of Europe's labour markets. Rather, it implies an updated, rational and simplified system of regulation and incentives' (EC 1993: 150). A special place in the strategy was reserved for the development of human resources. The Commission advocated increased investment in education and vocational training and, more broadly, a shift from passive income supports to more active incentives. The strategy called for increased investments on the part of national governments. However, the Community wanted to 'play an important supporting role by providing a forum where a common broad framework strategy can be agreed' and by 'underpinning national measures with complementary Community action, whether in the form of financial support through the European Social Fund…or through networking and other measures designed to ensure the transfer of good practice and experience' (*ibid.*: 164). The Commission stated:

> Generally speaking, the Community should set firmly and clearly the essential requirements and the long-term objectives for measures and policies in this area in order to make it easier to develop a new model for growth, competitiveness and employment.
>
> (EC 1993: 149)

The Commission concluded that in order to achieve this new model of growth, competitiveness and employment the Community should play a central role in formulating the basic requirements and the long-term goals and objectives.

The idea of the Commission did thus not refer to a basically different macroeconomic view. The supply side remained the primary point of reference. At best, one could discern traces of a demand-oriented approach in the plan for Trans-European Networks (TEN), and even these traces were highly controversial (cf. König 1994). New, and more important than these 'inclusions', was the fact that in the White Paper the Commission called into question the division of labour between member states and European institutions. It attempted to tie the European level in more tightly in the formulation of the general conditions that were intended to force a guided transition from the old 'Keynesian welfare state' to an innovation oriented competitive 'Schumpeterian workfare state' (Jessop 1995; see also Chapter 3 of this volume). This attempt clearly went a step further than the deregulation of the Single Market strategy (see Figure 5.1, first column).

This attempt to reform the integration project from above failed utterly. The heads of state and government leaders at the 1994 Summit in Essen stuck to an unaltered integrative logic. The initiatives of the Commission in the employment field were no more than acknowledged. Some of the political guidelines were advocated to the *national* governments in the form of seven recommendations, but the integrated strategy – core contribution of the White Paper – was torn apart. The competency of the EU was restricted to the sphere of the common currency and the completion of the internal market, while the responsibility for employment policy was to be assumed exclusively at the national level. The member states were called upon to take the very general conclusions and recommendations of the European Council into account in their national employment policy and to report annually on their progress. The Council of Ministers and the Commission in their turn would then report to the European Council (European Council in Essen 1994; see Figure 5.1, second column). With this strictly inter-governmental approach to co-ordination the possibilities for a

Figure 5.1 European employment policy: phases of development

Post-Maastricht crises	1993	1994	1996/7	1997	1997	2000
	White Paper	**EC Essen**	**IGC**	**EC Amsterdam**	**EC Luxembourg**	**EC Lisbon**
Policy-profile	• Keynesian • Schumpeterian • neo-liberal	• (Schumpeterian) • neo-liberal	• Schumpeterian • (neo-liberal)	• Schumpeterian • neo-liberal	• Schumpeterian • neo-liberal	• Schumpeterian • new-Keynesian consensus
model of employment policy	• measures • intervention	• non-binding co-ordination	• non-binding co-ordination • measures • otherwise indefinite	• co-ordination • incentive measures	• convergence method	• employment pact • employment is fit into structural policies and new methods of open co-ordination
model of labour market reform	• human-resource management	• flexibilization	• controversial or indifferent	• without specific profile	• Benchmarking • active labour market policy/employability	• Benchmarking • emphases on education/employability
division of labour responsible for	• new	• unchanged	• partially new	• partially new	• partially new	• partially new
• **macro-economic**	EU	EU	EU	EU	EU	EU
• **employment policy**	EU	MS	EU	EU	EU?	EU (and social partners)
• **labour market**	EU + MS	MS	MS	MS	EU + MS depends on implementation process	EU + MS depends on implementation process
Advocacy-coalition/ conflict-constellation	Commission vs governments	governments vs Commission	Sweden Austria Belgium Denmark vs Germany, (France), (GB)	France vs Germany	L&S Council vs. ECOFIN DG V vs DG II PES vs EPP France vs Germany parts of the core vs parts of the periphery	'third way' consensus
range of political agenda	expansion	restriction	expansion	restriction	in the run-up expansion, then restriction	Schumpeterian expansion

abbreviations: MS: member states DG: Directorate-General L&S Council: Council (labour & social affairs) EPP: European People's Party PES: Group of the Party of European Socialists

European response to the new social and economic challenges were exhausted. The possible reorientation of the integration project foundered on the dominant internal-market logic and the established national/European divide.

The Inter-Governmental Conference (IGC) 1996

The IGC of 1996 – preparations for which were made in a Reflection Group – was concluded at the Amsterdam Summit of June 1997. It made clear that the Essen decisions succeeded in moderating the explosive theme for the moment but failed to resolve the underlying tensions. The unemployment theme was once more put on the agenda, this time more clearly as a political issue. The explanation for this is that the member-state governments were on the one hand increasingly restricted in their problem-solving capacity by the exigencies of the upcoming monetary union, while demand for effective policies increased. Moreover, the new member states Sweden and Austria had experienced an upsurge in unemployment since the early 1990s, which was directly related to the EU accession in public opinion (Michelsen 1997; Tidow 1996; Bieler 2000). During the preparations for the IGC a number of governments insisted on placing the employment question on the agenda, and the differences around this issue sharpened considerably (Jopp and Schmuck 1996: 248).[2]

The results of the negotiations are known: a so-called 'Employment Title' was incorporated into the new EU Treaty. At first sight this result can be seen as the lowest common denominator between the two groups and as such understood through an analysis of the preferences and the relative bargaining positions of the participants (Moravcsik and Nicolaïdis 1999). A more detailed analysis of the negotiations and of the position papers of the member-state governments (as well as of the societal actors involved) allows us to paint a finer picture, which undermines this 'two-camps theory' (cf. Tidow 1998). Instead we see that the contradictions and conflicts within the different camps as well as the restrictive context of the 'New Constitutionalism' (Gill 1998) have substantially determined the course of events, from the definition of the initial negotiating positions onwards. The decision to put the employment theme on the agenda was taken as early as 1995, in the Reflection Group. With the exception of the British, everyone agreed that the goal of high employment levels should be enshrined more clearly in the Treaty to show the citizens that their worries were being taken seriously (Reflexionsgruppe 1995a). But when some governments desired to move beyond new formulations and cosmetic changes and demanded concrete European policy instruments, relations in the group polarized (Reflexionsgruppe 1995b). Nevertheless, these forces too were unable to formulate 'hard' alternatives. They did point analytically to the relation between macro-economic and employment policy, but the link became weaker as the proposals towards institutionalization of employment policy became more concrete during the negotiations. This is because the central presuppositions of the overall integration project remained unquestioned even by the most critical participants:

- The fundamentals of economic and monetary union should remain untouched.
- The first responsibility should remain with the member states and the division of labour between the national and the European levels should remain unchanged.
- There should be no financial cost involved; some participants ignored the financial question altogether, others were willing to consider certain financial allocations, but strictly within the existing budgetary framework (cf. Tidow 1998).

Against this background, it is perhaps not surprising that during the IGC there were indeed general references to 'employment' policy, but substantively the attention focused more and more on questions of (European) labour-market restructuring. The macro-economic design of the integration project was more or less explicitly addressed by some, but at no point during the Conference were real alternatives discussed in earnest. Even the protagonists of a more active European posture such as Austria and Sweden had very little in common: they agreed that there ought to be some form of co-ordination and monitoring. But they were divided even on the question of whether this represented simply a codification of the Essen follow-up or, rather, an enlargement and refinement of the Essen results. The most sensitive issues were the relation between employment policy and macro-economic policy, the desire for truly European regulations and instruments, and the obliging nature of European directives.

Austria took the lead in the debate on the one side, arguing for full employment as an explicit objective of macro-economic co-ordination (Österreich 1997). This position was later supported by the European Parliament (1997). On the opposite side, Sweden, supported perhaps remarkably by the European trade unions, pressed for subordination of employment policy to the wider objectives of orthodox macro-economic stability (Sweden 1995; EGB 1996). In hindsight we may conclude that Sweden was successful in shaping the direction of developments. Its interventions were in line with the road taken in Essen and the 'path dependency' of subsequent developments was thus reinforced. However, these institutional path dependencies were not solely responsible for the final result of the negotiations. Only the unquestioned acceptance of the continuity of the integration project in combination with the substantial differences in the protagonists' camp created the space within which a compromise could be constructed. In addition, procedural aspects, too, influenced the negotiations. The employment issue was repeatedly discussed during the first months of the IGC (Weidenfeld 1998). Notwithstanding the persistent opposition of the French, British and German governments, the Irish Presidency succeeded in orienting the debates towards a separate Title on Employment. The need, however, to reach consensus among the protagonists caused the ambitions to be clearly toned down some time before the decisive phase. In the end, the compromise reached hardly represented more than the lowest common denominator among the 'progressive' forces (Irish Presidency 1996). It is for this reason not surprising that as early as the autumn of 1996 the German government signalled that it would be able to live with the foreseeable proposals of the Irish Presidency (*Agence Europe*, 7 October 1996).

Although the fall of the conservative governments in Great Britain and France in the spring of 1997 shifted the co-ordinates of power in the EU institutions, this did not lead to a new dynamic in the concrete elaboration of an Employment Chapter. The new French government, in its bid for hegemony, did for the first time raise questions about the direction of the integration project. It failed, however, to generate an inspiring conception around which a new majority could have formed. On the contrary, the French government watered down its initial call for European economic governance – a potential focus for the crystallization of an alternative hegemonic project – considerably by embedding it in the existing political set-up, and thus delayed a potential conflict indefinitely. The German government was able in the final bargain to water down even further the employment policy paragraphs. In the end the protagonists considered the naked existence of an Employment Title in itself a victory. The fact that the actual substance of the new Treaty regulation was not at all a concern of public interest made it much easier for the protagonists to celebrate this and to make it more palatable to the national public.[3]

Ironically in light of the resolve to avoid this, the Amsterdam Summit and with that the end of the IGC were heavily influenced by the theme of the Economic and Monetary Union (EMU). It even came to a direct issue-linkage between the two themes. The Pact for Stability and Growth, which had to be agreed along with the Treaty revision, originated from a German initiative to secure member-state fiscal and budgetary rectitude after the creation of the single currency. Germany demanded that the existing sanctions for economic and budget policy would be both broadened and sharpened. This Stability Pact, the principles of which had been agreed at the Dublin Council in December 1996, was to be drafted in its final version in Amsterdam. As the French Socialists made their support for the intensification of the neo-liberal project dependent on a simultaneous deepening of common macro-economic policies, the run-up to the Summit led to hectic attempts to find the basis for a bargain. At the Franco-German summit in Poitiers it was agreed simply to append a declaration on growth and employment to the existing text of the Stability Pact (*Agence Europe*, 16–17 June 1997). This declaration offered no new points of view: it reiterated the neo-liberal credo that the reduction of unemployment would depend on improved competitiveness and macro-economic stability (European Council 1997b). It was decided that the European Investment Bank and the European Investment Fund would expand their activities. In particular, a facility was created to finance high-technology projects in small and medium-sized enterprises; in addition, new credits were made available for areas such as education, health and (urban) environment, and possibilities were examined to make available long-term loans for big infrastructural projects (*ibid.*). In comparison with the robust Stability Pact, supported by two European directives, the Declaration on Growth and Employment appeared rather toothless. Even if it may seem as though the French concessions on the Stability decision were bought with a German concession regarding the Employment Title, this hardly amounts to a typical package deal. The 'compromise' remained asymmetrical and the Employment Title fell far short of the expectations of those who had hoped to achieve a real modification of the integration project (see Figure 5.1, third column).

The Amsterdam Treaty revisions

With the Treaty revision a high employment level is now legally part of the objectives of the Union (Art. 2, TEU), and as a consequence the Community is explicitly engaged in the 'promotion of the co-ordination of the employment policies of the member states with a view to the reinforcement of their effectiveness through the development of a co-ordinated Employment Strategy' (Art. 3, TEU). Key to the new Treaty clauses is the procedure of this co-ordination (Art. 128, TEU), which is structured after the example of the macro-economic co-ordination mechanism, without, however, providing for sanctions (see Figure 5.2). Conclusions of the European Council are to bring the Commission to develop guidelines that must be taken into account by the member-state governments in their national employment policies. The member states report annually to the Commission on the successes (and failures). The Commission then composes a joint report from the European institutions, which serves as the basis for new conclusions on the part of the European Council. The final responsibility thus remains with the member states, a fact which runs as a red thread through the new Treaty text.

And yet new community powers can be detected. The Commission must contribute to a high level of employment by promoting and where necessary complementing the co-operation of the member states (Art. 127(1), TEU). The objective of a high employment level shall henceforth be taken into account when agreeing and implementing communal policies and measures (Art. 127(2), TEU). The Council can even decide on 'incentive measures designed to encourage co-operation between Member States and to support their action in the field of employment'. This wording carefully avoided the formulation of a full-blown employment programme. The pilot projects to be promoted shall exclusively serve to develop instruments for the evaluation and exchange of information (Art. 129, TEU). Finally, the Treaty created a committee for labour-market and employment affairs which – as the Economic Policy Committee – is seconded to the Council, and which must monitor and assess the national developments as well as co-ordinate co-operation with the Council of Economics and Finance Ministers (ECOFIN) (on the Treaty revisions, see also Roth 1998 and Keller 1999).

We have now introduced the most important actors. In addition, the social partners (employers' organizations and trade unions) are to be consulted with regard to the guidelines to be drawn up by the reformed Standing Committee on Employment (*Agence Europe*, 22 November 1997). Below this level we find a widespread and highly differentiated network of relationships that has been

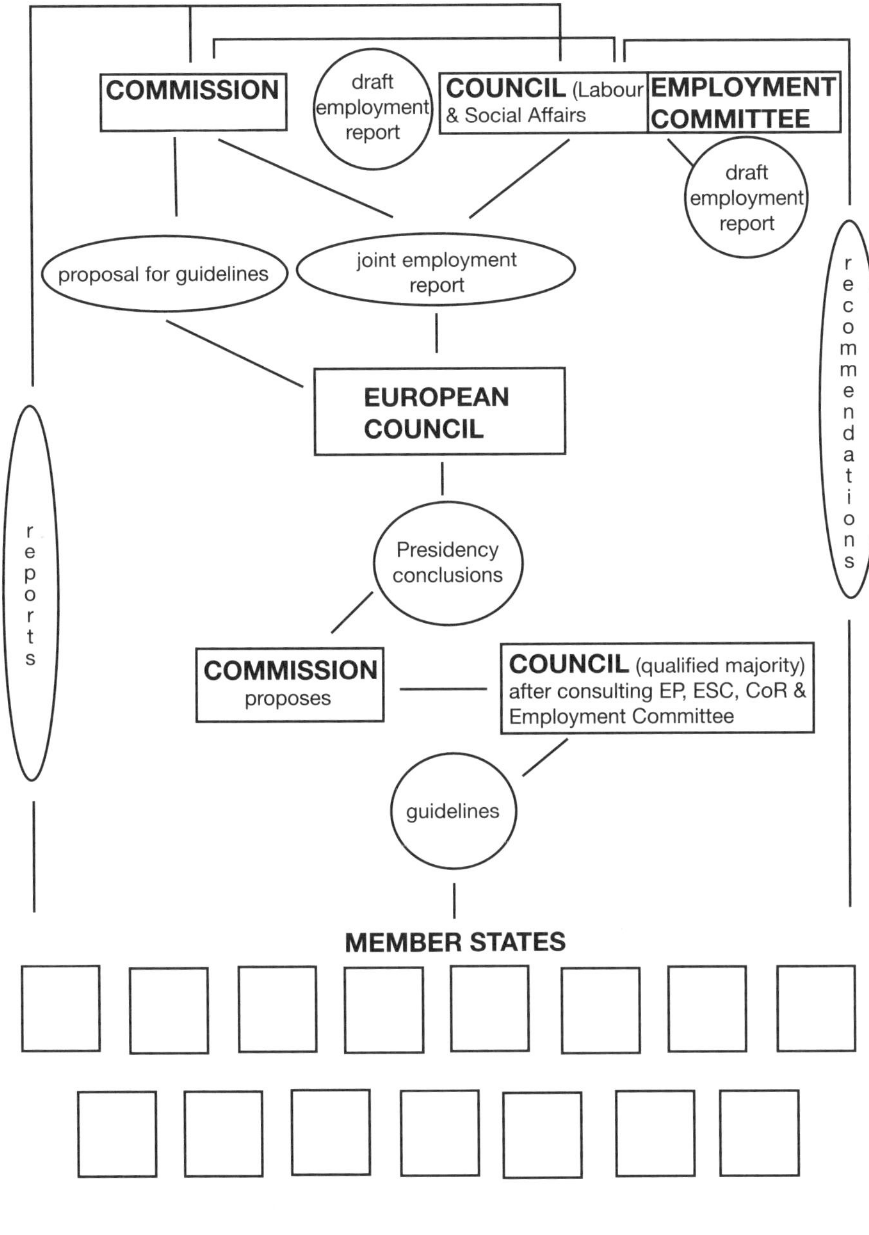

Figure 5.2 A co-ordinated strategy for employment

CoR Committee of the Regions
EP European Parliament
ESC Economic and Social Committee

Source: Art. 128, TEU.

formed over a longer period of time, in particular around the programmes of the ESF (Kaluza 1998; Heinelt 1996).

Financially, things pretty much remained unaltered. The Structural Funds remain the most important venues for autonomous Community initiatives.[4] Small changes relate to the credit policies of the European Investment Bank as well as to the shifts in the budget enforced by the European Parliament (European Council 1997a; *Agence Europe*, 13–14 October and 24 October 1997).

In substance the Amsterdam advances were not very inspiring. They were limited to a codification of the Essen decisions and the established practices since 1994. Even the new Committee was merely the institutionalization of an ad-hoc group of individual civil servants established after the Essen Summit. Its definitive structure had already been agreed when the struggle in the IGC over the Employment Chapter was still in full swing (*Official Journal of the European Community*, L6, 10 January 1997: 32). The new objective in the Treaty also added little: the Maastricht Treaty already referred to the need for a 'high level of employment'.

The restrictive conceptualization of employment policy was reaffirmed in Amsterdam. There was talk of 'employment policy', but what was meant in fact was 'labour-market policy'. And here, too, no Europeanization was intended: the European level was assigned a strictly supplementary role (see Figure 5.1, fourth column). The most decisive result of the Conference, therefore, was less of a substantive and more of a procedural nature. First, as consolation for the French it was agreed that the new Treaty clauses would be implemented before the new Treaty was ratified. To that purpose a Special Summit was called for autumn 1997, to be held in Luxembourg. Second, the codification of the co-ordination of national employment policies laid the foundation for a further dynamic and freed employment policy from the straitjacket of 'social policy'. This incremental development, however, also makes it clear that the tension between the continuity of the integration project and the societal transformation remained unresolved. The Amsterdam Treaty strengthened those forces that insisted on a partial modification of the integration project. In order to enhance our understanding of this contradictory relation it is perhaps useful to consider Antonio Gramsci's concept of 'passive revolution'.

The developmental logic of European employment policy: 'passive revolution' and 'molecular changes'

By 'passive revolution' Gramsci understood the introduction of change that neither is supported by a political base nor expresses a new formation of political forces – in other words, which lacks broad support and participation among the population. The core themes are exogenously inserted rather than endogenously developed in the course of popular political activity. It is a revolution from above, in which 'a State replaces the local social groups in leading a struggle of renewal' (Gramsci 1971: 105–6). In analogy to Gramsci, we can interpret the strategy of the Commission in this way: 'through the legislative intervention…and by means of the corporative organisation relatively far-reaching modifications are being introduced into the country's economic structure' (*ibid.*: 120). This attempt, as we saw, largely failed. However, we can partly discern a process here that Gramsci has attributed to the passive revolution: 'molecular changes which in fact progressively modify the pre-existing composition of forces, and hence become the matrix of new changes' (*ibid.*: 109).[5] This matrix for new changes has taken the form of the emergence of the new political arena and explains the dynamic of employment policy.

The balance of forces between the European institutions had already shifted – albeit just marginally – with the European Council in Essen. The position of the Commission was made more legitimate and eventually stabilized and even slightly strengthened in Amsterdam. The co-ordination mechanism agreed in Essen served national actors, as shown above, as a point of entry for their demands, leading eventually to the Employment Chapter. Even more important are some further molecular changes which, rather than manifesting themselves at the constitutional level, came to fruition in the margins of the formal agreements.

During the preceding years the Commission had already – in a sense destined by its own White Paper to do so – repeatedly placed its strategic objectives on the agenda by utilizing its right of initiative. On the one hand, this was possible because certain elements of its strategic plan could be elaborated and accentuated in the context of its formal competence (e.g. in the field of structural policy). The local employment pacts formed a key building block, enabling the Commission to bypass the national level to some extent in its implementation and testing at the local and regional levels of its programme for the Structural Funds. On the other hand, the Commission was able to pursue its comprehensive project of a socially acceptable and employment-friendly restructuring of Europe's political economy and to condense it in the concept of the 'European Social Model' (cf. EC 1995a, 1996a).

Molecular changes are also especially to be found in the follow-up to the Essen Council, and thus in the area of the co-ordination of national employment policies. For one thing, the results of the different national employment policies had to be rendered comparable. This required an evaluation instrument with which to measure economic performance. This task was entrusted to the Committee for Employment and Labour Market Questions. The professionalization and depoliticization of the co-ordination of employment policy gave rise to further points of entry, which the Commission condensed into a benchmarking process and with which it thus created a new European mechanism of intervention.

The political discussions between the member states therefore formed just a first level of policy-making, promoting certain further developments while cutting off others. How the Amsterdam framework was concretely filled in and how the intervention points were utilized constitute another level. Moreover, for an understanding of European employment policy it is necessary to detail its instruments and principles of operation. These did not take the form of the observance of formal Treaty obligations; nor did they mean a return to classical modes of regulation. New forms of governance were developed which defy classification in terms of the classical dichotomy between (re)distributive vs regulatory policies. In what follows we will therefore analyse the further development of employment policy at another level, looking more directly at the political profile of the new forms of intervention. This will allow us to see better the molecular changes that eventually contribute to a partial modification of the overall project of European integration.

The Luxembourg process and the benchmarking procedure

The French government had failed to prevail in Amsterdam and accepted the Stability and Growth Pact without direct compensation in the employment field. It postponed the real conflict (Dräger and Wolf 1999) by demanding a special summit that should concretize the new Treaty provisions and put them into practice immediately (without waiting for the formal Treaty ratification). In the run-up to the so-called Luxembourg Employment Summit the contours of an 'advocacy coalition' (Sabatier 1993) became discernible, consisting of the Luxembourg Presidency and the European Commission (Juncker, Santer and Flynn), which aimed to prevent another 'deregulation summit' and demanded more commitment in the co-ordination of employment policy. The anti-deregulation rhetoric became louder, not least because the Employment Chapter and the Stability Pact had already demarcated the political space. In contrast with the open situation at the IGC, the politicization of the employment issue no longer threatened the overall hegemonic project.

Ignoring the stipulations of the Treaty, the Commission had already drafted proposals for nineteen employment guidelines before the Summit and thus established itself successfully as process manager. The guidelines were grouped in four pillars (employability, entrepreneurship, adaptability and equal opportunities) and clearly confirmed the supply-side orientation of the follow-up to the Essen Summit. However, the Commission also attached quantitative objectives to the guidelines, thus following up considerations expressed in the White Paper. This made it difficult for the member states to reject the guidelines themselves: political debate focused on the quantification instead. Many actors referred back to the 'convergence method' to characterize the 'new' European employment strategy. This underlined that they continued to favour a partial modification of the old integration project and demanded a substantive employment strategy. The partly very concrete proposals of the Commission brought these conflicting viewpoints to the surface anew. In addition to the differences between member states (which were, of course, affected by the fact that quantitative objectives affected countries with different unemployment rates differentially), conflicts within national governments also became visible, for instance between finance ministries and employment ministries. Likewise, the otherwise so closed European Parliament was clearly divided over the application of the guidelines, and even within the Commission itself the proposals apparently caused dissension (*Frankfurter Rundschau*, 7 November 1997; *European Voice*, 30 October–5

November 1997; *Agence Europe*, 22 October 1997). In the final interstate bargaining process the Commission proposals were only slightly altered. The most important change was the weakening of the quantitative objectives (cf. European Council 1997b) in order to prevent the European level from gaining real influence over national policy-making.

But focusing on quantitative objectives or on modalities of sanctionable convergence criteria is misleading when estimating the effects of the new policy procedure. Such a viewpoint spoils our understanding of how European employment policies actually work (Deppe *et al.* 2000). At the latest with the Luxembourg Summit, it became clear that other – only seemingly weaker – regulatory mechanisms were developed. Apart from 'management by objectives' (Lönroth 1998), which typifies the co-ordination process, the so-called 'benchmarking' of labour-market practices proved particularly effective (Tidow 1999). Both forms of intervention aim to open up national labour-market regimes to new practices diverging from the established ones. These forms of intervention aim to transform and restructure labour-market regulation in the member states without transcending the boundaries of the hegemonic project outright. They require no hard regulatory directives from above. By strengthening competitive elements and by the diffusion of common problem-solving philosophies they facilitate harmonization from below. The European strategic points of reference must be processed within national institutional frameworks, which in turn are themselves modified and restructured as a result of these transnational pressures.

On the first view, it seemed that the Luxembourg process implied no more than an additional task for the national labour-market administrations. The present and planned future measures (programmes and legislation) have to be brought together in the National Action Plans (NAP). But the conclusion of the first annual cycle already showed, however, that the Commission criticized the quality of the various NAPs in unusually sharp tone and utilized the pressures of publicity to obtain stronger substantial commitments (Tömmel 2000). In the second year the Commission went even further and called on the Council of Ministers (foreseen as a possibility in Article 128 of the TEU) to adopt political recommendations towards the member states (EC 1999c). In this way, national and European levels were tied together more closely, as national officials were forced to respond to the criticism and to engage with the problem-solving approach predominant at the European level. This does not constitute hierarchical control over the policies of the member states or an immediate reformulation of the NAPs. It does, however, set in motion a process of communication between the European and the national level in which individual measures must be presented and founded in a systematic context. The European political process thus provokes not just an evaluation of the national programmes, but also, simultaneously, a discussion of the distinct substantive policy orientations. The broad scope of the guidelines forces various ministries (Economy, Culture, Social Affairs, Labour) to present a common plan and to co-ordinate their separate policies.

Common problem-solving philosophies are, however, generated through benchmarking in particular. Where the co-ordination process engendered by

Luxembourg is limited to the convergence of overarching objectives, benchmarking prepares the way for the convergence of the means and thus of the formulation and implementation of concrete policies. This characteristic management tool entered European policy discussions in 1996. Not for the first time, it was the European Round Table of Industrialists (ERT) which proved to be a successful agenda setter (ERT 1996; see also Chapter 7). Benchmarking involves the continuous search for and use of 'best practices' that significantly improve 'competitiveness'. Processes which had hitherto been shielded from the market are exposed to (artificial) competition. Through a comparison of one's key data with those of the 'best' performer one attempts to clarify one's strengths and weaknesses in order then to adopt the 'best practices' in one's own 'enterprise'. In the mid-1990s the Commission intensified its efforts to develop the discourse of benchmarking in the sphere of labour-market policy. Its own think tank RESEARCH provided the scientific basis for this endeavour (Tronti 1998). If we compare the employment reports of 1996, 1997 and 1998, we can trace this development: where at first the *European* labour market took centre stage and subsequently the *national* employment performances, finally not only were these two related to each other, but nationally successful strategies and measures were abundantly praised and implicitly held up as examples to the other member states (EC 1998a).

These key data, which are used for the comparison of national employment policies, are underpinned by specific rationality criteria. Notwithstanding their selectivity they are claimed to represent comprehensively the complexity and diversity of various labour-market performances and problems. Benchmarking no longer uses neo-classical textbook recipes as its reference, but the real experiences and policies of the member states, thus emphasizing the – always contradictory – specific historical and institutional development of national regimes.

> In other words, the new benchmarking procedure seeks to build fairly close and meaningful connections between national labour regimes without requiring much institutional harmonisation. Balancing policy convergence and institutional diversity is the centrepiece of the new employment strategy.
>
> (Teague 1999b: 54)

The chances of success for these forms of intervention are, of course, not so much promoted by subversive activity on the part of the Commission as by the fact that a new form of articulation between politics and economics has pervaded the regulatory channels (Felder 2001). The substance of the new policies is equally compatible with the hegemonic orientation of the European project and with the strategic selectivity of the national-state projects and their new search for competitiveness. This is brought out in particular in the ideology of the 'new' social democracy (the 'Third Way'), which unquestioningly supports the assumptions of the integration project and its macro-economic orientation (as Bieling as well as Ryner and Schulten show in this volume; Chapters 4 and

10). The insertion of elements of competition in the sphere of policy formation, which undermines the normative underpinnings of politics and makes it into an appendix of economic management thinking, is therefore just one side of the coin. The other side will transpire when we analyse in more detail the substance of the reform proposals for labour-market policy that are expressed in the guidelines as well as in the preferred 'best practices' (see Figure 5.1, fifth column).

In essence the reform proposals revolve around a conception of employment policy that is best described by the term 'employability'. This concept is really at the heart of all current debates about labour-market reform (Blancke *et al.* 1999). The European Commission in particular has been concerned since a few years ago to give this trendy concept a more solid foundation (Gazier 1999). Employability refers not only to a different conception of the problem of unemployment, but also to a new understanding of labour-market policy and, with that, to a new role for the state. Unemployment, in this view, is explained from the supply side: it signifies the inadequate ability of the individual to be employed. Lifelong learning and the investment in human capital has thus become an individual imperative necessary to being able to follow the structural changes in the economy and to remain employable. The performance cuts in passive transfer payments are not simply the result of cost reduction, but further the erosion of established industrial relations ideologically as well: under the terms of the ongoing modernization no vested rights can be guaranteed, and thus the duty to seek employment is strengthened. In order to enhance the 'access ability' (Philpott 1999) of the unemployed the workfarist system (see Chapter 3 in this volume) is complemented by an active state labour-market policy. The shift in emphasis from passive to active labour-market policy thus refers to a qualitatively different (rather than weaker) expenditure profile. The focus is less on cost-intensive employment measures and more on qualification, education and training, and stronger independence. More than before, these measures are now related to the actual and future needs of the labour market, whether by enlarging the capacity for prospective analysis or by means of publicly financed public–private training initiatives.

'Employability' refers to this labour-market policy in a narrow sense. As the bearer of human capital, labour power itself has become a resource for economic innovation, structural change and competitiveness. Official labour-market policy thus aims not only at the unemployed, but at the total workforce and at the constitution and reproduction of its ability to be employed and its 'performance ability' (Philpott 1999). Labour-market policy is thus disengaged in two ways from the context of social policy, and embedded in the context of economic, competition and structural policy. Politics is reformulated as public human resources management (HRM).

In sum, we can conclude that the European employment agenda was indeed initially shaped by the direction of the integration project and the intergovernmental harmonization of national policy projects. However, it now also influences the national restructuring processes to the extent that the contours of a Schumpeterian labour-market policy are not just conceptually elaborated at the European level but now feed back actively into the national level of policy-making. The classical division of labour between the European and the national levels is thus increasingly blurred (Deppe *et al.* 2000).

The macro-economic policy mix of Cologne

The results of Amsterdam and Luxembourg already institutionally anchored European employment policy. In fact, however, it was labour-market policy which now acquired a clear European bias. However, a new elaboration of the macro-economic dimension of the integration project was still to be achieved. The Socialist government of France in particular linked its search for a 'European economic government' to its political project (Uterwedde 2000). And the European trade unions too reflected, with their call for an employment-oriented policy mix, the increased pressures on wage determination resulting from the introduction of the Euro (Gabaglio 1999). When the conservative coalition lost the German elections and Social Democracy became the leading force in Europe, conditions for the linkage of the European employment strategy to overall macro-economic policy improved. European Social Democrats openly advocated a change of direction (SPE-ECOFIN-Gruppe 1998). This re-politicization of the European project found its clearest expression in the joint strategy paper of the French and German finance ministers (Lafontaine and Strauss-Kahn 1999). The restrictive set-up of European macro-economic policy had to be relaxed in order to gain more political freedom of action.

With the European Council of Cologne this link-up was finally realized. The limitation of employment policy to aspects of labour-market policy so dominant until then seemed to have softened. Already at the Summit in Pörtschach Gerhard Schröder, the new German chancellor, had called for a 'European Alliance for Jobs' and demanded an extra European contribution to employment. In the course of the German Presidency the haze gradually lifted and it became clearer what was meant. The (old) social-democratic agenda was elaborated under a new political aegis: not Lafontaine and Strauss-Kahn, but Blair and Schröder turned out to hold the quill pen.[6] A macro-economic dialogue was introduced in which the parameters of monetary, financial and wage policy would be discussed. The ministers for labour and social affairs, the ECOFIN council, the European social partners and the central bank presidents meet regularly, with the Commission also attending. However, the notion of 'policy mix' in the Cologne decisions represents a semantic reminiscence of Keynesian economic management only, and does not yet mark a substantive change of policy. Not only was the priority of stability-oriented objectives confirmed and fixed in the conclusions of the European Council, but the independence of the actors concerned and their policy autonomy were also strictly observed. Truly new was therefore only the inclusion of trade unions and employers in the European discussion forum, and the attention to wage policy.

To interpret these recent developments as the contours of a 'regulated capitalism' (Pollack 1998) is premature. We see, rather, once more the incrementalist incorporation into the existing integration project of a demand that admittedly does not question monetary union as such, but does strongly politicize its neoliberal character. Institutionally, the hope for a regulated capitalism is contradicted by the absence of a wage-negotiation mandate for the European social partners. In particular, the trade unions face the problem that their structural weakness vis-à-vis the employers is not reduced (Streeck 1995b; Schulten 1998), and nor are the conditions created for a tripartite bargaining arena. On the contrary, the unions are now confronted with the fact that – after the political fine-tuning of fiscal and monetary polices was again confirmed – the employment policy misery could still, as before, backfire against wage policy, which was assigned a decisive role as a strategic variable in the struggle for competitiveness and employment. This development brought to light the penetrating change in macro-economic policy which Stephen Gill has called 'New Constitutionalism': monetary and exchange-rate policy have been extracted from the national context and subordinated completely to the fight against inflation. Expansionary demand-oriented growth strategies are excluded under the pressure of fiscal rectitude. Redistribution is possible only to the extent that international competitiveness is not endangered, and is furthermore regressive as a result of policy competition. Even the critics of monetarist policy remain imprisoned by this restrictive frame in their demand for a 'neutral' and shock-evading fiscal and monetary policy.

The employment pact of Cologne keenly reflects this 'new-Keynesian consensus' (Teague 1999b). The link-up between the separate policies was in principle recognized and a 'political' arrangement accepted, but this 'co-operative macro-economic policy mix' leaves the central strategic core of monetary and fiscal policies unaffected. Moreover, the social partners are required to subordinate their wage agreements to the price stability objectives of the European Central Bank (ECB) in this way to create the real basis for employment growth. The Cologne employment pact completed the institutional link-up of wage policy to the project of monetary union. The project of a 'social Europe' was pushed into the background. The guiding principle is not so much the balance between economic efficiency and social justice as it is the balance between the national state and the institutional make-up of the new Euro-zone (Teague 1999b). On the European level we see the reproduction of a tendency that had already characterized national wage policy: the shift towards supply-side corporatism (Traxler 1995) where 'social pacts' support the domestic economic imperative. And just as domestically the core of employment policy has shifted towards the regulation of the labour market, so labour-market and structural policy remain the central sphere of action at the European level. This gradual shift manifested itself clearly six months later in Lisbon (see Figure 5.1, final column).

The conservative forces in the EU above all attempted to reign in the space for interpretation in the area of employment policy. Immediately after Luxembourg they had already stressed the need to view the internal market policy as a source of employment and to rehabilitate the 'Cecchini logic' of deregulation and supply-side restructuring as employment policy. At the European Council in Cardiff the continuity of this strategy was confirmed

(European Council in Cardiff 1998). At the special Summit in Lisbon in 2000, too, employment was on the agenda formally speaking, but in fact it amounted to a new reform initiative of structural policies (European Council in Lisbon 2000). The Portuguese Presidency, at the special wish of the British and Spanish governments and after preparatory work by the Commission, launched, among other things, an ambitious Internet offensive designed to make Europe fit for the 'New Economy' (Portuguese Presidency 2000). The challenging goal of making the EU into the most dynamic economic bloc in the world may be overreaching, but is not for that reason undesirable. More decisive is that the conclusions from Lisbon and a special emphasis on education represent a further shift towards supply-side restructuring primarily designed to boost competitiveness and innovation, while social concerns over unemployment recede even further into the background. Yet the new employment policy has lost its critical impetus as an instrument for eliminating social inequality. It has become a tool to reform the conduct of individuals and institutions in all sectors to make them more competitive and efficient. For this, the EU transferred the benchmarking procedure as a 'new method of open co-ordination' to other policies.

Conclusion

At least since the mid-1990s, employment policy has stood in the centre of European debates. The changing balance of social and political forces has been inscribed in the orientation of policy. The continuous renegotiations of the political boundaries of the theme, and the political and institutional resolution of conflicts have characterized this process. However, if we look beyond the political conjuncture we see also that the hegemonic orientation of the integration project was never seriously challenged. The central premises of the trajectory of the Single Market and monetary union were not put in question. Under these conditions, those pushing for a modification failed, and had to fail, to generate an attractive model that could have served as a point of crystallization for a counter-hegemonic project. In this sense all attempts to reorient the integration project by means of a new employment policy were futile. Figure 5.1 summarizes the separate phases of this process clearly.

Nevertheless, the employment dimension of the EU did acquire an autonomous existence. In the course of the successive political confrontations, employment policy was freed from the narrow confines of social policy and established as a separate political arena. This institutional embedding relates both to the creation of a co-ordination mechanism and the annual formulation of guidelines as well as to the establishment of the employment pact. These 'molecular changes' have redrawn the terrain for the political debate at the European level. They have produced new entry points for those aiming at stronger regulation of employment policy. The possibilities of re-politicizing this field have thus been enlarged. This effect has been reinforced by the partial regrouping of the political and administrative *rapports de force* achieved by the new measures. For not only have the ministers for economic affairs been involved in the formulation of employment and labour-market policy, but the ministers for social affairs and employment have also become involved in the dialogue on macro-economic policy. At the national level the formulation and implementation of the NAPs cut right through the established ministerial division of labour, and at the European level the role of the Commission *vis-à-vis* the Council has been strengthened. The conflict between the objectives of economic policy and of employment policy, we might expect, could surface more clearly than before and will hence require institutional answers. Since the tension between social disintegration and the pursuit of national competitiveness which lies at the heart of European employment policy cannot be resolved with the present set-up, a renewed politicization cannot be ruled out. Whether these contradictions will in fact become acute will depend, above all, on the extent to which common (hegemonic) ideals dominate the reorganization of labour-market policy and to what extent competitiveness and employment are conceived as complementary.

Against this background, a major role will be played by the new regulatory mechanisms developed for the European employment strategy. 'Management by objectives' and 'benchmarking' are precisely geared towards generating and diffusing shared ideals for the reorganization of labour-market policy. Instead of hierarchical supervision of national policy, it is through the joint elaboration of problem-solving strategies that the European and the national level are tied more closely together. The technocratic problem-solving approach facilitates the depoliticization of conflict.

In terms of the substantive profile of the various reform proposals, the continuity of supply-side elements is conspicuous. Qualitatively new are the concerns over a 'productivist reconstruction of solidarity' and a new form of supply-side 'egalitarianism' which no longer aims at a de-commodification of human labour but instead opts for 'equal opportunities for commodification' (Streeck 1999: 12; see also Chapter 6). The issue of the marketability of individuals, which neoliberalism has silently taken as axiomatic, is being made into the key component ('employability') of the employment strategy, also and perhaps especially in the new programmes of Social Democracy (see Chapters 8 and 10). European employment policy is much more than just symbolic politics. Its present importance arises from the fact that it has become a key factor in the ongoing transformation of the nationally defined Keynesian welfare state regime into a Europeanizing Schumpeterian workfare state regime (see also Chapter 3).

Notes

1 This development can, on the one hand, be interpreted as part of its 'Russian doll' strategy in the sense that partial supranationalization also served its own institutional interests, while, on the other hand, the Commission tends to be very sensitive to questions of legitimacy because it is more strongly affected by them than national institutions.

2 The strongest opponents at the time were Germany, Great Britain and France, while the Austrian and Swedish governments were supported primarily by their Belgian and Danish counterparts.

3 The German Sozialdemokratische Partei Deutschlands (SPD) criticized the reluctance of the German government sharply and even threatened to withhold its parliamentary approval, without even once explicitly outlining its minimum criteria for an acceptable outcome.

4 Significantly, the Structural Funds were not explicitly referred to in the Employment Title, and thus their status as instruments for labour-market policies was not enhanced.

5 Although these 'molecular changes' possess an incremental character, the notion of 'passive revolution' (in contrast with that of 'incrementalism') emphasizes intended and strategic reform options rather than ad-hoc measures and an orientation towards maintaining the status quo. At the same time, the trajectory of change is hemmed in by political and ideological constraints and alternative options are excluded (on incrementalism, see Lindblom 1975).

6 See also the Schröder–Blair Paper (1999). It is remarkable that the European dimension in this strategic paper of the 'Third Way' is almost completely absent. Only in the cases of the liberalization of world trade and the completion of the internal market is the EU assigned any role at all.

6 Economic and Monetary Union, employment and gender politics

A feminist constructivist analysis of neo-liberal labour-market restructuring in Europe[1]

Brigitte Young

A dilemma: the European Monetary Union and the scepticism of Nordic women

In connection with the Danish referendum on 28 September 2000 to join the European Economic and Monetary Union (EMU), the German daily newspaper *Frankfurter Rundschau*[2] signalled with the headline 'Courting the sceptical women' that all was not well with the EMU. That the majority of Danish voters declined joining the EMU, by a margin of 53 to 46 per cent, is largely the result of the scepticism of Danish women. One of the many opinion polls two days before the referendum suggested that support for the EMU among men was 51 per cent, in comparison to only 30 per cent among women. Many women worry about the danger to the social welfare state, which is how the Danish political scientist Anette Borchorst describes the uneasiness women feel toward joining the EMU. More women than men see the European Union (EU) and the introduction of the Euro as a threat to the universal social system. It is feared that the impending drive toward European tax harmonization will replace the tax-financed social system with the more common European insurance-financed social system. European tax harmonization, according to Drude Dahlerup, spokesperson of the anti-European 'June Movement', would imply redistribution away from the universal welfare system and the loss of women's employment opportunities.[3] Thus the fear of losing jobs and 'people's pension' is the driving force behind the scepticism of many Danish women about joining the EMU (*Frankfurter Rundschau*, 12 September 2000: 2).

It is thus not surprising that Sweden, confronting an equally EU-sceptical fraction of women voters, is taking the female 'exit' threat seriously. Sweden, for the first time since joining the EU in 1995, chaired the Presidency from January 2001. A country notoriously sceptical about the idea of European integration, it has also refused to join the EMU. This was all the more interesting since Sweden, holding the EU Presidency in the first six months of 2001, had an important role in the preparations for the introduction of the Euro in January 2002.[4] Realizing the high stakes in terms of its domestic and foreign reputation, Sweden went on the offensive and presented a clear outline of the goals it wanted to pursue during its first Presidency.[5] Prime Minister Persson announced that the letter 'E' marks Sweden's presidency: 'E' not only for Europe, but also for 'enlargement', 'environment' and 'employment'. Sweden wants to build on its successful strategy in the labour market and emphasize 'education' and 'equality' to improve the European employment situation.[6] Sweden thus became the first country presiding over the EU specifically to stress equality between women and men as a goal to pursue while at the helm of the Presidency.

Nordic scepticism among the female population and their power to use the 'exit' option seems to have borne fruit. If Sweden and Denmark want to join the EMU, a goal Prime Minister Göran Persson strongly pursues for his country, then both Sweden and Denmark have first to overcome the scepticism of many of their women voters. Sweden courts its women with the promise not to sacrifice the existing achievement in gender equality and is ready to confront the other fourteen members of the European Union with a solidaristic gender regime that is unique to Sweden. In the same vein, the Danish minister of the interior, Karen Jesperson, appeals to the sceptical female voters that only by joining the EMU are the conditions for a stable welfare system guaranteed. A 'no' vote could lead to isolation and endanger the Danish economy. Another strategy of the Danish 'yes' fraction is to shift the debate to issues of human rights and culture, and away from economic issues such as the convergence criteria agreed upon in the Maastricht Treaty to usher in the EMU and foreign exchange rates.[7]

What makes this 'puzzle' of Nordic recalcitrance so interesting is that for the first time a large section of women voters hold the key to joining the EMU. This is all the more interesting because the Nordic countries have always been regarded as exemplars of progressive welfare-state development (see also Chapter 10). The question I want to pursue in this chapter is whether the Gordian knot between the present construction of the EMU, with its aim of maintaining rigid price stability, and the Nordic promise to preserve the present level of social programmes can be reconciled. This chapter differs from many other feminist approaches to the EMU and equal opportunities policy in that it combines a constructivist understanding of the EMU with feminist political economy. There is an extensive literature on equal opportunities policies in the EU and their impact on women in member states (Walby 1999; Ostner and Lewis 1995; Rubery 1998; Hoskyns 1996; Young 2000).[8] Much of the published works interpret European employment and equal opportunities policies within a narrow policy focus. Very few feminist scholars situate employment policies within the larger context of economic globalization, with its emphasis on deregulation and political disengagement from the economy.

Instead of a policy approach, the intention of this chapter is to focus on the macroeconomic environment of the EU and analyse the effects of the institutionalization of the EMU on reconstituting a new 'ordering rationality' (Rosamond 1999: 658) that regulates and constrains actors' behaviour and limits policy options. Most economic accounts have privileged a rational choice or neo-institutional account of the EMU. Much less attention has been paid to the interest- and identity-forming roles of institutions. This chapter stresses the active role of institutions in creating systems of beliefs and norms (Christiansen *et al.* 1999; Checkel 1999). A constructivist approach is particularly well suited to pursue the question of how the EMU is involved in constructing the identities and interests of member states and groups within them (Checkel 1999; Rosamond 1999).

The first section of the chapter gives a short overview of the present debate on EU gender and equal opportunities policies. It concludes that the present policy studies are too narrow in focus and suggests that the macroeconomic environment of the EMU is essential to understanding both the limits and opportunities of labour-market policies for women. However, the argument does not stop here. The subsequent section goes on to interpret the EU as a 'strategic site of centrality' (Sassen 1998b) in the global economy. Investigating the discursive construction of globalization and European integration, it will argue that the EMU constitutes a new governance framework to make member-state governments more responsive to the discipline of market forces and correspondingly less responsive to social-democratic forces and gender-friendly processes. Next we focus on the 'content' of the new disciplinary governance framework by highlighting the effects of the EMU's monetary policy on the creation of new norms and systems of beliefs that are much more commensurate with neo-liberal practice and discourse. Essentially, we will ask the question of what interests are legitimized by the EMU's unilateral focus on price stability. Then we return to the question of gender and equal employment politics. Utilizing the tools from feminist economics, three forms of bias are discussed that need to be avoided if macroeconomic policies are to promote equal opportunities for women and men in the EU. Failing to consider the social content of macroeconomic policy, so the thesis of this chapter goes, will make it difficult, if not impossible, to live up to the promise the Danish and Swedish pro-EMU factions have made to their female constituencies of maintaining the Nordic model.

EU employment policies and gender politics

Few of the feminist analyses of EU employment and equal opportunities policies have paid attention to the EMU and its institutional effects on social construction. Scholars have mainly stayed within the confines of particular policy studies. As a result, we have scholars who focus on EU labour-market policies (Walby 1999; Cook 1998) and others who study the welfare state (Ostner and Lewis 1995; Elman 1996; Rossilli 1997; Hoskyns 1996). Only some feminist economists have taken into account the macroeconomic environment and macroeconomic policy framework that provide the context in which the policy programmes are implemented (Rubery *et al.* 1998). As a result, the dominance of the Maastricht convergence and stability criteria over issues that deal with employment targets and the resulting supply-side-oriented measures contained in the employment guidelines are largely disregarded in policy studies.

Despite the different policy foci, feminists agree that with the start of the Amsterdam Treaty the EU entered a new phase of European employment policy characterized by a growing recognition of the importance of gender issues. However, feminists disagree about the impact of the EU equal opportunities directives on women in member states. Scholars that work in the tradition of welfare policy overwhelmingly conclude that the EU equal opportunities policies have a mostly limited impact or are ambivalent at best about their effect on women (Ostner and Lewis 1995). In contrast, Sylvia Walby (1999, 1997) presents the strongest defence of equal opportunities laws and argues that the EU has made significant changes to the governance of gender relations.

In this argument between European welfare specialists and labour-market analysts we face two different policy foci. They draw on different political theories with regard to citizenship rights and concepts of national sovereignty and the normativity that comes with it. In short, feminist welfare specialists are associated with social democracy and corporatism, while the issue of equal opportunities is situated within a liberal framework: 'Welfare has tended to make demands on the state, offer collective solutions to dilemmas, and be dependent upon taxation. Equal opportunities needs a more minimal type of regulatory state, ostensibly offers a more individualistic solution, and does not require taxation' (Walby 1999: 60). Welfare policy analysts argue further that member states are an obstacle to the implementation of supranational regulation. In contrast, Walby focuses on the power of European law and suggests that many feminists have underestimated the power of European law to override national social regulation. The argument between welfare policy specialists and labour-market analysts has provided important insights into different gender perspectives and approaches.

If we include a political economy approach, the focus shifts to the impact of the global macroeconomic environment that constrains both welfare and labour-market policies. From this perspective, the Maastricht Agreements and EMU represent a dramatic shift towards a disciplinary neo-liberal discourse of capitalism to produce the conditions for global economic production (Gill 1998; Young 2000). The implications of all this for a social and gender-friendly Europe, as the Danes and the Swedes seem to promise their female constituencies, are at best contradictory. At worst, the promises are quite unrealistic. The deflationary macroeconomic environment resulting from the Maastricht criteria is counterposed to the social and employment guidelines enacted by the EU. Adopting the Maastricht guidelines has led to economic retrenchment in all member states, which has involved cutting, or at best stabilizing, welfare and social expenditures (Teague 1998). Given the supply-side measures contained in the employment policies, it is difficult to see how effective the EU will be in creating higher rates of employment and thus fulfil the equal opportunities promises. Yet the equal opportunities employment agenda rests on the promotion of women's employment. The European Commission has foregone, and even implicitly denied, any demand-side intervention in the economy. Instead, at the centre of the approach is a focus on the supply side. Improving the skills of potential workers and facilitating easier access to the job market by providing child-care facilities are believed to promote the employment of women (Rubery 1998).

But here we confront a catch-22 situation. Women are entering the labour market in increasing numbers, and the EU, rhetorically at least, encourages such a move, particularly in the light of Danish and Swedish recalcitrance to join the EMU. At the same time, the EMU creates the environment for a demand-constrained employment scenario. As Rubery (1998) has pointed out, these developments contribute to the problem of job shortages. To promote the employment of women in the absence of an active job-creating policy and in the context of a restrictive fiscal environment seems like trying to square a circle. Neither the employment guidelines nor the Joint Employment Report even mention the public sector as a vital promoter of women's employment and facilitator of labour-market integration, and yet it is difficult to see how in the absence of the revival of the public sector the private sector can generate the required job growth to absorb the increased labour supply. The strict monetary goals of the EMU and fiscal targets circumscribe the policies that are needed to promote the EU's equal opportunities objectives. In other words, the neo-liberal macroeconomic environment shuts the door to a public-sector employment strategy, which, in fact, is the key to the Nordic equal employment model (Theobald 1999).

Concluding that the introduction of the EMU is commensurate with a new neo-liberal governance framework tells us little about the forces that drive these processes. The next section will thus place the EMU in the context of the political economy of globalization.

The EU as a strategic site of globalization

The meaning of globalization is central to the argument pursued in this chapter. We want to find out to what extent a particular discourse of economic globalization serves to shape the European integration process, and how in turn the discursive practices influence the creation of new norms, values and practices within the EU. In other words, does a particular discursive construction of globalization set the boundaries for the politically feasible within the EU? Which political strategies are thereby excluded, and which new opportunities are made possible? Political feasibility is understood not just as a question of objective and exogenous structures of the global economy. Political ability to act is a social construction that is repeatedly redefined and constituted through a particular rhetoric of globalization. Defining globalization as a 'discourse of power' (Gill 1998) suggests that the present privileging of a particular reading of globalization is, as Hay and Watson (1998) have pointed out, only tangentially related to the realities of the global economy. Although a particular neo-liberal version of globalization has become hegemonic, this does not mean that alternative discourses do not exist that challenge the dominant assertions. The large demonstrations starting at the Ministerial Meeting of the World Trade Organization (WTO) in Seattle in late 1999 and in Washington, DC, in the spring of 2000, continuing right up to the G7/G8 Summit in Genoa in 2001, have shown that many oppositional narratives to globalization exist (Gill 2000b).

In defining globalization as a 'discourse of power', a particular reading of the constructivist approach[9] is suggested that maintains that there is an inherent connection between the social construction of the external environment and the interests that actors acquire (Ruggie 1998; Wendt 1992; Rosamond 1999; Checkel 1999). Unlike methodological individualism, with its emphasis on rational actors that push the European integration process forward (Sandholtz and Zysman 1989),[10] constructivists focus on the complex effects of institutionalization both in shaping the actors' expectations and in generating shared beliefs and norms within a policy context. In most economic analyses of the EMU, institutions play virtually no role in creating systems of beliefs and conventions (Christiansen *et al.* 1999; Checkel 1999). Realists assume that actors' interests are given. They arrive at this conclusion because they assume a radical separation between subject and object (Kratochwil and Ruggie 1986). According to this logic, only objective forces have the power to influence the behaviour of actors. Constructivists, on the other hand, attempt to dissolve the dualism between structure and agency. Their environment does not structure agents' interests. 'They help to make their environment and their environment helps to make them' (Rosamond 1999: 658). Introducing an inter-subjective meaning into the study of institutions opens a much-needed space to raise questions about the origin and reconstruction of identities, the impact of institutional rules and norms and of political discourses. In other words, constructivists suggest that not only interests but also identities are important in explaining political processes (Christiansen *et al.* 1999).

If we apply this insight of a norm-creating process to the establishment of EMU, then we can argue that the EMU is more than an economic project. The introduction of the Euro as a new European denomination has helped to create a world according to a particular neo-liberal logic that then shapes actors' behaviour according to this logic. Starting with the Maastricht convergence criteria and the Stability Pact, we can argue that these organizational structures have supplied a new ordering rationality that has subsequently defined the structural boundaries in terms of both its limits and the opportunities in which actors can operate. One of the most powerful insights that constructivists provide is the inseparability of (economic) structures and the social construction of norms. According to this interpretation, the EMU is thus not just an important new institution that sets monetary policy for all member states. More importantly, the EMU and the introduction of the Euro help to constitute a new European identity. That money is involved in constructing national identities is not exactly a new insight. Karl Marx noted the close relationship between money and national identity. 'Money as money' does not only function as standard of value, as means of circulation and of payment, and as credit. Historically money has always had an identity-creating and a legitimating function in the development of modern nation-states:

> Money thereby directly and simultaneously becomes the real community [Gemeinwesen], since it is the general substance of survival for all, and at

> the same time the social product of all. But as we have seen, in money the community [Gemeinwesen] is at the same time a mere abstraction, a mere external, accidental thing for the individual, and at the same time merely a means for his satisfaction as an isolated individual.
>
> (Marx 1973: 225–6)

The introduction of the Euro as an identity-creating entity is no exception. Thus the European EMU can be seen as one, if not the central, constitutive moment of a common European identity.[11]

The new rules and norms of the EMU governance framework

If we conclude that Sweden and Denmark cannot reconcile the promise to maintain the present level of the universal welfare system and joining the EMU, then we need to ask what is the role EMU plays in constructing new norms and conventions that effectively rule out Keynesian-type demand management in the member states. In answering this question, it seems that the role of money and the definition of money in the neo-liberal orthodoxy play a central role. The role of money is important because at the centre of a monetary union is the definition of money. As pointed out earlier, money is not just an abstract measuring device. Much more important is the interest- and identity-forming effect that money generates (see Gilbert and Helleiner 1999). In order to explicate the norm-creating function of money it may be helpful to compare the effects money, more precisely monetary theory, has in Keynesian economics and in neoclassical economics. The intent of this exercise is to show that the orthodox monetary theory espoused by the EMU is based on assumptions that create norms favouring the interests of finance capitalism and contradict the Keynesian assumptions of a full-employment economy.

According to classical theory, money does not enter into the 'real' economy. Neo-liberals have revived the classical orthodoxy about the 'neutrality of money' (Hein 2000), which assumes that money supply and the rate of interest on money have no influence on the real factors of the economy (such as employment, production and economic growth). Money only has an effect on the level of prices. It was John Maynard Keynes, in *The General Theory of Employment, Interest, and Money* (1997), who challenged the classical assumptions of money as something separate from the general theory of supply and demand. According to Keynes, monetary and financial policies determine changes in the scale of output and employment as a whole. It is this conflict about the neutrality of money, on the one side, and the influence of money on real economic variables, on the other, which is at the centre of the normative construction of the neo-liberal globalization discourses. Despite the existence of a large amount of quantitative econometric studies to justify one side or the other, it is not statistics that can resolve the puzzle. It is a question of the basic beliefs and theoretical foundations that underpin the two contrary positions (Flassbeck 1999).

More important than who is right and who is wrong in this historic struggle among economists about the role of money is the question of the effects of these two divergent monetary theories. Which shared norms, understandings and normative principles are mobilized and which ordering rationality is created that in turn shape interests and constrain the behaviour of actors within the global economy? If we follow the fundamental assumptions of an expansive monetary theory, then money has a double role in influencing the 'real' economy. First, the rate of interest on the money influences the stability of wage income and economic growth, as was the case during the Fordist period after World War II. Here, we have a growth model that links real wage rates to productivity rates and to anti-cyclical monetary and fiscal policy. The Keynesian welfare state had the additional function of regulating demand and generalizing norms of mass consumption, and thereby contributing to full-employment levels of demand. In addition, the Bretton Woods monetary system and the General Agreement on Tariffs and Trade (GATT) trade regime meant that the circulation of free-floating international currencies stabilized Keynesian economic management through state control over the national money (Jessop 1994). In this Fordist model of managed economic growth, the level of interest rates played a major role in facilitating full-employment policies. Monetary institutions pursued a policy of holding the real interest rate below the growth rate of the gross domestic product (GDP) (Hein 2000). A national distributional consensus was thus secured through a corporatist male-dominated class compromise between capital and labour. Not only did the Keynesian full-employment model ensure a certain level of economic stability, but it also helped to foster an identity of national citizenship within the redistributional model of European social democracy (Altvater and Mahnkopf 1996).

In the present regime of a market-led global financial system, or, as Giovanoli (2000) refers to it, a 'private international monetary system', the geometry has been fundamentally altered. The drive toward deregulation and the creation of global financial markets has led to an increasing competition on the exchange-rate markets. To avoid capital flight, interest rates are used to defend the national currency. In other words, the centre of monetary policy pursued by central banks has shifted to securing assets based on their own currency (Guttmann 2000b). With the transformation of the credit system from commercial loans to securities as the principal form of credit we also witness a change in the central banks' monetary policy that favours the private-commodity elements of money.

Increasingly, the social and the private dimensions of money are in conflict with each other. Money as a social institution reveals itself as both a public good and a private commodity. It is a public good in that stable valuation and smooth circulation are in the interest of all. It is a private commodity inasmuch as private agents trying to gain income from financial activities create it. If the private-commodity elements of money become dominant, as is the case right now,

> [the] economic system suffers from all the negative consequences of money's commodification into a vehicle for bank profit – more pronounced cyclical

> fluctuations punctuated by financial crises, greater price instability, and widening income-distribution gaps between rich and poor as the result of increasingly unequal access to money and credit.
>
> (Guttmann 2000a: 5)

The bias towards private-capital investors has shifted the emphasis in macroeconomic policy to price stability and controls against inflation (Soskice 1999b). In this exclusive emphasis on price stability (shared by the European Central Bank, ECB) economic growth as a policy goal has lost its theoretical validity. Focusing on interest rates to defend the national currency has meant much higher long-term real interest rates than was the case in the previous Keynesian period. We have reached a peculiar point in economic development where since the early 1980s the real interest rates of many countries have been higher than the rates of growth in GDP in those same years. Instead of money being invested in productive growth, money flows into investments with the highest capital gains, a preference which cements the importance of securities markets while at the same time restricting long-term growth and job-creation capacities (Hein 2000).

The institutionalization of restrictive monetary policy signals a fundamental shift in the theory of money from a belief in the power of money to influence economic variables to a belief in the neutrality of money in neo-liberal discourses. However, this shift in monetary policy is not restricted to monetary and economic variables. The particular discursive construction of globalization in the EMU has also supplied a new ordering rationality within the EU that helps to create a new world according to this rationality. Hans Tietmeyer, the former president of the German Bundesbank and one of the chief architects of the EMU, expressed this new rationality very poignantly at the European University Institute in Florence in 1996:

> Therefore the fundamental truth holds: The members of the EMU will only have a chance to solve their problems if the Euro remains stable over the long run.... Because financial markets judge countries, they not only look at the actual data but also try to estimate how far a country is able and prepared to solve its long-term problems.... Financial markets can punish an expansive monetary policy and an undisciplined fiscal policy right at the start. They can disinvest capital from that country and charge a higher capital interest rate.... The Monetary Union needs an implicit political 'quasi-union'. This means, first, the maintenance of a stability culture and, second, the readiness of fiscal politics, if not to give up sovereignty, then to regulate and set limits.... The stability pact asks countries whether they are prepared to maintain the stability of the common currency at the expense of pursuing their own fiscal policies.
>
> (Tietmeyer 1996; my translation)

To invoke the power of neoclassical orthodoxy as the only reality for constructing the new EMU implies that the neo-liberal discourse of globalization and the construction of the EMU are mutually constitutive processes. More importantly, the power of financial markets has been used, as Hay and Watson have pointed out, 'to act as an exogenous enforcement mechanism for domestic policies which aim to re-define existing notions of citizenship by limiting the state's role as guarantor of minimum social rights' (Hay and Watson 1998: 8).

So far, we can conclude that the Nordic promise to its female constituency to safeguard the present social and employment system cannot be sustained within the context of the restrictive monetary regime institutionalized by the EMU. The question now arises whether European women will have to subordinate themselves to the dictates of the private-commodity elements of money or whether there is an alternative that would lead to a more gender-friendly Europe. This issue will be addressed in the next section.

A feminist alternative: deconstructing macroeconomic assumption

Feminist economists (Bakker 1994, 1999; Elson 1995, 2000; Elson and Gagatay 1999, 2000; Benería 1999; Young 2001b) have called for a paradigmatic shift to 'engender the macroeconomy', arguing that gender is a major factor in reconstituting the 'new geography of power' in a globalized economy. From the perspective of a gendered political economy, markets and states are viewed as institutions imbued with structural power relations that have asymmetrical class and gender dimensions. Markets are 'embedded' in social relations, and co-operation, reciprocity, trust, redistribution and care are vital to the functioning of any market economy. Missing from standard economic narratives are the 'non-market relations' which structure all markets and are important for the conditions under which people come to the market. As Isabella Bakker reminds us, 'markets are as much political and cultural institutions as they are economic entities' (1994: 4). An engendered view of the macroeconomy would not only include markets and states; it would also include social reproduction made up of non-monetized and non-market activities that provide the necessary conditions for production and exchange relations to take place.

As a first step in engendering the study of macroeconomics, we need to *demystify* the economic rhetoric and ask whether the highly technical language in the Maastricht Treaty and in the Stability Pact signed in Dublin in 1996 is not also a weapon to fight against an alternative vision of globalization. Hans Tietmeyer and others may speak about the disciplinary effects of the market on nations. Yet we need to ask what 'prudent' monetary policy means? Who are the winners and losers from this finance-led globalization, and how can globalization and European integration benefit the many instead of the few? An emerging issue is the gender dimensions of international financial markets, and feminist economists have started to articulate their ideas of how the global financial architecture has to be changed to provide alternative political spaces for inclusive class, gender and race relations.

Diane Elson and Nilufur Cagatay (2000) have, in their recent work, identified and critiqued three interlinked assumptions upon which neoclassical macroeconomics rests. These are:

1 The deflationary bias: overemphasis on deflating the economy whenever the markets show any signs of rising inflation or whenever short-term capital is pulled out of, mostly, developing countries.
2 The commodification bias: the bias that turns many public services into privatized commodities, to be sold to the public by newly privatized businesses or to be delivered by a public sector operating on business principles and levying user fees for its services.
2 The male-breadwinner bias: the assumption that women are dependent on males. Built on this bias are entire social-service systems that have created a 'two-channel welfare state' (Nelson 1990), carved out of a set of specific gender, race and class relationships. In the first channel, men are the breadwinners and have direct access to citizen entitlements, while women are relegated to the second channel and can get access only as dependants of men.

These biases are mutually interlinked. For example, the commodification bias fuels the growth of financial institutions, as pensions and health insurance are increasingly privatized; and the growth of financial institutions in search of high interest rates fuels the deflationary bias in monetary policy. In terms of the deflationary bias, much has been said in the previous section on the negative distributional effects that result from the central banks' singular focus on price stability. Given that the EMU does not have an equivalent EU fiscal institution, the member states have to subordinate their fiscal policies, as Hans Tietmeyer so clearly pointed out, to the restrictive monetary policy set by the EMU. In other words, the macroeconomic policies do not only have a negative distributional impact, in that social expenditures either decline or, at best, are stabilized at the present level. They embody a profoundly unjust social content, in that they favour financial interests at the expense of the majority of citizens. As a result of their triple dependence on the welfare state as social workers, clients and consumers, women are particularly at risk. They may lose their jobs or have to accept part-time work resulting from the public cutbacks; they may be faced with fewer services; and/or they may have to cope with outright cuts in benefits and services. It is this scenario of endangering both employment opportunities and social services that has made Swedish and Danish women so sceptical about joining the EMU.

Intertwined with the deflationary bias in macroeconomic policy is also the breadwinner bias. The particular Fordist compromise of the World War II period between capital and labour stipulated that the workplace and the 'family wage' were tailored to the needs and interests of the male worker and 'his' dependent family. It is true that the strong breadwinner models associated with continental Catholic societies are not found in Scandinavian countries

(Pfau-Effinger 2000). However, even in Nordic countries labour markets are highly segregated into private markets mainly reserved for males and a public market occupied largely by women. The important aspect of the breadwinner bias is its normative content that males have a 'natural right' to the role of breadwinner and that women have to justify their labour-market integration. As a result, economic narratives do not take into account the unpaid work done in the home by women, because this type of work is regarded as 'natural' (G.S. Becker 1974). Despite the massive integration of women into the labour market since the 1970s, the economic discourse and public policies have continued to draw on the separation between family and work (Young 2001b).

In addition to the deflationary and the breadwinner biases, there is also the increasing commodification discourse that is linked to the deflationary bias. Many public services are turned into market-based and individualized services available to those who can afford them. These changes have produced new social hierarchies based not just on gender but also on class and race. The 're-privatization discourse' (Fraser 1989) seeks to repatriate the economic and social to the domestic enclave. Re-privatization of the domestic sphere means that many social services once again become part of the non-monetized private sphere. The commodification bias has thus fundamentally challenged the very notion of what is public and what is private. In the process, it has worsened gender-specific social divisions.[12] The growing participation of professional women in the labour market is accompanied by the largely 'invisible' development of a 'service class' that is involved in cleaning, childcare and in many other household-oriented service jobs. Growing numbers of migrant and immigrant women are involved in the informal labour market to provide these services. An invisible link has thus emerged between women's increasing participation in the formal labour market and the informal labour-market roles of migrant and immigrant women. In the process of scaling back the social state, women have responded differently according to their social and class position. They are forced to work double or triple shifts to accommodate these added care functions at the household level. For women in the lower-skilled professions, the loss of publicly provided care services often makes the difference between seeking employment and staying at home. In the case of business and professional women, they increasingly 'solve' the marketization bias by relying on inexpensive undocumented migrant women, creating a new international division of labour at the level of the household. On the one side is the 'mistress' and on the other stands the 'maid', separated by different racial, ethnic, class and national identities and backgrounds (Young 2001a).

To conclude, the triple bias of deflation, commodification and breadwinner is built into the theoretical frameworks of economics. In terms of practice, the 'costs' of these biases are largely distributed along ethnic, gender and class lines. With globalization and European integration, the democratic aspects of economic decision-making have largely been moved to the transnational and international level and removed from the national level. Democratizing the process of macroeconomic policy-making is, as Elson and Cagatay (2000) point out, a crucial element of a 'transformative' approach to macroeconomics.

Transformative implies that democratizing the economic process is more than adding the 'social' or gender dimensions to the macroeconomic framework. It means changing the fundamental assumptions of macroeconomic policy-making in the context of global challenges.

Conclusion

This chapter started with the EU's dilemma that a majority of Swedish and Danish women have little confidence in the EMU ensuring a 'social' Europe. Focusing on the debate between neoclassical and Keynesian scholars on the role of money and monetary policy, this chapter then analysed whether the Nordic promise to its female constituency to maintain a gender-friendly social system can be reconciled with the EMU's orthodox belief in price stability. In fairness, it has to be said that the EMU is still a project under construction. Neither the institutional structure, nor its operational dimensions, nor its functional scope are fully in place. Despite the 'institutional underdevelopment', the main thesis here is that the EMU is more than an economic project. Deriving theoretical insights from a combination of constructivism and political economy, the chapter illustrated that the institutionalization of the EMU, with its exclusive emphasis on price stability, reflects a shift from the European social norms of a stakeholder society to a disciplinary market-based capitalism. This has created a new ordering rationality that (re)draws the structural boundaries in terms of both opportunities and constraints that shape interests and influence the behaviour of actors within the EU.

The exclusive focus on deflationary monetary policy and the fiscal constraints that are imposed on individual member states provide little leeway for member states to embark on Keynesian-type social-democratic and gender-friendly strategies. The focus of the present finance-led growth model implies that fighting inflation and not economic growth will remain at the centre of macroeconomic policy. The result will be an increasing commodification and privatization of public goods, with the resulting negative distributional effects on women and marginalized groups. However, the alternative is not to return to a Keynesian-type policy. Instead, feminist economists argue for an examination of the implications and gender dimensions of the international economic architecture. By focusing on three biases – deflationary, commodification and breadwinner – the paper concludes that the fundamental class, race and gender assumptions built into the present economic models have to be made transparent. Feminist economists are calling for an alternative macroeconomic framework to promote social justice and gender democracy.

Notes

1 An earlier version of this chapter was published as B. Young (2002) 'On Collision Course: The European Central Bank, Monetary Policy, and the Nordic Welfare Model', *International Feminist Journal of Politics* 4(3): 295–314.

2 *Frankfurter Rundschau*, 'Buhlen um die skeptischen Frauen' (Courting the sceptical women), 12 September 2000: 2.

3 The Danish activity rate of women in the labour market, with Sweden's and Finland's, is among the highest in Europe: Denmark 78.2 per cent, Finland 70.4 per cent and Sweden 73.2 per cent. The average European activity rate for women is 58.1 per cent (*Eurostat* 1997).

4 A solution was found: during the discussions of the finance ministers of the Euro-12 group the Swedish finance minister, Bosse Ringholm, would leave the room when monetary and interest-rate policies were debated. The chair would then pass to the Belgian finance minister, since the EU Presidency was to pass to Belgium in the summer of 2001.

5 For a detailed list of goals, see the Swedish website: http://www.eu2001.se.

6 *Frankfurter Rundschau*, 'Im Zeichen des E. Unter Schwedens EU-Präsidentschaft geht es im kommenden Halbjahr um Eingemachtes wie Erweiterung und Euro' (Under the letter E. During the Swedish Presidency of the EU in the coming six months, the issues tackled will be enlargement and the Euro; 21 December 2000: 6).

7 *Frankfurter Rundschau*, 12 September 2000: 2.

8 For the different views on this debate, see Young (2000).

9 The particular strand of constructivism presented in this chapter leans on the early insights of Kratochwil and Ruggie (1986); these insights have subsequently been largely taken over by neo-Gramscian and critical approaches, while they have been abandoned by many later constructivist analysts, who have in a sense re-entered the mainstream of international relations theory (the editor).

10 For Sandholtz and Zysman (1989) the driving forces for the introduction of the Single European Market of the EU were the increasing economic internationalization and the changing domestic constellations of the European nation-states starting in the 1970s.

11 This assumption differs from that of many legal scholars, who argue that the role of law and the European Court of Justice are in fact the constitutive moment of the European integration process (Jørgensen 1999; Shaw 1999; Weiler 1997).

12 The argument which follows is based on Young (2001a).

7 European unemployment and transnational capitalist class strategy

The rise of the neo-liberal competitiveness discourse

Bastiaan van Apeldoorn

> Structural reform increases the EU's job creating potential and is therefore fundamental to the task of reducing the high levels of structural unemployment. It will do this by enhancing the EU's competitiveness and sustainable long-run economic growth rate, as well as its ability to deal with globalization and technological change.
>
> (EC 1999b: 2)

> This process [of creating higher levels of employment over the longer term] also inevitably involves job creation and job destruction: (new jobs requiring new skills replace old jobs involving old skills; successful firms take the place of the less successful; some sectors decline while others expand. The creation and growth of new enterprises is a crucial factor in renewing the economy.) A spirit of enterprise, and a climate conducive to entrepreneurship, will accelerate structural change and contribute to the development of new markets, products, services and jobs. In this context, the overall aim of improving the competitiveness of EU enterprises remains paramount.
>
> (EC 1999a: 3)

Introduction

As is illustrated by the above quotations, the shift from a Keynesian welfare state (KWS) to an Schumpeterian workfare state (SWS) identified by Bob Jessop in Chapter 3 can also be observed at the level of European supranational governance. The process of 'creative destruction' that Schumpeter saw as at the heart of capitalism's dynamism increasingly takes place transnationally, with increasingly less regard for national borders and the national states that once saw it as among their principal tasks to control those borders. Indeed, states have now abandoned the task of economic border control, and, with that, several (although surely not all) of the regulatory and redistributive functions that were part and parcel of a post-war capitalism in which markets were embedded in (national) societies and states *correcting* for market outcomes.

In fact, states have now taken up very much the opposite tasks: abolishing border control (though not with regard to the movement of persons); opening up ever more sectors to international competition; creating new markets and deregulating existing ones; in sum, promoting the marketization and commodification of ever greater areas of social life. Since its relaunch in the mid-1980s with the internal-market programme, the European integration process is clearly part of this transformation process. Indeed, one could argue that the promotion of market competition has become the main function of the European Union (EU), inasmuch as its institutions, in the absence of any supranational *state-building*, have, in the words of Wolfgang Streeck, been reduced 'to the role of a *supranational liberalization engine*' (Streeck 1998b: 5; emphasis in original). In the preceding chapter Stefan Tidow has shown how it is within this context that we also have to understand the current efforts of the EU to create a common employment policy, or rather to formulate a common framework within which national employment and related policies are formulated. According to Tidow, the social content of this Europeanization of employment policy clearly reveals the imprint of the current neo-liberal integration project.

In this chapter I will argue that this neo-liberal project is ideologically underpinned by what I will identify as a *neo-liberal competitiveness discourse*, and I will examine how, and through the agency of which social forces, this discourse has been constructed within the transnational political arena of the EU. Competitiveness is the key concept in EU policy-making, constituting a master policy discourse to which other policy discourses are subordinated. The meaning of the word 'competitiveness' is not fixed, however, but has to be actively articulated through the *agency* of groups that have a particular interest in defining the term in certain ways. This chapter will seek to show how in these ideological struggles neo-liberal forces have prevailed by not only making competitiveness into the overriding goal of European governance but also articulating competitiveness with a programme of neo-liberal restructuring, in particular so-called labour-market reform in which workers are required to 'adjust' to the 'new conditions' that global capital imposes. At the supranational European level 'flexibility' and 'adaptability' on the part of the workforce have thus come to be seen as the panacea for Europe's unemployment problem.

The main argument here will be that this dominant approach to the (un)employment question has to be understood as the outcome of *transnational* political and ideological struggles over the new *European order* emerging out of the relaunched integration process (van Apeldoorn 2002). In contrast to both intergovernmentalist and supranationalist accounts of European integration, the approach adopted here – grounded in *a transnational historical materialism* (see, for example, van der Pijl 1998; Overbeek 2000) – takes as its starting point that the *social forces* underpinning the evolving European order are not necessarily internal to the EU nor to its member states, but must, rather, be situated within a global political economy in which capitalist production and finance are undergoing a sustained transnationalization and globalization. The latter processes can be argued to engender what, following the pioneering work of Kees van der Pijl (1984, 1998), could be conceptualized as a process of *transnational class formation*. The class-theoretical premise underlying this research agenda is that the class domination by which capitalist societies are characterized cannot be understood from a structuralist perspective which merely focuses on the structural domination of capital over labour, but that the reproduction of this power of capital – and of the capitalist class – has to be explained also in terms of collective human agency within concrete social power struggles taking place on the structural terrain of the accumulation process (on the relation between structure and agency, see also Chapter 1).

As I have also argued elsewhere (van Apeldoorn 2000), an important manifestation of the agency of an emerging European transnational capitalist class can be found in the strategic role played by the European Round Table of Industrialists (ERT), an elite forum mediating the interests and power of the most transnationalized segments of European capital. Here, my focus will be on the role of the ERT in the transnational debates around the European employment question and in shaping the ideological framework in which European employment policy is formulated. The following analysis will show that the ERT has in fact been one of the most important 'authors' of the new transnational European discourse on competitiveness.

The remainder of this chapter is organized in four sections. The first puts the contemporary political economy of European unemployment in a historical context of the past two decades, in which rival *transnational* social forces have formulated contending responses to the global crisis affecting European capitalism. Here, I will argue that from the 1970s a neo-liberal discourse developed claiming that the solution of Europe's economic woes (including mass unemployment) lay in the removal of institutional rigidities that prevented the efficient operation of the labour market and, in the context of the relaunching of the European integration process in the mid-1980s, favouring the internal market as one instrument in realizing this deregulatory programme. This emerging neo-liberal project, however, initially had to contend with what I identify as the rival projects of neo-mercantilism and (transnational) social democracy. The second section introduces the case of the ERT and examines its transnational class strategy *vis-à-vis* the European unemployment question. It shows how, after a neo-liberal shift in its own ideological orientation, it became increasingly active in advocating a profoundly neo-liberal restructuring of Europe's labour markets. The third section argues that this emerging hegemonic project has been premised upon and legitimated through a neo-liberal *competitiveness discourse* and that this discourse has shaped European socio-economic governance, not least in the area of labour market and employment policies. The final section concludes that the new paradigm behind the current 'European employment strategy' is inextricably bound up with the interests and strategy of Europe's transnational capitalist elite, leaving bleak prospects for resolving Europe's persistent unemployment crisis.

European unemployment in the 1980s: global crisis and rival European responses

The present European unemployment crisis and the policy responses formulated must be understood within the context of the crisis of the KWS, which from the 1970s onwards was confronted with unemployment levels it was never intended to deal with, straining it financially and undermining its legitimacy. This crisis unfolded within a global context of intensifying competition in which European industry was perceived as suffering from a lack of *competitiveness*, in particular *vis-à-vis* the United States and Japan. From the 1980s onwards, this perceived competitiveness deficit has come to be a central element within the transnational European socio-economic policy debates, with different interpretations of (the causes of) this deficit conditioning the formulation of different responses to the crisis of European capitalism.

Initially, governments pursued their own divergent national responses, ranging from the Thatcherite experiment in the UK, through the 'socialist experiment' in France, to the continuation of the *Modell Deutschland* in spite of the neo-conservative turn in Germany. Breaking with this pattern of national divergence, from around 1983 an elite consensus began to take shape in favour of a *European* solution to the crisis. Europe's political leaders had come to accept the idea advocated by large parts of European big business that only the creation of a European 'home market' could restore competitiveness in the face of intensifying US and Japanese competition, and thus bring Europe back on to a path of growth and employment creation. It was thus that the internal-market programme was born with the Commission's White Paper of 1985, expected, in very optimistic assessments, to create millions of new jobs (CEC 1988: 167).

Although in the end 'Europe 1992' – in the absence of any substantial positive integration – turned out to be one big market liberalization operation, what can be interpreted as a neo-liberal project was at the time only one among different contending responses to the ongoing economic crisis. The rising dominance, or, indeed, eventual hegemony, of neo-liberalism should therefore not be interpreted deterministically as the inevitable outcome of prior structural change, but can only be explained *ex post* as the product of (transnational) political and ideological struggles. In particular, the neo-liberal interpretation of the internal-market programme was initially contested by what is here identified as a *neo-mercantilist* interpretation, on the one hand, and a *social-democratic* one, on the other. The rise of the neo-liberal project, and the way neo-liberal ideas on competitiveness in the 1990s came to define the terms of the European unemployment debate, should thus be placed within the context of a wider *transnational* struggle over European order.

The neo-liberal ideology of 'Eurosclerosis'

The neo-liberal response to the crisis of European capitalism has to be understood in the context of the crisis of the institutionalized class compromise that had underpinned the post-war European model. The class alliance between 'big capital' and 'big labour' started to unravel when at the end of the 1960s productivity gains began to decline whereas wages continued to rise – resulting in a falling share of profits within the income distribution (Mazier 1982: 52; Boltho 1982: 24). This led to an outright profit squeeze – whilst at the same time fuelling inflation – when in the recession of the 1970s workers continued to resist any decline in their living standards. They could do so because of the strong bargaining position labour had built up during (and due to) the full-employment regime, which thus had become a burden to capital. As the Polish economist Michael Kalecki (1990) wrote many years before, from the perspective of the capitalist class the risk inherent in a sustained full-employment regime is that it tends to undermine its political and social power *vis-à-vis* an ever more self-confident working class: '[the capitalists'] class instinct [thus] tells them that lasting full employment is unsound from their point of view, and that unemployment is an integral part of the "normal" capitalist system' (Kalecki 1990: 351). The rising bargaining power of organized labour would, moreover, also eventually lead to inflation, hurting in particular the interests of money capital. These developments, then, could lead to the formation of 'a powerful alliance…between big business and rentier interests, and they would probably find more than one economist to declare that the situation was manifestly unsound' (*ibid.*: 355).

Indeed, the crisis of the 1970s was soon met by an intellectual (but at the same time ideological) offensive on the part of neo-classical economists against the Keynesian post-war consensus. The unemployment that the Western economies were already facing in the 1970s was in this view not the fault of 'the market', but, rather, of the systematic interference with that market, leading, in the words of Friedrich von Hayek, to 'a distortion of the system of *relative* prices and wages' which would normally 'establish themselves with free markets and stable money' (von Hayek 1991a: 271). In order to restore those markets and stop inflation, the full-employment policy had to be abandoned and employment deliberately (albeit temporarily) further reduced.[1] Employment could subsequently be restored by policies aimed at reforming the *structure* of the labour market, as here government regulation and 'monopolistic' trade unions were depriving this market 'of the function of guiding labour to where it can be sold' (von Hayek 1991b: 318). Nevertheless, the goal of *full* employment had to be seen as unattainable and undesirable, as there was argued to be a so-called *natural rate of unemployment* below which inflation would be pushed to unacceptable levels. Indeed, the hallmark of the new economic policy orthodoxy became the complete reversal of post-war macro-economic priorities, from the maintenance of full employment to the maintenance of price stability.

The ideas advocated by right-wing intellectuals like von Hayek, Milton Friedman and others can be argued to be linked to the interests of a transnationalizing capitalist class centred, in the first instance, around global financial capital and intent on breaking the power of organized labour (Overbeek and van der Pijl 1993). The emergent neo-liberal hegemonic project succeeded indeed during the 1980s in reversing the (Keynesian) post-war consensus. In the early 1980s several European states started to put monetarism into practice, with millions of workers losing their jobs as, in the words of Milton and Rose Friedman, an 'unpleasant side effect' (Friedman and Friedman 1980: 273). Subsequently, so-called labour-market reform, going under the banner of 'flexibility', has come to replace the discredited Keynesian demand management as the principal instrument of employment policy. As will also transpire from this chapter, flexibility is defined so as to make labour-market reform mainly a deregulation exercise, eroding established workers' rights. Although the concept of flexibility has been given different meanings, it has in practice increasingly been defined in terms of external or *numerical* (rather than internal or *functional*) flexibility; that is, enhancing – through the relaxation of hire-and-fire rules, the promotion of temping, the decentralization of wage bargaining, etc. – the control of management over the number of people employed, their working hours and their remuneration.[2] Although for obvious reasons most employers (especially those employing post-Fordist production techniques) in fact have an interest in both forms of flexibility, numerical flexibility is advocated with regard to the great majority of workers, whereas investment in functional flexibility is restricted to a small group of core workers which is then also offered better pay and job security (see, for example, Harvey 1989: 150ff.). This flexibility discourse has been used by international institutions such as the Organization for Economic Co-operation and Development (OECD) to launch ideological offensives against more institutionalized (or co-ordinated) market economies by accusing them of unemployment-creating labour-market rigidities. The evidence in support of the claim that neo-liberal flexibility as such leads to higher employment is hard to find.

Although in the early 1980s neo-liberal social forces had yet to achieve hegemony within the European arena, the neo-liberal discourse on the causes of Europe's alleged decline did significantly influence the policy climate in Europe, and as such also played its part in paving the way for Europe's renaissance in the mid-1980s. Here, the rising power of neo-liberal ideology first became manifest in the discourse of 'Eurosclerosis', which bemoaned the alleged structural decline of the European economy *vis-à-vis* the other economic blocs and blamed this decline on a number of 'rigidities' inherent in the European mixed economy, caused in particular by interventionist governments, trade unions acting as Olsonian distributive coalitions and 'excessive' welfare states draining resources from the private sector (Grahl and Teague 1990: 20). In other words, the *market-correcting* institutions that had made up the post-war model of European capitalism were seen as hurting competitiveness and impeding the necessary adjustments to the changing global economy. The internal market was conceived of as an opportunity to free Europe from these rigidifying institutions, as market liberalization was expected – through the enhanced mobility of capital – to lead to regulatory competition (Scharpf 1999: ch. 3), *inter alia* putting Europe's labour markets under deregulatory pressures. Liberalization was hence offered as the main solution to Europe's unemployment problem. As indicated, it was not until the 1990s that this neo-liberal restructuring programme was consolidated at the level of policy-making within continental

Western Europe. In fact, in the 1980s neo-liberalism as an ideological project had to contend with rival projects for the relaunching of the European integration process through the internal-market programme.[3]

The struggle over European order

In contrast to the neo-liberals, advocates of the *neo-mercantilist project* blamed Europe's loss of international competitiveness less on labour-market rigidity, trade union power or the welfare state, and more on the fragmentation of the European market, insufficient economies of scale and the perceived technology gap *vis-à-vis* the US and Japan. This project thus constituted a defensive regionalization strategy in which the internal market was conceived of as the creation of a European 'home market' in which 'European champions' would be able – thanks to the larger economies of scale – successfully to confront the growing non-European competition. Such a regeneration of European industry was to be further promoted by an active pan-European industrial policy (in particular in the area of new technologies) and protected against outside (especially Japanese) competition through European tariff walls and import quota (Pearce and Sutton 1986).

The *social-democratic project* for European order sought to re-embed the new European market in a supranational framework of social regulation and thus protect and consolidate the so-called 'European social model' against the potentially destructive forces of neo-liberal globalization. This project developed within the context of the initial success of the internal-market programme and was advocated most prominently by Jacques Delors, who as president of the Commission sought to move the integration process beyond market integration and towards state-building, hence promoting his vision of an 'organized capitalism' (for an account of this Delorist project, see Ross 1995b; Delors 1992). This involved complementing the internal market with a 'social dimension', the implementation of which set the Delors Commission on a direct collision course with Europe's employers' class. Notwithstanding this confrontation between neo-liberalism and transnational social democracy, Delors and other fellow modernists had accepted the argument that the European social model could not be saved by preserving the post-war social democratic commitment to the KWS and its full-employment regime. The welfare state had to be restructured and market forces – although not to be left 'unorganized' – were to be promoted, as it was these forces upon which the competitiveness of the European economy, and thus employment, in part depended.

As I have argued elsewhere (van Apeldoorn 2002), neo-liberalism and neo-mercantilism can be interpreted as contending strategies on the part of rival groups or 'fractions' within the ranks of Europe's evolving transnational capitalist class.[4] Throughout the 1980s and into the 1990s the main dividing line within this transnational elite was between, on the one hand, a 'globalist' fraction consisting of Europe's most globalized firms (including global financial institutions) and, on the other hand, a 'Europeanist' fraction made up by large industrial enterprises primarily serving the European market and competing against the often cheaper imports from outside Europe. The perspective of the former has tended towards neo-liberalism, whereas the latter came to promote the neo-mercantilist project. It has been in the context of the struggle between these two rival projects, as well as the later social-democratic challenge to neo-liberal Europe, that we have to place the eventual rise to hegemony of neo-liberalism. It was a struggle that was waged, in part, within the ranks of an emergent European transnational capitalist class. It is thus now time that we examine the role and strategy of this transnational capitalist class more closely.

Transnational class strategy, unemployment and the rise of the neo-liberal project: the case of the ERT

In analysing the role of transnational class strategy in the construction of the neo-liberal underpinning of the European (un)employment strategy, I focus on the ERT, which is interpreted as the principal platform for Europe's transnational capitalist class, whilst at the same time being a key organization through which that class (fraction) has taken shape (van Apeldoorn 2000; Holman 1992). Founded in 1983 by the heads of firms like Volvo, Philips, Fiat, Siemens and Nestlé, the ERT today consists of around 45 chief executive officers (CEOs) and chairmen of Europe's biggest and most transnational industrial corporations. The membership of the ERT is personal (rather than corporate), but the fact that its members together control a large part of European transnational capital – a majority of the members' companies are Fortune 500 firms[5] and about half are among the 100 biggest transnational corporations (TNCs) of the world (UNCTAD 1997) – of course goes a long way towards explaining the huge political influence that this group of people can command. Generally recognized to be one of the more powerful business groups in Europe – if not the most powerful one (Gardner 1991: 47–8; Greenwood 1997: 113) – the ERT is, in particular, credited with bringing the completion of the internal market back on to the European agenda and thus with being one of the driving forces behind Europe's relaunching (Cowles 1995; Holman 1992; van Apeldoorn 2000).

The ERT can be viewed as an elite organization of Europe's evolving transnational capitalist class in which – transcending the more conventional forms of corporate lobbying in the EU – the interests of that class (fraction) are organized, shaped and synthesized into a comprehensive strategy which, while effectively representing the perceived material interests of European big business, ideologically transcends those interests as well by appealing to a wider set of interests and identities. In contradistinction to UNICE (the EU's official employers' organization), which represents a more 'corporatist' class interest (defending the vested interests of the European employers' class), the ERT, as a private club of transnational capitalists, seeks to elevate its class strategy to a higher, more universal level – that is, to the level of hegemony.[6] The ERT hence does more than defend relatively clear-cut (narrow) corporate interests, but, rather, seeks to define the *general class* interests of transnational capital –

that is, to formulate a relatively long-term and forward-looking strategy oriented towards the shaping of European socio-economic governance. As former ERT vice-chairman David Simon explains, precisely because it brings together around

> 45 bosses who run businesses, they [the ERT members] will tend to take a more strategic view than an association...because after all that's what they're responsible for, they're responsible for direction and strategy. [The ERT thus] tries to concentrate on strategy and direction for the economy at large.[7]

The role of the ERT must thus be seen as operating primarily at the level of ideas and ideology formation.

From neo-mercantilism to neo-liberalism

In the years after its founding, the ERT became dominated by representatives of the Europeanist fraction. Its strategic orientation in the 1980s tended towards a *neo-mercantilist* regionalism, the heart of which was the promotion of a big European home market, in which Europe's regional TNCs could grow to resist and challenge rising global competition (ERT 1983). Although the completion of the internal market did favour the creation of economies of scale, the kind of industrial policies that the neo-mercantilists had hoped would nurture the growth of 'Euro-champions' were never really developed beyond very limited technology co-operation programmes like ESPRIT.

Instead of creating a 'Fortress Europe', the internal-market programme in the end only led to a further opening-up of Europe's national economies to the global economy. In the transnational struggle over Europe's relaunching, neo-liberal social forces were quickly gaining the upper hand over those that favoured a neo-mercantilist interpretation of the internal market. This struggle was also fought out within the ranks of Europe's transnational business elite as united within the ERT – in which the Europeanist fraction slowly lost its dominant position and itself gradually abandoned its earlier neo-mercantilist perspective. Not only did many 'globalist' companies (re)join the ERT, but the older ERT companies became more global themselves (van Apeldoorn 2002). Concomitant with the changing composition of its membership, the ideological and strategic orientation of the ERT gradually shifted from a neo-mercantilist Europeanism towards a neo-liberal globalism. The broadening of ERT's membership with many prominent exponents of the globalist fraction (such as the heads of global giants like Unilever, Shell, BP and La Roche) also allowed it to develop more into an elite forum for the *whole* of an emergent European transnational capitalist class. The ERT of the 1990s has thus become a forum within which this class came to redefine its interests along neo-liberal lines and from which it has sought to shape the discourse in which European public policy-making is embedded.

ERT's neo-liberal discourse on unemployment

The neo-liberal shift of the ERT in the 1990s reflected a general reorientation of the European transnational bourgeoisie with both the (former) globalist and the Europeanist fractions now united within the Round Table's ranks. Whereas in the early 1980s the response to economic crisis was still defensive, and indeed protectionist, the deep recession of the early 1990s – which was again accompanied by rising levels of unemployment – met with a rather unambiguous call for further neo-liberal restructuring – that is, deregulation; labour-market flexibility; 'downsizing' of the public sector; and an unequivocal commitment to global free trade (ERT 1993b, 1994). These themes came to occupy a much more central place within ERT's strategy as it abandoned its earlier strategic orientation of protective regionalism, in which the threat to European industry was first of all perceived as stemming from (unfair) outside competition. Indeed, it is in the area of social, labour-market and employment policies that ERT's current discourse has become most unambiguously neo-liberal.

The ERT for the first time explicitly dealt with the issue of unemployment in one of its first reports, *Making Europe Work* (1986), which appeared at the time when the European unemployment rate was just reaching record post-war levels. The report identified labour-market rigidity as one of the causes underlying European unemployment, but its tone was still moderate, with the largest part being devoted to an analysis of the impact of demographic and technological change on the structure of employment. In particular, it advocated more investment in (allegedly employment-creating) new technologies, including appropriate (partly publicly financed) programmes at the European level.

In a report on *European Labour Markets* published four years later (ERT 1990), the ERT's ideas were already shaped by a much stronger neo-liberal discourse. This report is a key document with regard to ERT's current perspective on employment policy inasmuch as it already contains most of the elements of the neo-liberal (labour-market) restructuring programme that the ERT advocated throughout the 1990s (but without, as yet, doing so in the name of competitiveness). Written by a working group led by the later ERT chairman and major representative of the 'globalist' fraction Helmut Maucher (the then CEO of Nestlé), it anticipates the consolidation of ERT's neo-liberal turn a few years later. The core thesis of this and later reports (ERT 1993a, 1997, 1998) is that 'institutional rigidities' of the European economy lie at the heart of Europe's unemployment problem (ERT 1990: 3 and *passim*). These rigidities, including 'social protection' and 'too high and downward rigid wages' (*ibid.*: 18), make it difficult for the labour force to adapt swiftly to the exigencies of 'accelerated technical development' (*ibid.*: 3). In addition to these 'structural causes' of unemployment, the report also emphasizes 'individual reasons' for unemployment, pointing to 'the attitudes and behaviour of the employed and unemployed', 'the degree of actual willingness to work', 'excessive wage aspirations, [and] unrealistic expectations concerning job quality' (*ibid.*: 3, 14). Thus, in formulating an 'agenda for action' to combat European unemployment, the ERT suggests that seeking to '[i]ncrease the awareness of, where necessary, *individual responsibility* for unemployment' should also be an integral part of national employment policies, countering 'the present degradation of work ethics' by '[t]he development of motivation and positive attitudes [with regard to work]' through education at school and in TV and advertisements (*ibid.*: 41). This discourse clearly reflects the ideology of the SWS, in which the social *right* to welfare in case of unemployment is replaced by the social *duty* to work under the conditions and against the price set by the market. The transition to the 'workfare state' implies the hollowing out of the welfare state, inasmuch as the social security provided by the latter creates a problem of 'moral hazard' (*ibid.*; see also Chapter 3).

Focusing on the *supply-side* of (un)employment – i.e. the conditions under which labour power as a commodity is offered on the market – the ERT also pays considerable attention to improving education and training. Here, ERT has in fact been very active since the early 1990s in promoting ideas like 'lifelong learning' and the 'learning society', concepts that have since also entered into the policy discourse of the EU (see, for example, ERT 1992, 1995; EC 1995b). The new approach in the field of training that the Round Table advocates – an approach in which flexibility is again one of the 'keywords' (ERT 1990: 38) and emphasis is put on the continuous learning of general, 'multi-purpose' skills – fits the requirements of the new flexible accumulation paradigm and its need for a core workforce that can add functional flexibility to the numerical flexibility provided by the peripheral workers.

At the heart of these and later ERT recommendations with regard to European employment policies, however, we find the call for deregulation as 'the key instrument', implying that 'job security' must ultimately be sacrificed for 'necessary labour market flexibility' (*ibid.*: 43). The 'cancer of over-regulation' is a 'direct factor behind excessive [*sic*] unemployment' (ERT 1997: 14) and there is thus 'a crying need for greater flexibility in labour laws at [the] national level' (ERT 1998: 26). At the time the aforementioned 1990 report was written, the ERT was, however, also still worried about re-regulation at the *European* level, or what it perceived as the threat of 'a politically strengthened Commission' increasing 'its scope of action in the *fields related to labour markets and employment policy*' (ERT 1990: 8, 29) and thus creating 'new, centralised and overly harmonised regulations [that] will add to the large number of labour market rigidities already existing in EC countries' (*ibid.*: 3). The latter, of course, expresses ERT's clear opposition to the Delorist (social-democratic) project of a social dimension to the internal-market programme. Indeed, ERT's activities in the area of labour-market policies at this time (and the aggressiveness of its tone) to an extent has to be understood as part of the mobilization of transnational capital against these social-policy initiatives of the Delors Commission. It was a time of direct *confrontation* with a social-democratic project that was just gaining momentum in the context of the success of Europe '92, whereas the defeat of this Delorist project, which became apparent post-Maastricht with the very watered-down social protocol (Ziltener 2000; van Apeldoorn 2002), would later allow for a strategy of *hegemonic articulation vis-à-vis* social-democratic social forces, a strategy, as we shall see, that would centre around the concept of *competitiveness* as the uniting slogan.

Thus, ERT's 1993 follow-up report on labour markets identifies the 'twin problem of *slow economic growth and a lack of competitiveness* as a major factor underlying Europe's insufficient job generation' (ERT 1993a: 4). Well aware of the negative employment effects of the cost-cutting strategies that their companies had adopted, this report gloomily warns that 'a hard core of persistent unemployment will remain into the next century', but adds that this core might yet be reduced if Europe is willing to 'flexibilise and upgrade the supply of labour' as '[o]nly a readapted labour force and more flexible labour markets can ensure that economic growth will translate into significant job growth' (*ibid.*: 8, ii). With respect to the measures proposed, the emphasis has shifted even more towards the reduction of costs, and in particular those of labour, the ERT arguing for both wage moderation and wage flexibility (with 'lower wages, where necessary') as one of the preconditions for 'durable employment and European competitiveness' (*ibid.*: 15–16). Indeed, the Round Table bluntly states that '[a] very large amount of the effort to adjust European labour markets will rely on labour' (*ibid.*: 15).

The Round Table's discourse in fact makes it clear that what is needed is not merely – to use Peter Hall's terminology – a *second-order* policy change, i.e. a change of instruments, but a *third-order* change, which is 'marked by the radical changes in the overarching terms of policy discourse associated with a "paradigm shift"' (P.A. Hall 1993: 279). The desired 'adaptation' of labour thus necessitates a fundamental restructuring of state–society relations. Again, the ERT is well aware of this, and, speaking the language of hegemony, it calls for the creation of a 'new social consensus':

> Enabling Europe to return to high employment growth requires more than replacing policy instruments, it calls for a change of our economic and social structures. But governments are only able to change structures when there is a *new social consensus*, i.e. the convergence on principles and, ultimately, agreement on the goals that [*sic*] for change among the social partners, governments, the opinion leaders and, ultimately, population.... We need a consensus on the European level that *only a healthy, efficient and competitive private sector is able to provide sufficient jobs, and that markets should be left to allocate labour efficiently*.
>
> (ERT 1993a: 9; emphasis in original)

Creating this new consensus means that the existing 'distorted [*sic*] social balance' (*ibid.*: 2) has to be changed. As indicated, the key concept in the discourse in which this nascent hegemonic project of Europe's transnational capitalist class is articulated is that of 'competitiveness'. Competitiveness has come to function as such a key concept because of its potential to represent the 'general interest', as it appeals equally to neo-liberals, neo-mercantilists and social democrats. But what competitiveness actually means, and how it is to be achieved, is an open question decided in concrete struggles.

Below I argue that competitiveness is increasingly being defined in neo-liberal terms and that the ERT has been one important forum promoting such a definition.

Constructing a new social consensus: the neo-liberal competitiveness discourse

Commenting on the concept of competitiveness, a senior ERT official explains the way in which this has become the key concept as follows:

> The members of the European Round Table perceive it as their role to make some input into policy-making at the European level on those issues which are of crucial importance for the economic strength of Europe, what we are now calling the sort of general term of competitiveness. *And 'competitiveness' is now a useful word but it is really like a paper bag into which you put things.*[8]

What the ERT has been trying to put in the bag – that is, the meaning it has sought to attach to the concept of competitiveness – is increasingly of neo-liberal origin. A comparison with the way competitiveness was defined in the 1980s is revealing here. Although competitiveness as a political catchword has only recently risen to its current heights, it was already much talked about in the 1980s, not least by the ERT. In fact, within the context of the transnational struggle over Europe's socio-economic order between the rival projects of neo-liberalism, neo-mercantilism and social democracy, we may also distinguish three concomitant contending discourses on competitiveness.

In the neo-mercantilist discourse – one that could be read in some of ERT's earlier publications – competitiveness means enhancing the global market power of European industry *against* non-European competition through government intervention and protectionism: it means being able to compete in the global marketplace by first shielding oneself from the forces of globalization, in order then to enter the fray on the basis of increased strength achieved through *non-market* means. Partly convergent with this is what could be interpreted as a social-democratic competitiveness discourse that in part came to underpin the Delorist project at the end of the 1980s. In the much more market-centred vision of the 'new social democracy' (Geyer 1993) promoted by Delors competitiveness was to be achieved not by negating the market but by 'organizing' it in such a way that its productive capacities are developed. This translates into an employment strategy that does not focus on deregulation but, rather, on investment in education, training, high technology, infrastructure, etc., with productivity-enhancing policies aimed at improving the capacity of *labour* (rather than just capital) to adapt to the exigencies of the global economy, thus avoiding unemployment and protecting workers' income (Reich 1992; see also Albo 1994).

Being a central element, then, in all three projects, a goal to which all mainstream European socio-economic and political forces were wedded, we can understand how competitiveness has come to be such a 'useful word' for the ascending neo-liberal forces seeking hegemony. As we saw in the previous section, what the ERT in this context has thus been trying to 'put in the bag' called competitiveness has increasingly become elements of a neo-liberal discourse on labour-market reform, a restructuring that the ERT argues is a precondition for both 'wealth-creation and employment' (ERT 1994: 1). By articulating competitiveness to these latter goals, the Round Table effectively appeals to wide sections of society, including the political and social forces bound up with social democracy or organized labour. The concept of competitiveness thus, I argue, became the lynchpin of a process of hegemonic articulation in which an essentially neo-liberal ideology is articulated with elements of contending orientations, such that their 'potential antagonism is neutralised' (Laclau 1977: 161).

Competitiveness, employment and European socio-economic governance

The first testimony (at the EU level) of the power of the new competitiveness discourse was the Commission's White Paper on *Growth, Competitiveness and Employment* (EC 1993), which has since become one of the main intellectual reference points in the EU socio-economic policy debate. The White Paper, written under the direction of Jacques Delors and often seen as his last political will, was intended as a response to the post-Maastricht recession that had pushed the unemployment rate to a new post-war record. The paper was the first Commission document that put the issue of unemployment squarely on the EU agenda, declaring that we should 'once again make employment policy the centre-piece of our overall strategy' (*ibid.*: 11; see also Chapter 5 of this volume).

Different pieces of evidence suggest that the ERT had a significant input into the development of this key Commission document. At the press conference after the December 1993 Brussels Summit at which Delors had presented his White Paper, the then Commission president recalled his consultation with industry and the support he had received for his proposals from the ERT (*Agence Europe*, no. 6127, 12 December 1993). The week before, Delors had also participated in the press presentation of the ERT report *Beating the Crisis* (ERT 1993b), which was conceived as its contribution to the Commission's future economic strategy (*Agence Europe*, no. 6122, 6 December 1993). As a senior ERT official commented on the relation between these two reports:

> It was very parallel, and we saw their drafts and they saw our drafts. And one of my friends, a very senior official in the Commission, he said to me, there is basically no difference between them…: very similar, growth, investment, competitiveness, and employment. What we have tried to is to get these things fixed together in people's minds…the message is the same, these things all go together, you won't fight unemployment if you don't fight for competitiveness, you won't get growth if you don't have investment.[9]

Indeed, a careful reading of the two reports does reveal some striking similarities. Most importantly, they share the basic premise that higher growth and employment can only be achieved through promotion of the competitiveness of European industry. Moreover, the strategy (with regard to these objectives) outlined by the White Paper also echoes that of *Beating the Crisis*. In the Commission document, the road to higher employment follows a strategy based on the three 'inseparable elements' of:

1 A 'macro-economic framework which instead of constraining market forces…supports them'.
2 Structural adjustment of policies 'aimed at increasing the competitiveness of European industry and at removing the rigidities which are curbing its dynamism'.
3 '[A]ctive policies and structural changes in the labour market and in the regulations' (EC 1993: 61).

The paper of the Commission straightforwardly identifies labour-market inflexibility – to 'be traced back to specific institutional, legal and contractual circumstances in each country' – as a major cause of Europe's *structural* unemployment (*ibid.*: 16, ch. 8). Contrary to Keynesian theory, and contrary to some analyses (see Chapter 11 of this volume; see also P.A. Hall 1998) of the effects of the Maastricht criteria, cutting budget deficits is seen as helping to overcome recession by freeing public resources for private investments (*ibid.*: 65–7). The greatest significance of the White Paper, however, lies in the way it articulates the objectives of growth and employment with that of competitiveness, an articulation that has since become central to the emerging policy consensus around European unemployment.

Notwithstanding all this, Delors' White Paper was still largely an attempt at a compromise between neo-liberals and social democrats, agreeing 'with [the] liberals about the need to deregulate labor markets and make the welfare state less rigid, but within a broader context designed to prevent social divisions from themselves rigidifying' (Ross 1995b: 225). Next to the emphasis on investment in 'trans-European networks' and in the 'information society' – policies that had also been advocated by the ERT, but as part of a different strategy – typical Delorist themes such as the social dialogue also pointed to traces of a social-democratic competitiveness discourse. Since then, however, competitiveness is increasingly being defined in neo-liberal terms within the Commission's policy discourse. As indicated, the ERT has constituted a key forum within which this neo-liberal competitiveness discourse has been articulated.

The ERT's promotion of the concept of competitiveness has certainly contributed to the rise of that concept within European governance. A first testimony to this was the setting-up by the EU of a Competitiveness Advisory Group (CAG) at the beginning of 1995, just over a year after the ERT had first proposed the creation of such a group (ERT 1993b: 27). The CAG membership consists of CEOs as well as leading trade union representatives and other 'eminent persons' (usually former politicians), but is dominated by the former group.[10] At the time of its founding, three ERT members joined the 13-member council, and at present Marco Tronchetti Provera (of Pirelli) maintains the links between the two groups. It should not surprise us, therefore, that the 'advice' this group has so far given (in six-monthly reports to the European Council) closely resembles that of the ERT, with both the Round Table and the CAG spreading the new competitiveness gospel.[11] As a senior official of the ERT remarked: 'One thing that is quite important in this whole scenario is multiplicity of messages and delivery systems around the whole theme'.[12]

As an operationalization of its competitiveness ideology, the ERT has, in tandem with the CAG, started to promote the concept of *benchmarking vis-à-vis* the Commission and the member states. Benchmarking means 'measuring the performance' of individual firms and sectors, but also of nations, against that of the 'best competitors' in the world (ERT 1994: 4). Since launching the idea the Round Table has organized several seminars with Commission and government officials to promote the concept.[13] In its report *Benchmarking for Policy-Makers*, the ERT is very explicit about how policy-makers should 'measure' competitiveness – the country or (macro-)region that is most competitive is the country that is most successful in attracting mobile capital: 'Governments must recognize today that every economic and social system in the world is competing with all the others to attract the footloose businesses' (ERT 1996: 15). Attracting transnationally mobile capital is, of course, also seen as beneficial to employment creation. In this context, the ERT proposes the following checklist for 'benchmarking employment': the level of 'labour costs/performance, indirect labour costs and income levels, the flexibility of labour; working and factory hours, mobility of labour, [and] termination costs' (*ibid.*: 13). The Maastricht criteria are also mentioned as a successful application of the benchmarking concept (*ibid.*: 18). Significantly in the context of the current labour-shedding restructuring that is taking place in part under the discipline of Europe's growing capital markets (see also the final section of this chapter), the ERT sees 'shareholder value' as the principal benchmark for private enterprise itself: 'The overriding measure of competitive performance for any commercial enterprise is the return it is able to provide its shareholders' (*ibid.*: 9).

The ideological potential of a concept like benchmarking, and indeed its capacity to appeal to a wider set of forces within society and to incorporate them into the emergent hegemonic bloc, is also not lost on the Round Table capitalists, as the report stresses that benchmarking is 'not just an analytical device' but also 'carries a symbolic message':

> At a time when the European model of society is experiencing some difficulties, and change may be perceived as painful (though not nearly so painful as the results of not changing), *the role of symbols* in mobilising human effort may become more important, and benchmarking can be part of this.
>
> (ERT 1996: 7)

Competitiveness and benchmarking have also accordingly become the key concepts within the public (socio-economic) policy discourse of the EU.

Analysing the policy documents of the Commission, one also sees how these concepts are mobilized to promote a programme of neo-liberal restructuring aiming to remove, in the words of the director-general for industry, the remaining 'rigidities and distortions...that prevent Europe from fully exploiting its potential' (EC 1997a: 5). ERT's promotion of the concept of benchmarking *vis-à-vis* the Commission has been particularly successful. In the same month that the ERT published its report on benchmarking, the Industry Directorate-General came out with a document entitled *Benchmarking the Competitiveness of European Industry*, in which it suggested that benchmarking should be used as a central policy guideline at all levels of EU governance (EC 1996b: 16). In a follow-up communication the Commission explicitly acknowledges the input of the ERT as the first business organization to draw the Commission's and the Council's attention to the benchmarking concept (EC 1997b: 3). In this communication – and at the request of the Council of Ministers[14] – the Commission launched a number of concrete initiatives to put the concept of benchmarking into practice, including the establishment of a High Level Group on Benchmarking, made up by 'experts' from industry, and the initiation of a number of so-called pilot projects in different member states to start identifying Europe's 'weaknesses and inefficiencies' at the enterprise, sectoral and public-policy level (*ibid.*).

Invoking the inevitability of globalization and 'hence' the need for adaptation, the Commission defines benchmarking as a tool for improving competitiveness and, with that, as 'a tool for promoting the convergence towards best practice' (EC 1996b: 16; 1997b). This involves the global 'comparison of societal behaviour [*sic*], commercial practice, market structure and public institutions' (EC 1997b: 3). As the High Level Group on Benchmarking – chaired by a board member of Investor, the investment company controlling the global Wallenberg empire – makes clear in its first report, the object of all these 'comparisons' is to promote rapid 'structural reforms' that will allow Europe to adapt to the exigencies of globalization: 'this involves further liberalisation, privatisation..., more flexible labour laws, lower government subsidies, etc.' (High Level Group on Benchmarking 1999: 13). Similarly, in a language much more radical than that of Delors's White Paper, the Commission identifies labour-market reform as a 'vital factor for the competitiveness of European industry', calling for 'a radical rethink of all relevant labour market systems – employment protection, working time, social protection, and health and safety – to adapt them to a world of work which will be organised differently' (EC 1996b: 11). The report even goes so far as to state that 'evidence suggests' that there is a direct causal (negative) relation between the level of labour-market regulation and the level of employment (*ibid.*; see also EC 1997a). Labour-market flexibility, finally, is also at the heart of the formulation in the so-called employment chapter of the Treaty of Amsterdam. In fact, the objectives of employment and labour-market flexibility are mentioned in the same single sentence, the latter being the means of achieving the former: 'Member States and the Community shall...work towards a co-ordinated strategy for employment and particularly for promoting a skilled, trained, and adaptable workforce and labour markets responsive to economic change' (Art. 109n., Treaty of Amsterdam).

Conclusions: transnational capital and European unemployment

The employment chapter of the Treaty of Amsterdam has been one step in the development of what the Commission calls a 'European employment strategy' (EC 1999c) This development started with the Delors White Paper, was followed by the European Council employment Summit held at Essen, and has since been further institutionalized in the so-called 'Luxembourg Process' of EU-approved and -monitored National Action Plans (NAPs). This *Europeanization* of employment policy (see Chapter 5; cf. D.R. Cameron 2000) does not represent a new form of *positive* integration beyond the *negative* integration of the market, as in fact no common employment policy is pursued but, rather, national policies are co-ordinated within an overall European framework.[15] This framework is first and foremost a normative one, formulating a new *policy paradigm* for employment policy, establishing the *benchmarks* for national policies by formulating 'guidelines' (see, for example, Council of the EU 1999) and 'recommendations' (see, for example, EC 2000a). The fact that employment policies remain primarily the responsibility of the member states (the Amsterdam Treaty is very clear on this) already points to the limits of this new European answer to the persistent employment crisis, in particular given the constraints imposed by the internal market (and the regime competition it engenders) and EMU plus Stability Pact (in fact outlawing Keynesian macro-economic policies). As Wolfgang Streeck writes:

> [A]s long as the management of unemployment continues to be considered, in the sense of the Essen agreement, as a *Hausaufgabe* [homework] of national governments acting under international institutional and market constraints, the privileged means for it is to increase labour market 'flexibility'.
>
> (Streeck 1998b: 21)

It is, however, also the European employment 'policy' itself that is oriented towards promoting that latter goal of neo-liberal restructuring.

Based on the 'four pillars' of 'employability', 'entrepreneurship', 'adaptability' and 'equal opportunities', the so-called European employment strategy reflects a shift from the Keynesian paradigm of *market-correcting* and market-steering macro-economic full-employment policies, sometimes complemented by micro-economic interventionism, towards a new *transnational* policy paradigm of *market-making* employment policies. Not redistribution, but creating the opportunity to participate in the market is the object of these policies. 'Employability' thus stands for *marketability*; thus, again in the words of Streeck, '[defining] the responsibility of public policy, not in terms of *de-commodification* of individuals, but to the contrary of creation of *equal opportunities for commodification*' (Streeck

1999: 6; emphasis in original). This is to be further promoted by improving the 'adaptability' of workers, i.e. through the flexibilization of labour. Indeed, the whole employment strategy is clearly based on the premise that labour-market flexibility is the key to reducing unemployment. It is thus that in its latest 'Joint Employment Report' the Commission notes with satisfaction that member states have made substantial 'progress in reforming the labour markets' and claims this as an important factor behind the recent slight drop in the EU unemployment rate (EC 2000b: 2).

In sum, then, the EU's employment strategy and related 'social' initiatives do not represent a belated move towards the Social Europe Delors wanted to construct, but, rather, in its present form represents the consolidation of the neo-liberal hegemonic project, inasmuch as it completes the incorporation of social democracy (which, being in power in the large majority of EU countries, of course both had the opportunity and the electoral motivation to put employment high on the European agenda). The social-democratic project does see elements of its competitiveness discourse return in the European employment strategy, but in such a way that the proclaimed goals of high employment and social cohesion are rendered compatible with the neo-liberal goals of market-making and market liberalization. It is thus that Hans-Jürgen Bieling (in Chapter 4) speaks of '*communitarian* neo-liberalism'.[16]

In this chapter I have argued that this hegemonic project in the post-Maastricht context has come to be ideologically underpinned by a neo-liberal competitiveness discourse, a discourse that has penetrated all areas of European socio-economic policy-making, including the recently emerging field of employment policies. Here, too, 'competitiveness' is a key word, time and again articulated with the necessity of labour-market reform, etc. The second purpose of this chapter was to show that this discourse has in fact been produced within the struggle between rival transnational social forces and, as such, has also been shaped by the agency of those forces. Here, I argued, a critical role has been played by the ERT as a platform of Europe's evolving transnational capitalist class. I showed how the ERT, since its own neo-liberal reorientation, has promoted a programme of neo-liberal restructuring, in particular of European labour markets, and has succeeded in articulating this programme with the concerns of other social forces through the concept of competitiveness. This ideological commitment to neo-liberal competitiveness makes it increasingly difficult even to think about alternative approaches to the EU's unemployment crisis. The content of European employment strategy, and the fact that it, for instance, totally ignores the question of aggregate demand, is testimony to this.

As long as the policy responses to European unemployment are informed by a neo-liberal competitiveness discourse that serves the interests of the most transnationalized segments of European capital, the prospects for any alternative policy response remain bleak. What does this imply for the prospects of Europe's unemployed? Europe's transnational capitalist class is well aware that employment creation is not to be expected from Europe's TNCs. Indeed, in recent years many of Europe's largest firms have been consistently cutting back their workforces.

Despite – insofar as there is a contradiction here – the fact that these firms made record profits throughout much of the 1990s, they also laid off workers with each new round of restructuring. Whereas the success of Fordism was based on expanding aggregate demand by paying high(er) wages to what became a relatively secure workforce, the present accumulation regime is based on cost-cutting and labour-saving 'rationalization' (Harvey 1989). This accumulation strategy must be understood not only in the context of intensifying global competition, but also in the context of the rise of money capital after the crisis of Fordist productive capital. Profits are increasingly made within, or at least siphoned off to, the sphere of circulation, rather than made within and reinvested in the sphere of production. This has certainly been the trend in the US and the UK, where, according to Lazonick and O'Sullivan (2000), the rise of a new *shareholder-value* ideology has been associated with a shift in corporate strategy from what they call 'retain and reinvest' to 'downsize and distribute' (to the shareholders, that is). Although in the US this has not led to higher unemployment, it did lead to a significant reduction in the number of relatively secure and well-paid jobs (*ibid.*). There are indications that this rise of a new shareholder-value capitalism can also be observed within continental Europe, and that the money-capital perspective (which is the perspective of the shareholder who stands outside the firm and the production process and is exclusively oriented towards financial return) comes to prevail within industry and within production itself (van Apeldoorn 2001). The fact that the industrialists of the Round Table now also invoke 'shareholder value' as the fundamental benchmark for the performance of industry (ERT 1996: 9; see above) does not bode well in this respect, and may also be taken as an indication of the extent to which financial and *rentier* interests now dominate Europe's transnational capitalist class.[17] This, then, is one reason why we may expect the current intense restructuring within European industry to continue at an unabated pace.

In this Schumpeterian process, 'the work of modernisation', the ERT writes, inevitably 'leads to creating some jobs but shedding others' (ERT 1997: 2). The ERT implicitly admits that its companies have been responsible for much of the shedding and that the creation of new jobs will have to come from small and medium-sized companies in their 'partnership' with large companies, i.e. through increased subcontracting, etc. (*ibid.*). It is unclear how the contracting-out of jobs that used to de done within the TNC by workers with relatively secure and full-time jobs to small and medium-sized enterprises employing part-time flexible workers is in itself going to contribute to higher employment. The ERT would answer that if overall competitiveness is improved through deregulation and flexibilization, market forces will be released that will in themselves generate new jobs. Here, the United States – 'the current best' against which 'Europe needs to benchmark itself', according to present ERT chairman Morris Tabaksblat (Tabaksblat 2000) – is the leading example. Whether the extremely deregulated labour market – with an increasing number of workers having peripheral 'MacJobs' – of the US could be realized in Europe without fundamentally undermining the social consent that is necessary for any hegemonic project is rather doubtful, even if the current trends towards a more Anglo-

Saxon shareholder capitalism are likely to put more pressure on Europe's labour markets. Here, the so called 'Dutch Model', popular within 'Third Way discourse' but also often invoked by Europe's transnational capitalists, seems to have more hegemonic potential. Nevertheless, when the next global recession hits, the limits of that model may also become more apparent (see also Chapter 9 of this volume). The long-term prospects of the neo-liberal European project are therefore unclear. If and when it enters into a crisis, the most disconcerting thought is that given the social-democratic conversion to (much of) neo-liberalism there will probably not be any politically viable alternative on the left.

Notes

1 Thus, von Hayek wrote in 1975 that 'substantial unemployment' was now inevitable and that governments should prepare their electorates for this (von Hayek 1991a). Milton Friedman, one of the intellectual fathers of monetarism, likewise called for the acceptance of higher unemployment as an 'unpleasant side effect' of the necessary cure for inflation, namely slowing down the growth in the quantity of money (Friedman and Friedman 1980: 273–6).

2 Numerical flexibility expresses the freedom of employers to vary, according to need, the number of workers (hire-and-fire rules), the hours worked, as well as individual wage levels (hence labour as a flexible input); whereas functional flexibility refers more positively to the functionality of the worker in terms of his or her skills and his or her adaptability to varying needs in the production process (with a high degree of functional flexibility marking a contrast to the traditional Fordist worker). Functional flexibility, therefore, speaks more to a progressive social-democratic discourse, whereas numerical flexibility is clearly the centrepiece of the neo-liberal strategy.

3 For a more elaborate account than can be presented here, see van Apeldoorn (1998).

4 The social base of the Delorist social-democratic project is more difficult to identify; indeed, it largely lacked a strong social base, which helps to explain its failure in the face of neo-liberalism. However, support for this project obviously came from parts of the trade union movement but may also be linked to certain parts of industry, in particular inasmuch as there was at least a potential convergence of interests between the social-democratic and neo-mercantilist projects.

5 *Fortune's* 1998 Global 500; see http://cgi.pathfinder.com/fortune/global500. For a list of current ERT members (as well as other up-to-date information on the ERT), see the ERT website: http://www.ert.be.

6 The term 'hegemony' is, throughout this chapter, used in a Gramscian sense. For Gramsci, hegemony signified a mode of governance that rests upon a set of institutionalized practices and norms 'freely accepted' by subordinate groups but nevertheless expressing a structure of domination (Gramsci 1971: 169–70 and *passim*).

7 Interview, London, 12 September 1996.

8 Interview, Brussels, 24 May 1996.

9 Interview, Brussels, 24 May 1996.

10 For a list of present and former members, as well as other information on the CAG, see http://europa.eu.int/comm/cdp/cag/publications/rapport4/index—en.htm.

11 See the CAG's first four reports, as collected in Jacquemin and Pench (1997).

12 Interview, Brussels, 24 May 1996.

13 Interviews, London, 12 September 1996, and Brussels, 24 May 1996 (see also *Agence Europe*, 23 November 1996).

14 At the Industry Council of 14 November 1996. The Council recently called on the Commission again 'to ensure the ongoing development of benchmarking' at all levels (see EC, *Bulletin EU*, 4 1999, point 1.3.79).

15 It is thus that we may interpret the Europeanization of employment policies as what Knill and Lehmkuhl (1999) call the *framing* mode of Europeanization, a form of Europeanization that operates by altering the beliefs, norms and expectations of actors, as distinct from *positive integration* (which imposes a legally binding European model on the member states) and *negative integration* (which removes economic barriers, thus affecting the power resources of domestic actors). The Europeanization of employment policy can be argued to go beyond framing inasmuch as it also provides for the formulation of NAPs, the implementation of which is then supranationally monitored.

16 In a similar vein, Streeck notes that the social democracy of the 'Third Way' 'seems to become indistinguishable from an *activist liberalism* which pursues social justice through intervention in the distribution, not of market outcomes, but of the capacities for successful market participation' (Streeck 1999: 6). Elsewhere (van Apeldoorn 1998, 2002) I have argued that the current neo-liberal project in continental Europe, because of the incorporation of not only social-democratic elements but also concerns of the (former) neo-mercantilists, has transformed European neo-liberalism into what I call an 'embedded neo-liberalism' that is distinct from the more orthodox Anglo-Saxon neo-liberalism. Embedded neo-liberalism, however, does not reflect a return of the 'embedded liberalism' of the post-war order but, rather, the need for neo-liberalism to accommodate the concern of certain social forces – which are stronger in continental Europe than, for instance, in the Anglo-Saxon heartland – in order to become hegemonic.

17 Although the ERT is principally a club of CEOs of industrial firms, to the extent (there are in fact also signs of resistance) that these managers have internalized the shareholder-value ideology they may also become the representatives of financial capital (also because industrial TNCs themselves increasingly make money outside production).

Part III

The articulation of global and EU tendencies with national dynamics

8 From Thatcherism to New Labour

Neo-liberalism, workfarism and labour-market regulation[1]

Bob Jessop

Introduction

For some, the landslide victory of the Labour Party in 1997 held the promise of a reversal of the socio-economic transformation of Britain which had been effected by nearly 18 years of Conservative government. Great Britain had become the exemplar of European neo-liberalism, and the return of the social democrats seemed to announce at least a partial end to that development. It did not take long for the Blair government to disappoint these hopes. In many ways, rather than repealing the changes of the Thatcher years Labour took the neo-liberal transformation of Britain yet a step further.

Blair's self-described 'New Labour' government is openly committed to a radical and modernizing reform of the British state apparatus and its economic and social policies. It is also actively promoting its version of neo-liberalism in Europe and the wider world. Often presented as the 'Third Way', New Labour strategy could also be described as the 'American Way';[2] and, indeed, the consolidation of a Blairite neo-liberalism in Britain could become a Trojan Horse through which a transatlantic neo-liberal project penetrates further into the European Union. For, while Blair is keen for Britain to opt out of some EU institutions and policies of a neo-corporatist or neo-statist character, he does not hesitate to lecture fellow social democrats on the economic effectiveness and moral superiority of New Labour's programme and America's enterprise culture. Likewise, Blunkett, then secretary of state for education, trumpeted the success of the British presidency in 'replacing the old agenda by putting jobs, skills and employability at the heart of Europe' (DfEE 1998). This is also reflected in British pressure for a minimalist social chapter, resistance to French and German proposals on job creation, and pleas for recognition of its 'New Deal' for the unemployed as a model policy for Europe (Gray 1998: 6). The Thatcher and Major governments shared similar objectives for at least ten years before New Labour's landslide election victory in 1997 at home and abroad. But there are some interesting discontinuities as well as significant continuities with Conservative neo-liberalism, which, while insufficient to fully justify the label 'Third Way', do mean that New Labour is developing its own distinctive version of neo-liberalism. Elsewhere I have described the latter as 'Thatcherism with a Christian Socialist face' (Jessop 1998b).

This chapter will consider how far and in what respects the distinctive features of this approach represent either major departures from the overall neo-liberal project and/or minor supporting and flanking measures to make that project more sustainable in the long run. The continuities and discontinuities are illustrated mainly from the field of labour-market policy, but I also refer to other reforms in the welfare state. In addressing these questions, I draw on and extend my earlier arguments about the shift from the Keynesian welfare national state (or KWNS) to the Schumpeterian workfare post-national regime (or SWPR) (see Chapter 3).

From Thatcherism to New Labour

Neo-liberalism varies in its form and objectives. At its most ambitious, in trying to effect a transition from authoritarian state socialism to liberal-market capitalism following the collapse of the Soviet bloc in 1989–90 it involves a radical experiment in *system transformation*. Just such an experiment was promoted by the Reagan and Thatcher governments and some key international institutions under neo-liberal influence (for example the International Monetary Fund (IMF), the World Bank and the Organization for Economic Co-operation and Development (OECD)), with some rather equivocal (or, perhaps, cynically opportunistic) support from 'nomenklatura capitalists' in the post-socialist societies. At its weakest, neo-liberalism involves little more than an ad-hoc set of *policy adjustments* within modes of regulation and welfare regimes in capitalist societies that remain basically (neo-)statist, (neo-)corporatist, or otherwise non-liberal in character. This weak form of neo-liberalism can be identified in some continental European societies in the 1980s and early 1990s. Nonetheless, given the political, intellectual and moral climate during this period and its domination, if not hegemonization, by the transatlantic neo-liberal power bloc, it was often misinterpreted (enthusiastically or despairingly) as proof of a general neo-liberal turn in capitalist formations. In between system transformation and policy adjustment comes a *neo-liberal regime shift*, i.e. a fairly comprehensive shift of economic and political regime within an already capitalist social formation that entails fundamental restructuring and strategic reorientation compared with the previous regime. Just such a regime shift occurred under Thatcher and Reagan in the 1980s, as well as in the two anglophone economies in the Southern hemisphere, Australia and New Zealand. Given our focus on Europe, however, this chapter focuses on the neo-liberal regime shift in Britain.

A major step forward in this shift was initiated in 1979 with the election of the first Thatcher government. It is true that the first elements of this neo-liberal turn had been gradually initiated in the guise of (partly externally imposed and purportedly reluctantly accepted) economic and social policy adjustments during the last three years of the previous Labour government (see Leys 1989; Artis and Cobham 1991; Holmes 1985); and it is also true that it took a further three years before the new Thatcher regime was fully consolidated and began to embark on its radical neo-liberal programme to 'modernize' the economy, state and civil society and to promote an enterprise culture (for a periodization of Thatcherism and a discussion of its relative discontinuity with 'old Labour', see Jessop *et al.* 1988; Jessop *et al.* 1990). Nonetheless, 1979 marked an important symbolic defeat for the post-war mode of economic regulation, its institutionalized class compromise between capital and labour and its associated forms of crisis management. And in this sense it greatly facilitated further development and consolidation of neo-liberalism.

Consolidated Thatcherism (including here the Major government, which could be interpreted as 'Thatcherism with a grey face') combined a distinctive 'two nations' authoritarian populist hegemonic project, a centralizing 'strong state' project, and a neo-liberal accumulation strategy. It is crucial to distinguish these three aspects of Thatcherism, not only because they developed unevenly in the Thatcher–Major years, but also, and more importantly for our purposes, because the so-called 'break' with Thatcherism initiated by New Labour's Third Way affects Thatcherism's hegemonic more than its state project[3] and leaves its neo-liberal accumulation strategy more or less intact. Thus, whilst New Labour certainly retains an authoritarian populist approach in many areas, it has equally clearly moved towards a more socially inclusive hegemonic project. This addresses the limitations of the possessive individualism favoured by neo-liberalism and recognizes the need to re-embed market forces into a broader, more cohesive social order. It aims to re-moralize the neo-liberal accumulation strategy around a populist 'one nation' hegemonic project that will reduce social exclusion without undermining the economic well-being of 'Middle England', whose members have delivered Blair two general election victories despite a loss of support in Old Labour's heartlands.[4] This project clearly reflects Blair's strong Christian socialist leanings and marked antipathy to collectivism and corporatism.[5] In this context, social inclusion is to be secured primarily through labour-market attachment and the economic regeneration of marginalized communities; and individual, family, and child poverty are to be alleviated mainly by a series of 'stealthy' (rather than proudly proclaimed) redistributive measures that ideally involve redirecting revenues within what would still remain rigid fisco-financial parameters. In this sense the emphasis on communitarian themes and policies could prove to be little more than a flanking measure to ameliorate the effects of a neo-liberal accumulation strategy (see Chapter 4). For, in this latter regard, New Labour has largely followed in the tracks of the neo-liberal regime shift it inherited, as can be seen by examining the main elements of neo-liberalism as pursued in the Thatcher–Major years.

The principal elements of consolidated Thatcherism's neo-liberal accumulation strategy comprised:

- *liberalization*, promoting free-market (as opposed to monopolistic or state monopolistic) forms of competition as the most efficient basis for market forces;
- *deregulation*, giving economic agents greater freedom from state control and legal restrictions;

- *privatization*, reducing the public sector's share in the direct or indirect provision of goods and services to business and community alike;
- *(re-)commodification* of the residual public sector, to promote the role of market forces, either directly or through market proxies;
- *internationalization*, encouraging the mobility of capital and labour, stimulating global market forces and importing more advanced processes and products into Britain as a means of economic modernization;
- *reduced direct taxes* to expand the scope for the operation of market forces through enhanced investor and consumer choice (see Chapter 3).

These six mutually reinforcing neo-liberal policies formed the micro-economic basis of its supply-side strategy as the complement to Thatcherism's macro-economic counter-inflationary strategy based on monetary and financial restraint. They also shaped the broader structural and strategic shift from a flawed Atlantic Fordism and KWNS towards an ill-defined post-Fordist mode of growth and half-hearted SWPR. The path beyond the post-war Fordist mode of growth was understood during the Thatcher–Major period primarily in terms of a shift from industrialism to post-industrialism, flexibility rather than rigidity in the social relations of production, and an increased role for small and medium-sized firms in job creation. This was believed to require state action to promote enterprise, innovation and competitiveness, to subordinate a broad range of social policies to the demands of greater labour-market flexibility, and to lower overall social expenditure qua cost of international production. In pursuing these objectives, however, Thatcherism fell well short of realizing an SWPR. For its economic policy was more Ricardian than Schumpeterian, social policy was more concerned with cost-cutting than promoting economic regeneration and, despite the transfer of economic and social policy functions to public agencies and/or public–private partnerships that bypassed elected local authorities, there were still strong 'nationalizing' tendencies reflected in micro-management by the central state.

It is tempting to attribute New Labour's electoral victory in 1997 to a cunning combination of 'an organizational fix and floating signifiers'. For its organizational reforms enabled the leadership to distance New Labour from its past and to assert control over its future; and its resort to sound bites and malleable 'big ideas' enabled it to leave its strategic line and detailed political programme undefined as far as the electorate was concerned.[6] Following its election, the New Labour government seems to have been content, at a minimum, to administer much of Thatcherism's legacy with regard to the six main planks of neo-liberalism, as if considering their effects to date as so many economically or politically irreversible *faits accomplis*. It also committed itself to further liberalization and deregulation in many areas; to the privatisation, or at least corporatization,[7] of most of what remains of the state-owned sector; and to the extension of market forces into what remains of the public and social services at national, regional and local level, as well as to the spread of market forces into the provision of such services elsewhere in Europe and the rest of the world. Its policy on this last point reflects its firm attachment to the internationalization of the British economy, as evidenced in its welcome to inward investment, its active promotion of the international interests of British-based (but not always British-owned) financial, commercial and industrial capital, and its support for the Washington Consensus on the benefits of free trade in services on a world scale. Indeed, New Labour has warmly embraced the logic of neo-liberal globalization as a whole, proudly proclaiming to all and sundry at home and abroad its inevitability, desirability and truly global benefits. Finally, it also accepted the income-tax rates and spending plans of the last Conservative government as the basis for its own first period of office,[8] not just for prudential electoral reasons but also on more principled grounds, reaffirming during the 2001 election campaign its commitment to maintaining the current top rate of income tax. This explains why New Labour prioritizes attempts to reduce unemployment in order to cut the social assistance bill and to raise tax revenues, to discover areas where cuts can be made to free up resources for its social agenda and to introduce social policies that 'would make a difference at little or no cost' (Blair 1996; cited in Panitch and Leys 1997: 252).

Nonetheless, neo-liberalism has been modified compared to the Thatcher and Major years. This has enabled New Labour to contrast some of its key policies with those of the 18 years of 'Thatcherite misrule' and has even led some commentators to claim that it has rejected neo-liberalism. Against such self-serving and/or ill-judged interpretations, however, some basic points about neo-liberalism need to be recognized. For it is an evolving economic and political project that has already passed through several stages, that can be adjusted as its effects unfold in different fields and on different scales, and that has to be adapted to changing economic, political and social circumstances. In particular, as the neo-liberal regime shift comes to be consolidated significant changes in the state's role should be anticipated. The transition period was marked by a concern with *rolling back* the exceptional forms of state intervention linked to attempts at crisis management in the previous regime (Atlantic Fordism), as well as the more normal forms of intervention associated with the KWNS; and by a concern with *rolling forward* the institutional architecture for a new regime, securing the balance of forces needed for this and establishing the new forms of state intervention deemed appropriate to that regime should it be successfully consolidated. This period has been followed by the first steps on the road to a *routinization of neo-liberalism.* Thus more emphasis has been given to securing the operation of the emerging neo-liberal regime through normal politics, to developing supporting policies across a wide range of policy fields and to providing flanking mechanisms to compensate for its negative economic, political and social consequences. All of these measures are being pursued, of course, in a context marked by continuing political worries about state unity and territorial unity, political legitimacy and re-election, as well as more general concerns with the future of social cohesion (on these aspects of political practice, see Poulantzas 1973; Jessop 1990).

Some of the discontinuities with the Thatcher–Major years are related to New Labour's aim to adapt neo-liberalism to new exigencies on a global,

European and national scale. In particular, its economic strategy reflects a further intensification of the dominant neo-liberal mode of globalization and the increasing equation of post-Fordism with the alleged transition to the so-called 'knowledge-based economy'. Thus, within the framework of a strong commitment to expanding the European single market and maintaining the dominant position of the City of London, New Labour is developing a strategy for a *knowledge-driven economy*. This was first clearly articulated in the Department of Trade and Industry's (DTI) White Paper *Our Competitive Edge: Building the Knowledge-Driven Economy* (1998), in which the more formal neo-liberal arguments about competitiveness inherited from the Thatcher–Major years were combined with more substantive claims about the importance of information and communication technologies, the information economy, the culture industries, the knowledge base and human capital as the crucial foundations for competitiveness in an irreversibly globalizing economy. This is consistent with the fact that, whilst manufacturing continues its relative decline, the UK has become the world's second-biggest services exporter after the USA – overtaking Germany and France – on the basis of an explosive growth in such creative industries as fashion, film, pop music and advertising as well as continued strength in financial services, computing and information technology.[9] At least discursively, then, the 1998 White Paper marks a shift from a more Ricardian to a more Schumpeterian approach to competitiveness. In this sense, New Labour is less concerned to manage the transition from rigid labour markets to flexible labour markets in response to the crisis of Fordism – a task already largely achieved under Thatcherism – than to create a neo-liberal (rather than neo-statist or neo-corporatist) framework conducive to a 'knowledge-driven' globalizing economy. Its accumulation strategy in this regard can be seen, in the language of transnational historical materialism, as a new 'comprehensive concept of control' that seeks to reconcile and realign the interests of financial capital and a knowledge-intensive productive capital.

Likewise, New Labour's social strategy reflects the continuing desire not only to subordinate social policy to the alleged economic imperatives of global competition but also to address the marked increase in social polarization and exclusion that has accompanied the neo-liberal project as pursued by the Thatcher–Major governments. This is especially important given the markedly uneven development of the British economy during the Thatcher–Major years – with overheating in London and the South more generally and, in the North, de-industrialization and relative economic stagnation. This is reflected in a series of flanking measures to improve the efficiency of flexible labour markets as well as to temper the social costs of labour-market reforms and other neo-liberal economic measures. These were nonetheless limited by cost constraints in the first two to three years of the New Labour government and by worries that they might create political space for opposition to the New Labour project. Initially more impressive in their rhetoric, aims and institutional design than in their often niggardly and mean-spirited implementation, therefore, these measures have recently become the centrepiece of the second New Labour government.

The primacy of neo-liberalism in this changing policy mix can be discerned in many aspects of New Labour strategy. Thus Labour continued to move consistently towards neo-liberalism in its economic policies from its disastrous 1984 general election defeat to its landslide 1997 general election victory (see, especially, on a wide range of policies, Hay 1999). We can also note the subsequent trend for the neo-liberal and the disciplinary bias of many of its economic and social policies to increase from their initial policy formulation through local experimentation to full-scale implementation (for example, in the field of labour-market policy, see Dolowitz 1997; Haughton *et al.* 2000). This impression of neo-liberal primacy is reinforced when one contrasts the constancy and conviction that marks the pursuit of neo-liberalism both rhetorically and practically with the oscillation and hesitation in those aspects of New Labour discourse and actions that seem to run counter to neo-liberalism.[10] Moreover, whilst it toughs out opposition from party members, trade unions and new social movements, New Labour has always proved highly sensitive to business criticism about its alleged neglect and/or backsliding regarding the market mechanism. Business is also over-represented in scores of official review and advisory bodies and is being given an increasing role in the creeping privatization of public and social services. Initially this could have been dismissed as a pragmatic desire to win the *trust* of business on the grounds that this would make it electable and help to secure a period of economic stability and growth that would provide the resources to reform the welfare state. But it now appears that New Labour has embraced the City agenda and neo-liberalism more generally and pays less attention even to regional chambers of the Confederation of British Industry (CBI), Chambers of Commerce and other representatives of the domestic economy, let alone the trade unions. Indeed, it appears to have replaced the Conservatives as 'the party of the City, the big transnational corporations and the Foreign Office – the overseas lobby' (Ramsay 1998: 115).

The neo-liberal approach to labour-market reform

Five main features characterize the Thatcher legacy on labour markets:

1 De-industrialization, with a consequent weakening of the strongest and most militant trade unions;
2 Legislation directed at trade unions' capacity to engage in strike action and collective bargaining, and to represent their members in other respects;
3 A general de-legitimization of corporatism and tripartism as means of co-making and co-implementing economic, social and political policy;
4 The flexibilization and deregulation of labour markets;
5 The development of neo-liberal 'welfare-to- work' strategies.

The first of these features is a *fait accompli* that had already fundamentally changed the social basis of the party and its links with the trade union movement well before 1997. Blair also long ago warmly embraced the second feature.

Indeed, he created political capital for himself with the power bloc and the wider electorate through his sustained attacks on the economic and political power of trade unions as well as on Clause IV of the Labour Party constitution, which committed it to the nationalization of the commanding heights of the British economy. Moreover, although the first Blair government did introduce some measures favourable to unions (for example in the field of union recognition and family-friendly employment policies), major concessions were made to business regarding their content, scope of application and timing of implementation. Third, not only does New Labour continue to reject corporatism and tripartism, it is also just as enchanted as the Thatcherites with entrepreneurs, business leaders and the business community more generally. Thus the business elite continues to have privileged access to the Labour Party and the Labour government, has a leading role in policy advice and policy evaluation, and has secured key positions in an increasing range of public–private partnerships. New Labour's continuation, elaboration and consolidation of the fourth and fifth legacies of Thatcherism are the main focus of the remainder of this chapter.

The Thatcher–Major years witnessed a growing turn to neo-liberal workfarism, with Major himself being the first to float the idea of 'workfare' to replace welfare before he became prime minister. The shift towards 'soft' workfare can be dated from the introduction in 1986 of the Restart Programme (itself modelled on US experience), which *invited* the unemployed to search for work and accept job or training opportunities in return for benefits. The turn to 'hard' workfare was initiated with the Social Security Act 1989, which *forced* individuals not only to look for employment but to accept private-sector jobs in return for continued state aid (Dolowitz 1997: 4). Under this Act it was no longer necessary that 'suitable' employment be offered, only employment; and it was no longer considered a 'good cause' for refusing an offer if that employment involved part-time, low-waged or seasonal work and/or if the hours were excessive. Not only was this hard workfare approach tougher than in the rest of Europe, it was even tougher in its demands to accept any job and more punitive in its application than the US model on which it was based (*ibid.*: 12).

This approach was taken further with the publication of the *Jobseeker's Allowance* scheme (1994) and the subsequent passage of the 1995 Jobseeker's Act, which combined unemployment and income support into a new Jobseeker's benefit and further tightened the qualifications for access to benefit. This approach was extended yet again a year later with the introduction of the Project Work pilot schemes, which are US-style workfare programmes that offer the long-term unemployed 13 weeks' intensive training in job finding and work preparation. After this period, individuals without regular employment must participate for three months in work-experience projects; those who refuse to participate or do not complete the programme lose benefit progressively. Far from rejecting the tough demands of these schemes, New Labour welcomed them. Indeed, Blair vetoed proposals from the Labour Party to scrap the Jobseeker's Allowance and advocated workfare in a series of 'tough love' speeches on rights and responsibilities. Likewise, Gordon Brown indicated his intention as shadow chancellor to extend the Jobseeker's scheme to 18–24-year-olds. It is hardly surprising, then, that the Jobseeker's Allowance remains the cornerstone of labour-market policy in New Labour's welfare-to-work policies.

Blair had pledged that his government would be a 'welfare-to-work government'. He also claimed that 'the greatest challenge for any democratic government is to refashion our institutions to bring [the] workless class back into society and into useful work'.[11] This point was echoed by Brown, the chancellor, who signalled New Labour's intention to 'rebuild the welfare state around the work ethic' (*Guardian*, 26 July 1997), and by Peter Mandelson, the flawed *éminence grise* behind New Labour strategy for many years, who argued that 'a permanently excluded underclass actually hinders flexibility' (Mandelson 1997: 17). A key feature of this reorientation towards workfare is the recognition that a permanent underclass (or surplus population) of individuals who are unemployable and/or have opted for a life of welfare dependency increases inflationary pressures as labour markets tighten. Thus it is a deliberate aim of New Labour policy to force the unemployed – including lone parents, the disabled and those who have taken early retirement on benefits – into the labour market at entry-level, low-wage jobs in order to expand the labour pool and reduce wage-inflationary pressures (for details of this rationale, see Layard *et al.* 1991; for current policy, see Layard 1998).[12] It follows that unemployment is no longer seen in terms of a *shortage of jobs* and hence of a need to manage aggregate demand in order to secure *full employment*, but is interpreted instead in workfarist terms as the product of a *shortfall in job-readiness* that is reflected in a lack of *full employability*. This means, in turn, that the appropriate response to unemployment should no longer be short-term job creation until demand management reflates the economy but, rather, policies to force the unemployed into work (with employers subsidized by the state and/or their employees receiving top-up social security benefits as necessary) in order to reinforce the *work ethic*, reduce welfare dependency and generate social-security savings and/or tax revenues that can be applied to more worthwhile social ends.

In this context it was little surprise that the first New Labour budget (July 1997) made its 'New Deal' for the unemployed its largest single new public spending commitment, with a £5.2 billion budget financed from a windfall tax on the profits of the utilities privatized during the Thatcher–Major years. This initiative built on the earlier Project Work and Job Seeker's Allowance approaches but modified these (US-inspired) policies in the light of later developments in American workfare programmes. The New Deal is a typical neo-liberal programme and is intended to eliminate welfare dependency. It is an active labour-market attachment programme that emphasizes rapid integration into the private labour market with sanctions for non-compliance; it also emphasizes low-cost, privatized delivery, with performance-related rewards for the intermediaries who seek to 'attach' the unemployed to work or training. It provides a central plank in the government's efforts to improve the pathways into work of specific target groups, such as young workers, the disabled, lone parents, the long-term unemployed aged 25–49, partners of the unemployed, and those aged

50 years or older. The aim in each case is to integrate those without work into the labour market on the grounds that opportunities for employment are the best form of welfare support.

The New Deal for young people (defined as 18–24 years old) who have been in receipt of Jobseeker's Allowance for six months is emblematic here. It is also reckoned to absorb 70 per cent of the total projected spending on the New Deal programmes (Robinson 2000: 19).[13] The young unemployed are offered four routes from welfare into work: (subsidized) private employment (including, in approved cases, self-employment), full-time education for those with basic-skills needs, activities with an environmental taskforce or voluntary-sector employment. To stay at home on full benefit is not an option. Before starting on one of these routes, young people enter the 'gateway', i.e. they receive counselling and are given tailor-made plans suited to their particular needs and circumstances. The options are not regarded with equal favour: the highest preference is for unsubsidized employment, then subsidized employment, then education courses and then environmental taskforce or voluntary service (with these last two options often serving as a deterrent to non-participation). Participation in the scheme is compulsory, and non-participation leads to increasing levels of benefit withdrawal. Employment Service regulations require most claimants to be contactable for a minimum of 40 hours per week and to be available for work, if offered, in less than 24 hours. The unemployed must sign a Jobseeker's Agreement and are subject to a Jobseeker's Direction, i.e. a requirement that they undertake specific actions to improve employability. A range of providers in each locality can operate these gateway services, either individually or in partnership. Local partners can include central, regional and local government; businesses; trade unions; and voluntary community organizations. Nonetheless, an increasing role in provision has gone to private business, both because of New Labour's ideological preference and because payment in arrears combined with tough auditing and administrative requirements make it hard for non-commercial bodies to take a lead role.

Within the context of New Labour's welfare-to-work strategy, a recent innovation is the establishment of Employment Zones. Whilst formally separate from the New Deals, they are part of the same overall concern to improve employability. They are supposed to work through capacity building at the individual and institutional level in areas with high levels of economic inactivity and/or registered unemployment. Thus they blend local workfarism with labour-market policy, and their delivery involves a 'Third Way combination of pluralistic governance and local partnerships, galvanized by inter-locality competition and national performance targets' (Haughton *et al.* 2000: 670). Their rationale is to cut the unemployable surplus population so that inflationary pressures are reduced and resources freed for other social programmes. Consistent with the general pattern of welfare-to-work programmes under the Conservative and New Labour governments, however, 'there appears to be a shift within Employment Zones from innovation-based local partnerships, practising progressive and sustainable welfare reform through experimentation, to a workfarist local regime of labour market discipline and regulation' (Jones and Gray 2001: 5).

In addition to its labour-market attachment policies, New Labour has developed an anti-poverty strategy to address the widely acknowledged fact that, far from having reduced inequality through the so-called 'trickledown' effect, the neo-liberal reforms of the Thatcher/Major years seriously aggravated it. Thus, in contrast to the Thatcherite view that economic growth would solve any residual problems of social exclusion, New Labour sees social exclusion and the existence of an underclass as obstacles to economic growth (cf. Cochrane 1999: 199). This distinctive feature of New Labour policy has been well expressed in the following statement:

> In place of the indifferences and neglect of the Conservative years, when unemployment was simply the price that had to be paid for controlling inflation and when the prevailing governmental response to the existence of poverty was one of denial, Labour has launched a raft of new policies and initiatives in this area while setting itself exacting poverty-alleviation targets.
>
> (Haughton *et al.* 2000: 670)

The background to this change of approach can be deduced from the following data. Whereas average real income increased by 44 per cent from 1979 to 1996/7 and the real income of the top 10 per cent rose by 70 per cent, the real income of the poorest 10 per cent fell by 9 per cent. Couples with children account for the largest group in poverty (22 per cent of the total), with the result that more than 1 in 3 children were in poverty in 1996/7 compared with 1 in 10 in 1979. There was also a change in the geography of poverty, with the gap between affluent and poor wards increasing between the 1981 and 1991 censuses, so that the very poorest were more concentrated in areas of acute need (Benington and Donnison 1999: 64). In response to such problems, Blair announced in March 1999 a 20-year programme to eradicate child poverty as a central part of New Labour's overall strategy to alleviate all forms of poverty and to reduce social exclusion. This was necessitated by the rise in workless households, especially those containing children, over the previous 30 years. Thus 17 per cent of households were workless in spring 1999 (just over 1 in 6) when the scheme was announced; these households contained 4 million adults and 2.6 million children (13 per cent and 18 per cent of the respective populations). These proportions were roughly three times larger than those found in the 1970s and four times those in the late 1960s at the height of the Fordist boom. Unsurprisingly, 90 per cent of these households were poor and, as working poverty had also increased, around 1 in 3 children was now living in a 'relatively poor' household (Dickens *et al.* 2000: 109–10). New Labour's assault on child poverty is based on the principles of a 'modern' (*sic*) welfare state rather than the old Beveridgean model with its assumption of lifetime employment for the male head of household. Among the most distinctive features of the New Labour approach is a requirement that lone mothers seek employment once their youngest child becomes 4 years old (again, this is an innovation borrowed from the USA). It has also introduced a programme of childcare support (promising to create 50,000 extra childcare places), as well as other policies intended to 'make work pay' for those with dependent children. The overall package of measures includes the national minimum wage, a raising of the threshold at which employees pay National Insurance contributions, a reduced rate of 10 per cent for the first tranche of taxable pay, the Working Families Tax Credit (WFTC), a Child Care Tax Credit for low-income households where all parents are in work, and a range of other plans to integrate the tax and benefit system.

It is important to note the financial cost of these transfer payments for the working poor. In the fiscal year of 2001–2, for example, New Labour's forecast spending on the New Deal programmes was just £900 million; in the same year, it spent an extra £6,000 million on increased benefits and tax credits aimed at low-income families. This suggests that

> [a] strategy appears to be emerging, by design or by accident, of trying to use job-search-focused programmes to move people into regular employment in a relatively cost-effective way and then to subsidize households, especially with children, so that their net incomes can rise above the poverty line. Most of this expenditure could be classified as good, old-fashioned fiscal redistribution to the poor. Even the precise instruments are not new, as the UK introduced its first income supplement for poor families in 1973....So there is less new about the New Deals than appears at first sight, and they may turn out to be less important than the Labour government's programme of fiscal redistribution in improving the lifetime incomes of disadvantaged households [and thereby reversing the dramatic increase in income inequality of the 1980s and 1990s].
>
> (Robinson 2000: 25; my comment)

The incoming Labour government established a Social Exclusion Unit (SEU) in the Cabinet Office, with a brief to 'develop integrated and sustainable approaches to the problems of the worst housing estates, including crime, drugs, unemployment, community breakdown, and bad schools etc' (Mandelson 1997). The main focus of the SEU in its first years, however, has been education and crime rather than social security. Overall responsibility for the latter has remained with the Treasury, which has, indeed, increased its control over welfare strategy policy more generally (Deakin and Parry 2000). The effort to eradicate social exclusion is based on a wide range of experimental poverty programmes that typically involve tightly focused partnership- and area-based initiatives. Symptomatic of these are the New Deal for Communities, which comprises 17 such programmes; six multiple action zones to pursue 'joined-up government' action across the fields of health, education and employment in six inner-city areas; and 250 Sure Start education schemes for children in poor families. These policies are being pursued within a broader framework of policies to target social welfare at poor families – the most important of which is the family tax-credit guarantee for the working poor. But none of this detracts from the impression that New Labour scores highly on 'work for those who can' and poorly on 'security for those who cannot'.

Another supplement to the welfare-into-work programme is commitments to educational reform at all levels from nursery education, through universities, to lifelong-learning programmes, as well as a range of programmes to promote a knowledge-driven and service-based economy. But these policies, too, are neo-liberal in inspiration, rhetoric, content and implementation. In the education field, for example, they are associated with increasing use of market proxies, inter-provider competition and, even, for failing schools, privatization; and they use market incentives to modify educational and career choices and to induce institutional restructuring at all levels from primary schools to advanced research.

The most likely result of the welfare-to-work scheme in its present form is an increased crowding in low-wage job markets, exerting downward pressure on pay amongst the working poor and further destabilizing contingent employment. Given the uneven geography of unemployment, this policy approach inevitably works out differently in areas of high and low labour-market demand. In the former, welfare-to-work reforms may well help channel some people into work more effectively. In areas of demand deficit, however, the reforms will at best take people off the unemployment register and engage them in some form of useful job-preparation activity. At worst, moreover, given the strong coercive element in some programmes, pushing people off benefits into work creates a downward spiral of job insecurity and low pay that harms all those seeking a footing in this precarious segment of the labour market (Haughton *et al.* 2000: 671).

'New Labour' neo-liberal?

New Labour has followed willingly in the footsteps of Thatcherism in promoting a shift from a Keynesian welfare national state to a Schumpeterian workfare post-national regime. Having pioneered Keynesian demand management under Attlee, the Labour Party under Blair now advocates full employability achieved through micro-government rather than full employment achieved through macro-economic management; and, having set up the post-war welfare state, it now sees welfare dependency and welfare statism as problems to be eliminated through a mandatory neo-liberal programme of workfarism and the introduction of market forces and business practices into the delivery of income support and public services. In both respects it has embraced the general neo-liberal strategic line developed during the Thatcher–Major years and, in particular, the increasingly hard welfare-to-work programme that was developed in the USA under the Reagan, Bush senior and Clinton presidencies. Thus, whilst Blair is on record as admiring many of the achievements of Thatcherism, he also enthusiastically contributed to an emerging Transatlantic dialogue with the Clinton Administration to advocate the 'Third Way'. In line with this emerging bipartisan Anglo-American neo-liberalism, New Labour has intensified the strategy it inherited of promoting workfare and putting systematic downward pressure on public spending on universal welfare benefits – most notably in pensions, housing provision, long-term disability insurance, long-term healthcare and higher education – as well as making welfare benefits more selective (or 'targeted' in the jargon of neo-liberalism). However, whereas the Conservatives would have used the savings generated by these measures to cut taxes, New Labour is attempting to use them to effect a longer-term and covert redistribution of welfare spending to the very poor through carefully targeted means-tested benefits. This is intended to limit the most serious forms and effects of social exclusion – to promote both economic efficiency and social justice – without upsetting the crucial swing voters of Middle England.

Given the arguments and analysis above, to what extent can we describe the New Labour government as moving Britain along a neo-liberal path towards an SWPR? First, New Labour certainly adopts a Schumpeterian rhetoric, stressing innovation for global competitiveness, the need for an enterprise culture, the promotion of a knowledge-driven economy and the development of a lifetime 'learning society'. Indeed, as Rustin has recently noted:

> the fundamental assumption of the Blair project is that unless Britain can reach the standard of performance of its global competitors, in virtually every aspect of life, there is no hope of achieving lasting improvements in well-being. 'Getting competitive' is the name of its game. This frame of thinking is shaping most fields of government policy.
>
> (Rustin 1998: 7)

However, just like the preceding Conservative governments, New Labour rejects the levels of taxation and public expenditure needed to pursue a consistent Schumpeterian strategy. Instead it is more inclined towards a neo-Ricardian strategy, i.e. one that is oriented to weak competition based on deregulating enterprise and reducing relative unit labour costs in the interests of allocative efficiency rather than one that is oriented to greater dynamic efficiency based on developing strong competition around enhanced structural or systemic competitiveness (K.R. Cox 1995: 218; Messner 1997). In this respect it believes that it is following the American road to economic prosperity rather than one of the various continental European or East Asian roads. But Blair and his colleagues do not seem to recognize that many conditions for US success, if such it were, cannot be repeated elsewhere. There can be only one world debtor running massive trade deficits among leading capitalist economies; only one economy able to print the most liquid international currency to finance its debts; only one major economy able to exploit a global brain drain to sustain its technological prowess despite decrepit public education; only one economy able to impose its definitions of intellectual property and other standards to benefit its own producers; and so forth. Political conditions in America and Europe are also quite different despite the latter's growing Americanization in political as well as popular culture.

Second, it is obvious that New Labour is committed to a workfare strategy in which social policy is subordinated to the twin requirements of labour-market flexibility and of maintaining downward pressure on the social wage qua cost of international production. This involves both more and less than an active labour-market policy – which is widely acknowledged as a common trend across the advanced capitalist economies. For it inflects that policy in a neo-liberal rather than neo-corporatist or neo-statist manner, and is therefore more likely to promote 'flexploitation' than 'flexicurity'. The former term usefully refers to 'the anti-worker aspects of flexibility' (Gray 1998: 3).[14] The latter term, although anglophone, was coined by the Dutch in 1995 to refer to the rebalancing (through neo-corporatist bargaining and social pacts) of increased labour-market flexibilization on the one hand and social and employment security on the other (Wilthagen 1998).[15] In contrast to the preceding Conservative governments, however, New Labour's approach to workfare is more a 'One Nation' inclusionary than a 'Two Nations' exclusionary strategy. This shift in approach has a dual motivation. For not only does New Labour believe in an American-style welfare-to-work strategy that uses welfare as a springboard into the labour market rather than as a safety net for the unemployed, but it also hopes that this will gradually reduce public expenditure, releasing funds for other social priorities, including education, health and alleviating child poverty. This second motivation is well expressed in a statement by Mandelson, which followed the sentence quoted above on the extent to which the underclass needed to be eliminated as a fetter on flexibility:

> [But] flexibility on its own is not enough to promote competitiveness. It is the job of government to play its part in guaranteeing 'flexibility plus' – plus higher skills and higher standards in our schools and colleges; plus partnership with business to raise investment in infrastructure, science and research; plus an imaginative welfare-to-work programme to put the long-term unemployed back to work; plus minimum standards of fair treatment at the workplace; plus new leadership in Europe in place of drift and disengagement from our largest markets.
>
> (Mandelson 1997: 17)

There is little hard evidence as yet, however, that New Labour's economic and social policies are having the promised beneficial effect in boosting the enterprise culture and competitiveness as opposed to getting people off the unemployment register and reducing welfare spending. Much of the beneficial effect of New Labour policies is more plausibly attributed to the favourable international economic situation (including the continued overvaluation of sterling with its downward pressure on wages and prices) that prevailed in its first four years in office and to the more traditional macro-economic measures that it has been following. In the future, the much-expanded commitment to fisco-financial redistribution by stealth will further enhance this. The most comprehensive estimates of the impact of changes to the tax and benefit system in the first three New Labour budgets, in combination with the national minimum wage, suggest that the worst-off quintile of households will gain by around 8 per cent on average, whereas the best-off quintile will gain by around

0.5 per cent (Immervoll *et al.* 1999). The second term of office should see further improvements in this regard. However, as Glyn and Wood note, since the bottom quintile receive more than 80 per cent of their post-tax income in the form of benefits and these are indexed to inflation rather than earnings, around one-half of the so-called 'redistribution' achieved by Labour's budgets and other measures (such as the minimum wage) simply prevents the poorest falling *even further* behind as benefits rise more slowly than earnings (Glyn and Wood 2001).

The post-national character of New Labour's strategy is ambiguous. On the one hand, there is a clear commitment to devolution (witness the Welsh Assembly and Scottish Parliament, plans for regional assemblies in England, and, beginning with London, the introduction of city mayors). And, albeit more for political than economic motives, New Labour also has a more pro-European stance to put alongside the pro-Americanism or pro-Atlanticism it has inherited from the Thatcher/Major years. But this pro-EU stance is more concerned with the creation of a single market that might benefit UK-based (if not always British-owned) international financial and service firms than it is with developing a strong Social Europe or a federal European state. New Labour supports a strong European approach to the single market, security issues, the environment and labour immigration; but it opposes a uniform European approach to labour markets, trade unionism, social welfare and social inclusion. Its decision to delay participation in the single European currency system also suggests continuing caution about the European project. In this sense there is more rhetoric than reality behind New Labour's commitment to giving Britain a leading role in Europe.

Finally, there has been much New Labour talk about extending citizenship, implementing communitarian values, building a stakeholding society, promoting public–private partnerships and pioneering a 'Third Way' between laissez-faire market capitalism and top-down national economic planning and bureaucratic welfarism. Indeed, a key theme of the current modernization debate is that joined-up government and citizen-centred services require a greater degree of both vertical and horizontal integration – that is, closer co-ordination between different tiers of government (local, regional, national and European) and different spheres of society (public, private, voluntary and the grassroots community) (Benington and Donnison 1999: 61). Nonetheless, there is still a strong role for the state in Blair's 'New Britain'. This is particularly clear in the enhanced disciplinary role of the state – whether with regard to promoting the enterprise culture among the unemployed;, the constant monitoring and disciplining of individual hospitals, schools, universities, local authorities, government offices, privatized utilities and so on; the pursuit of a 'zero-tolerance' strategy towards hooliganism; or the increasingly authoritarian response to asylum seekers, refugees and economic migrants.

Notes

1 In writing this paper I have benefited greatly from discussions and collaboration with Martin Jones, Jamie Peck and Nik Theodore, on whose publications I have also freely drawn (see references).

2 I owe this point to Theodore and Peck (1999: 486).

3 Thus, whilst New Labour has developed strong centralizing instincts, a penchant for centralized micro-management of local social and economic policy initiatives, and a frenetic desire to discipline the Labour Party and control the wider political agenda, it has also conceded – albeit reluctantly – some (at least potentially democratic) constitutional reforms at national, regional and urban levels. Even in these regards, however, decentralization has been marred by 'control freakery'.

4 On the rationale behind this strategy, see Benington and Donnison (1999: 68–9).

5 Gordon Brown shares Blair's ethical socialism and commitment to the work ethic but, as can be seen from his expensive programme of redistribution by stealth, is less hostile to an active role for the state. Against this social conscience, however, must be set Brown's passionate and unfathomable support for the Private Finance Initiative, an expensive means of purchasing capital goods on annual rental from profit-making enterprises.

6 Extensive effort went into reassuring the City of London, however, that the economy was safe in New Labour's hands.

7 Corporatization refers to the transformation of publicly accountable state-owned enterprises into corporate entities operating according to commercial criteria and protected by a cloak of commercial confidentiality, even if they continue to receive state funding. A recent example is the transformation of the Royal Mail into Consignia. The most controversial new privatization under Labour is that of the National Air Traffic Services, but there has been a creeping privatization of many social and public services, including health, education and pensions.

8 In practice, New Labour broke with these plans with regard to health and education for a mixture of reasons to do with restructuring and electoral calculation.

9 Since 1970, the annual average growth rates for services and manufacturing have been 2.6 and 0.7 per cent, respectively. Services now account for around two-thirds of total economic output.

10 At different times New Labour has invoked 'the stakeholding society', 'the giving society', 'communitarianism', 'social citizenship', 'social capital', 'partnership' and, of course, 'the Third Way' to distinguish its approach from Thatcherite neo-liberalism. But these are rarely followed through in practical terms in case they threaten the neo-liberal project. Instead, New Labour has proceeded to implement its social programme through 'stealth' rather than by mobilizing the socially excluded behind a radical hegemonic project. On New Labour discourse more generally, see Fairclough (2000).

11 Speech at the Aylesbury Estate, Southwark, 2 June 1997.

12 This has been dismissed as a forlorn hope on the grounds that wage pressures are not really significant in the low-wage sector of the labour market (Haughton *et al.* 2000: 671).

13 This is equivalent to £2,240 million and compares with 15 per cent of the total spend devoted to the New Deal for 25–49-year-olds, 1 per cent for the over-50s, 6 per cent for lone parents, 6 per cent for the disabled and 2 per cent for the partners of unemployed people (Robinson 2000: 19).

14 For arguments that welfare-to-work as practised in the UK will not necessarily lead to social inclusion, see, among others, Cook *et al.* 2001; Glyn and Wood 2001; Haughton *et al.* 2000; Hyde *et al.* 1999; Jones and Gray 2001; Peck and Theodore 2000.

15 For a more general review of 'flexicurity'-type active labour-market arrangements in Europe that are non-liberal in form, see Schmid (1998).

9 Competitive corporatism?

National and transnational elements in the Dutch employment 'miracle'

Uwe Becker

Introduction

In the Netherlands the employment rate has risen by more than 30 per cent since 1985. This is an exception to the general European trend. For between 1960 and 1995 the long-term development of employment in relation to working-age population growth was negative in Western Europe (about −0.3 per cent annually). In the less populous USA, by contrast, it was positive (about 0.5 per cent annually; Standing 1999: 137). So in the western world as a whole, economic growth was nearly 'jobless' in relative terms. Given that the bulk of the exports, imports and foreign investment of the western countries has been an intra-western affair, one could get the impression of employment growth as a zero-sum game of competing territorial states. And it is just in terms of a zero-sum game that the main proposals for raising the number of jobs in national economies are made. The catalogue of demands is well known: bring down wage costs below the level of the main competitors, deregulate the labour market, reduce taxes on labour and particularly on capital, cut welfare benefits. In an open, transnational economy these changes are said to be exigencies of globalization.

The Netherlands seems to have met these criteria, particularly wage restraint (which has been extraordinary since 1979), better than most European countries, and this is argued to be the source of its employment 'miracle' and of its recent emergence as a 'model' country. A special feature always added to this picture is the harmonious cooperation between capital and labour rendering wage restraint and welfare cuts into unproblematic consensus-based processes. In the country itself the employment success gave rise to a model discourse, and in international discussion the Dutch case is put forward by some writers (specifically by Martin Rhodes, for example in Rhodes 2001) as an example of competitive corporatism. Is it such an example, and is competitive corporatism a viable strategy for territorial states to raise employment? Has international competition to be understood as a zero-sum game? These questions will be dealt with briefly in the final part of this contribution. In the main part, we first investigate whether the 'miracle' is really due to a successful, consensus-based adaptation of the Netherlands to a globalizing economic environment. The answer will be that this explanation is not particularly strong and that domestic processes have been at least of equal importance.

Sharply climbing employment, stagnating broad unemployment

By the year 2000 the Dutch economy was widely being called, with reference to geographic peculiarities of the country, the 'delta' or 'polder' model. This 'delta' economy is under full steam; employment is still rising, unemployment declining; in contrast to other success stories, such as the US and Britain, overt poverty is very limited; the people are very satisfied with their country and its institutions (European Commission 1998b: B 4–6 and 27); producers' and consumers' confidence in the continuation of Dutch prosperity is high; and the international valuation of the country's economy could not be better – the Economist Intelligence Unit has just declared the Dutch 'business environment' as the world's best for the years 2000–4 (*Economist*, 20 May 2000). Everything seems to be fine, the positive image of the delta model has become a dynamic force of its own, and economic as well as employment growth seem to be self-sustaining at the moment.

In the early 1980s the situation was very different: the Netherlands was a low-employment country, and like other countries it was hit by the second oil crisis. Moreover, because of a sharply rising inflow of women into the labour market, participation rates started to grow at the very moment that employment declined. Unemployment rose, and at its peak, in the summer of 1983, it reached more than 14 per cent. Thereafter the situation improved, although until 1990 the Netherlands still lagged clearly behind most of the surrounding states in terms of both employment and unemployment. In the subsequent decade, however, when stagnation and decline hit other countries, employment continued to rise and registered unemployment fell further (see Table 9.1). In Europe, the only countries with a record comparable to the Dutch one are Denmark, where participation and employment stabilized at a high level and unemployment went down, and Austria, Switzerland and Norway, where unemployment remained below 5 per cent. A special case is Ireland, Europe's 'tiger economy'. Outside Europe, Dutch employment growth was equalled in New Zealand (until 1996) and in the US unemployment also fell below 4 per cent.

However, this picture must be qualified. Although Dutch employment growth since the mid-1980s is very impressive, the country has really only caught up with the European average. Moreover, the high increase is almost entirely due to the female labour force doubling since 1973, when Dutch participation rates for women were extraordinarily low. In the late 1960s the previously Christian-conservative Netherlands became a rapidly secularizing 'permissive society', and with a certain time lag more and more married women went from the kitchen into paid employment. In a context of poorly developed facilities for public childcare (SCP 2000: 202), the overwhelming majority of them took part-time jobs. They have won some economic independence in this process, although the effect should not be

Table 9.1 Participation, employment and standardized unemployment rates (per cent of age groups 15–64 and 55–64) 1983–96/9

	Participation		*Women*		*55–64*	*Employment*			*Part time*			*Part time, women*		*Standardized unemployment*		
	1983	1999	1983	1999	1999	1983	1990	1999	1983	1990	1996	1983	1996	1983	1990	1999
Austria	65.6	71.6	49.7	62.7	30.7	62.9		68.2	8.4	8.9	14.9	20.0	28.8	9.9	7.0	7.2
Australia	68.8	73.6	51.9	64.5	46.9	62.1	67.9	68.2	17.5	22.6	25.2	30.4	40.0			3.7
Belgium	60.5	64.6	44.5	56.0	26.2	53.5	54.4	58.9	8.0	10.9	14.0	19.7	30.5	12.1	6.7	9.0
Canada		75.9		69.8	49.9		70.3	70.1		17.0	18.9		28.9		8.1	7.6
Denmark	79.6	80.6	72.8	76.1	56.6	71.8	75.4	76.5	23.3	23.3	21.5	43.7	34.5		8.4	5.2
France	67.4	67.8	55.6	61.3	37.4	62.0	59.9	59.8	9.6	11.9	16.0	20.1	29.5	8.3	9.0	11.3
Germany	67.5	71.2	52.5	62.3	44.7	62.2	64.1	64.9	12.6	15.2	16.3	30.0	33.8	7.7	4.8	8.7
Great Britain	75.9	76.3	62.5	66.4	52.1	67.0	72.4	71.7	18.9	21.3	22.1	41.3	42.7	12.4	7.1	6.1
Italy	60.1	59.6	40.1	45.6	28.9	55.0	53.9	52.5	4.6	4.9	6.6	9.4	12.7	8.8	9.0	11.4
Ireland	62.8	66.3	37.8	54.3	45.7	54.0	52.3	62.5	6.7		11.6	15.6	22.1	14.0	13.4	5.8
Netherlands	59.0	73.6	40.2	64.4	36.6	52.0	61.1	70.9	21.0	31.6	36.5	49.7	66.1	12.0	6.2	3.3
New Zealand	65.3	75.2	45.7	67.4	59.9	61.6	67.3	70.0	15.3	19.6	22.0	31.4	36.8		7.8	6.8
Sweden	83.0	78.5	78.3	76.0	68.6	80.2	83.1	72.9	24.8	23.3	23.6	45.9	39.0	3.5	1.7	7.2
United States	75.2	77.2	63.5	70.7	59.3	68.0	72.2	73.9	18.4	16.9	18.3	28.1	26.9	9.5	5.6	4.2
European Union		69.0		59.5	41.4		61.6	62.6		13.3	15.2		28.7		8.4	9.2
OECD		70.4		59.5	51.6		65.2	65.9		14.3	15.1		25.7		6.1	6.8
Switzerland		82.2		74.5	73.6		79.6	79.7		25.4	27.4		52.2			3.5*

Notes:

* Swiss unemployment 1998 instead of 1999.

Because of a significant statistical break for the EU countries after 1996 the part-time figures for 1999 are not included here.

The statistical series presented in the table include many 'breaks'. In the case of the Netherlands as well as the other EU countries there was a break in the series for part-time work after 1996, when the OECD decided to reproduce the much lower *Eurostat* figures instead of national Dutch ones. This series, however, only starts in 1990, so that no comparison with earlier years is possible. The table, therefore, only presents the OECD part-time figures until 1996. Furthermore, the US figures on employment as presented in the table reflect neither the second jobs many people hold nor the rise in employment among persons older than 64 years. Together with the rising working-age population, these developments may explain why, despite sharply rising numbers of jobs, the USA employment *rate* remained almost unchanged through the 1990s.

Source: OECD 1999, 2000a; OECD 1997 for the part-time rates.

exaggerated. The average female contribution to the household income of couples with both spouses working is only 30 per cent (*NRC Handelsblad*, 17 April 1999).

The explosive growth in part-time work is, however, not solely a female affair, since male part-time work is also very high, at more than 16 per cent. In part, the development of Dutch part-time work has been a process 'from below'; in the late 1970s and early 1980s public employers, particularly in healthcare and education, offered part-time work as a solution to job shortages. In the first instance, part-time employment was neither an aspect of public policy nor supported by the unions. 'It just came our way', a civil servant is quoted as saying (Schmitter and Grohe 1997: 539). Today, part-time work is also the destination of the majority of the unemployed, if they find a job at all. Nearly three-quarters of unemployed women getting a new job and about 40 per cent of unemployed men move into part-time contracts. In most other European countries slightly more than 10 per cent of the males move this way and roughly two to three times this percentage of women – only in the UK and Germany is their percentage 50 per cent (O'Reilly and Bothfeld 1996: 23).

When a rising employment rate is first of all due to part-time jobs, the expansion of the relative labour volume (full-time equivalents related to the 15–64-year-old population) will be less dramatic than the overall employment rate suggests. This is exactly the case in the Netherlands: employment has increased sharply since the early 1980s; the relative labour volume, however, much less. In 1983 it was 46.5 per cent, in 1990 it had risen to 52 per cent and in 1998 to 54 per cent (the employment-rate figures are 52, 61 and 69 per cent, respectively). In Denmark and the US the actual labour-volume rate is approaching 70 per cent; in Germany it is still slightly higher than in the Netherlands (SCP 2000: 298).[1] Perhaps part-time work is the future prospect for distributing life chances in societies that can no longer create full-time full employment, but at the moment, and put in comparative perspective, the high percentage of part-time jobs renders the Dutch employment miracle less miraculous.

Almost all new jobs have been added in the service sector (SCP 1998: 363; OECD 2000a[2]). This development is a widespread phenomenon throughout the OECD world. Special to the Netherlands is the strong increase (from about 9 to 14 per cent of total employment between 1984 and 1998) of business and professional services (banking, insurances, support services such as automation, bookkeeping), which in part was realized by processes of 'outsourcing' by large firms. In relative terms, the decline in employment in manufacturing and agriculture/fishery has been completely compensated for by the growth of these branches. The shares of the distributive (wholesale, retail), personal (hotels, recreation) and social (government proper, health, education) services have largely remained stable or, as in the large social/government sector, slightly declined (OECD 2000a: 87). In absolute terms, this means that job growth in these branches was roughly in line with the overall increase in employment of about 30 per cent, whereas producer service employment has risen spectacularly.

When we look at unemployment an ambiguous picture becomes apparent. Registered unemployment is low, yet this figure only covers people actively seeking work. In fact the term 'registered unemployment' is misleading, because the people counted under this label are surveyed but not registered at all. Non-employment is much higher. It includes:

- A high percentage of retired persons of 55–64 years old (see Table 9.1). This general feature of continental European Union (EU) countries contrasts with the Anglo-Saxon world, Switzerland and Scandinavia.
- A large number of people no longer seeking a job and receiving unemployment benefits or social assistance. Surveyed unemployment numbered 200,000 people at the end of 1999, yet the number of unemployed receiving benefits was 550,000. And the labour-service offices had registered some 600,000 people seeking work. Moreover, in 1998 there were more than 400,000 people receiving social assistance (SCP 1999: 68; *NRC Handelsblad*, 18 November 1999; SCP 2000: 337), while it is an open question how many of them were hidden unemployed.
- A large proportion of the people registered under the disability scheme. Currently, their number is about 930,000 (nearly 14 per cent of the economically active population). This number is 50–100 per cent higher than in most comparable countries (*NRC Handelsblad*, 28 January 2000; SCP 2000: 361). In fact, the Dutch disability scheme turns out to be a specific regulation for nearly half a million long-term unemployed.

Taking all these figures together, the Dutch picture is still one of medium employment, low labour volume and high non-employment ('broad unemployment' declined slightly from 1984 to 1986 and stabilized on the 1986 level of about 24 per cent until 1996; SCP 1998: 382). Alternatively formulated, one could say that unemployment has shifted substantially from 'registered' towards other categories of non-employment and that total Dutch unemployment has hardly declined since the mid-1980s. Under the pressure of labour shortages, this picture changed only somewhat in the final years of the 1990s.

Finally, it should be noted that ethnic minorities fare very badly in the Dutch labour market. Dutch society prides itself on its 'tolerance', but it is a traditionally segmented society where the segments, although tolerating each other's peculiarities to a high degree, are rather closed. As a result, unemployment of people (males) from Turkey and Morocco is six times higher than that of the indigenous population, with that of males from Surinam and the Dutch Antilles four times and that of other minorities five times higher. The figures for minority women are more favourable, but their participation rates are low. Given that, on average, ethnic minorities are lower skilled than 'indigenous' people, the higher unemployment of the former is particularly striking when one takes into account that the unemployment rate of all Dutch low-skilled employees in relation to the general unemployment rate is favourable (Standing 1999: 162; OECD 2000b: 179). As a result of the high unemployment of ethnic minorities the overall unemployment rate of immigrants (including westerners) is three times that of indigenous persons. In France and Germany the immigrants' rate is 60–70 per cent higher, in Australia it is equal and in the USA it is even lower (SCP 1998: 247; *NRC Handelsblad*, 17 October 1998; Leslie *et al.* 1997).

Employment growth by a corporatist beggar-my-neighbour strategy?

The explanation of the Dutch 'miracle' most often heard is that it was realized by wage restraint. This explanation is clearly breathing the air of a zero-sum game. Competition is understood as price competition where the expensive countries will lose jobs to the cheaper ones. Aspects such as quality, product image and comparative advantages (as well as demand and expectations) are largely neglected, and the main trade partners are supposed to be competitors in the same markets. So, to be more competitive wages have to be brought down, or in any case to increase less than the gross domestic product (GDP). Exports will grow then, imports will increasingly be substituted, profits will rise, they will trigger investment, and this will enhance economic as well as employment growth. Or in the words of the director of the Dutch Central Planning Bureau (CPB): 'wage restraint is good for our position in international competition, for exports, for profits, for the investment climate, and hence for employment' (*NRC Handelsblad*, 26 November 1999).

This construct may perhaps not meet the standards of sophisticated economic theory. Yet it has been the message hammered into the Dutch public by the employers, the government and particularly the CPB since the late 1970s. The argument was largely based on an econometric study by the CPB of the Dutch experience of the restrictive 'guided wage policy' during the 1950s (Therborn 1986:154f.), a period judged to have been a success story. Current wages, by contrast, were considered too high, profits too low for the necessary investment. Time and again the CPB presented figures pointing to a rising 'rate of labour income' (share of labour income in total income), a construction of this advisory agency itself which did not take certain elements of GDP into account. So initially, in the late 1970s and early 1980s, wage restraint was launched as a necessity. Two decades later this had become largely undisputed wisdom in the Netherlands and, having been disseminated by Visser and Hemerijck's *A Dutch Miracle* (1997: 13, 27), it is now internationally repeated as factual evidence (Levy 1999: 263; Rhodes 1997: 15; 2001: 14).

However, the empirical basis for the necessity of Dutch wage restraint is rather weak. Whereas the CPB's labour income rate rose from 87.8 per cent in 1974 to 91 per cent in 1981, the more common wage rate declined from 76.4 to 66 per cent (Albeda 1984: 41). And, as Table 9.2 indicates, in comparative terms profits have never been particularly low in the Netherlands. The 'operating surplus' presented in the table is a gross figure and includes the income of self-employed people, which, however, is roughly the same in the countries compared. The data show that during the 1970s profits fell in all countries, but that in most of them the next decade brought some increase again. The Netherlands is no exception to this trend, and its profit decline in the 1970s was

Table 9.2 Comparative profit and investment rates 1960–89 (annual averages)

	Operating surplus (in per cent of GDP)			*Gross fixed capital formation (in per cent of GDP)*		
	1960–73	1974–9	1980–9	1960–73	1974–9	1980–9
Belgium	34	25	29	22	22	18
Canada	26	25	26	22	24	21
Denmark	30	24	24	24	22	17
France	32	25	24	24	24	20
Germany	30	23	23	25	21	21
Netherlands	32	25	29	24	21	20
Sweden	21	15	17	23	21	19
Switzerland	31	25	23	28	23	25
UK	21	18	20	18	19	17
USA	25	22	21	18	19	17

Source: Huber and Stephens (1998: 365f.; based on OECD, National Accounts).

no more severe than in Belgium, France, Germany, Sweden and Switzerland. Most striking is perhaps – though the peculiarities of national fiscal systems as well as the relative importance of capital exports have to be taken into account – the large difference in the Netherlands between profits and investment, particularly in contrast to Sweden, Switzerland and the USA.

Moreover, unit labour costs have never been particularly high in the Netherlands, not even in the late 1970s, the period preceding the years of continuous extraordinary wage restraint. From 1974 to 1979 they rose by 5.7 per cent, whereas the figure for the OECD countries as a whole was 8.3 per cent and that for the European Community 10.5 per cent (the respective percentages for 1968–73 were 6.1, 5.2 and 7.0, and those for 1980–3 were 2.1, 5.8 and 8.7; Therborn and Koole 1989: 20).

Whatever the merits of the CPB's construction, the forces pushing for wage restraint were successful, and in the early 1980s a period of extraordinary wage restraint started – in fact, wage growth has lagged behind GDP growth continuously since 1979 (SCP 2000: 290). Subsequently, wage moderation developed from an asserted necessity into a general strategy of creating competitive advantages. Wage restraint has been 'Holland's single most important weapon in international competition', the CPB wrote in 1995 (Visser and Hemerijck 1997: 26). And economist van der Ploeg proudly wrote that 'since 1980 real wages in manufacturing have risen by a mere 3 per cent, whereas in France and Germany the corresponding figures are 28 and 40 per cent respectively' (van der Ploeg 1997: 319). These seem to be very large differences (though the percentages address manufacturing only), but to illustrate the dimension of wage restraint one can also point to Dutch contract wages, which increased between 1983 and 1997 by 29.5 per cent, compared to an aggregated inflation of 30 per cent (van Empel 1997: 19).

Because the period of extraordinary wage restraint coincided, though only since about 1985, with the rise in employment, wage restraint is presented as a success formula that, according to the CPB, explains half of employment growth since the mid-1980s (Visser and Hemerijck 1997: 113). The CPB computers have been fed, however, with a specific microeconomic causal conception of the macroeconomic relationship between wages and employment. An empirical test of the neo-classical chain of lower wages causing investment growth by higher profits, more exports and, as a consequence, higher economic growth and more jobs does not support the theory. Capital income in fact rose, from about 10 per cent of GDP (in terms of the 'rate of capital income', which is inversely related to the 'rate of labour income') in 1983 to 20 per cent in 1990, and since then it has been on a level of about 17 per cent (Kool *et al.* 1998: 319).

The average rate of domestic investment, however, did not rise at all in this period (*ibid.*), and until 1995 export growth remained below the average level for the EU (Salverda 1999: 225). Furthermore, economic growth in the 1990s only slightly exceeded the European average (though in the final years of the decade the difference became larger). Taking into account the very low employment rate in 1983, until the end of the 1980s wage moderation did not correlate with higher than average employment growth. And it must not be forgotten that in the entire period job growth took place in the service sector, a sector much less vulnerable to international competition than manufacturing.

It does not appear, therefore, that higher profits have directly led to job growth. The big companies, particularly the banks, have made some spectacular acquisitions abroad, however. According to research by ABN-AMRO Bank, 4 out of 10 big enterprises do not know what to do with their profits (*de Volkskrant*, 25 February 1999). Sometimes they pay their stockholders enormous dividends, as Unilever did – one of the largest European companies with an annual turnover of *ca.* €90 billion. After announcing a super-dividend totalling 16 billion guilders, Unilever's CEO said: 'we don't need the money' (*de Volkskrant*, 24 February 1999). Wage restraint for enriching shareholders?

A brief comparative investigation further weakens the view underlying the idea of a Dutch model, that wage restraint is the best medicine against unemployment and for generating new jobs. Looking at the data in Tables 9.1 and 9.3, a clear co-occurrence of slow wage growth and an improved labour market exists only in the Netherlands and in New Zealand and the US. Reverse cases, superficially also supporting the theory of employment increase by wage restraint, are France and Sweden. Here, rising unemployment and a stagnating employment rate correlate with wage increases roughly matching economic growth.

Germany is more difficult. There, after 1983, unemployment went down and employment up without significant wage moderation. In the 1990s the opposite occurred: wage restraint went together with a stagnating employment rate and rising unemployment. Australia is also such a hybrid case. There, wage increases were particularly low after 1983, but a correlation of wage restraint and employment growth only exists until the early 1990s, whereas unemployment only slightly declined over the entire period. Finally, in Britain, Austria, Denmark and

Table 9.3 Comparative international economic growth and labour costs in the Netherlands

	Real growth GDP (annual average)			*Development of wage costs[1] per employee*		*Relative unit labour costs[2]*
	1986–96	1997	1998	1985–94	1990–4	1996
Australia	3.4	3.6	5.1	1.9†	4.4†	120
Austria	2.5	2.5	3.3	17.9‡	5.5‡	
Denmark	1.8	3.1	2.9	9.6*	5.3*	200
France	2.0	2.3	3.2	10.2	5.8	150
Germany	2.6	2.2	2.8	14.1	4.1	150
Great Britain	2.3	3.5	2.1	15.7†	5.1†	160
Italy	1.8	1.4	1.4	20.1*	10.3*	90
Netherlands	2.6	3.6	3.8	7.3**	3.9	110
New Zealand	1.8	3.0	0.8	1.5	3.4	
Sweden	1.3	1.8	2.9	15.1	1.5	140
Switzerland	1.1	1.7	2.1	15.1‡	3.3‡	
USA	2.5	3.9	3.9	2.2**	0.9**	100

1 real, including indirect costs;

2 the absolute level is indexed in relation to the US (=100);

† 1987–96 and 1992–6;

‡ 1986–95 and 1991–5;

* 1984–93 and 1989–93;

** 1987–94.

Source: OECD (1999: 16; 1997: 2, 5, 7, last column), *Economist*, 19 December 1998.

Switzerland wage increases roughly paralleled economic growth, but the employment rate rose or remained relatively stable at a very high level. The figures of these countries do not support the theory discussed here. The same probably holds for the United States in the 1970s and early 1980s, where more than a decade of low wage increases did not bring about any visible employment effect.

When we consider unit labour costs the picture becomes even more complicated, particularly in the cases of Denmark, where very high unit labour costs and also a current-account deficit combine with employment growth and low unemployment in the second half of the 1990s, and of Italy, where unit labour costs are lower than elsewhere and where unemployment benefits are very low but employment is also very low (see U. Becker 2001 for a more extensive account). Even if one looks comparatively to co-occurrences or non-co-occurrences of (relative) wage decline and employment growth which do not necessarily point to causal relationships, the supply-side equation of higher profits by lower wages and rising employment is not generally convincing.

This implies that the zero-sum view of Dutch employment growth being due to a beggar-my-neighbour strategy seems not to be valid. The beggar-my-neighbour interpretation of the Dutch development is found not only in critical examinations (see, for example, A. Martin 2001) but also in articles praising the 'delta model'. Van der Ploeg, for example, points to the 'Dutch miracle of wage moderation spurring job growth' (1997: 310) and repeats the supply-side argument of higher profits facilitating investment (*ibid.*: 311). Answering the question of whether the Dutch formula could be exported, however, he considers the 'danger that, if all the countries of Europe follow the Dutch example, aggregate demand gets choked off' (*ibid.*: 319). This argument would have been true if wage restraint had brought about the intended effects. It did not. The causal relationship between wages, profits, investment and employment seems to be more complicated.

Interestingly, in a comparative investigation the Sociaal en Cultureel Planbureau (SCP), in its 2000 report (SCP 2000: 308ff.), comes to a similar conclusion: in terms of economic growth, wage-moderation countries do not differ from other countries. They differ, however, in terms of productivity development. Wage restraint, so the argument runs, renders investment in new technologies less attractive. Lower productivity increases and more labour-intensive growth are the result. Comparative figures (see also OECD 2000b: 180) seem to support this theory. The Netherlands, where wage restraint has been most drastic, has the lowest growth in productivity. Does this mean that in the end the wage-restraint formula has been successful in an indirect way? It does not! The SCP and OECD figures relate to productivity growth per employee. But this is a flawed yardstick in the matter at stake.

To eliminate the effect of employment redistribution toward part-time work, productivity development has to be calculated on a per-hour basis. Doing this, the Netherlands emerges as a case where productivity growth (2.47 per cent per year) from 1979 to 1994 was slightly above the OECD average (2.34 per cent; Buchele and Christiansen 1999: 96). The annual rise in unit labour costs, by 1.1 per cent against an OECD average of 2.9 per cent in the period 1987–97 (OECD 2000a: 16), points in the same direction. Wage restraint was not an alternative course to productivity growth; it was added to it. The conclusion, therefore, must be that wage restraint was not the main cause of the Dutch development, neither directly nor indirectly by facilitating labour-intensive production. This assessment is borne out by recent processes: driven up by labour shortages, de facto wage development no longer lagged behind economic growth in 1998–2000, prices of industrial products rose by two-digit figures (*NRC Handelsblad*, 25 and 31 July 2000), and yet investment is expected to reach a record high. This was the front-page headline of the *Financieel Dagblad* on 17 June 2000 – on the same day that *de Volkskrant* wrote on its front page that Dutch profits had declined in the past few years.

Flexibility and welfare retrenchment

Global competition, it is said, forces national states to flexibilize their industrial relations, to lower direct taxes and to cut back welfare expenditures. With respect to the first, Alan Greenspan of the US Federal Reserve Board recently said that 'the greater ease with which employees can be laid off in the U.S. has counter intuitively created a greater incentive to hire, and thus reduced unemployment in the U.S. to levels unimaginable in all but a few countries in Europe' (*Wall Street Journal Europe*, 29 August 2000: 6). One of the countries he had in mind was probably the Netherlands, of which his former colleague Tietmeyer, of the German Bundesbank, once said that its labour-market flexibility should be taken as an example by his country (*NRC Handelsblad*, 21 December 1996).

The impression of a particularly flexible Dutch labour market enhancing employment is, however, largely unsustainable. It is more generally doubtful whether flexible, American-style hire-and-fire rules facilitate employment growth (OECD 1999: 47; Nickell 1997: 72). But, that caveat aside, in the Netherlands it is not particularly simple to dismiss employees. According to the *Competitiveness Report* of the World Economic Forum, Dutch dismissal legislation was 3.47 in 1994–6 on a scale of 0 (very rigid) to 10 (very flexible), a figure much lower than in Britain and the US (Empter and Esche 1997: 193).[3] By autumn 2000 there was political discussion of whether the regulation that every dismissal case had to be brought to court should be abolished. On the whole, flexibility is not special to the Netherlands (Smulders and Klein Hesselink 1997). It is top of the list in part-time work, and the possibilities for 'flex-work' are above the European average, yet on most other criteria, for example night, weekend and home working or extra hours, the Netherlands scores below average. And it should not be forgotten that wage flexibility is restricted by a still relatively high minimum wage and the great reach of collective wage agreements – though companies have the possibility of setting their own wages within the framework of these agreements.

With taxes the situation is more complicated, yet probably not much different from the case of flexibility. A new tax system was introduced in 2001, but in international comparison the new rates are still on the higher edge. The top marginal tax on labour income will be 49 per cent, starting at an income of about 50,000 guilders (the current top rate, 60 per cent, starts at 110,000 guilders, or €50,000). An interesting detail is that the awareness of international tax competition made Dutch newspapers recommend that the government had a further look at the new rates after the German parliament had approved a tax reform in July 2000 (*NRC Handelsblad*, 17 July 2000; *De Telegraaf*, 18 July 2000). Corporate taxation is a more complicated matter. The marginal tax rate on retained earnings is not particularly low (*Economist*, 26 August 2000: 97; SCP 2000: 82), but since 1975 effective corporate taxes as a share of GDP have declined more than in any other comparable country, from about 12 per cent to 7 per cent. This level roughly equals the British and American ones and is considerably lower than in most EU member states and Japan (*Economist*, 26 August 2000: 4). Moreover, foreign investors have the possibility of negotiating special rates called 'rulings'. It is these rulings that made the European Commission rank the Netherlands first of those member states violating the rules of fair tax competition (*NRC Handelsblad*, 10 November 2000: 17). It appears that the beggar-thy-neighbour spirit is clearly present in Dutch efforts to adjust taxation to changing international circumstances.

An idea also fitting into the currently dominant economic discourse is welfare state retrenchment. Not only wages, but also social assistance and social-security benefits have to be brought down. In this case, again, the Netherlands is praised from abroad. Journals like *Business Week* (7 October 1996) or *Wirtschaftswoche* (20 February 1997) wrote that other countries should look to the Netherlands for how to trim the welfare state for the future. Such comments overlook the fact that the Dutch welfare state, though it has shrunk to some degree, is still one of the most generous and comprehensive social-security systems in the world. In order to reduce costs and/or budget deficits resulting from population ageing and rising non-employment, most western states raised social-security contributions or (indirect) taxes, cut back provision levels, changed eligibility criteria and introduced more means testing. State intervention became somewhat discredited, individual responsibility became more emphasized, and duties were stressed as much as or even more than rights (R.H. Cox 1998).

The Netherlands took part in this nearly general western process of retrenchment and reorientation. In order to reduce the budget deficit and to improve the possibility of creating low-wage jobs the minimum wage (2,406 guilders per month in 2000 for adults) was frozen for a number of years, and is down from two-thirds of the average wage in 1978 to half this income now (OECD 1997: 13). Elementary welfare provisions related to the minimum wage – basic pensions, social assistance – have moved down simultaneously. General child and student allowances were frozen for many years, most gross replacement rates were cut from 80 to 70 per cent of previous earnings, and eligibility rules were tightened. As a result, the income of the mean household of welfare recipients (including pensioners) declined from 92 per cent of the average household's income in 1977 to 79 per cent in 1995 (SCP 1998: 12).

Retrenchment started, however, from a very high level and in comparative terms, the current level of Dutch welfare is still relatively high and comprehensive (U. Becker 2000). Consequently, the Netherlands belongs to the countries with the lowest poverty rates, though its rate has doubled to about 6 per cent since the late 1970s. Regarding long-term poverty, Headey *et al.* (1997: 341f.) found a percentage of only 2.1 for the period 1985–9, a figure sharply in contrast with the US percentage of 16.5. What is true for poverty seems also to be true for income inequality. In terms of the Gini index, the Dutch figure increased by about 10 per cent from 1975 to 1994, but, again, the Netherlands still belongs to the countries with the lowest level. These Gini figures have to be taken with a pinch of salt, moreover. They refer to household income, not to individual earnings, whose differentiation has increased by more than 10 per cent (see below, pp. 169–72). They also conceal a comparatively large wage gap between the sexes.

To summarize, some tendencies in the direction of what Bob Jessop calls the 'Schumpeterian workfare state' (see Chapter 3) are identifiable in the Netherlands. Until now, however, it would be an exaggeration to use this concept to describe the Dutch welfare system. The overall level of this system is still relatively generous, and where cuts and changes have taken place they were sometimes undermined by welfare policies of the communities (providing additional social assistance or exemption from local taxes) or even by the labour-market parties in their collective agreements. This happened, for example, with respect to the sickness and disability schemes, where cuts by the government were largely 'repaired' by the joint action of capital and labour (*Financieel Dagblad*, 12 July 2000; supplement on the disability scheme). Most striking and measurable, however, is that whatever changes have taken place in the welfare system they have not brought non-employment down. The inflow into employment from the various categories of non-employed people is very low (SCP 2000: 341).

Wassenaar, a myth created in the 1990s

Successful or not, the whole Dutch strategy of welfare cuts and wage restraint is presented as based on a consensus between employers and unions, and the agreement of Wassenaar[4] in November 1982 to exchange wage restraint against working-time reduction as its origin. The ideological importance of the discourse on the Wassenaar Accord can hardly be exaggerated and deserves close scrutiny. This view is supported by the fact that the Netherlands is generally considered a 'bargaining democracy' and that its industrial relations are embedded in corporatist institutions, of which the bipartite Foundation of Labour – where the Wassenaar Accord was signed – and the tripartite Socio-Economic Council are the most important. After a period of polarization in the 1970s, Wassenaar, it is claimed, paved the way back to consensus. But did it? And, more generally, has the extraordinary Dutch wage restraint really been based on consensus? The second question is a tricky one because 'consensus' is a soft category. Unequivocal evidence is scarce and interpretation is very prominent in dealing with the question of whether something called consensus deserves this name.

There is much evidence, however, to call the Wassenaar thesis a myth that was created in the euphoric context of the 1990s. It was only then that the unions repeatedly adhered to wage restraint as a necessary condition for employment growth. Looking for a starting point of this agreement with the employers, Wassenaar was remembered. Until the end of the 1980s the situation was very different. Employment began to increase only after 1985, and in subsequent years it was no special Dutch phenomenon. It also occurred in countries where wage restraint was not as drastic as in the Netherlands or where it did not take place at all. So, in those years there was no reason to praise wage restraint. And one has to keep in mind that in the Wassenaar Accord, which was only a declaration of intent and opposed by some sectoral unions (Hemerijck 1995: 214), the union federations Federatie Nederlandse Vakbeweging (FNV; socialist, 'general'; representing about two-thirds of organized labour) and Christelijk Nationaal Vakverbond (CNV; Christian) agreed on a formula of working-time reduction in combination with a proportional retreat in wage income or wage growth. This did not contradict the Keynesian idea of wage increases in line with productivity growth, and in this spirit it was interpreted by the FNV (1983: 5ff.) as an agreement on a 'cost-neutral' redistribution of work. The FNV even hoped that concessions on the wage front could be compensated for by productivity growth.

The *post-festum* construction of Wassenaar as an agreement on wage restraint as the basis for economic and employment growth downplays the differences which existed beyond the mid-1980s between the unions on the one hand and the employers, the then Christian-Liberal government and advisory bodies such as the CPB on the other hand. The unions' recipe for fighting unemployment was not wage restraint – in fact, the FNV (1984: 6) warned of a wage-restraint race between the countries of the EU. Their, as well as the oppositional Labour Party's (Partij van de Arbeid; PvdA), recipe was redistribution of work. A look into the annual reports of the FNV (1983–1999), programmatic writing of the PvdA and politico-economic journals reveals that this was true at least until 1986/7. There was even discussion of a proposal to bring the working week down to 25 hours by 1990 (Crone 1984).

The unions were not successful, however. Wage restraint continued, but working-time reduction hardly made progress. The unions criticized this time and again, and in spite of a number of Wassenaar-like 'agreements' no real consensus emerged. In 1989 Steven Wolinetz (1989: 93ff.) described the climate between unions and employers in the previous years as 'icy'. The unions had become ideologically weak in a context where critical economic thinking had gone into 'hibernation' (Therborn and Koole 1989: 25); they lost members and did not have a strong bargaining position. After the civil-service workers had lost a long wage battle in 1983, they confined themselves to complaining. Hemerijck, analysing these developments from some distance in time, described the unions of the mid-1980s as being in a 'sorry state' (1995: 215).

The entire configuration only changed in the 1990s, when the improvement in the employment situation became increasingly visible, after 1994 particularly in comparison to other countries. Whether or not there was really a causal relationship between lower wages and higher employment, their co-occurrence became evident, and employers, Christian Democrats, Liberals, 'experts' and now even a growing number of Social Democrats adhered to a supposed causal nexus. The latter had become more liberal in the course of the 1980s, and in the new government coalition of 1989 they replaced the Liberals as the junior partner of the Christian Democrats. In this context the unions could think about accepting the wage-restraint formula as a way of returning to some influence in corporatist consultation.

In its 1990 annual report the FNV wrote: 'Looking back to the 1980s one can notice that the line of controlled wage development set going in 1982 has been effective. By this strategy a substantial growth of the number of fulltime and part-time jobs has been realized in the second half of the 1980s' (FNV 1991: 7; translation by the author of the piece). The unions began to share in the creation of the Wassenaar myth, and the internationally praised Dutch consensus on wage restraint took shape. According to the Social and Economic Council, the foundations for a restoration of confidence were laid in 1992 by a unions' and employers' agreement 'to breathe new life into the consultation economy' (SER 1998: 8). And in December 1993, only after the government had threatened a statutory wage measure (Delsen 2000: 26), capital and labour agreed that future wage increases would have to remain limited (Stichting van de Arbeid 1993: 3). Now, particularly after 1995, the unions began to demonstrate 'model consciousness', and they were proud of being part of an internationally appreciated system.

The preceding overview suggests that the Dutch unions embraced wage moderation as the most qualified formula to enhance employment growth only from about 1990 and particularly after 1995. This can be interpreted as an ex-post legitimation of their factual acceptance of wage cuts in nearly all the years of the previous decade. Visibly growing employment and the decline of 'registered' unemployment made it possible to present this acceptance as a wisely chosen strategy. The more employment rose in subsequent years, the easier it became to change to the position of a protagonist of wage restraint. The unions jumped on to a moving train. Possibly, they have even become convinced that the wage-restraint formula is the only right one, or at least that it is suitable in a common, 'competitive corporatist', beggar-thy-neighbour effort of capital and labour.

How can we explain that until the late 1980s the unions did not explicitly consent to the wage-restraint formula, though they accepted it in practice? The latter becomes understandable when one takes into account that the balance of power shifted towards capital in those years. The 'sixties' were over, union membership decreased, Labour's electoral support declined, and intensifying international competition as well as capital mobility formed the basis for this development. Similar processes occurred in other countries too, but there the unions did not turn to wage moderation of the Dutch extent and duration. This is particularly true for the British unions, which were hit by the Thatcher government and operated in a context where the social wage – seen as a power resource of labour – was relatively low. Therefore, the change in the distribution of effective power resources cannot fully make plausible why the Dutch unions acted as they did.

An extra factor pushing the development in the Netherlands into the direction it eventually took was probably the very structure of Dutch consensualism. In a consensualist culture, which has a long tradition in the Netherlands (Daalder 1974), the definition of the general interest is a matter of negotiation and compromise. Corporatist institutions are the roof under which capital and labour have to find agreement on such a definition. Whenever compromise and rational agreement are impossible, however, there will be no agreement at all or the general interest and the strategies most suitable to its realization will be defined by its hegemonic interpretation. In the Dutch case, this seems to have been the special supply-side economics as it was repeatedly put forward by the CPB, by subsequent commissions of experts as well as by the Christian-Liberal government. It should be added that expert bodies, particularly the CPB, have a very high esteem in the Netherlands (Klamer 1990: 94; Andeweg and Irwin 1993: 223).

In Dutch consensualist culture the very rules of the game demand consensual behaviour of the participants in socio-political bargaining or decision-making processes. They have to avoid conflict, to argue carefully, in order to avoid taking a clear-cut point of view and to look for the common good. Non-adherence to these rules means disturbing the atmosphere of consensualism and results in excommunication (van der Horst 1994: 236–41). For those in a weaker position, the most suitable way to adjust to these rules is to conform, if not in words then at least in deeds, to the opinion that is most supported from the outside, particularly by the academic world or by government bodies with a strong impact because of their scientific experts such as the CPB. So, consensualism turns out to be a mechanism for sustaining hegemony; in fact, it transforms dominance into hegemony.

On balance, 'Wassenaar' is largely a myth, and the famous Dutch consensus on the wage-restraint formula is a myth as well. It did not exist in the 1980s, and practical acceptance of this formula by the unions can be interpreted as an adjustment to changed power relations as well as to the rules of the game of Dutch consensualism. These factors did not disappear in the subsequent decade, but at that time it had become opportune for the unions to join the forces that praised wage restraint.

Alternative explanatory factors: income differentiation and the house-price 'bubble'

If the wage-restraint formula provides a rather weak explanation, what else brought about the impressive growth of Dutch employment? One reply should be that comprehensive answers to this question do not exist. Explanations of complex economic processes cannot undergo 'hard' tests, and in spite of the sophistication of mathematical models it is extremely difficult to identify all, often mutually interdependent, relevant variables and to quantify causal relationships. Against this background, the following does not claim to present *the* alternative explanation of the 'Dutch miracle'. It only points to a few features barely mentioned in the mainstream delta-model discourse.

First, one could do what Schwartz (2001) has done with respect to Denmark: ask how important luck has been in the Dutch development. According to Delsen (2000: 33f.), luck in the sense of favourable contingent circumstances should not be underestimated. In the years after 1983 the Dutch economy simply participated in an upward international business cycle largely accelerated by the so-called 'perverse Keynesianism' of the Reagan era in the US. In these years, the Netherlands started to catch up with its neighbours, and it was to its advantage that economic restructuring was not hampered by regions of traditional heavy industry such as the British Midlands, the German Ruhrgebiet or the French province of Lorraine. In the early 1990s, then, the country took a particular advantage from German unification, and in the recession thereafter the Netherlands was favoured by international demand for just those goods it produced (chemicals, food).

There is another lucky – domestic – factor that appears to have influenced the development of Dutch employment in the 1990s. The few countries that showed considerable employment growth from 1994 until the end of the century and which are currently discussed as 'models' (the Netherlands, Denmark, the

USA and Ireland) all experienced sharply rising house prices (*Economist*, 29 May 1999). And except for Ireland they all had generous possibilities of tax relief on mortgage interest. Uniquely in the EU, Dutch house owners and their American counterparts are even allowed to offset the whole of their mortgage interest payment against taxable income (in Denmark the percentage is 46.4; Haffner 1998: 171). Moreover, with rising house prices Dutch house owners (about 50 per cent of households) are allowed to take out mortgages on the 'overvalue' of their real estate under the same conditions.

The supposed causal mechanism at stake here is that rising house prices are creating a so-called wealth effect that is a stimulus for consumption growth based on loans. When rising house prices are accompanied by rising stock prices and the extension of stock ownership to broader layers of society, as was the case in recent years, the wealth effect is even stronger. And the stimulus to spend increases when money is cheap because of generous tax relief on mortgage interest payments. A house and stock price-bubble-induced consumption bubble is lurking. Once it exists, it keeps domestic demand and employment growing – as long as it does not burst, as it did in Japan and Sweden in the late 1980s. Without doubt there has been such a demand bubble in the USA in recent years (Brenner 2000). Total household debt jumped from 85 per cent of personal income in 1992 to 103 per cent in 1999, and between 1996 and 1999 domestic demand rose by an annual average of 5.3 per cent, whereas economic growth was only 4.1 per cent. And in Denmark, to temper private borrowing and spending the government decided to reduce tax relief on mortgage interest from 46.4 to 32 per cent (*Economist*, 22 January 2000: 21; *Financial Times*, 5 April 2000).[5]

In the Netherlands, the conditions for a mortgage-induced demand bubble are most favourable because of higher taxes than in the US and higher tax relief than in Denmark. In 1998 houses had become more than twice as expensive as a decade before, and in 1999 and the first half of 2000 prices rose by another 34.8 per cent (*de Volkskrant*, 11 July 2000). When a house is worth twice the amount of the mortgage the owner can get an extra mortgage on 70 per cent of the 'overvalue'. Many people took this opportunity. In addition, the interest rate moved down to about 5 per cent until 1999. This implies a rate to be paid after tax reduction of only 2.5 per cent for people in the tax group of 50 per cent, starting at an income of *ca.* 50,000 guilders. Given an inflation rate of 1.5 per cent the real interest rate was only 1 per cent. Until the end of 1997, these mortgages could be used, without any restrictions, for rebuilding houses, buying cars or for buying life insurance and stocks; thereafter some rather soft restrictions were introduced (from 2001 tightened restrictions came into force).

By taking advantage of this provision, Dutch households in 1996 and 1997 alone pumped some 50 billion guilders into their economy. This is roughly the same amount as that lost by wage restraint.[6] In 1999, according to the Dutch central bank, once again some 18 billion mortgage guilders went into consumption. 'We are consuming mortgages', a spokesperson for the central bank commented on these developments (*de Volkskrant*, 31 August 1999).[7] And the OECD wrote that private consumption had become buoyant 'by the significant, albeit declining, wealth effect stemming from the boom in house prices in the past few years' (OECD 2000b: 117).

This wealth effect has not only brought about an extensive use of mortgages for consumptive ends, however. It generally spurred borrowing. As a result, savings declined by 11 billion guilders from 1998 to 1999. Leaving aside pensions and life insurance, savings even went into the red by 2 billion guilders in 1999, whereas in 1997 and 1998 their balance was positive, at 13 and 7 billions, respectively. This is comparable to the development in the US where net savings declined from nearly 6 per cent of GDP in 1992 to −4 per cent in 1999 (*NRC Handelsblad*, 19 July 2000 for the Netherlands; *Economist*, 22 January 2000 for the United States).

The phenomenon of rising demand caused by extensive mortgage use could be called 'mortgage Keynesianism', for it is a form of subsidized income that is used here. The question is how important this extra income has been for the expansion of the labour market. This is not exactly clear and is therefore a point of dispute. According to the central bank one-fifth of economic growth in 1998 and 1999 came from mortgage-financed consumption, and for the year 2000 the bank calculated a decline in growth by 1.5 per cent if there had been no mortgage spending at all (*NRC Handelsblad*, 23 July 2000). Willem Buiter, until 1999 a member of the board of the Bank of England, looking at the whole of mortgages, share prices and the number of shareowners, both of which have more than doubled in recent years, and at the growing general indebtedness of Dutch households, predicts that a harsh decline of GDP by 15 per cent would not be impossible if house and share prices were to fall by 20 per cent (*de Volkskrant*, 17 June 1999).

Such critical voices are only sporadically heard. In May 1999 the OECD warned that the Dutch economy could be hit severely by a rise in interest rates (*de Volkskrant*, 19 May 1999), and from time to time the Dutch central bank also releases warnings. The private banks, however, with their interest in selling mortgages and loans, do not see any problem at all (*NRC Handelsblad*, 17 July 1999). A continuation of the stock-market decline that began in April 2000, a further, perhaps 'hard', slowdown in the American economy, the change from a positive to a negative wealth effect in the US and elsewhere, and the subsequent consequences for the global economy could, however, change the entire picture dramatically. Since the Netherlands has a bubble of its own it could be one of the countries hit most severely.

The argument based on rising house prices, just like the wage-restraint formula, is growth-centred. Given the continuing rise in productivity in manufacturing, however, economic growth will only have a significant positive employment effect at very high rates of growth. In the Netherlands such rates only occurred in the second half of the 1990s, but employment has risen strongly since the mid-1980s. Therefore, this increase can only have come about by a considerable extension of the less productive service sector. In fact it did, in absolute as well as in relative terms. But why did this happen in the Netherlands whereas in France and Germany employment stagnated? Part-time work does not provide an exhaustive answer. Perhaps the missing link can be inferred from the USA, where the service sector developed with similar speed. There this is said to be partially caused by income differentiation (D. Cohen 1998: 44–61). The underlying idea (Iversen and Wren 1998) is that certain parts of the private services, particularly personal services, will grow relatively independently from the pace of economic growth when these services, because of low wage costs, are cheap and when sufficient purchasing power to buy such services emerges. In the USA the required divide in income seems to have occurred.

Does the Dutch development, at least to some extent, resemble this aspect of the 'American jobs machine'? The size of the personal-services sector is much smaller in the Netherlands than in the USA (OECD 2000a: 87), the 'rich-people-buy-cheap-services' nexus must be less prominent, and the usual indices for net income distribution show much lower inequality as well as a much lower increase in it. With respect to the question at stake these statistics are problematic, however. Regularly, they only count (predominantly male) full-time full-year earnings and household incomes. The former has not significantly changed in the past two decades (OECD 1996b), and the latter only grew slightly more unequal. But this may be misleading because the number of households with two incomes has risen sharply (by about 50 per cent from 1982 to 1994; SCP 1998: 225) because the strong increase in female part-time work. On average, part-time jobs are paid 14 per cent less per hour than full-time jobs, however (*ibid.*: 376). Therefore the distribution of household incomes possibly conceals increasing differences in individual per-hour earnings.

An indication of such a trend is the rise of 41 per cent from 1983 to 1994 in the Theil co-efficient of inequality of the total distribution of wages (including the wages of the growing number of part-timers; SCP 1998: 368). For many years the lowest wage scales have been moving in the direction of the minimum wage, which, by being 'frozen' for several years, has sharply declined since the late 1970s, from two-thirds of average income to half. And an increasing number of new jobs, particularly part-time and flexible jobs in the service sector, are offered at a level just above the minimum wage (Delsen 2000: 67; SCP 1996). This trend began in the early 1980s, together with the 'explosion' of female employment (Elfring and Kloosterman 1989; Kloosterman 1994: 177). One has to be cautious here because the statistical base is only fragmentary, but the conclusion to be drawn seems to be that the combination of a per-hour wage differentiation with a rising number of two-income households has brought about increasing demand for as well as the supply of relatively cheap services. The extent and effects of these processes, which are less pronounced than in the US, have still to be studied, but this is true for demand-induced developments as a whole.

In the Dutch politico-ideological climate of the 1980s, which was dominated by austerity goals, the freezing of the minimum wage was intended to reduce the budget deficit (because basic benefits are related to the minimum wage) and, as a second aim, to force the reintegration of the low-skilled unemployed. The latter plan largely failed, but the operation had the effect of creating a labour market for female and juvenile part-timers.

Conclusion: an example of competitive corporatism?

In sum, wage restraint has not been the main cause of the impressive increase in employment in the Netherlands. Intended to advance the Dutch position in international competition, it was barely effective – it did not even enhance labour-intensive production. And the famous consensus on the wage-restraint formula only took shape at a moment when employment had already increased for nearly a decade and when there was some superficial plausibility that this formula was successful. In the 1980s, the unions only reluctantly accepted it – the Accord of Wassenaar in 1982 as the starting point of the Dutch miracle is a myth. As the main ingredients of the Dutch-model discourse, wage restraint and consensus appear to be highly ideological.

The assumption of an international zero-sum employment game proved to be wrong. Global competition is not only about wage costs and prices. This, however, did no harm to the Dutch economy because other mechanisms fuelling job growth emerged. The Netherlands participated in an international upswing in the 1980s and took advantage of German unification as well as of some more favourable circumstances. Most important was the redistribution of work toward part-time jobs, and in the 1990s the country got an extra boost from a house-price and stock-market bubble. Finally, there is the employment effect of income differentiation. Its base was the lowering of the minimum wage in real terms. This operation as well as welfare retrenchment as a whole did not reduce broad unemployment, but it created a fundamental condition for the attraction of relatively cheap part-timers to the service sector.

In a world where boundaries are breaking down, countries and companies cannot evade global competition, and in one way or another they have to adjust to the policies of transnational institutions such as the European Central Bank (ECB) and to transnationally dominant conceptions of economic life such as liberalism or Keynesianism. Moreover, they depend on global and, still more important, regional business cycles. All this, however, is not completely new. Under capitalism, territorial states have always had only limited economic autonomy. Perhaps it is continuously diminishing, but it has not totally vanished. The Dutch case demonstrates that domestic processes are still very important for economic and employment development. Much more than the beggar-thy-neighbour policies, it was the unplanned and unco-ordinated mix of work redistribution, consumer demand and service-sector growth that brought about success.

The lesson to be drawn from this is that there are still possibilities for successful national employment policies. To create a demand bubble by intention is impossible and unhealthy, and in Euroland the (currently) restrictive stance of the ECB limits any form of Keynesianism. Some space for fiscal policies to influence demand, however, remains. And the stimulation of part-time work is a purely domestic matter. The same is largely true for extending employment in the service sector. Income differentiation, with its problematical effect of enlarging inequality, is only one alternative. The other one is the Scandinavian way of creating jobs in the public services of healthcare and education. This possibility depends, of course, on the willingness of the people to pay the necessary taxes, and given the increasing international mobility of capital it depends more and more on the willingness of the wage-earners to pay high income and indirect taxes (Iversen and Wren 1998). Perhaps this willingness is eroding, and perhaps this is an international trend (George 1998). Nonetheless, turning this tide would first of all be a national effort.

Whatever route is chosen, competitiveness of the national economy is a general condition; competitiveness in terms of location, productivity, quality, price and – something that has become important in certain branches, e.g. cars – image. It is in this context that one has to ask whether 'competitive corporatism' is a viable option. The idea is that by a capital–labour consensus on wage moderation and labour-market flexibilization productivity growth will be guaranteed and new jobs created, and that generous standards of social welfare and a low level of inequality can be secured. In this sense, competitive corporatism is thought to be a Third Way-style social route of keeping competitiveness in the age of globalization. And the Dutch development serves as the example (Rhodes 2001; see also Chapters 4 and 10 of this volume).

The example presented, however, is the rosy-cosy development according to the Dutch-model discourse which has been criticized in this chapter. A diffusion of competitive corporatism in line with the devices of the real Dutch case would imply the generalization of ineffective and counterproductive beggar-thy-neighbour strategies with respect to wages and taxes really endangering the world economy to become a zero-sum game. Would that be a social route? Moreover, the concepts of corporatism and consensus deployed in this theory are highly problematical. Besides the fact that corporatism needs a favourable breeding ground, it always includes power relations, and corporatist bargaining always operates in the context of more or less hegemonic discourses. Whatever is called a consensus depends on these relations. So, the question is whether the unions would have the power to secure welfare and equality standards in exchange for concessions on the wage front. Another question is on what common national interest – the roof of corporatism – labour and capital should agree in a situation where more and more companies operate as transnational players.

These arguments are not necessarily against any form of 'competitive corporatism'. They point to weak elements in this theory. Perhaps there is even an alternative to the currently discussed variety – at least where corporatism is feasible at all. Apart from the possibility of transnational – for example European – unions meeting transnational capital (largely hypothetical at this moment), one could also think about the acceptance of the national–transnational divide between unions and employers. Unions would have to concentrate on the strong aspects of their national environments – infrastructure, reliability, skill levels, networks – which relate to what P.A. Hall and Soskice (2001) call 'comparative institutional advantages'. In a global competition that is understood as quality competition these advantages could be the very power bases of labour. Mobile capital would have to learn that it has something to lose by abandoning the welfare state altogether.

Notes

1 For the figures on 1983 and 1990 as well as the calculation of the labour volume, see U. Becker (2001: 40, n. 7).

2 The OECD also reports a slight increase in employment in manufacturing (2000a: 108). If one adds up the figures it presents about the different service branches (*ibid.*: 84–8) this information becomes doubtful, however.

3 For Britain, Denmark (scoring surprisingly low), Germany, New Zealand and the USA the figures were 7.34, 8.08, 4.02, 7.43 and 6.97, respectively. These figures reflect managers' views. On the same scale, research by the OECD on the dismissal legislation in 1989 revealed scores of 4.91 for the Netherlands, 8.42 for Britain, 7.72 for Denmark, 1.58 for Germany, 9.49 for New Zealand and 9.75 for the USA (Empter and Esche 1997: 193).

4 Wassenaar is a wealthy suburb of the Dutch seat of government the Hague, making the location particularly symbolic for what took place there.

5 See also the internet site of the Federal Reserve Bank: http://www.federalreserve.gov/boarddocs/. For Denmark, see Finansministeriet, *The Danish Economy: Medium Term Economic Survey*, Copenhagen 1999, part 1: 6 (http://www.fm.dk/udgivelser/publicationer/survey99).

6 In 1992 household income made up 80 per cent of total disposable income; in 1997 this share was 75 per cent. Maintained at the level of 80 per cent, the households' disposable income would have been 27 billion guilders higher, in two years about 50 billion (data from Central Bureau voor de Statistiek).

7 The data are taken from *NRC Handelsblad* (8 September 1998 and 22 February 2000). The figures on consumed mortgages are estimates that fluctuate somewhat. So on 23 June 2000 the *NRC Handelsblad* reported that according to the Dutch central bank 39 billion guilders taken from mortgages had gone into consumption and shares in the period from 1996 to 1999, an amount that is lower than the CBS estimate for 1996–7.

10 The political economy of labour-market restructuring and trade union responses in the social-democratic heartland[1]

Magnus Ryner and Thorsten Schulten

Introduction

In an essay written at the beginning of the 1990s, Robert Cox (1993; see also 1987: 289–98) held up the hope that European regionalization might give rise to a counter-hegemonic project that would challenge neo-liberal global governance. His argument was based on the idea that the 'state capitalism' prevalent in continental Western Europe and Scandinavia potentially provided the basis for an alternative economic rationality that might clash with the hyper-liberal tendency with its roots in interests centred in the Anglo-Saxon world. Hence, the sovereignties pooled through the fledgling European Union (EU), Cox argued, could potentially become the locus of mobilization for social forces that, *contra* neo-liberalism, were concerned with a more equitable and socially reflexive development of the world order. A crucial factor in whether or not such a development would take place, according to Cox, was whether European social forces could transcend their nationalist economic corporate consciousness. In this chapter we analyse one category of civil societal agency in this part of Europe which is crucial for the realization of this potential: the trade unions. It is generally acknowledged that the strategic orientation and capacity of organized labour is critical to the prospects of realizing the potential to synthesize economic rationality with social equity within what Cox called 'state-capitalism' (and what later has become known as 'Rhineland capitalism'; Albert 1993).

Our analysis of socio-political developments in the 1990s does not augur particularly well for Cox's hopes. The prevailing tendency of restructuring of 'Rhineland capitalism' is towards integration into a world and regional order increasingly reflecting the Anglo-Saxon neo-liberal ideal, and potential sources of antagonism have been successfully managed in a way that favours such neo-liberalism. It should be pointed out in this context that we argue that trade unionists have not so much internalized the ideological *contents* of neo-liberal norms. Although trade unions sometimes seem to accept elements of the neo-liberal agenda, they usually continue to critique neo-liberal restructuring and search for strategies of opposition. However, the *institutional forms* that are at their disposal, whether on the national or regional level are increasingly *integrated into* a neo-liberal form of governance that expresses the structural power of capital. It is the loyalty of trade unions to these fora in, for example, their fight against unemployment that interpolates trade unions into the neo-liberal power bloc.

Our argument is based on a multi-level analysis which relates global developments to the emerging European political-economic space, and to the national level, especially in Sweden, Germany and, to some extent, the Netherlands. The Netherlands is an interesting point of reference because it is the case of successful articulation of 'Rhineland capitalism' to neo-liberalism *par excellence*. Sweden is interesting for the opposite reason; it is the paradigmatic case of a realized social democracy. Germany is interesting because of the importance of the German state in the forging of any regional hegemony in the EU.

In the first part of the chapter we analyse the nature of 'post-Fordist' transformation and the socio-economic forces that it engenders in capitalism, especially in the areas of the labour market and in work organization (see also Chapter 3). It is our premise that this is the appropriate context in which to situate questions concerning unemployment and employment. The second part of the chapter focuses much more directly on trade union strategy and its structural and institutional context as discussed in the first section. We show how unions have been forced into a defensive position as issues pertaining to the restructuring of work and the labour market are increasingly being captured by neo-liberal socio-political forces engaged in a project of neo-liberal deepening. Unions have been politically captured by a neo-liberal politics of 'competitive corporatism' and competitive austerity at the national level, not only in the Netherlands but also in Sweden and Germany, as well as in most other EU countries. At the European level they have been politically captured through a new form of 'symbolic Euro-corporatism', expressed through the so-called 'European social dialogue' and the common employment strategy. Such symbolic corporatism offers little of substance, but that ensures that the unions become part of the increasingly problematic effort of ensuring the legitimacy of the neo-liberal integration project. We conclude by discussing two prospective strategies for escaping these traps of political capture: the attempt to co-ordinate bargaining transnationally among European trade unions and the attempt to reform the European Monetary Union (EMU). In the former case, the unions are trying to develop joint bargaining principles in order to prevent downward competition on wages and working conditions, which became even more likely under the conditions of EMU. In the latter case, unions have been disappointed by the direction taken by social-democratic governments in power. The defeat of the Lafontaine-wing in the German government especially constitutes a lost opportunity for the trade unions. This defeat, however, also expresses their weakness in the political arena at the turn of the twenty-first century.

Capitalist restructuring of work and labour markets

No serious analysis of trade union strategy can ignore the paradigmatic transformation of work organization and labour markets since the early 1980s as a result of economic, social and technological change. In this section we will seek to identify the specific causal powers at work in this transformation and relate them to one another in order to clarify the structural constraints and prospects for trade union action in Europe. In particular, we invoke regulation-theoretical research, which relates technological change to the different moments in the overall circuit of expanded capitalist reproduction and explains how such change may or may not help sustain the coherence of this circuit and hence maintain order in capitalist society (e.g. Aglietta 1979; Lipietz 1985; Boyer 1989). The conclusion of regulation-theoretical research has been that nothing inherently neo-liberal is implied in the logic of contemporary socio-economic restructuring. Rather, different potential 'post-Fordist' accumulation trajectories have been identified. Some of these not only are compatible with the labour-inclusive aspects of Fordism – full employment and an *ex ante* integration of the expansion of mass production and mass consumption in economic development – but could also potentially be made compatible with more ambitious aspirations of industrial democracy (e.g. Leborgne and Lipietz 1988; Boyer 1997).

Regulation-theoretical research has reached these conclusions through theoretically informed empirical research of different experimental corporate responses in the Organization for Economic Co-operation and Development (OECD) region to the 'crisis of Fordism'[2] expressed through the 'stagflation' of the 1970s and the attendant profits squeeze. These responses entailed different mixes of cost-cutting strategies and production-technological innovation, and they have set the conditions for a new phase of capitalist development based on new core products and processes. At the most abstract level, 'post-Fordist' production is based on cybernetic automation of industrial processes and a breakdown of information bottlenecks. This allows for increased capital intensity, a reconnection of conception and execution without productivity losses (especially through computer-assisted integration of design, management and manufacturing, CAD/CAM), as well as more flexible adjustment to demand (Kaplinsky 1984). One of the most important contributions of regulation theory has been the ideal-typical sketch of different possible regimes of post-Fordist capital accumulation. Here, macroeconomic implications are inferred from the observation of microeconomic experimentation in the 1980s (Leborgne and Lipietz 1988).

Post-Fordist possibilities

Certainly, *flexible neo-liberalism* provides the basis of one possible post-Fordist trajectory. Here, the economies of CAD/CAM and 'general-purpose machines' are facilitated through the elimination of collective bargaining and the use of individual contracts, incentives and threats, and numerically flexible wages, all used to create an 'enterprise-corporate' culture. Flexible neo-liberalism implies labour-market polarization, with a shrinking core workforce with enterprise-corporate contracts and a growing periphery of precariously employed. However, on the basis of corporate experiments in Sweden, Germany and

Northern Italy, Leborgne and Lipietz (1988) argue that another trajectory is more compatible with trade unionism. The premise of the *negotiated-involvement* model is that numerical flexibility of wages is not essential for post-Fordism but wages can continue to be set through bi- or tripartite collective bargaining. Rather, co-determination provides an organizational form for *functional flexibility* – or 'networking and skill to adjust volume to demand without productivity-losses' (Amin 1994b: 20–1) – compatible with the application of CAD/CAM technology and general-purpose machines. In this model, active labour-market policy facilitates workforce training and mobility, and collective bargaining provides for a solidaristic distribution of work, wages and leisure in exchange for public goods such as the stable supply of a skilled workforce and public provisions cutting social overheads (such as healthcare and childcare). The final ideal-type is the *neo-Taylorist* model, where new technology is merely used in a Fordist way to increase capital intensity and to extend further the separation between conception and execution.

Considered from the point of view of the functionalist requisites for expanded reproduction, the different models have different macroeconomic strengths and vulnerabilities. One central strength of the negotiated-involvement model is that collectively bargained wages and social entitlements (operating as 'automatic stabilizers') could still integrate expanding production with demand and consumption *ex ante*. This would mean that flexible adjustment and economies of scope could be combined with other economies, like capacity utilization and returns to scale, adequate investment levels, and a stable environment and time-horizons for 'learning by doing'. At the same time, however, this model seems to *presuppose* stable and expanding aggregate demand. Apart from the role that demand expansion in and of itself plays in productivity increases, this is because of the limited scope for cost cutting during contracting demand in the negotiated-involvement scenario. Hence it requires a Keynesian dimension. This is further reinforced by the fact that it is associated with tight labour markets that increase the capacity of labour to sustain solidaristic wage policy and assert demands for meaningful co-determination in the production process (Sandberg *et al.* 1992; Pontusson 1992b). Furthermore, wage rigidity tendentially shifts the burden of adjustment to capital as it requires capital accumulation at lower profit/value-added ratios and/or as it sets higher demands for innovation – a 'Schumpeterian dimension'. This in turn sets a higher demand for stable and predictable access to sources of finance and other public goods such as vocational training.

A weakness of the flexible-liberal model is that (especially downward) wage flexibility set *ex post* may mean that it encounters difficulties in generating sufficient demand for a sustained new growth phase and it may be associated with wide business-cycle fluctuations. It may also have difficulties in generating adequate public goods such as vocational training (Albo 1994: 150–3). But the former problem might possibly be compensated for by intensified consumption by the upper middle class, and especially a reduced turnover time in consumption in, especially, the service sector. Moreover, the financial sector has also become very flexible in terms of managing slumps and booms, through risk management and credit extension (Harvey 1989: chs 10 and 11). It should be noted, however, that these are services for which it exerts rents, although the financial sector itself is responsible for much of the risk (Strange 1989). One should also not forget territorial expansion as a possible mechanism to sustain accumulation.[3] Moreover, of course, numerical wage flexibility allows for wage reductions as an instrument to sustain profit rates. Together these measures may prove sufficient to displace contradictions in capital accumulation.

The nature of the financial sector is a critical factor upon which the direction of post-Fordist capitalist development hinges. The currently predominant trend towards more market-based and globalized finance operates tendentially both as an obstacle to negotiated involvement and as an impetus for flexible liberalism. The balance-of-payments constraints and the shortening of time-horizons in investment associated with globalization and marketization of finance constitute severe obstacles to the welfarist, Keynesian and Schumpeterian requisites of negotiated involvement. With regard to the latter prerequisite, increased markets for risk management and increased competition in corporate finance spurred on by informatics are important. They provide incentives for a breakdown of voice-based links between banks and firms, as well as a relative focus on financial transaction as such (including mergers and acquisition), as opposed to production-process innovation. With regard to the former prerequisites, rents exert inhibiting costs on the prospects for public-sector expansion as well as fiscal and monetary stimuli, especially in the present context of high debt ratios. Whether this takes the form of higher deficits, increases in inflation (in relation to other currencies) or taxes, currency markets will punish such moves with higher interest rates and 'risk premiums' on currencies. Moreover, in a context where all states try to run surpluses to reduce their debt burden the result is a reduction in demand growth in the world economy and 'competitive austerity'.[4] At the same time, the increased importance of risk management as an economic activity and the rent it exerts provide the basis for an expanding financial services industry, organized along flexible-liberal lines (Sassen 1991). This may provide neo-liberal accumulation with a 'core product'. The consequence of all these trends is that global finance operates as a formidable bias for flexible neo-liberalism and against negotiated involvement. Hence, the question of *regulation* of financial markets is central to the question of whether flexible liberalism or negotiated involvement prevails as the hegemonic regime of accumulation.

A regime of accumulation based 'purely' on neo-Taylorism is unlikely. Due to expensive overheads it requires stable market outlets, but undermines these through increased capital intensity, unemployment and a breakdown of the Fordist *ex ante* wage relation. However, the model remains relevant because a 'fallacy of composition' is possible (what is 'irrational' on a macro level might be rational for the individual components), engendering an 'organic crisis of production'. But, perhaps more importantly, there is evidence that suggests that no concrete case of economic restructuring follows the ideal types 'purely', but, rather, they articulate elements from all models. Taylorist practices might survive as a subordinate mode in the dual economy or 'sunset' sectors (notably in the consumer-service sector). Moreover, corporate strategy may employ elements of the different models in attempts to combine economies of scope and scale. For example, corporations may combine flexible processes with a scale and mergers designed to retain price-setting privileges in their markets (Amin and Malmberg 1994). The mixing of Fordist/Taylorist elements makes scale more relevant and decreases the capacity of market adaptation of flexible liberalism to fluctuating and sluggish demand. However, insofar as strategies of scale have become transnational, it also generates further balance-of-payments constraints for the reflationary requisites of a negotiated involvement strategy, as well as constraints on industrial policy.

Post-Fordist restructuring in Europe

The European monetary regime seems to operate against the interest of organized labour in the regulation of the process of post-Fordist restructuring. This is because, whether in the guise of the European Monetary System (EMS) or the post-Maastricht and post-Dublin 'Stability Pact' EMU, it is exactly this organization that provides the institutional framework through which global finance exerts market discipline in Europe. This is not merely a question of global markets constraining individual states. Through the monetary arrangements of the EMS and the EMU, states, here represented above all by central banks and finance ministries, deliberately use these markets as steering mechanisms to exert monetary discipline and its primacy over employment and social commitments. In the EMS, this policy was exerted through the *Exchange Rate Mechanism* (ERM), which generalized the monetarist norms of the German Bundesbank and its management of the 'anchor currency' (the Deutschmark) on the basis of the strict norm of price stability. Other states then 'imported' the stability through the internationally determined rate of interest (and the 'risk premium' that market operators required to hold other currencies as opposed to the Deutschmark). When the third stage of the EMU was completed, this 'automatic' form of adjustment was exchanged for treaty provisions in the form of the *convergence criteria* that became the basis for the *Stability Pact.*

This European monetary regime, which constitutes the commanding heights of European economic governance, is primarily designed to avoid inflation at any cost. It has, however, had detrimental effects on the European model of 'Rhineland capitalism' and its prospects of institutionalizing a viable post-Fordist mode of regulation. Already before the Maastricht Treaty had been signed, Lipietz (1989) and Boyer (1990) warned of the effects that competitive austerity would have. According to Boyer, most European labour-market institutions tended to be a problematic 'hybrid' where neo-Taylorist forms predominated in a mix with either flexible-liberal or negotiated-involvement forms. In the context of sluggish demand, they were unlikely to accrue flexibility benefits from one (market-flexible wages) or the other (concerted macro-level wage-economic policy integration), and the likely outcome, he argued, would be mass unemployment.

Branch-level wage-negotiation systems would hence be at a crossroads, and would have to adjust either to the flexible-liberal model or the negotiated-involvement model. But the latter would require stable and sustained growth in aggregate demand, and an effective social charter that would prevent flexible-liberal 'defections' from this regime. A Single Market without these provisions would most likely increase core–periphery tensions. Low-productivity regions, competing for scarce and increasingly mobile investment resources in a context of increased regional specialization, would have no resort to exchange-rate adjustments. These regions would increasingly have to rely on social cutbacks to such an extent that it would even endanger social standards in the core, as they would be increasingly subject to 'social dumping' and a shortfall of export demand (see also Shepley and Wilmont 1995).

Developments in Sweden, Germany and the Netherlands in the 1990s verified these fears. The promising corporate experiments with negotiated-involvement strategies have on the whole been discontinued and have given way to more flexible-liberal strategies. While there have been important contingencies affecting this development, there is strong evidence that the disciplinary neo-liberal monetary regime has played a critical role in determining this development. This is mainly because it has engendered pro-cyclical policies combined with highly volatile exchange and/or interest rates.

Despite the fact that German monetary policy has been at the core of the disciplinary neo-liberal monetary regime in Europe since the 1970s, the exceedingly strong position of the manufacturing export sector has made it possible for Germany to combine this with a more social-market-oriented domestic growth model. This encouraged negotiated-involvement solutions in the 1980s. Since the mid-1980s Germany has seen a shift from a primarily technology-oriented path of rationalization towards more organization-oriented rationalization strategies. The introduction of new forms of work organization seemed to create a basis for a new 'modernization compromise' between capital and labour since it was hoped to improve labour productivity and working conditions at the same time (Bahnmüller 1996).

Against that background, it was also possible to integrate the unions into the power bloc that underpinned disciplinary neo-liberal monetary policy in Europe (Streeck 1995c). In fact, the 'hard Mark' policy reduced the real price for industrial inputs (especially oil) and consumer goods and thus increased the scope for real wage increases. This, combined with the fact that pegged exchange rates prevented competitive devaluations by potential West European competitors gave Germany strong incentives to support the EMS (eg. Riemer 1982; Lankowski 1982). German unions would have preferred a more employment-oriented economic policy and an expansion of social services qua the Scandinavian model (Markovits and Allen 1984). However, co-determination, the German apprenticeship system and other forms of selective labour-market policy, as well as working-time reductions made it possible to contain unemployment (which nevertheless rose), maintain a solidaristic wage and work policy, and manage limited wage dispersion (Swenson 1989: 177–223; Flecker and Schulten 1999).

In the 1990s, however, it seemed as if competitive austerity had caught up with German developments. German industrial development was subjected to powerful pro-cyclical shock generated by the attempt to unify the former German Democratic Republic (GDR) with the Federal Republic of Germany (FRG) without altering the regime of monetary and financial governance. Part of the problem was the rapid increase in the interest and exchange rates resulting from the combination of tight monetary policy and pro-cyclical policy (*inter alia*, OECD 1991–9). Another problem which became prevalent in the middle of the 1990s was the reduction of demand in, especially, the European export market. This development is directly linked to the generalization of German-style monetarism through the Maastricht Convergence Criteria and the Stability Pact, as well as to the generalized effect of Germany's aforementioned post-unification macroeconomic policy stance. A final factor behind this development was the structural implications of incorporating the GDR into the Federal Republic. Given the lack of competitiveness of industry in eastern Germany and the burden it puts on transfer payments, reunification has seriously undermined the prospects for the export-oriented growth model and the prospects of combining monetarism and the social market in Germany (Bonder *et al.* 1992). Mass unemployment and increased capital intensity have also generated a fiscal crisis in Germany's pay-as-you-go social-insurance systems. With pressures towards increases in claims and decreases in revenue, individual social contributions have increased in order to make up the gap, but this has increased unit labour costs further, inhibited service-sector employment growth and further enforced the incentives to substitute labour for capital (Esping-Andersen 1996).

As a result of this, German corporations favour more flexible-liberal solutions, emphasizing outsourcing, wage segmentation and cost reductions, which fundamentally questions the modernization compromise of negotiated involvement. Under the conditions of increased competitive pressure and a growing 'short-termism' coming from shareholder-value orientation, many companies have turned away from negotiated involvement towards a strategy of flexible neo-liberalism which often includes strong elements of a 're-Taylorization' of work (Bahnmüller 1996; Schumann 1998; Schulten 1999a; Dörre 2000).[5] Outsourcing and the shifting of adjustment costs to subcontractors have contributed to an uneven development within economic sectors. This has, in turn, increased the pressure on unions to accept 'negative wage drift' – that is, local concessions to the sectoral wage norms (*Flachentarif*) negotiated centrally. The implication of this is a creeping erosion of the German system of collective bargaining (Flecker and Schulten 1999).

All in all, demands for neo-liberal reform in Germany have become increasingly pervasive. Contrary to the predictions of many in the 1980s, this is not accompanied by demands to abandon corporatist institutions.[6] Rather, following the example of the Netherlands, corporatist procedures are seen as the main form through which such restructuring is to take place. Corporatism is seen as a way of engaging trade unions, weakened by mass unemployment, to establish welfare-state retrenchment in nationwide concession bargaining aimed at containing wage demands, to secure increased wage segmentation and to reduce and differentiate social insurance benefit levels, in exchange for increased employment. This is the rationale of the position of business and employers, as well as of the increasingly predominant social democratic 'Third Way modernizers' of the Social-Democratic/Green government, in Germany's 'Alliance for Jobs' negotiations (Bispinck and Schulten 2000).

In contrast to Germany, the Netherlands is widely regarded as a successful model for post-Fordist restructuring.[7] Following the 'Dutch disease' (Therborn 1986) of the 1980s, with high unemployment levels and low participation rates, in the 1990s the Netherlands saw a prospering economic development and were able to bring official unemployment down to 3.5 per cent in 2000 (Centraal Planbureau 2000). The 'Dutch miracle' has been interpreted as a successful 'self-transformation of a negotiated economy' which led to an adjustment of social security and labour-market regulation on the basis of strong corporatist arrangements (Visser and Hemerijck 1997; Hemerijck *et al.* 2000). The results of these arrangements have been moderate wage developments and less generous social insurance. They have also led to new institutionalized provisions for temporary and part-time work (through employment with temporary-work agencies or *uitzendburos*), as well as new labour-market policy programmes, which mainly aim to strengthen the employees' employability. It should also be pointed out, however, that Dutch income inequalities are increasing at the fastest rate in the OECD (albeit from a comparatively low level; Clayton and Pontusson 1998). Most of these reforms have been made with and through active trade union collaboration for the sake of promoting employment.

There is a broad consensus that the large extension of part-time work was a major source of employment growth in the Netherlands. Furthermore, taking into account the still very high number of early retired, the Dutch 'job miracle' is to a large extent the result of a significant redistribution of work (Schmid 1997). In addition to that, most authors believe that the moderate wage developments have been another major source of the Dutch employment record. Thus, the Dutch case appears to prove one of the core tenets of neo-liberal ideology, namely that wage restraint creates employment. The latter might also be the major reason why the Netherlands has become a 'model case' for policy-making elites in Europe in their search for 'best practice' (eg. EC 1997c). More recently, however, some authors have argued that even in the Dutch case the relation between wages and employment is far from clear (Kleinknecht 1998; Reuten 1998; Schulten 1999b; see Chapter 9 of this volume for a detailed analysis).

Despite the impact of strong corporatist arrangements, what has often been underestimated in explaining the employment record of the 'Dutch model' is the role of both structural and cyclical economic development. First of all the Netherlands successfully managed to extend their service sector, which became the major field for the creation of employment (Visser and Hemerijck 1997). Furthermore, particular niches of the Dutch economy offer particularly good conditions for the expansion of high value-added service production (especially considering its position as a transportation hub). Finally, employment growth in the Netherlands has a strong cyclical dimension. Its phase of expansion was the mid-1990s, which was a period of high economic growth, driven in particular by growth in exports on the one hand and a sharp increase in private consumption on the other (Centraal Planbureau 2000; see Chapter 9 of this volume for more detail).

Developments in Sweden in the 1980s pointed towards a more advanced level of negotiated involvement, where there was a tendential development towards generalizing it to the entire economy. The development of an extensive service sector, absorbing surplus labour from manufacturing and, even more to the point, creating employment opportunities for women, set Sweden and its Scandinavian neighbours apart (Esping-Andersen 1990). Keeping a commitment to 'decommodification' and continuing to draw on the general prescriptions of the 'Rehn–Meidner model' (Hedborg and Meidner 1984; Erixon 1994),[8] this strategy was based on high tax rates, solidaristic wage policy and selective labour-market policy (especially vocational retraining and sophisticated employment exchanges). Here, some of the market-determined surplus of the high-productivity export-oriented manufacturing sector was redistributed to finance public social services. The service sector, in turn, served 'reproductive functions' (childcare, healthcare, and the prevention and rehabilitation of injuries) and generated user-producer networks in a national system of innovation by pursuing spin-off effects between healthcare and the pharmaceutical sector, for instance.

What most of the benevolent accounts of these developments ignored, though, was that the Rehn–Meidner model had presupposed the 'double screen'[9] of the Bretton Woods system. The Bretton Woods system ensured international demand expansion for Sweden's dependent economy (Mjöset 1987). At the same time, its provisions for credit regulation made it possible to render low and stable interest rates compatible with strict counter-cyclical fine-tuning of the domestic economy. This facilitated capital accumulation at low rates of profit (A. Martin 1986; Ryner 2002: ch. 4). When Europe's monetary regime became monetarist and centred around the Bundesbank, Sweden initially tried to shield employment promotion by devaluing the Krona and flanking this with incomes policies. When this failed to contain inflation, Swedish policy-makers embraced the European monetarist regime: capital markets were deregulated and interest-rate discipline was exerted (Notermans 1993), first through the pegging of the Krona to the EMS, and later through an explicit inflation target and a commitment to the Stability Pact. Whilst formally Sweden remains outside the Third Stage of the EMU, its economic policy is entrenched in the European monetary regime. Swedish monetary policy, and to a lesser extent fiscal policy, generated a highly pro-cyclical and volatile development in the late 1980s and early 1990s that pre-empted the negotiated-involvement trajectory. The last of the post-Bretton Woods devaluations in 1982 generated an export and profits boom. When the monetary regime was changed in 1985 the effect was pro-cyclical rather than anti-cyclical. Credit-market deregulation increased the money supply through credit expansion. It seems that the Swedish Social Democratic Party

(Sveriges socialdemokratiska arbetarparti; SAP) government had hoped to contain inflation by increasing the discipline on trade unions, by increasing the sensitivity of the interest rates to international credit markets (Ryner 1999; Ryner 2002: ch. 7). But this rather astonishing breach of the post-war accord between unions and the state had the opposite effect. Interest-rate increases added to the inter-union rivalry that wage drift in the export sector combined with attempts at a wage freeze in the public sector had already engendered. Co-ordinated wage bargaining at the macro level broke down, with the encouragement of the employers, who at this time were working for a decentralization of wage bargaining (De Geer 1989). In addition, productivity growth stagnated: corporations increasingly invested abroad (Andersson 1993);[10] too-high profit rates retarded transformation pressure in the economy (Erixon 1989) and generated a speculative bubble in real estate, that subsequently burst in the downturn of the early 1990s. The downturn became very sharp. The attendant increase in unemployment from 2 to 9 per cent in a few years, the bailout of bankrupt banks and increases in interest rates (resulting from speculation against the Krona), as well as an underfinanced tax reform (Ljunggren 1993), forced austerity measures that led to negative annual growth in the period 1991–4 (OECD 1994). At this time, Swedish corporations assumed the more defensive corporate strategy of labour shedding, cost cutting and 'lean production' (*ibid.*), and experiments such as that of Volvo were abandoned due to the needs of short-term consolidation (Sandberg 1994). The Swedish economy subsequently recovered in the late 1990s, but it is following a different growth trajectory with higher profit-to-social-wage ratios; reduced benefit levels in the social-insurance system; more inequality; a reduced public-service sector; and increased wage and income inequality – that is, labour-market segmentation; application of lean production; and disturbing signs of the reappearance of poverty (*inter alia*, OECD 1999; Statistics Sweden 2000; Eklund 1999; Mossler *et al.* 1999).

Trade unions between competitive corporatism and symbolic Euro-corporatism

The previous section illustrated that, while the logic of post-Fordism could be rendered compatible with a socio-economic development that would sustain and even extend the interests of organized labour (in the form of 'negotiated involvement'), the *mode of regulation* that is being instituted in Europe rather favours a regime of accumulation based on neo-liberal flexibility. Modes of regulation, however, do not emerge merely as automatic responses to functional imperatives; they are instituted through socio-political struggles, where accumulation strategies and hegemonic projects are advanced (Jessop 1990: ch. 7). Viewed from this vantage point the European monetary regime, first organized through the EMS and then the EMU, is at the apex of the institutional arrangement that organizes transnational neo-liberal hegemony in Europe. The main principle of rule of this institutional arrangement has been to use the territorial non-coincidence (Murray 1971) between the spatial scale of operation of global capital-market and nation-state policy to exert market discipline of the latter and make them serve neo-liberal interests and norms (Gill 1992, 1998).

This understanding of the European moment of transnational hegemony draws on Robert Cox's (1983: 137) adaptation of Gramsci's (1991: 1,561ff.) notion of the 'extended state' to make sense of transnational relations. As the 'Amsterdam School' has argued, this hegemonic project implies a particular configuration of capitalist class formation, where financial fractions and export-oriented and transnationally mobile productive capital have achieved class leadership in the forging of the European economy and fledgling civil society, and thus exercise profound influence on the process of European integration (Holman and van der Pijl 1996; van Apeldoorn 1998). However, hegemony, as a paradigm for exercising modern power, implies forging the consent of subordinate classes and groups. This implies adequate material concessions to these groups as well as a credible claim to represent the 'general will'. Ultimately this is the domain of political society and the state, and the international organizations that had grown out of state action and acquired a 'life of their own' sustained by economic transnationalization and transnational socialization.

> The concept of an international historic bloc means much more than an alliance of capitalist interests across boundaries. It implies that elements of more than one class were involved, its basis was more organic and rooted in materials and normative structures of society, that is in the governmental and social institutions of a number of countries.
>
> (Gill and Law 1993: 97)

Consider in this light the EMU. Whilst its configuration certainly most transparently represents the interests of transnationally mobile, export-oriented productive capital, it is not merely that. Insofar as it has ultimately been grounded in the authority of the Bundesbank, it also presupposes the integration of German organized labour into the 'German model'. In addition, one can only explain why the EMU obtained the configuration that it did by referring to 'non-economic' factors, such as the French concern with a too-dominant Germany in the EU. Ultimately, the European monetary governance assumed the shape of the EMU as opposed to an extension of the EMS because an end to German unilateralism in European monetary policy was a French quid pro quo for accepting German unification (Sandholtz 1993). These additional dimensions of the EMU have been necessary in order to ensure the requisite *universalization* of norms that a hegemonic project presupposes (Bieling and Steinhilber 2000). As a result, the complexities of the state–society configurations that constitute historic blocs tend to become contradictory. For example, with the EMU the principle of territorial non-coincidence has been attenuated since the exit option of swaps from one European economy to another has disappeared. As a result, the Stability Pact, a framework for broader transnational economic governance, had to be created. The problem with such a broadening, from the point of view of neo-liberal hegemony, is that such a framework is more vulnerable to being captured by an alternative political project. It is in this context that one best views the vehemence with which Oskar Lafontaine's attempts to infuse more Keynesian elements into these institutions were met (Lafontaine 1999).

Given the strong position of the trade union movement in the 'Rhineland capitalist' area and the well-entrenched corporatist structures, the relatively successful integration of the trade unions on the national and European level remains an important resource of political legitimation and stabilization for the EU. In other words, it is also important to consider the role of the trade unions in the transnational state–civil society complex of the EU. In what follows we show how the trade unions have been politically captured by the hegemonic project of neo-liberal restructuring in Europe, despite the biases that it has engendered in post-Fordist restructuring. We argue that this integration is based on integrating trade unions into segmented 'national competitive corporatisms' on the one hand and into a 'symbolic Euro-corporatism' on the other. And, indeed, it is the trade union concern with unemployment in the context of unions' weakness in the light of capital mobility that provides the main impetus of this integration.

Competitive corporatism

One of the most notable misjudgements of the literature on post-Fordism was that if the neo-liberal variant was to prevail this would be synonymous with the end of national corporatism (e.g. Lash and Urry 1987). This prognosis was no doubt based on a projection of the crisis of the Fordist corporatism of the 1970s, but in retrospect one must conclude that the evidence at the turn of the twenty-first century points towards a revival of corporatism. With the exception of the United Kingdom and France, in all European countries there exists some form of national concert between the state, capital and labour (Ferner and Hyman 1998; Fajertag and Pochet 2000).

The contents and the function of the new post-Fordist social pacts have, however, changed in relation to those in the Fordist era. Changes from 'demand-side corporatism' to 'supply-side corporatism' (Traxler 2000) or from 'social corporatism' to 'competitive corporatism' (Rhodes 1998) are some of the formulations that have been used to capture the change. The social corporatism of the 1950s, 1960s and 1970s was part and parcel of the Keynesian policy paradigm of macroeconomic steering. As such it was based on a 'social compromise' whereby trade unions accepted productivity-oriented wage norms in exchange for redistributive taxation, welfare-state expansion and extension of co-determination rights (Mesch 1984). Competitive corporatism, on the contrary, has as its primary objective of regulation the increase of national competitiveness. It is intended to contribute to this objective by facilitating a comprehensive restructuring of wage, social and tax policy, which is achieved through one or another form of *national social pact* (Hassel 1999), such as the Dutch Wassenaar Accord and its successors (Visser and Hemerijck 1997; see Chapter 9 of this volume) or the German 'Alliance for Jobs' negotiations rounds (Bispnick and Schulten 2000).[11] The three defining features of these pacts are:

1 Committing the trade unions to wage restraint, wherein wage increases remain below productivity increases, and wherein an increased segmentation of wages and incomes is accepted.
2 Flexibilizing the labour markets and welfare-state institutions and reducing social wage costs.
3 Restructuring the taxation system so that taxation gradually shifts towards indirect taxes and in particular so that corporate taxation rates are reduced.

These social pacts fundamentally change the nature of the 'social compromise', which becomes increasingly asymmetrical and unfavourable to labour: trade unions are asked to provide certain effective guarantees in exchange for the rather vague, and by no means ensured, hope that this will induce increased employment. Furthermore, this social compromise precludes any demands to actually redistribute realized profits. Finally, trade unions are expected to adopt the neo-liberal credo that it is high social wage costs and an over-regulation of business that have caused the economic problems of European welfare states. In sum, 'social pacts are not fundamentally about an alternative to [neo-liberal] reforms. [They are] rather about securing the social acceptability of such reform through the political capture of the parties of the labour market [into this reform project]' (Hassel 1999: 10; our translation; see also van Apeldoorn's notion of embedded neo-liberalism in Chapter 7).

The revival of corporatism in Western Europe is, above all, a reaction against the legitimation deficit of the neo-liberal hegemonic project in the 1990s. The 'hard neo-liberal line' was not able to prevail in any West European country except the United Kingdom (see Chapter 8). Although the trade unions were on the defensive in most countries, they were still strong enough to defend the inner institutional core of the Fordist welfare state (Bieling and Deppe 1997). Whereas the trade unions successfully blocked neo-liberal restructuring when they were provoked in open confrontation, competitive corporatism has proved itself an effective medium for co-opting the trade unions into this restructuring. From the point of view of the trade unions, the new opportunity for corporatist participation was also seen as an opportunity to break with the politically defensive posture of the 1980s and to regain recognition as a respectable national 'social partner'.

Symbolic Euro-corporatism

The neo-liberal integration project in Europe, as organized through the Single Market and the EMU, poses many fundamental problems for the trade unions. In particular, there is a clear danger that it will result in competitive austerity and deregulation which successively hollow out national social and labour-market standards. (Schulten and Bispnick 1999; see also Chapters 4 and 5 of this volume). But despite this, with the exception of the position taken by some Scandinavian unions in the domestically oriented sectors and perhaps the French Confédération du Travail (CGT), the neo-liberal integration project has in general not been questioned by the trade unions in Northwestern Europe (however, the trajectory of neo-liberalism was more complicated in the Mediterranean countries: see Chapter 11). At the beginning of the 1980s, the position of trade unions within the EU began to converge on this question (Deppe and Weiner 1991). The position taken has aptly been described as a 'yes, but' position (Dölvik 1997: 528). On the one hand, trade unions have supported the Single Market and the EMU; on the other hand, unions have criticized the failure to develop social policies to flank this development.

This criticism by the trade unions was taken up at a rather early stage in the EU institutions. In the mid-1980s the European Commission, under the leadership of Jacques Delors, insisted on the necessity of a 'social dimension' to European integration. This social dimension was to include social minimum standards, but above all 'quasi-corporatist' structures on the European level (Dölvik 1997; Falkner 1998; Keller and Sörries 1998; EC 2000c). The initiative for the so-called 'Social Dialogue' was taken at Val Duchesse in 1985. The aim of this initiative was to create a central forum for the 'social partners', by which was meant those peak associations of workers and employers that the Commission officially recognized. This initiative institutionalized regular meetings between representatives of the European Trade Union Confederation (ETUC) and the Union of Industrial and Employers' Confederations of Europe (UNICE), as well as the European Centre of Enterprises with Public Participation (CEEP). These meetings resulted in a number of joint position papers. These have been of little consequence, however, since they took the form of advisory, general and voluntary documents without any binding force.

The scope of the Social Dialogue was significantly broadened as a result of the Social Chapter of the Maastricht Treaty of 1991. First, not only did the European social partners gain rights to be consulted on all social policy initiatives, but they also gained the right to substitute Commission proposals for legislation through their own agreements or through their own joint initiatives. As a result, bi- and tripartite contacts have increased substantially at the European level and this has resulted so far in three central European Social Partner Agreements, in the areas of parental leave (1996), part-time work (1997) and a-typical employment conditions (1999) (for details, see also Chapters 5 and 6). Given the modest substance of these agreements, they have not improved upon existing national regulations in most member states. Nevertheless, they are attributed a strong symbolic value by trade unions as possible embryonic forms of a European collective bargaining system. However, sceptics point out that such an optimistic interpretation is hardly warranted since there is no evidence that the social partners' fundamental differences in principles on such a system are in the process of being overcome (Keller and Sörries 1998). As before, the employers are only interested in agreements when they believe that such agreements will avert more unfavourable EU directives.

The actual political significance of the Social Dialogue can be discerned from the very few substantial results: It serves to politically capture the trade unions into the political development of the EU by serving the institutional self-interest of the European trade union *organizations* in Brussels and by forever nurturing their functionalist hopes of an albeit slow but progressive development of European social regulation. The political capture of the trade unions into the integration project has proved important in light of the 'post-Maastricht' legitimation crisis of the early 1990s, when political forces that were critical or even hostile to the EU gained in political support (Deppe and Felder 1993).

It is also against the background of this legitimation crisis that one should understand the establishment of employment policy as an issue at the level of the EU, which further extends the institutional involvement of trade unions and employers' associations at European level (see Chapter 5). Besides these official 'quasi-corporatist' structures on the EU level, a rather comprehensive informal network has developed between representatives of the European employers' associations and trade unions and officials of EU institutions. A particularly closely knit network has developed between the ETUC, its sectoral affiliates and the Directorate-General for Employment and Social Affairs (former DG V). Last but not least, ETUC has profited from the Commission's strong political and financial support, which has underwritten its organizational infrastructure for many years (A. Martin and Ross 1999). From the point of view of trade unions, however, this support is double edged. On the one hand, it increases the potential capacity to act on the EU level. On the other hand, it generates political dependencies that are of considerable consequence for the formulation of positions and strategy within the European trade union organization itself.

To sum up, a wide-ranging network of bi- and tripartite institutions has been developed on the EU level since the early 1980s. These have opened up many opportunities for trade unionists to participate in EU politics, but without granting trade unions the capacity to influence or modify, let alone change, the underlying neo-liberal integration dynamic. 'Symbolic Euro-corporatism' ensures that the trade unions can maintain their credo in a 'European social model' while at the same time participating in and contributing to an integration project that is progressively destroying this very 'model'. The EU has in this sense developed an efficient regulatory system that ensures that European trade unions are integrated into a hegemonic bloc whose essential political will it is to sustain a neo-liberal trajectory of socio-economic development.

Contradictions in trade union integration and tendencies towards trade union autonomy in European governance

The first part of this chapter outlined a number of possible trajectories of post-Fordist capital accumulation. It concluded by pointing to how a mode of regulation is being institutionalized in Europe around the EMU that pre-empts a development that would be consistent with the interests of organized labour. In the second part of the chapter we explained how trade unions have nevertheless been integrated into the EU-wide neo-liberal hegemonic project that underpins this mode of regulation and accumulation strategy. This should not be understood in terms of an internalization of the ideological substance of neo-liberalism among trade unions. Trade unionists are aware of the problems that neo-liberalism poses for the interests they represent, and they articulate substantive critiques and policy alternatives to neo-liberalism. If it could be argued that there is any ideological internalization at all, it would be that trade unions have committed themselves so much to the institutional *forms* of the neo-liberal European integration project despite the meagre results. But, even at that level, the integration of the trade unions into European neo-liberal restructuring should not be seen as a functional effect of the 'strategic action' of the ruling class. It should, on the contrary, be seen as a result of permanent social struggle and a permanent process of social compromise formation on a socially biased terrain. As such, the integration of the trade unions remains structurally unstable, and this always provides the potential for 'counter-hegemonic' projects.

Moreover, the contradictions of the neo-liberal restructuring process themselves put the incorporation of the trade unions into the neo-liberal project on the national and European levels into doubt. Since the mid-1990s there have been several notable instances where trade unions have turned directly against the logic of neo-liberal restructuring. The most important impulse came from France, where a far-reaching public criticism of neo-liberalism has developed that has reached beyond the borders of France to other EU countries (Bourdieu *et.al.* 1997). The French movement started with strikes in the public sector in 1995, followed by many further protests, of truck drivers, farm workers and the association of the unemployed. Beyond this, there have been many instances of resistance against neo-liberal hegemony that point towards the brittleness of the social compromise of competitive corporatism. Swedish unions organized protests against public-service retrenchment throughout the mid-1990s; and especially in the public-sector unions, connected with the feminist movement, Euro-scepticism remained strong. In Denmark and Norway in early 1998 and 2000, respectively, general-strike conditions emerged when the rank and file voted against packages that had already been accepted by the central union leadership. Finally, even in the model case of competitive corporatism, the Netherlands, the trade unions find it increasingly difficult to assert wage restraint, and in early 2000 they were forced to increase their wage demands as a result of pressure from the rank and file.[12]

Beyond this 'pressure from below' there are a number of interesting instances where corporatist trade union elites have attempted to articulate policies and strategies that transcend neo-liberalism. We shall conclude by accounting for two instances: attempts to formulate a change of policy within the EMU and tendencies towards Europe-wide co-ordination of sectoral bargaining.

A different EMU?

In the first section we pointed out that contradictions in the EMU point towards a potential transcendence of neo-liberalism. This is because neo-liberal discipline has fundamentally been based on financial markets and economic policy operating on different spatial scales. The global scale of financial markets imposes market discipline on national economic governance through the exercise of a potential 'exit option' should policy not conform to neo-liberal norms. A regional currency potentially undermines, or at least radically reduces, this exit option, and at least theoretically it opens up the space for an interventionist and even Keynesian macroeconomic policy stance on the European level.

Whilst competitive corporatism can be based on a monetarist stance, provided that the export sector is strong enough, the logic of competitive austerity points to the difficulties of generalizing such trade union consent to the EU as a whole.[13] One interesting development in the mid- to late 1990s was the development in both Sweden and Germany towards a Euro-Keynesian position among sections of trade union elites in response to the internal tensions that these unionists faced within their own labour movements. It should be noted that the theme of an alternative European monetary regime was totally absent from the policy of these unions prior to the 1990s. Swedish trade unions had essentially advocated a crawling peg in which the Swedish currency would gradually depreciate to underwrite Sweden's higher employment ambitions in case these generated higher inflation than in the EMS area (Bergström 1993). German unions did not question the EMS as long as the German export sector underwrote their bargaining strategy throughout the 1980s and the early 1990s.

In 1997 the economists of the Swedish blue-collar confederation Landsorganisationen i Sverige (LO) reconsidered their position. They suggested that trade unions would co-operate with the initiatives by the government to reinstate co-ordinated macro bargaining, to be ensured by a state mediation institute with expanding powers to restrain the strike and lockout weapons. Since such co-operation would contain inflation, however, the LO economists argued that in exchange the Swedish government should adopt an employment-promoting *macroeconomic* stance and regulations against tax competition in the EU, and if this was realized they proposed that LO could accept Swedish EMU membership. The LO economists also saw this as part of an intra-union deal to re-establish solidaristic wage policy: the export-oriented unions would retain their commitment to solidaristic wage bargaining and restrain their wage demands within the wage norm. This would create a space for proportional wage increases in the public sector, which in turn would refrain from inflationary leapfrog bargaining. The expansionary macroeconomic policy would constitute a gain for both factions of LO (*inter alia*, LO 1997a, 1997b, 1997c, 1997d). Such an accord would not have been without significance for the prospects for negotiated involvement and unionized service employment growth (or working-time reductions) based on the public-service model. However, in addition to the fact that Sweden is a minor player in the Council of Ministers, Swedish social-democratic monetary policy has been notoriously disciplinary neo-liberal since the mid-1980s, and in this respect the proposal of the LO economists fell on deaf ears.[14] It has also not been taken up within the trade union movement itself, which remains divided on the issue of Europe, with the metalworkers quite comfortable with competitive corporatism and symbolic Euro-corporatism, and the public sector remaining a hotbed of Euro-scepticism.

A potentially more potent development took place in Germany at the end of the 1990s, when the trade unions, in the wake of the unemployment crisis, supported Oskar Lafontaine's (1999) line of a more employment-oriented demand-managed economic policy and a common taxation policy to be forged on the European level (e.g. Welzmüller 1999, Putzhammer 1999). When Lafontaine subsequently became minister of finance there was a real prospect for such a development through Franco-German co-operation (Lafontaine and Strauss-Kahn 1999). One major result of this 'short spring of Euro-Keynesianism' was the establishment of a new Macroeconomic Dialogue at the European level under the German EU Presidency at the EU Summit in Cologne in June 1999 (European Council 1999). The Macroeconomic Dialogue contains a joint forum of representatives from the EU member states (ECOFIN Council and Labour and Social Affairs Council), the European Commission, the European Central Bank (ECB) and the European trade union and employers' organizations, the principle aim of which has been defined as the 'co-ordination of economic policy and improvement of mutually supportive interaction between wage developments and monetary, budget and fiscal policy' (*ibid.*).[15] Although the Macroeconomic Dialogue has explicitly recognized the independence of the ECB, the neo-Keynesian forces around Lafontaine promoted it as an instrument to emphasize the ECB's responsibility for employment creation and to politicize its monetary policy. This approach was strongly supported by major sections of the German trade unions, which demanded a close macroeconomic policy co-ordination at European level, including:

- an employment-promoting collective bargaining policy whereby real wages increase in line with productivity growth under consideration of price developments;
- an anti-cyclical fiscal policy aiming at sustainable growth as well as a budget policy which supports growth and employment;
- a monetary policy that supports growth and employment via a policy of low interest rates without threatening price stability (DGB 2000; our translation).

Lafontaine's removal from power and Germany's subsequent turn towards a more supply-side oriented economic policy have decisively weakened the prospects of this; and, as a result, hopes for a more employment-oriented EMU have to be sorted under the category of 'symbolic Euro-corporatism'. So far, the Macroeconomic Dialogue has been little more than hidden backroom talks with no substantial effect on European economic or monetary policy.[16] Moreover, there is a danger that the Macroeconomic Dialogue might become another instrument that puts trade unions under pressure to subordinate their wage policy to the constraints of the neo-liberal EMU regime. Nevertheless, the Macroeconomic Dialogue has in principle created a new European institution that has at least the potential to influence the ECB's policy, and it depends to a large extent on the European trade unions themselves whether or not this potential will be used for the promotion of alternative economic views.

Towards transnational wage co-ordination?

Another set of contradictions emanates from the fundamentally contradictory interrelationship of competitive corporatism and symbolic Euro-corporatism. The latter hold out the promise of universal norms for labour-market and social regulation, whereas the former and institutionally more important moment is fundamentally based on regime competition. In this context it is doubtful that the myth of symbolic Euro-corporatism can be sustained and ensure a stable social integration of trade unions. Indeed, symbolic Euro-corporatism serves the particular organizational interests of ETUC itself. In contrast, the nationally based trade unions must confront the disappointments and disillusionment that are generated by the social problems that symbolic Euro-corporatism is supposed to address but cannot resolve. This could mean that the trade unions retreat into defensive national strategies in order to defend their labour-market and social standards.

The alternative to this is broader and stronger autonomous trade union action on the European level. It should be noted in this context that notable progress has been achieved in the area of wage bargaining in the last few years. Against the background of the EMU, some trade union organizations – in particular the European Metalworkers' Federation (EMF) – have begun to co-ordinate their national wage policies at the European level (Schulten and Bispnick 1999). The basic idea is that through such co-ordination trade unions can autonomously agree upon and determine common criteria and goals for the national level and avoid wage and social dumping. With such concepts for a European solidaristic wage policy, trade unions consciously resist the neo-liberal logic of national regime competition. Instead, they try to perform their original function: to mitigate competition over wages and working conditions through a reconstruction of this function on the European level.

Such a reconstruction requires stronger autonomous trade union organization on the European level. However, in contrast to national developments, the development of trade union organizations on the European level hitherto followed a 'top-down' trajectory. As such, trade unions may exist as *social institutions* in Europe, but not as *a social movement* (Turner 1996). As before, trade union struggles against neo-liberal restructuring take place almost without exception at the national level. The European trade union organizations play no role in these struggles; nor do national trade unions in this context co-operate internationally to any significant extent. While the trade unions often have developed rather intensive co-operative relations with other social movements on a national level, co-operation between trade unions is almost non-existent on the European level.

In early 2000 the French group of social scientists Raisons d'Agir (2000) therefore proposed a call for an assembly of the General Estates of the European Social Movements. The goal for such an assembly, they proposed, would be to 'elaborate a Charter of the social movement, and building the foundations of an international structure bringing together all the intellectual and organizational forms of resistance to neo-liberal policies' ('Charta 2000. Für die Einberufug von Generalständen der sozialen Bewegungen in Europa', *Die*

Tageszeitung (taz), 29–30 April 2000). It is hoped that this initiative could become the foundation of a 'counter-hegemonic network'. Time will tell what role trade unions might play in such an alliance. However, for the moment it can be assumed that they wanted to be both part of the ruling bloc and part of the counter-movement against this bloc.

Notes

1 Ryner gratefully acknowledges the financial support that the Social Sciences and Humanities Research Council of Canada (SSHRCC) and the Jean Monnet Fellowship Programme of the European University Institute in Florence provided for his share of the research.

2 In the Fordist phase, production was organized according to Taylorist principles, applying product-specific machinery on a large scale. Adequate market outlets were in this context ensured through *ex ante* regulation in the form of collective bargaining and Keynesian economic policy (which provided a sense of certainty that mass investments would be met with adequate market outlets). Mass consumption could thereby validate mass production, which in turn underwrote mass consumption through productivity increases (repressing inflationary tendencies in Keynesian regulation and, more fundamentally, the organic composition of capital). Stagflation signalled the breakdown of Fordist circuits of valorization. While many factors intervened in the economic crisis (including, for example, the oil crises, the breakdown of Bretton Woods, inflationary Keynesianism and mounting government debt), Lipietz (1985) argues that in the last instance the crisis was induced by Taylorism reaching its organizational frontier of labour-process innovation. Significant economies could no longer be yielded through the fragmentation of work moments and the separation of conception from execution. Especially important in this context were the legitimization and motivation constraints manifested through labour-force resistance. (Workers resisted changes through absenteeism, sabotage or wildcat strikes). As a result, returns to capital decreased and continued demand expansion could not be underwritten through productivity increases. This expressed itself through stagflation and fiscal crisis.

3 This is the stuff analysed by the classical Marxist theories of imperialism (the dynamic whereby profit rates are sustained by expanding into territory where higher rates of exploitation of labour are possible, and/or where surplus capacity and products can find a market outlet). This is not without relevance to the dynamic of the 'emerging markets'. Harvey discusses this in terms of 'spatial displacement' (1989: 183–4).

4 As Albo puts it:

> [E]ach country reduces domestic demand and adopts an export oriented strategy of dumping its surplus production [by keeping wage increases below productivity growth and pushing down domestic costs], for which there are fewer consumers in its national economy given the decrease in workers' living standards and productivity gains all going to the capitalists, in the world market. This has created a global demand crisis and the growth of surplus capacity across the business cycle.
>
> (Albo 1994: 147)

5 According to Krieger and Fröhlich (1998), with regard to new forms of work organization and employee involvement Germany has a significant 'modernization gap' compared with its main European competitors.

6 The main institution advocating the case for abandoning corporatist institutions in Germany was the Confederation of Industry (BDI), but especially after the victory of the SPD and the Greens and the increased awareness of Dutch developments in Germany, it is increasingly accepted by those favouring neo-liberal 'modernization' that this is best ensured through corporatism.

7 We include this short section on the Netherlands because of the particular importance of the supposedly unique 'Dutch model' in the debates elsewhere, for example in Germany and at the European level. However, we do not enter into a more detailed discussion. The reader is referred to Chapter 9, by Uwe Becker, who shares our position and examines the Dutch case in detail.

8 As discussed above under the heading of 'negotiated involvement' (p. 179), the Rehn–Meidner prescribed co-ordinated wages for the economy as a whole, which prematurely forced low-productivity enterprises out of business to free up resources for high-productivity enterprises that could sustain high wage levels and tax levels.

9 On the 'double screen', see Ruggie (1982). The double screen refers to the institutional arrangements of the Bretton Woods system that made it possible to render compatible international co-operation for international economic expansion, on the one hand, and policy autonomy for domestic macroeconomic stabilization policy, on the other.

10 There were two main reasons for the outflow of foreign direct investment: corporations were seeking agglomeration economies on the European continent and there was a shortage of labour in Sweden. It should be noted in this context that the average rate of productivity growth of Swedish corporations was −0.1 per cent in Sweden and 5.5 per cent abroad.

11 No such 'social pact' has formally been formed in Sweden on an enduring basis. Nevertheless, a bipartite agreement signed by all the main trade unions and employers' associations for the last major wage-negotiation round of 1997 served some of the same purposes (Dölvik and Martin 2000). Negotiations on a 'growth pact' broke down in 1998, however, as LO refused to accept Sveriges arbetsgivareförbund (SAF) ultimatum on taxes and numerical flexibility.

12 It should be noted that in the latter cases resistance has emerged in places where competitive corporatism has been successful, and this points toward its internal limitations: it is a type of accord that can be forged when unions are weak as a result of high unemployment levels. In these conditions wage restraint in exchange for employment enjoys a measure of support among the rank and file. But such a policy is hard to sustain when the economy enjoys growth and lower unemployment levels and when workers demand their 'fair share' of economic prosperity.

13 In this regard it is worth pointing out that competitive corporatism is based on particularistic 'niche strategies' of economic development based on the experience of small states. This stands in a necessarily contradictory relation to the ambition of developing a universal concept (Bispinck and Schulten 2000).

14 Whilst since joining the EU the Swedish government has acted for a Europe-wide employment policy, its orientation has always been one-sidedly supply-side focused and it has always accepted the framework of the EMU as untouchable (Sweden, Ministry of Foreign Affairs 1997: 31–2; Lund 1996). It should be noted that the official responsible for formulating this position for the Amsterdam Inter-governmental Conference, Gunnar Lund, belonged to the small group of officials that reconfigured Swedish macroeconomic policy in a disciplinary neo-liberal direction.

15 The Macroeconomic Dialogue contains a two-stage approach including meetings at a 'technical' and at a 'political' level: at *technical level* a new working group with representatives from member states, Commission, ECB and trade unions and employers' associations was established to discuss recent developments in the different macroeconomic policy fields. The working group should meet two times a year: first, before the Commission adopts its recommendation on the annual Broad Economic Policy

Guidelines (BEPG) and, second, after presentation by the Commission of its autumn forecast and its Annual Economic Report. In addition to that there will be two annual meetings at *political level* between the decisions-makers of all parties involved. The first meeting should take place before the drawing up by ECOFIN Council of the draft BEPG and the second before the adoption by the European Council of its conclusion in respect of the Employment Guidelines (European Council 1999: 13).

16 Since all parties involved in the Macroeconomic Dialogue agreed on strict discretion, almost nothing is known about the course of the joint talks and the topics discussed.

11 Mediterranean labour and the impact of Economic and Monetary Union

Mass unemployment or labour-market flexibility?

Leila Simona Talani and Emma Cerviño

Introduction

In the wake of the new millennium, the challenge facing Europe is defined by the identification of new priorities and the solution of old problems. Most important among them is the problem of unemployment. However, the implementation of new policies, particularly those related to the establishment of a European currency union, provides mixed answers to similar challenges.

Indeed, the macroeconomic consequences of the adoption of a single monetary and exchange rate policy for all Economic and Monetary Union (EMU) member states are still the object of a heated debate among academics and policy-makers. This debate tends to reflect the traditional division between Keynesian approaches to macroeconomic policy-making and monetarist ones. Whereas the former school of thought underlines the restraining effect of tight monetary and fiscal policies on the aggregate demand, and thus their recessive bias, the latter puts the emphasis on the supply-side consequences of the Maastricht way to EMU triggering the elimination of labour-market rigidities.

However, the debate on the impact of EMU on European countries' growth and unemployment rates can also be read in terms of its consequences for the existing balance of power between the different socio-economic actors. In fact, the path to EMU, as defined by the Maastricht Treaty and by the subsequent agreement on the Stability Pact, directly and substantially affects the powers and prerogatives of trade unions in their traditional policy realms. In particular, the statutory European Central Bank (ECB) goal of a low and stable inflation rate has undeniable consequences for the limits within which trade unions are able to conduct wage policies. Moreover, the implementation of monetary policy by the ECB, through the decisions over the level of European interest rates, undoubtedly affects investment decisions and, consequently, the level of unemployment. Finally, the rigid limitations on the conduct of national fiscal policy imposed by the Maastricht Treaty for the transition to EMU and by the Stability Pact for its aftermath are deeply modifying the terms of the debate over the survival of the welfare state in all its components. Therefore the trade unions' position on further progress on the way to monetary union must be read in terms of a reaction to this process of institutionalization and of the attempt to regain the terrain lost since the beginning of the process of monetary integration.

This contribution seeks to analyse both the theoretical debates over the consequences for growth and unemployment rates of the establishment of EMU, and the empirical evidence on its impact on the bargaining powers of the European trade unions.

To this end, the research will be divided into two sections. The first deals with the economic literature on the labour-market and employment consequences of the Maastricht way to EMU. The problem here will be to assess whether the recessive bias of the Maastricht criteria and the Growth and Stability Pact (GSP) and their consequences in terms of unemployment will be offset by the implementation of measures aiming at the liberalization of labour markets. In the second section the analysis shifts to the political-economy level, with the aim of verifying to what extent the implementation of EMU is the result of and/or has contributed to changing the existing balance of power between the different socio-economic actors. Attention is focused in particular on Southern Europe, namely Italy and Spain. Here, after giving a general introduction to the characteristics of the so-called 'southern cluster' or 'Mediterranean regime', the analysis moves to the relations between EMU and the changes in the labour-market structures and the power position of the trade unions in the two countries.

Mass unemployment or labour-market flexibility as a consequence of EMU?

The establishment of EMU will be read as a major institutional undertaking whose economic outcomes are not only constrained but also defined by its institutional framework. That is to say that the economic consequences of EMU are specific to the way in which this particular currency union has been devised and this, in turn, is the product of a unique historical process. Therefore, the purpose of the present contribution is not to analyse the economic impact on unemployment of currency unions in general. The focus of this analysis is on a particular type of currency union: the one defined by the Maastricht agreement on EMU in 1991 and refined by the adoption of the Stability and Growth Pact by the European heads of state and government in 1997. It will not, however, discuss why EMU has this particular institutional configuration because, although it is an issue of major importance, this has been addressed widely in the literature.[1]

From an institutional point of view, the Maastricht Treaty and its protocols solved the long-lasting controversy between the 'monetarist' and the 'economist'[2] approaches to monetary union. This was possible, on the one hand, by establishing a rigid institutional framework with a clear-cut economic objective (that of pursuing price stability) and a three-stage timetable to achieve EMU (cf. Gros and Thygesen 1998) and, on the other hand, by devising a set of convergence requirements that applying member states had to respect before entering. These requirements included permanence in the 'new' Exchange Rate Mechanism (ERM) (within 15 per cent bands) for at least two years; inflation rates no more than 1.5 per cent higher than the average of the three most virtuous member states; interest rates no more than 2 per cent higher than the average of the three most virtuous member states; a debt-to-gross-domestic-product (GDP) ratio not exceeding 60 per cent, subject to conditions; and, most importantly, a deficit-to-GDP ratio not exceeding 3 per cent (Art. 104(c) and Art. 109(j), Treaty on European Union; TEU).

The economic viability and the political (or political-economy) rationale of the Maastricht criteria has been the subject of a number of studies from the most varied academic points of view, which is why the issue will not be tackled here (see note 2). It is important to underline, however, that their strict anti-inflationary aim was even strengthened by the adoption of the GSP (Eichengreen and Wyplosz 1998: 71). The pact confirms the objective of a deficit-to-GDP ratio not exceeding 3 per cent and commits EMU member states to a medium-term budgetary stance close to balance or in surplus. It also defines the terms and sanctions of the excessive-deficit procedure. Exemption from respecting this fiscal criterion within EMU is allowed only in the case of a decline in GDP of 2 per cent or more and of a temporary and small excess deficit. With a GDP declining by between 0.75 and 2 per cent, the decision on exemption from sanctions is left to the Council of Ministers. With lower decreases in GDP, the excessive-deficit procedure will be implemented in any case, and countries will be obliged to keep up to 0.5 per cent of their GDP in non-interest-bearing mandatory deposits with the ECB until excess deficit is reabsorbed. If this does not happen within two years, deposits are transformed into outright transfers (Gros and Thygesen 1998: 341).

The major question to answer at this point is how, if at all, the implementation of this particular kind of currency union will influence EMU member states' performances in terms of unemployment. There are two ways of tackling the issue. The first is to assess to what extent this particular form of currency union contains a recessive bias, thus reducing the level of output ceteris paribus. The other way is to see how the establishment of EMU has been linked in theory and, in the following section, in practice to the flexibility of labour markets. These two streams of reasoning might have opposite outcomes. Indeed, while the former would point to an increase in the level of unemployment, the second could lead to its decrease. However, the tricky aspect lies in the fact that the first way of reasoning might be used to further the second, thus adding to its economic rationale and fostering its political feasibility.

The first stream of economic reasoning assesses the overall recessive effects of the implementation of the Maastricht fiscal criteria and/or of the GSP. Some authors have argued that the effort brought about by the implementation of the Maastricht criteria, and in particular of the fiscal ones, as well as the determination to stick to the ERM in a period of high-interest-rate policy, can explain the upsurge of European unemployment in the 1990s (Artis 1998). Of course, economic analyses are far from reaching an agreement on the issue. Indeed, the counter-arguments tend to underline the necessity of fiscal consolidation and anti-inflationary policies. Others point out that the time period over which unemployment has been growing in Europe is too long to be easily explained in macroeconomic terms (Nickell 1997). However, deflationary policies implicit in the implementation of the Maastricht way to EMU seem to have eventually worsened the level of European unemployment, at least by increasing the equilibrium rate of unemployment (a phenomenon called hysteresis in the literature; e.g. Artis 1998; D.R. Cameron 1997, 1998, 1999).

Moreover, some econometric simulations show that the implementation of the stability pact from 1974 to 1995 in four European countries (notably, Italy, France, Germany and the UK) would have limited economic growth by reducing the annual growth rate. This would have led to cumulated output losses of around 5 per cent in France and the UK, and of 9 per cent in Italy. The economic-theory rationale of these results is, of course, that the GSP constraints would limit (and will limit in the future) the use of automatic stabilizers to counter recessive waves, thus increasing the severity of recessions. This, however, will happen only if member states are not able to achieve a balanced or surplus budgetary position, allowing them to use automatic stabilizers during mild recessive periods in the appropriate way without breaching the Maastricht/GSP threshold (cf. Eichengreen and Wyplosz 1998: 93).

There is the counter-argument that the GSP gives credibility to the ECB anti-inflationary stances, thus reducing the level of interest rates required to maintain the inflation rate below 2 per cent and boosting the economy. Finally, even if the recessive bias of the fiscal criteria and the GSP were proved, this would not necessarily lead to a higher unemployment level (Artis and Winkler 1997; also Buti *et al.* 1997).

However, there is another way in which the Maastricht criteria and the Stability Pact might affect unemployment, a more indirect way, which is enshrined in the more general issue of how EMU will influence the European labour structures. This, in turn, is related to how member states should react to asymmetric shocks that might arise. By definition, autonomous monetary policy and exchange-rate policies are not available to react to idiosyncratic shocks in a currency union. At the same time, common monetary and exchange-rate policy should be used with caution since they can have mixed results if other members of the Union are in the opposite phase of the business-cycle. Thus, economic theory leaves few options: fiscal policy, labour mobility and relative price flexibility.

Indeed, a country could react to an asymmetric shock by using national fiscal policy, both as a counter-cyclical tool, through the action of automatic stabilizers, and in the form of fiscal transfers to solve more long-term economic disparities (as in the case of Italian Mezzogiorno). However, in the special kind of monetary union analysed in this paper, the Maastricht criteria and, to an even bigger extent, the requirements of the GSP constrain substantially the ability of member states to resort to national fiscal policy to tackle asymmetric shocks.

Alternatively, some authors suggest that the redistributive and stabilizing functions of fiscal policy be performed at the European level. Regarding this, the proposals range from increasing the size of the European budget, to pooling national fiscal policies, to establishing a common fiscal body which would act as a counterbalance to the ECB (e.g. Obstfeld and Peri 1998). The feasibility of similar proposals looks at least dubious in the light of the difficulties EU member states encounter in finding some agreement on the much less challenging task of tax harmonization (Overbeek 2000). Moreover, whichever discussion about fiscal policy one has, this inevitably triggers a discussion on the loss of national sovereignty and a related one on political unification whose outcomes are still far from being unanimous. Overall, there does not seem to be a compelling will on the part of EU member states to reach an agreement on the creation of a common fiscal policy or to find some way to increase the size of the EU budget so as to introduce a stabilization function.

Given the difficulties of using national fiscal policy to tackle asymmetric shocks and the lack of any substantial fiscal power at the European level, economists suggest the option of resorting to labour mobility. The EU does indeed provide an institutional framework in which labour mobility should be enhanced. The Treaty's articles regarding the free movement of workers, the Single Market programme and recent provisions in the Third Pillar of course represent this. However, economic analyses show little evidence of mass migration in response to asymmetric shocks in the EU (unlike in some respects in the US) (Obstfeld and Peri 1998). Indeed, few European policy-makers, if any, would seriously endorse temporary mass migration as a credible way to react to national economic strains, for obvious political as well as social reasons.

There thus remains only one policy option for national policy-makers to tackle the problems arising from asymmetric shocks: increasing the flexibility of labour markets so that 'regions or states affected by adverse shocks can recover by cutting wages, reducing relative prices and taking market shares from the others' (Blanchard 1998: 249). Not only this. Since reform of the labour market is clearly a structural intervention, it will help eliminate the structural component of unemployment as well as the cyclical one, if it is still possible to distinguish between the two (Artis 1998).

Indeed, the employment rhetoric and strategy officially adopted by EU institutions in the last few years shows clearly that the European Union has chosen to give priority to labour flexibility as 'the' means of tackling the problem of unemployment in Europe. For instance, the White Paper on *Growth, Competitiveness, Employment* (EC 1993) made no mystery of the fact that the way to increase employment passed through structural changes in the European labour markets.

Calls for full support of structural changes by the social partners at both the national and European level were then reiterated in the conclusions of the European Council meeting at Essen in December 1994 and in the course of the European Council meeting in Florence on June 1996.[3] Importantly, the Community strategy for employment was to be closely tied with the provisions on economic and monetary policy (see Art. 126(1) and Art. 128(2), TEU). This aspect was emphasized by the European Council of Vienna (December 1998), where the European heads of state and government called for more co-ordination between the employment and the broad economic policy guidelines. On this occasion the European Council also asked for the development of a European Pact for Employment. A report on the development of this pact was drawn up by the European Council in Cologne, which also endorsed it.

A very important step in the definition of the EU policy towards employment was represented by the insertion of a brand new title on employment in the EC Amsterdam Treaty (Title VIII, Articles 125–30). In the opinion of commentators, indeed, Amsterdam marks the final shift towards the liberal approach to employment that had taken place since the White Paper and the Essen European Council decisions (e.g. Duff 1997). Of course, one should not overestimate the impact that the EU recommendations, initiatives or proposals have in terms of effective policy-making. However, the array of interventions in favour of a relaxation of labour-market protection in relation to the implementation of the Maastricht budgetary criteria denotes at least the existence of a clear direction in the Community employment rhetoric, if not strategy (for further elaboration, see Chapter 5).

But what does labour flexibility mean? How has it been implemented at the national level? What kind of changes does it imply? Does it really help solve unemployment? How did the relevant socio-economic actors react in the different European countries? Who wins and who loses from the implementation of a similar policy? An attempt to answer to these questions will be provided in the following sections, with special attention paid to the cases of Spain and Italy.

Flexibility vs exclusion: the Anglo-Saxon model as opposed to the Mediterranean

The expression 'flexibility of labour markets' as used by the scholars of industrial relations (e.g. Rhodes 1997) refers to three forms of flexibility:

1 Internal (or functional) flexibility in the workplace.
2 External (or numerical) flexibility *vis-à-vis* the wider labour market.
3 Greater pay flexibility at local levels.

Categorizing the level of flexibility/rigidity of European labour markets along the dimensions of internal and external flexibility, we can distinguish what in the literature is referred to as the 'southern cluster' (Rhodes 1997: 10–11). This is characterized by a remarkable shift, from very low levels of both external and internal flexibility of the 'legal' or 'licit' labour markets in the 1970s to a much higher level of flexibility in the 1990s. Contemporaneously these economies (first and foremost Italy and Spain) saw the growth of 'illicit' labour markets and a shift from labour exporting to labour importing (cf. OECD 1988).

This process took place amid heated struggles between socio-economic groups that inevitably changed the balance of power between them. In this context, the EU issues in general and EMU in particular provided an excuse to shift the power battle from the national to the European level. This shift was by no means neutral. In the move from the national to the international level, some groups acquired more strength and cohesion. Others lost a great deal of their bargaining power for reasons ranging from a decreased organizational or representative capacity to a structural bias of the EU institutional setting in favour of certain societal interests (cf. Holman 1996). This game of transnationalization is, indeed, much more easily played by the employers' organizations than by the unions, given the many cleavages within the European working class, reflected in the cumbersome functioning of the European Trade Union Confederation (ETUC) (see Talani 2000 for an overview; see also Chapter 10 of this volume). This contribution will underline how, by shifting the struggle around labour flexibility in Italy and Spain between employers and employees from the national to the European level, the relative power positions between the two groups were changed, which made it easier to introduce neo-liberal labour-market reforms.

Whether, then, these labour reforms represent the solution to the problem of unemployment in Mediterranean countries is indeed a different issue. As Esping-Andersen (1999) reminds us, a considerable gap exists between the widely accepted theoretical claim that deregulation will create jobs and the evidence that rigidities seem to matter only selectively. This is particularly true for Mediterranean countries like Italy or Spain, where institutional rigidities have often been offset by informal flexibilities like self-employment, black-market or illicit and illegal arrangements.

Moreover, similar labour rigidities must be read in the context of the societal structure of Mediterranean countries. The so-called Mediterranean model is often characterized as a *familial* one, i.e. one based on the assumption that the family male is the only breadwinner. This would explain why the exceedingly high levels of female and youth unemployment are not inconsistent with a high level of labour protection and a low level of social protection. The family is the locus of social protection, and wife and children remain dependent on the income of the father up to a very late age. The protection of the job of the father and husband thus becomes of fundamental importance to the entire society. This model differs substantially from the liberal model prevailing in Anglo-Saxon countries, where in the trade-off between flexibility and exclusion there is a tendency towards the former, with all that it implies in terms of a decrease in equality. And, indeed, in Anglo-Saxon countries a high degree of labour-market flexibility produces high levels of employment at the expense of a growing wage polarization between unskilled and skilled workers (see Chapters 3, 8 and 9).

Many claim that in the era of globalization the Anglo-Saxon model is the only viable one in view of the competitive pressures stemming from lower labour costs in less-developed countries. And, indeed, that is the basic argument used by the supporters of flexibility, particularly within employers' organizations. But apart from the fact that the impact of globalization on employment is far from clear (see Chapter 2), the price in terms of increase in inequality might not be worth paying in countries where the societal setting is opposed to the Anglo-Saxon one. This, however, is not the place to address the many complex issues influencing the future of employment in a globalizing world. Therefore we now turn to the analysis of the Italian and Spanish cases.

Italy and the process of European monetary integration: shifting the level of governance

In Italy, leading socio-economic groups (particularly big industry) have consistently used European issues and in particular those related to the process of European monetary integration to reduce the level of labour protection and increase the flexibility of labour markets (cf. Talani 2000).

To analyse this in more detail we will first deal with the decrease in labour-protection legislation in relation to Italian entry in the ERM of the European Monetary System (EMS). Subsequently we will be concerned with labour-market flexibilization as a consequence of EMU.

The struggle over the Scala Mobile

It is generally agreed that the first relaxation in Italian labour-protection legislation was represented by the abolition of the so-called *Scala Mobile*, the Italian wage-indexation mechanism. This was made possible by commitment to the EMS, with all that it implied in terms of strict anti-inflationary policies, which, in turn, both was a consequence of the new dominant position of Italian capitalist groups and contributed to further strengthening of their position.

The 'hot autumn' of 1969 marked the beginning of the 'era of union centrality' (cf. Lange *et al.* 1982: 97; see also Giugni 1981: 341; Regini 1981). This was an era in which Italian economic policy was characterized by prevailing concerns about the maintenance of the purchasing power of wages, the institutionalization of workers' rights, and the leading role played by the trade unions and their political counterparts in Italian socio-economic policy-making. The growing strength of trade unions during this period is reflected clearly in the ascending slope of their membership parabola, whose density rates increased constantly from 1969 onwards, reaching their peak in 1978 (with 49 per cent of the total employed, an 18.2 per cent increase with respect to the 1969 figure) (see Figure 11.1).

The era of union centrality reached its political apex in 1975, with the signing of an agreement between the union confederations and Confindustria to upgrade the *Scala Mobile*, a system protecting workers' wages against inflation. The agreement provided for a three-month payment of a fixed amount for each unit increase in the inflation rate, the so-called *punto di contingenza*.[4] The main features of the agreement, which was the product of collective bargaining and not the result of a parliamentary process,[5] were the relatively high and immediate degree of inflation protection paying equal amounts to all workers and thus reducing wage differentials, and the automatic character of the system. These elements rendered the agreement a powerful means to protect workers' purchasing power, marking a major victory for the union movement. However,

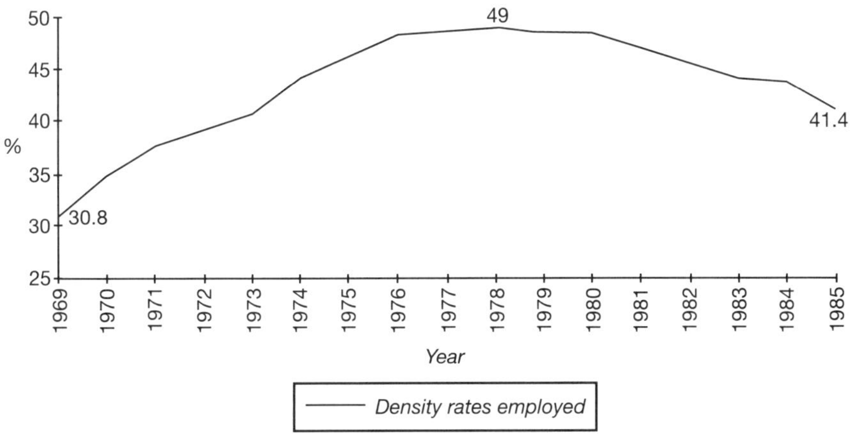

Figure 11.1 Density of union membership in Italy, 1969–85

Source: Centro Studi Economici Sociali e Sindacali (CESOS), *Le relazioni sindacali in Italia: Reports*; various issues.

the defence of this victory proved to be very problematic, and it eventually led, with the beginning of the economic crisis of the late 1970s to the early 1980s, to major conflicts not only between the unions and their social and political referents but also within the unions themselves.

In the face of the growing economic problems, particularly unemployment, the Italian union federation[6] in 1978 adopted a new strategic orientation, the so-called EUR strategy. This was based on a trade-off between fewer guarantees to the workers and more participation in investment decisions, and it was aimed at increasing employment through the new instrument of tripartite negotiations with the government and employers' representatives. Given the increasing involvement of the Italian Communist Party (Partito Comunista Italiano, PCI) in the governmental area, thanks to the pacification process between the PCI and Democrazia Cristiana (DC) (the so-called 'historic compromise'), this 'new course' of Italian unions appeared to secure their participation in the official sites of Italian economic-policy decision-making. On the contrary, in the light of the subsequent tragic end of 'national solidarity', the EUR strategy marked the beginning of a descending parabola of union bargaining power and political influence (Accornero 1994). The historic compromise suffered a serious blow with the 1978 kidnapping and subsequent murder of DC leader Aldo Moro, and was further discredited with the start of the 'Second Cold War' following the Soviet intervention in Afghanistan in 1979.

As already noted, the dismantling of the *Scala Mobile*, or at least the substantial reform of its mechanisms, and the reduction in state intervention in the economy constituted the main issues at stake in the domestic debate over the establishment of the EMS. Indeed, it was precisely in the course of this debate that the differences within the government majority and within the union federations over the future of the *Scala Mobile* became unbridgeable. Within the union movement itself the 'automatic' increases of the *Scala Mobile* were increasingly attacked. This is true especially for the Unione Italiana del Lavoro (UIL), which in this period was beginning to be controlled by the new Partito Socialista Italiano (PSI) of Craxi (see Merkel 1987 for a detailed account), and for the Confederazione Italiana Sindacati Lavoratori (CISL), traditionally linked to Catholic interests and to the DC. By 1982, for instance, both Pierre Carniti, secretary-general of the CISL, and Giorgio Benvenuto, secretary-general of UIL, favoured major reform of the wage-indexation mechanism within the context of tripartite negotiations. On the other hand, the Communist component of the Confederazione Generale Italiana del Lavoro (CGIL) was far less ready than the others to modify the system. The inconsistencies in the positions of the different unions eventually led to the first major blow to the *Scala Mobile*, represented by the accord of 22 January 1983 (see Lange 1987: 30). With this accord, for the first time since 1975 the unions accepted a reduction in the automatic inflation-indexed payments coupled with an eighteen-month freeze of wage bargaining in the private corporate sector. This constituted a major defeat, the significance of which should not be underestimated, even if the government agreed to protect the real purchasing power of workers by cutting taxes, limiting the rise of government-controlled prices and changing the family-allowance system.

Given the compromise nature of the 1983 accord and the fact that the balance of power between unions and employers was still shifting towards the latter, in late 1983 the unions agreed to pursue a possible revision of the 1983 accord. The issues at stake were still wages and job flexibility and, above all, the *Scala Mobile*, but this time Confindustria was taking a much tougher position and the unions reached the negotiation table without having achieved a joint position. The CISL and the UIL favoured further reduction in the *Scala Mobile*, while the CGIL made the reform of the system conditional on a government commitment not to distribute the costs of further economic growth and employment exclusively among the working class. The situation was further complicated by the government leadership of Bettino Craxi, which was characterized by a strong claim of the executive in taking hard economic policy decisions (*decisionismo*) and by an even stronger opposition to the PCI. The atmosphere was so heated that in early February 1984 the communist and the socialist factions of the CGIL split, assuming different positions on the *Scala Mobile* and on the need to consult the workers before signing any agreement. This step slowed, if not prevented, CGIL participation in any compromise. On 12 February the minister of labour, Gianni De Michelis, presented a draft accord that maintained the trade-off nature of the 1983 accord. It proposed a limitation in the number of units to be paid every three months during 1984, but it also promised that in the case of higher inflation rates fiscal interventions would compensate any unforeseen losses in the subsequent year. The CISL and the UIL promptly declared their willingness to conclude negotiations, while the CGIL, after a moment of hesitation, declared its unwillingness to accept the proposal, thus joining the PCI in its negative assessment of the manoeuvre. Open conflict broke out between the government, on one side, and the PCI and the communist component of the CGIL, on the other, when Craxi translated the basic terms of the 14 February protocol in a decree to be converted in law. Despite the campaign of the communists and their parliamentary allies, especially the deputies of the Democrazia Proletaria, and despite the massive popular demonstrations throughout Italy, this eventually happened on 12 June 1984. In June the PCI decided to pursue a referendum on Article 3 of the decree, concerning the cuts to the *Scala Mobile*. By late September more than the required number of signatures had been submitted. On 7 December 1984 the Central Office of the Corte di Cassazione declared the referendum constitutional. On 9 and 10 June 1985, after a long and bitter referendum campaign further complicated by the administrative elections of 12 May 1985, Italian voters finally defeated the PCI effort to overturn Article 3 when 54.3 per cent voted 'no' and only 46.7 per cent voted 'yes'.

The long battle over the *Scala Mobile* made it manifestly clear that the era of Italian political economy characterized by the market and the political power of the union movement and by the PCI's ability to act as a political 'guarantor' of union co-operation with government policy had come to an end. The battle over the *Scala Mobile*, transcending its economic meaning, became a struggle over the balance of power among the different Italian socio-political and economic actors. The issue at stake was control over the pattern of growth and distribution in the Italian political economy. With its conclusion, the outline of the political economy fundamentally changed and the era of union centrality ended, with the labour movement and the PCI as net losers.

What were the reasons for such a change? Analysts of industrial relations in Italy identify some tendencies in union organization during the late 1970s and early 1980s that might help to explain this phenomenon.[7] On the one hand, there was a renewed dependency of Italian industrial relations on the party system, after their relative autonomy during the early 1970s (cf. Lange and Regini 1989). This is demonstrated by the shift from the centralized political negotiations of the 1960s and early 1970s to the new tripartite agreements of the late 1970s and 1980s, in which the political parties and the government played a much more important and active role. On the other hand, unions found it increasingly difficult to perceive which interests to represent. A real representation crisis occurred during this period, and this, together with the new linkages with the political parties, led to a growing division within the union movement and to a progressive decline in their political and bargaining power (see Regini 1981: ch. 7).

These factors, however, are not enough to explain the change in power allocation, and greater attention must be paid to the fact that the phenomena under analysis took place in a period of deep economic change and crisis (see Vannicelli 1984: 404).

After the recession of 1970–1, Italy experienced a moderate recovery led by the depreciation of the lira after the abandonment of the European snake in the spring of 1973. This, however, proved to be only a palliative measure, to the extent that in late 1974/early 1975 an economic crisis came about in all its severity (Salvati 1984). Italian unemployment started to grow almost constantly from 1974 onwards, reaching double figures, 10.2 per cent, in 1984 without giving any sign of slowing down. Italian real gross domestic product (GDP) succeeded in recovering only slightly from its 1975 slump of −3.6 per cent with the devaluation of the lira in 1976. However, at the beginning of the 1980s it was again registering negative levels.

The Italian industrial and banking sectors tended to single out unsustainable labour costs as a fundamental cause of the country's crisis in the industrial sector. They consequently identify elimination of the wage-indexation system, so strenuously defended by the trade unions and left-wing political parties, as the only viable solution to the Italian economic crisis.

Turning to the purposes of this contribution, it should be recalled that the prolonged recessive phase, by weakening pressures on the labour market, limited substantially the workers' bargaining power, and encouraged the entrepreneurial and the financial sector to try to break those rules or institutions which limited their autonomy. However, the decrease in union bargaining power was not homogeneous. Certain strata of workers enjoyed greater protection under existing laws or by their crucial position in the productive process.[8] Thus, while the recession generally undermined the power bases of the union movement, it particularly reduced its capacity to represent the aggregate interests of the workers – that is, to act as a pre-mediator among a set of different interests. This is the role that enables a union movement to maintain a common position during negotiations.

Furthermore, structural interventions in industry, technological innovation, the growing importance of services, the spread of small companies, the shift to the immigration of foreign labour and the rise of the 'invisible' or 'black' economy are all phenomena which can be regarded as answers to the need, brought about by the recession, to increase industrial productivity and competitiveness. However, they all had the common effect of further fragmenting the social basis of the unions.

Thus, the context in which the 1984–5 failure matured was one characterized by a growing weakness on the side of the unions. Their power was undermined, on the one hand, by a deep representation crisis and an increasing difficulty in aggregating different interests, and, on the other, by a reduced capacity to obtain favourable measures in exchange for their consent to stricter economic policies. These developments are related to the underlying transformation of accumulation structures in Italy towards post-Fordist patterns (see Chapter 3).

Corresponding to the decline in the unions' capacity to influence socio-economic development is the opposite phenomenon of the rise of private company power. This has been an international and structurally determined phenomenon connected with the transformation of the global economy mentioned above. This structural development has also, at the same time, been dialectically interrelated with the political agency of big capital. Transnational corporations, being usually less affected by national regulations, called for deregulation in the domestic corporate sector and exported, mainly through the American channel, the Japanese conception of the 'firm as a community' giving rise to the development of a 'corporate identity'. This undermined previous social achievements in many European countries, in Italy in the form of the eventual abolition of the *Scala Mobile*, in which process the disciplinary effects of European economic and monetary integration proved very important.

EMU and labour-market flexibility

The tendency of the Confindustria to approach the problems of labour costs through the mechanisms by which they are determined, starting from indexation, was confirmed by the subsequent round of the battle over the *Scala Mobile*, which led to its definitive abolishment with the 1993 agreement.

After a long controversy between the CGIL, CISL, UIL, Confindustria and the government, the latter had, with Law no. 191 (13 July 1990) prorogued the *Scala Mobile* for the whole year 1991. However, from January 1992 the mechanism was again under the bargaining autonomy of the social partners. At the expiration of the deadline the government confirmed, with the Protocol of December 1991, its firm decision not to allow any other prorogation by law of the *Scala Mobile*. In fact, it stated that all the problems relating to a new general system of bargaining and to the structure of retribution should be tackled by 1 June 1992. The battle was likely to be extremely hard unless there was some external factor pressing the trade unions, or better still the CGIL, to accept the agreement on wage policy as the only possible alternative to the abyss. This external factor was represented by speculative attacks on the lira.

This does not necessarily mean that the Italian economic elite provoked the speculative attacks, but the Italian employers' class certainly acted within the limits of the possible. Indeed, the Protocol eventually signed on 31 July 1992 represented a major victory for the employers. The trade unions had agreed to the almost complete elimination of the *Scala Mobile* and had accepted the block of wage bargaining at plant level for the whole of 1993 in exchange of a forfeit sum of 20,000 lire ($8) per month for all workers.

The question of the structure of wage bargaining, not tackled in the Protocol, was left to further negotiations, leading to the agreement of 1993. The latter institutionalized the new balance of power between Italian social partners by introducing two levels of collective bargaining: the national and the plant levels. Moreover, it provided the take-off platform for future changes in social-protection legislation, particularly reform of the pension system (cf. Regini and Regalia 1997). Finally, it increased the level of flexibility in the Italian labour market by improving the Italian training system (boosting internal flexibility) and legalizing temporary-work agencies (improving external flexibility) (see Rhodes 1997: 14).

In the context of the decreasing bargaining power of the trade unions, some steps towards the deregulation of employment conditions had already been taken with Law no. 223/91, which modified the procedures of placement by introducing the so-called 'nominative call' in place of the 'compulsory call'. It also recognized collective redundancies as a possible solution for firms' crises, a measure which, together with the introduction of the new instrument of mobility insurance (a longer form of early retirement), was meant to guarantee Italian companies freedom to fire in the case of necessity (see Gualmini 1998). Coming to the hire side of liberalizing policies, Law no. 221 abolished the obligation of firms to choose workers from the so-called *liste di disoccupazione* (compulsory hiring lists) and introduced the principle of free choice.

In terms of job creation, some further initiatives were taken in the course of the 1990s, particularly by the Berlusconi government, on whose effectiveness, however, some doubts have been cast. Law no. 451/94 introduced the so-called 'public utility works',[9] which seemed to many to be yet another form of badly concealed *assistenzialismo* whose only outcome was to postpone the problem of unemployment for a very limited number of people. Moreover, some fiscal incentives for young employers starting new enterprises were introduced by the Berlusconi government, as was a law on ad-interim jobs. Finally, despite a long-lasting ideological debate on the reduction of working hours, no steps in this direction have so far been taken, even though there was an increase in the use of part-time contracts and solidarity contracts during the 1990s (*Economist*, 29 April and 5 May 2000).[10]

Notwithstanding an evident trend towards the reduction of labour protection and the increase of labour flexibility, the Italian unemployment level has not shown any particularly marked decrease in recent years and is still characterized by great differences in terms of region, age and gender (*Economist*, 29 April and 5 May 2000). Even the small reduction in unemployment in the last months of the year 2000 is related much more to a favourable phase in the Italian business-cycle than to the effectiveness of labour-market deregulation.

By contrast, Spain is often quoted as the most successful example of job creation driven by an effective employment policy geared towards increased labour flexibility and the reduction of labour protection. Indeed, since 1997 the level of unemployment in Spain has fallen from 20.8 per cent in 1997 to an astonishing forecasted 16.8 in the year 2000. Given the activism of the Aznar administration in terms of continuing the liberalization of labour markets initiated by the Socialist government in 1994, the temptation to correlate the two phenomena arises spontaneously. This is why the Spanish case deserves particular attention and why the following section is devoted entirely to its analysis.

Labour-market flexibilization in Spain

In Spain, too, the introduction of greater flexibility into the labour market in the 1980s has clearly affected trade unions' capacity of representation and their bargaining power in the political sphere. The changes introduced into labour legislation during the 1980s were aimed at increasing external (or numerical) flexibility by boosting temporary employment. The pressures stemming from the necessity of adapting the Spanish economy to the EU, and the particular institutional context of that period, made it very difficult for unions to reject these measures, whose major effect on employment was a huge increase in the number of temporary workers. Given the fact that the support of this category of workers to unions is very low, the result was a decrease in the capacity of representation of Spanish trade unions.

In the course of the 1990s a new strategy was adopted to make labour markets more flexible. The intention was always to increase the external (or numerical) flexibility, but in this case the stress fell on redundancy costs. In addition, some measures were approved to increase functional flexibility. In this new phase, the institutional context had changed and trade unions had some margin of manoeuvre to develop a strategy of opposition towards those measures. However, trade unions' efforts were not successful and the pressures stemming from EU membership prevailed over their protests. This outcome convinced the leadership of the trade unions to adopt a more co-operative attitude that allowed the employees' organizations to continue to play a role in the Spanish political arena.

The 1980s: the first measures toward flexibility and the crisis of representation in trade unions

The end of the Franco dictatorship and the transition towards a democratic system eliminated the obstacles to integrating Spain into the international context, and in particular into the European Community, for which a democratic political system was a precondition. However, the Spanish economy still needed important adjustments. The insulation of the country during the authoritarian regime and the delayed impact of the first oil crisis had destabilized the economy (cf. Fuentes Quintana 1988; Rojo 1987).

The first democratic government of Adolfo Suárez carried out the first attempts to stabilize the economy. However, the macroeconomic policy programme adopted was incomplete. The transition process, limited electoral support and the crisis inside the leading political party (Unión de Centro Democrático, UCD) restrained the government from implementing more thorough economic reforms (see Maravall 1995).

When in 1982 the Socialist Party won the elections, the consolidation of democracy and wide electoral support allowed the new administration to develop more determined macroeconomic policies (*ibid.*: 121). Indeed, with the aim of curtailing the inflation rate and the public deficit, the socialist government started implementing strict monetary and fiscal policies. The government was convinced that the only way to stabilize the economy was to improve the supply side of the Spanish economy. According to Maravall, the reasons for implementing such a policy rather than the Keynesian policy expected from a social-democratic government were what had been learnt from previous experiences, on the one hand,[11] and the influence of a group of post-Keynesian economists within the Ministry of the Economy,[12] on the other (*ibid.*: 128).

The implementation of an austere macroeconomic policy in order to correct the imbalance of the Spanish economy was justified by the process of integration into the international economy and, more concretely, by the aspiration to become a member of the European Economic Community (EEC). As Holman points out, 'the "extended relaunch" of the European integration provided both the institutional framework and the external legitimization for the implemented austerity policy' (1996: 125).[13]

The economic policy was accompanied by important changes in labour-market legislation. Spanish unemployment rates were amongst the highest in Europe and the blame was generally put on the rigidity of labour markets (Maravall and Fraile 1998: 4–5). This rigid system had been inherited from the authoritarian regime. Job security was the way in which the authoritarian regime compensated workers for the lack of collective liberties (Valdés Dal-Ré 1985: 304; see also Iriso Napal 1993: 321). However, in the context of global interdependence such legislation became obsolete.

The socialist government decided to make the labour market more flexible by changing labour legislation. The changes took place in 1984 with the reform of the Estatuto de los Trabajadores. This reform introduced '[t]he most important institutional change in the Spanish labour market of the last decade', the promotion of temporary employment (Bentolila and Dolado 1993: 113; our translation).[14] It was the first time in Spain that consistent and unitary legislation was introduced to boost temporary jobs. Apart from providing a whole range of facilities for the use of already-existing types of temporary contracts, the new legislation created new types of contracts and, in particular, 'temporary contracts for the increase of employment'. The novelty of this new type of contract was that it allowed temporary employment for non-temporary jobs since this contract could only be used for unemployed workers. According to Flórez, this legislation 'represented the end of the permanent job principle' (1994: 106; our translation).

The main advantage of temporary contracts is that they allow firms to react to economic fluctuations essentially by lowering firing costs. Indeed, while the firing cost of permanent workers is about 20–45 days of salary for each year of work, the firing cost of temporary workers is 12 days of salary for each year of work and in many cases there are no costs at all (Bentolila and Dolado 1994; 62). Government strategy, therefore, was intended to make the labour market more flexible by creating new temporary jobs with lower redundancy costs.

What was the reaction of Spanish trade unions to the introduction of this new legislation? Both unions, the Unión General de Trabajadores (UGT) and the Comisiones Obreras (CCOO), rejected temporary employment for non-temporary tasks because this might produce substitution of permanent jobs with temporary ones. This meant a worsening of working conditions for many workers, and the risk of producing segmentation of the labour market between permanent and temporary workers. However, their reaction to the bulk of new legislation was very different. Indeed, while the UGT accepted it, the CCOO rejected it. This trade unions reaction is explained by the institutional and economic context.

Since the beginning of the transition in Spain, the union movement has been divided into two families: the communist one represented by the CCOO and the socialist one represented by the UGT. This division strongly conditioned the strategies of these organizations. On the one hand, both unions competed for the leadership, which produced strong rivalry between them. On the other hand, their demands were strongly related to their allied political party.[15]

When reform of the legislation took place in 1984, the UGT maintained what Astudillo has called a 'relationship of solidarity' with the Socialist Party.[16] For that reason, although the new legislation had produced some discontent inside the UGT, this organization decided to accept it. In exchange for its support the union expected the government to increase social expenditure.

Moreover, the unemployment rate was so high that inside the UGT the idea gained momentum that it was better to create temporary jobs than not to create employment at all.[17] At the same time, the UGT believed that, as had been the case in the past, a moderate attitude would win benefits to the union. Since the end of the 1970s, indeed, the socialist union had followed a more moderate strategy than its rival union, the CCOO. This strategy consisted in participation in pacts with the entrepreneur organization (Confederación Española de Organizaciones Empresariales, CEOE) and with the government,[18] and it had benefited the union to a very large extent. In a period of political transition and economic crisis, such moderation coincided with the interests of the workers. The result was that in 1982, for the first time, the UGT took over the leadership of the CCOO (Astudillo 1998).

Therefore the UGT accepted the new labour legislation, notwithstanding a certain degree of opposition to it within the union itself, mainly because of the combined effects of both the economic and the institutional context. On the one hand, in fact, the urgent need to reduce the unemployment rate made this organization more willing to accept temporary jobs, as a way of boosting employment for young workers and women. On the other hand, the agreement on the increase of temporary contracts represented the price the UGT had to pay to maintain its privileged relationship with the Socialist Party and to maintain its leading role within the trade union movement.

The CCOO, on the contrary, maintained a critical attitude towards the new labour legislation. The members of this union believed that the reform only satisfied the entrepreneurs' interests and that the only effect it would produce in the labour market would be the substitution of permanent jobs for temporary jobs. The CCOO rejected not only the government's employment policy, but also the entire macroeconomic strategy devised by the socialist administration. In short, the CCOO adopted an attitude of total opposition to the government.

However, despite its disagreement with the new legislation the CCOO failed to organize demonstrations or any other kind of protest against it. There were two reasons for this. On the one hand, the effects of the new legislation were still uncertain. On the other, the mobilization of workers against temporary jobs was very difficult.

The new labour legislation soon produced effects on employment. The worldwide economic recovery in the mid-1980s made possible a rise in (especially temporary) employment. The result was that temporary jobs experienced huge growth in a very short period of time. In just eight years (1987–95) this form of employment rose as a proportion of total employment from 15 per cent to 35 per cent.[19] Temporary employment principally affects manual workers, especially women and young people, with few qualifications. It has spread in the private sector more than in the public sector. And, although there has been a generalized increase throughout the economy, temporary employment is particularly common in agriculture and the building and construction industry (Segura *et al.* 1991). As a consequence of such a growth, Spain became the EU member state with highest rate of temporary employment (for comparative data, see Chapter 9, Table 9.1).

The rise in temporary employment as a result of the reforms by the socialist government has negatively affected the functioning of the Spanish labour market. One of the most remarkable negative effects has been the segmentation of the labour market between temporary workers and permanent workers. The costs of reaction to the economic fluctuations fall most heavily on temporary workers and hardly affect permanent workers (Bentolila and Dolado 1993, 1994). As a consequence, the working conditions of temporary workers are very precarious. Temporary jobs usually last a very short time and rarely lead to a permanent job. This produces high levels of rotation from one temporary job to another, with workers condemned to remaining permanently in temporary employment (Bentolila and Dolado 1993; Dolado and Bentolila 1992; Polavieja 1998).

Temporary jobs normally also imply low wages. Some studies estimate that temporary workers earn less than permanent workers (Dolado and Bentolila 1992; Jimeno and Toharia 1992, cited in Bentolila and Dolado 1993, 1994).[20] Moreover, temporary jobs are related to adverse working conditions. These workers' limited capacity to protest and their interest in obtaining permanent employment leads them to accept worse working conditions than their permanent colleagues. The accident rate among temporary workers is significantly higher than among permanent workers (Recio 1991). At the same time, due to the short period of time these workers stay at firms, employers do not invest money in improving their skills and qualifications. This may have important effects on productivity (Dolado and Bentolida 1992).

The increase in temporary employment has also negatively affected the capacity of representation of Spanish trade unions. Membership rates and the results in union elections show that temporary workers have very low levels of support for trade unions.[21]

The main characteristic of union members and voters is, therefore, that both groups consist of permanent workers. The limited support for unions amongst temporary workers can be explained by the working conditions they face. On the one hand, temporary employment is higher in sectors and firms in which trade unions have a very limited presence, as in job agencies. On the other, temporary workers are afraid of redundancy, which in most cases reduces their tendency to join or vote for unions (Iriso Napal 1993: 324).

This is only part of the problem. If working conditions were the only reason not to join a union or to participate in union elections, temporary workers should have similar attitudes to trade unions as other workers. However, this is not the case. Polavieja's work shows that temporary workers have a more negative attitude towards unions than permanent workers (cf. Polavieja and Richards 1997). Indeed, Spanish trade unions have not been able to obtain the support of temporary workers. Permanent workers form their main constituency. This poses a serious challenge to the unions' representation capacity: the trade unions' objective of representing the working class as a whole has been seriously undermined. And the task of representing both types of workers is particularly difficult if we take into account the fact that the demands of temporary workers differ substantially from those of the traditional core constituency of trade unions.[22]

The effects of labour-market restructuring in the 1980s on the composition and organization of the Spanish working class have thus been considerable, and have, in particular, undercut the unions' representational capacity and workers' militancy.

A new policy for making the labour market more flexible and the change in unions' strategy

At the end of the 1980s the segmentation of the Spanish labour market due to the rise in temporary employment worried unions very much. This discontent with the consequences of the change in labour legislation was expressed not only by the CCOO but also by the UGT. The socialist union started voicing its feeling that the reform had not produced the expected results. It had indeed created employment, but a very precarious form of employment.

By that time, the institutional context had changed. In 1987 the UGT broke the solidarity pact with the Socialist Party in the 'labour sphere' and decided to co-operate with the CCOO in the development of a joint strategy on labour relations. According to Astudillo, the reason for this rupture was the growth of the economy in a context of union competition. During the mid-1980s the economy had experienced strong growth, which made workers increase their wage demands. In spite of this, the UGT continued to support the strict monetary policy of the government by accepting wage moderation. The result was that in 1986 the UGT lost workers' support in the union elections in favour of the CCOO, which had fought for wage increases. At the same time, the bad results of the socialist government's employment policy made UGT stop trusting in the economic policy of the government. However, in 1987 the UGT still wanted to maintain the solidarity relationship with the Socialist Party in the 'political sphere' (Astudillo 1998: 569–70).

The disagreement of trade unions with the economic policy developed by the government was shown in the general strike that took place on 14 December 1988. The CCOO and UGT decided to come out on strike after the government announced the introduction of a new measure to boost employment for young workers: *El Plan de Empleo Juvenil*. This new measure consisted of creating a new kind of job contract for young people. Trade unions strongly rejected this measure on the grounds that it would worsen even further the working conditions of young people. But the general strike also demanded what the unions called *la deuda social*: in a period of economic growth, unions demanded wage increases. These should also apply to people dependent on the state: civil servants, social-security recipients and lodgers. At the same time, unions demanded a rise in unemployment coverage. The strike was strongly supported by workers and made the government suspend the implementation of *El Plan de Empleo Juvenil*.

After the general strike in 1988 UGT decided to end the collaboration with the government in the 'political sphere'. The union considered that it was unable to influence the government on political issues.[23] Therefore the socialist trade union decided that the best way to obtain its social and political goals was to co-operate with CCOO on the development of joint policies, which were eventually presented in a document entitled *La Propuesta Sindical Prioritaria* (*PSP*) (Astudillo 1998). At the beginning of the 1990s, the objectives of trade unions were to reduce the proportion of temporary work in the labour market and to make the government increase social expenditure. With this purpose in mind the unions consented to carry out several agreements with the socialist government, but all of them related to very concrete issues.[24] On the other hand, the unions rejected several pacts that implied acceptance of the macroeconomic strategy of the government: *El Pacto de Competitividad* (1990), *El Pacto Social de Progreso* (1991) and *El Plan de Convergencia con la Comunidad Europea* (1992).

The Spanish government found it convenient to start a bargaining process with the unions and even to discuss an increase in social expenditure. The reason was that the minister of the economy, Carlos Solchaga, believed that if the government increased social expenditure the unions would accept wage moderation more easily. Furthermore, Solchaga thought that this strategy would promote his political position within the Socialist Party.[25]

For all these reasons, the unions were able to achieve many of their social and employment objectives. However, the unions' bargaining power soon faded away when in 1992 the economic crisis became more intense. On the one hand, given the trade unions' unwillingness to moderate their wage demands, the Spanish inflation rate – at 5.3 per cent – was above the level required in the Maastricht Treaty. On the other hand, the government's increase in social expenditure resulted in a bigger public deficit, which also was over the convergence requirements determined in the Maastricht Treaty. Finally, the unemployment rate grew to over 20 per cent. This situation seriously threatened Spanish chances of joining the EMU in the first wave, and this triggered the government's resolution to adopt a more restrictive set of policies. In the context of global interdependency, especially after the establishment of EMU, government policy was strongly constrained by the fulfilment of the macroeconomic results required by the EU.

The first restrictive measure in 1993 aimed at reducing the public deficit by making access to unemployment benefits more difficult.[26] Trade unions strongly rejected this reform and called for a half-day strike. However, the unions' action had no effect on the government. The need to reduce the public deficit in order to fulfil the Maastricht criteria to enter EMU became the government's first priority.

In 1994 the Spanish economy worsened. The inflation rate was still high (4.3 per cent), and the public deficit had grown further as unemployment reached 24 per cent. As a consequence, the government decided to implement new labour reform in order to reduce unemployment and to adapt the Spanish industrial-relations system to the global economy (*Boletín Oficial del Estado* 122/1994, 15805).

The reform had four main guidelines:

- The reduction of temporality in the labour market by limiting and simplifying contracts' modalities;[27] in exchange for this the government simplified the firing of permanent workers.
- The legalization of temporary work agencies.
- The introduction of measures to boost functional flexibility – on issues like wages, workers' mobility and working hours.
- The adaptation of the collective bargaining system to the competitive requirements of the global economy by eliminating the *Ordenanzas Laborales*, which were the basis for the rigid collective agreements inherited from the dictatorship regime.

The trade unions strongly rejected an agreement on this reform on the grounds that it resulted in a substantial diminution of workers' rights. According to the trade unions, in fact, the arrangements introduced to facilitate the firing of permanent workers would increase unemployment. Moreover, the legalization of job agencies was incomplete and did not sufficiently guarantee workers' rights. Finally, the collective bargaining introduced by the reform reduced trade union bargaining power in favour of the entrepreneurs, while the measures adopted to boost functional flexibility would worsen working conditions.

However, the content of the reform was not the only reason for the unions to reject an agreement with the government. There were also political reasons. By that time, indeed, the relationship between the UGT and the socialist government had become very uneasy. The UGT accused the government of betraying social-democratic principles and of adopting a neo-liberal policy. At the same time, part of the union leadership, especially of the CCOO, maintained positions that made it very difficult to reach an agreement. In particular, they were not ready to accept the introduction of greater flexibility in the legislation on firing.

Therefore the trade unions put pressure on the government not to carry out the labour reform. However, demonstrations and the protests organized by the trade unions did not sway political support for the government. The reason was that the government argued that the reform of labour legislation was necessary to reduce unemployment, to adapt the Spanish industrial-relations system to the European economy and to fulfil the convergence criteria for EMU membership. Therefore the context of global interdependency provided the government with the rationale to implement the labour reform, despite the disagreement of the unions.

The failure of the unions to stop the reform of 1994 resulted in a stark decline in their bargaining power. It was clear that their capacity to obtain important concessions from the government, demonstrated at the end of the 1980s and at the beginning of the 1990s, had by then disappeared. The defeat of 1994 also undermined the position of the more militant elements within the unions. As a result, a more moderate and co-operative strategy gradually gained more support. This turnaround was completed in 1994–5. The UGT leadership changed in 1994. In 1995 the CCOO ousted the most radical elements inside the leading group, leaving the CCOO to the moderates led by secretary-general Antonio Gutiérrez. The confrontational strategy developed by the trade unions after 1988 was abandoned.

The co-operative attitude of the unions began with the opening of a bargaining process with the CEOE in 1995. The results of this bargaining were proposed to the Popular Party (Partido Popular, PP), which won the elections in 1996, as the basis for a new labour reform. This reform, enacted in 1997, had three main objectives:

- the increase of permanent employment and the reduction of temporality;
- the articulation of the structure of the collective bargaining system;
- the introduction of minimum legislation for those sectors which were not covered by the collective bargaining.

This time the political context favoured the agreement. Indeed, the unions, the employers and the government had the same objective: the reduction of temporality and the re-establishment of employment stability. This was widely considered one of the most important problems of the Spanish economy. At the same time, reaching an agreement had a positive meaning in itself for both the social partners and the government. Indeed, all political actors had learnt from previous experiences that contested reform had a very bad effect on labour relations. It made many of the measures adopted ineffective and introduced uncertainty into labour relations. Moreover, the 1997 reform represented for the trade unions the opportunity to reduce temporary work, one of their priorities since the end of the 1980s, and it also allowed them to recover some political influence. On the other hand, for the new government an agreed reform would guarantee social and political stability, announcing it as a moderate administration. In fact, therefore, we may conclude that the 1994 defeat of union radicalism had prepared the ground for a more consensual and conciliatory variant of neo-liberalism, sometimes called 'embedded neo-liberalism' (see Chapter 7).

The concessions made, however, were not evenly distributed. On the part of the employers, an indispensable condition to reach an agreement was that trade unions were ready to make concessions to reduce firing costs. In exchange for reducing temporality, in fact, entrepreneurs demanded that the redundancy process be made more flexible and cheaper. The union leadership accepted this in order to reduce temporality rates. It was the first time trade unions agreed to make concessions of this kind.[28]

At the same time, trade unions had to change their traditional organizational structure of bargaining. This reform produced a much more decentralized bargaining process, signalling a gradual move from state corporatism to enterprise corporatism (cf. R.W. Cox 1987). As a consequence, the unions have had to strengthen their bargaining power at the firm level, where they have traditionally been very weak.

Conclusions

The unemployment consequences of the establishment of EMU along the lines agreed at Maastricht and confirmed by the GSP are still the subject of passionate discussions within the economists community. However, its political-economy consequences in terms of power relations amongst the different socio-economic groups at both the national and the transnational level look much less controversial.

Indeed, as we have indicated, the implementation of an EU employment strategy relying significantly on labour-market flexibility, for which the rationale is often neo-functionally linked to the establishment of EMU, is by no means neutral in its political-economy impact and substantially modifies the existing balance of power between employers' organizations and trade unions. Furthermore, the implementation itself of flexible labour-market policies was made possible by the strengthening of the employers' organizations' bargaining power enshrined in the institutionalization at the European level of the neo-liberal economic paradigm focusing on the implementation of strict monetary and fiscal policies.

If the process of globalization does modify the role of the nation-state from the welfare model to the Anglo-Saxon model or 'competition state' (Cerny 1990), it might be argued that the process of regionalization allows for a simplification of this process by strengthening the institutional power of transnational capitalist elites *vis-à-vis* organized labour in the shift from the national to the European level of governance. This game of transnationalization is indeed much more easily played by the employers' organizations than by the unions, given the many cleavages within the labour-interest representation groups and the disaggregating tendencies embedded in the present globalized capitalist structure. This dimension is particularly strong in what we have termed the Mediterranean model, where the relatively late arrival of welfare-state politics was overtaken by the onset of global restructuring and the implementation of the Single European Market programme.

If this is plausible, then it would seem that the process of transnationalization is a dialectical one in which the proactive role of organized transnational actors (see Chapter 7) and the restructuring of the world economy in the context of globalization mutually determine and reinforce each other. As far as this contribution is concerned, it seems clear that the redefinition of the power relations among socio-economic groups is well advanced in the two countries analysed, and furthermore that it occurred in dialectical interrelation with the process of European monetary integration.

Notes

1 See, for example, Crouch (2000), Dyson and Featherstone (1999), Eichengreen and Frieden (1998), Frieden *et al.* (1998), de Grauwe (1997) and Talani (2000).

2 The distinction between 'monetarists' and 'economists' emerged in the course of the discussions over the Werner Plan and referred to the strategy to be adopted during the transitional period. The 'monetarists' stressed the importance of achieving exchange-rate stability through European institutional arrangements, while the 'economists' pointed out the necessity of policy co-ordination and, ultimately, convergence before agreeing on the adoption of a European fixed-exchange-rate regime or a currency union. For more details, see Tsoukalis (1997).

3 The bases for the discussion were represented in the Commission communication entitled *Action for Employment in Europe: A Confidence Pact* (EC 1996a), the joint interim report on employment and the other documents before it, including the conclusions drawn from the Tripartite Conference on Growth and Employment held in Rome on 14 and 15 June 1996 and the French Memorandum on a European social model (see European Council 1996).

4 It is important to note that in the same year, 1975, the Bank of Italy committed itself to buying all unsold Treasury Bills.

5 Article 39 of the Italian Constitution indicates the requisites for a collective agreement to achieve the force of law, but this article has never been implemented.

6 The Italian UIL (a federation of CGIL and CISL) was established in 1972 and lasted until 1984, when, during the heated debate over the *Scala Mobile*, it was dismantled.

7 For a thorough analysis of the Italian trade union organization literature up to the early 1980s, see Giugni (1981: 324); for a more theoretical review of the relationship between industrial relations and political science, see Gourevitch *et al.* (1981: 401).

8 In the analysis carried out by Vannicelli, it is possible to identify four distinct groups of workers:

- the 'core' of the workforce, consisting of industrial workers, usually active in the union movement, who were affected by the economic crisis to a lesser extent;
- an expanding group of precarious workers, who were pushed by the recession into a condition of permanent, state-subsidized unemployment;
- women and young people with little hope of finding employment;
- a group of 'unofficially' employed people recruited by the 'invisible' or even 'black' economy (see Vannicelli 1984: 404).

9 The law allowed public administrations and some private organizations to promote projects for works of public interest and to use long-term unemployed selected from the *liste di disoccupazione* for a limited period of time.

10 Solidarity contracts allow workers to accept reduced working time to save jobs. They were introduced in 1984 and have been used so far only in a defensive way.

11 The crisis of the economic policy of the French government at the beginning of the 1980s and the crisis of the Labour Party in Great Britain in the 1970s. Other authors also point out the influence of the crisis of the economy policy of the socialist government in Greece in the 1980s (Holman 1996; Astudillo 1998).

12 Miguel Boyer and Carlos Solchaga, who were ministers of the economy between 1982 and 1993.

13 This was confirmed to one of the authors in an interview with Antonio García de Blas, a member of the head group of economists within the Ministry of the Economy.

14 Before this reform there had been several attempts to boost temporary employment, for example the *cuñas flexibilizadoras* in the late 1970s and the *Estatuto de los Trabajadores* in 1980. For a detailed analysis of this labour legislation, see Flórez (1994).

15 As already mentioned, the CCOO was very close to the Communist Party (Partido Comunista de España, PCE), and the UGT to the Socialist Party (Partido Socialista Obrero Español, PSOE).

16 Astudillo defines the relationship of solidarity as those 'in which social-democratic parties and unions share the same final objectives but, to avoid the possibility of subordination of one organization over the other, the tasks are divided: the political tasks for the party and the labour tasks for the union' (Astudillo 1998: 41; our translation).

17 This was the thesis defended by José Luís Corcuera, the union leader who pushed for the reform of 1984.

18 The UGT signed two bipartite pacts with the CEOE, the *Acuerdo Básico Interconfederal* (ABI, 1979) and the *Acuerdo Marco Interconfederal* (AMI, 1979), and one tripartite pact, the *Acuerdo Nacional de Empleo* (ANE, 1981), during the period of the UCD government. However, CCOO only participated in the ANE.

19 In 1985 90 per cent of job contracts were temporary, and in 1986 the percentage rose to 96 per cent (Castillo 1994: 63).

20 According to Jimeno and Toharia, temporary workers earn between 8.5 per cent and 11 per cent less than permanent workers (Jimeno and Toharia 1992). Wage discrimination is illegal in Spain. However, it is possible through the classification of temporary workers in lower occupational categories than those that they really deserve (Bentolila and Dolado 1994: 71).

21 The indicators of the power of representation of Spanish trade unions are membership rates and the results of union elections. There are important differences between these two indicators. Union membership implies affinity and commitment to the union organization. The union vote, however, only implies casting a vote every four years for the union of the worker's choice. Membership provides unions with an important source of funding. The results of union elections, however, give unions the right to participate in collective bargaining with employers. The union affiliation rate in Spain is low; in fact, at around 15 per cent it is one of the lowest in Europe. However, the level of participation in union elections is very high, with a turnout of around 75–80 per cent of the working population, almost exclusively permanent workers. Thus Spanish unions are considered to be organizations not of members but of voters (Jordana 1994: 139). Research shows that temporary workers hardly vote in union elections (a turnout of only 14 per cent, as revealed by a 1988 survey by the Spanish Centre for Sociological Research).

22 Different working conditions imply different, and even opposing, demands from each group of workers. Permanent workers' priorities are job security and higher wages. In contrast, the principal objective of temporary workers is to obtain a permanent job (Iriso Napal 1993). The interests of both types of workers are in conflict, especially in periods of economic crisis.

23 UGT was strongly against the minister of the economy, Carlos Solchaga, and wanted the government to remove him from office. The government, however, did not do so because Prime Minister Felipe González agreed with the minister's economic policy (Astudillo 1998).

24 The agreements were about a rise in social expenditure, a rise in the number of civil servants and the introduction of legislation to reduce the fraudulent use of temporary contracts. With these agreements the government satisfied the unions' demands in the general strike of 1988.

25 After the general strike of 1988 Felipe González thought about the possibility of withdrawing, and the deputy prime minister was involved in a political scandal. This situation within the Socialist Party made Solchaga think that he could become the next candidate to lead the government. A good relationship with the trade unions might help him to obtain this objective (Astudillo 1998: 249).

26 The minimum period of work to qualify for unemployment benefit increased from six to twelve months, and the average duration of such benefits was reduced from twenty to twelve months.

27 The high rates of rotation from employment to unemployment of temporary workers had produced a strong rise in the deficit of the unemployment benefit system. Therefore the government decided that it was necessary to reduce temporary employment.

28 Firing costs were reduced only for new permanent contracts, and the rights of those workers who already held a permanent job before the introduction of this new type of contract were left untouched.

Part IV

Conclusion

12 Conflicting views on how to address (un)employment in Europe

A tentative conclusion

Henk Overbeek

In the debates about employment policy both at the national and at the European level, we may, if we simplify the picture for the sake of clarity, conclude that two axes were crucial. The first regards the level at which policy formation takes place: the three levels identified here are the national, the regional and the global. The second concerns the mode of regulation;[1] here we distinguish between the dominant mode of capitalist regulation of the 1960s and 1970s (public regulation and Keynesianism); the straightforward opposite mode of market regulation, which we call neo-liberalism; and, finally, the emerging mode which aims to mitigate the socially disruptive effects of neo-liberalism without abolishing the primacy of the market that we could call 'corporatism' (or communitarianism, Chapter 4; or 'embedded neo-liberalism', Chapter 7). This results in nine boxes with stylized modes and levels of social and employment policy (see Table 12.1). There are, of course, especially as a result of the contestation between various interests, viewpoints and social forces, many overlaps and many intermediate forms and combinations. Nevertheless, Table 12.1 will make it possible to systematize the positions of various actors discussed throughout the preceding chapters.

Table 12.1 Modes and levels of regulation

	Level		
Mode	*National*	*EU*	*Global*
Public regulation	National Keynesianism	EU Keynesianism	Global Keynesianism
Public market-making	Competitive corporatism	Euro-corporatism	Global corporatism
Market regulation	Neo-liberal competition state	Neo-liberal regionalism	Neo-liberal globalization

National Keynesianism

In the post-war decades national Keynesianism was the hegemonic concept: we might say that the last (unsuccessful) instalment was the attempt by Mitterrand in 1981 to complete the Keynesian welfare state in France. The lesson of the Mitterrand episode has been not that a national solution is impossible in principle but, rather, that the abolition of capital controls (gradually introduced after the early 1970s and in Europe locked in with the advent of monetary union) has largely deprived governments of the means to enforce national policies against the preferences of transnational money capital (Helleiner 1995).

EU Keynesianism

In many political programmes of the Left the demise of national Keynesianism has led to the conclusion that the social objectives of Keynesianism may be salvaged by creating at the EU level the institutions and practices of Keynesian employment policy. Examples of attempts to put some kind of Euro-Keynesian programme into place were the proposals of the early Delors Presidency and, most recently, the Lafontaine proposals of 1999. The key argument of the Euro-Keynesians is that, whereas the enormous degree of openness of the national economies in Europe (with foreign trade as a percentage of gross domestic product (GDP) ranging from 60–70 per cent to 120 per cent or higher) precludes national avenues, the relatively lower degree of openness of the EU economy as a whole (around 40 per cent) would leave ample space for initiatives for Keynesian policies. With inter-European policy competition eliminated, it would become possible at the European level to implement a range of employment-boosting policies, provided the present limitations imposed by monetary union and the Stability Pact can be substantially amended (e.g. Coates and Holland 1995; Lipietz 1996; see also Chapter 10 of this volume).

Global Keynesianism

In response to the initially radical calls for a New International Economic Order in the mid-1970s, an independent commission of leading Social Democrats and reformist bourgeois politicians from North and South convened by Willy Brandt (the former West German Chancellor) wrote a report that has been characterized as a plea for Keynesianism on an global scale (Brandt Report 1980). This report is part of a series of similar reports (Tinbergen Report, Brundtland Report) often initiated in the United Nations (UN), of which the report by the Commission on Global Governance is the latest (CGG 1995) of its sort. All of these reports share the preference for reformist, redistributive programmes at the global level with a coordinating or even initiating role for UN organizations. With respect to employment and the global labour market, there have been calls for transnational employment policy (Emmerij 1994) and for a global social policy (Deacon 1997; Köhler 1999; Mishra 1999; de Swaan 1992, 1994).

Competitive corporatism

This concept has been proposed by Martin Rhodes to denote those cases where governments (usually of small open economies) have successfully convinced trade unions and employers to strike a deal (wage moderation in exchange for employment protection) in order to maintain 'competitiveness' (Rhodes 1998). Others have referred to this position as supply-side corporatism (see Chapter 5). Governments play a key role in this model, complementing this compromise with an active labour-market policy. Although protagonists of this strategy advocate an important initiating role for the state in the economy, this role is seen primarily as market-making, not as market steering. Adherence to strict budget controls is a key disciplining mechanism that limits possibilities for the state to actively *create* employment (Albo 1994). Examples of this strategy that are often identified are Ireland and the Netherlands (see Chapter 9 for a critical discussion; see also Visser and Hemerijck 1997).

Euro-corporatism

This label is used here to describe those forces at the EU level (e.g. the Delors Presidency and, less outspoken, the present Prodi Presidency) who press for what is in fact an EU variant of the strategy of competitive corporatism: proto-corporatist arrangements at the EU level (complementing national and regional arrangements) are encouraged in order to enhance the competitive position of the EU economy (e.g. the ambitious goals adopted at the 1999 Lisbon Summit to transform the EU into the most dynamic economic region in the world by 2010). Concrete efforts and policies in this direction (and this distinguishes Euro-corporatism from Euro-Keynesianism) are conceived strictly within the budgetary constraints imposed by the Economic and Monetary Union (EMU) and the Stability Pact, and are predicated on the accelerated full implementation of the Single Market in such new areas as energy provision and financial services (for more details see Part II of this volume).

Global corporatism

There are various strands of thinking that might be considered variants of one or another variant of 'corporatism' at the global scale: all those views favouring a combination of strong global institutions and involvement of 'global civil society' in a system of 'global governance' to guarantee ongoing 'responsible' globalization might be placed in this box. This means the whole range of options, from James Wolfensohn's view of development and the role of the World Bank to the advocates of creating some form of 'stakeholder democracy'.[2]

Neo-liberal competition state

The straightforward neo-liberal strategy takes its inspiration from such people as Friedrich von Hayek (1991a, 1991b) and Milton Friedman (Friedman and Friedman 1980). This strategy prescribes liberalization and privatization as the main instruments to enhance the self-regulatory capacity of 'the market' (Cerny 1990; see also Palan and Abbott 1996). In the OECD area the neo-liberal model is primarily found in the US and in the UK.[3]

Neo-liberal regionalism

Neo-liberal forms of regional integration rely on the wholesome effects of market enlargement and the removal of obstacles to the free movement of capital, goods and services (Gamble and Payne 1996), and under certain conditions also of labour (Pellerin and Overbeek 2001). The best-known examples of neo-liberal or 'open' regionalism are the project of the Single European Market and the North American Free Trade Agreement (NAFTA); since their adoption there has followed a rush of similar initiatives to establish free-trade areas all around the world. Most of these initiatives are at best still in the planning stage and it is far from clear that most will ever effectively move beyond that stage.

Neo-liberal globalization

Finally, at the global level the preferred neo-liberal mode of governance of the world economy is an informal, partly privatized, 'soft' one. Institutions and fora such as the G7 and the World Economic Forum facilitate ongoing globalization by a mix of market liberalization and discipline through creating a de facto neo-liberal constitution for the global economy (Gill 1995; van der Pijl 1998).[4]

The contributions to this volume illustrate many of the points summarily raised above. The terms of political debates in Europe about employment and labour-market issues have shifted considerably since the early 1980s. It is unquestionable that globalization has reduced the scope for national policy autonomy. The structural aspects of the globalization process, the rise of new communication and information technology, the very real (albeit by no means complete) globalization of financial markets, the transnationalization of production, the increased economic interdependence of national economies, all these changes are real and they do indeed exert a strong influence on the parameters for national policy-making.

We may not, however, conclude from this that national employment policy is no longer possible. Globalization, first of all, is not a process of homogenization: on the contrary, globalization in many ways accentuates difference as well as uniformity, and operates through the continuous creation of niches that can be utilized by national governments to pursue specific policy goals. What *is* largely impossible under the present globalizing regime is for governments to pursue – what are now usually called old-fashioned, socialist – strategies of de-commodification. Policies only have a chance of survival if they conform to the principles of market liberalization. Second, it is important to emphasize once more that globalization is also a project, and that governments themselves have at various stages decisively contributed to intensifying the globalization process: they are, to borrow the words of one critic, also *authors* of globalization (Panitch 1996). This means that the constraints that globalization 'imposes' are to a certain extent chosen and actively welcomed for (domestic) political and ideological reasons. This is true as well, in a much more institutionalized setting, of the European

EMU (see Chapter 12 in particular for an illustration of how 'domestic' actors instrumentalize 'external constraints' to pursue domestic political goals).

There are important differences between countries and between parts of the EU. As the studies in Part III of this book have made clear, these differences are the outcome of complex processes of dialectic interaction between internal, domestic processes and factors (institutional structures, historically shaped class structures, effects of previous policy trajectories) and external, international or global factors and processes. This means that niches for national strategies are possible. Simultaneously, as Ryner and Schulten address (in Chapter 10), the pursuit of national strategies (e.g. competitive corporatism) makes it more difficult for oppositional forces to forge transnational alliances. This is especially true, of course, to the extent that national competitive strategies imply an element of *beggar-thy-neighbour* policies (as was the case with the 'Dutch miracle'; see Chapter 9).

Spreading awareness of the constraints imposed both by globalization and by the effects of inter-European competition has contributed to the success of the European Commission in gradually claiming more competences in the area of employment and labour-market policy. But again, the contributions to Part II of this book have shown that the EU is very far from developing an EU-Keynesian approach. The balance of forces between Commission, governments, national social and political forces, and transnational capital has moved in the direction of an intermediate position between Euro-corporatism (a road that the Commission is actively pursuing) and neo-liberal regionalism (mostly the preferred strategy of transnational capital in Europe). As a result of the weight of the US and US interests at the global level, developments within the EU are tilted further in the direction of market liberalization, even though this effect is weaker in the area of labour-market policy than in such areas as business taxation or competition policy, where the freedom of movement for capital is directly at stake.

Alternative voices are weak. Even the modest attempt by Lafontaine and Strauss-Kahn in 1999 to introduce some Keynesian principles at the EU level was met with devastating hostility. The conjuncture for more radical proposals seems even more unfavourable. If the lessons of the 1970s are taken seriously, however, this does not necessarily imply that things will remain this way forever. A deepening recession in the world economy, rising unemployment and ideologically motivated pro-cyclical policies by most of Europe's governments, these by now quite likely developments are certain to lead to rising social unrest and to a new militancy in industrial relations, threatening the stability of European capitalism. In such circumstances a significant realignment of social forces becomes possible, accompanied by a sudden shift in the hegemonic discourse on economic management away from the almost religious belief in the virtues of the free market, and back to some conception of the need for public and democratic economic governance, this time firmly set in a transnational context where global, European and national movements and institutions emerge simultaneously as part of an overarching alternative to the present neo-liberal order.

Notes

1 The term 'regulation' is used here in an agnostic, a-theoretical and loose fashion. There is no direct reference to what is known as 'regulation theory' (for some detail on this, the reader is referred to Chapter 10).

2 Hewson and Sinclair (1999) provide an excellent overview of strands of global governance approaches.

3 In Chapter 8 Jessop discusses the degree to which Tony Blair's New Labour government pursues policies that are consistent with the earlier neo-liberal policy of the Thatcher governments and to what extent they deviate from the straight neo-liberal path in the direction of competitive corporatism.

4 Recently the role of private actors in this mode of global regulation has been highlighted in a number of important studies: Cutler *et al.* (1999); Higgott *et al.* (1999); R.B. Hall and Biersteker (2002).

Bibliography

Abrahamson, P.F. (1999) 'The Welfare Modelling Business', *Social Policy and Administration* 33(4): 394–415.

Accornero, A. (1994) *La parabola del sindacato* (Bologna: Il Mulino).

Addison, John T. and W. Stanley Siebert (eds) (1997) *Labour Markets in Europe. Issues of Harmonisation and Regulation* (London: Dryden Press).

Aglietta, Michel (1979) *A Theory of Capitalist Regulation* (London: New Left Books).

Ainley, P. (1997) 'Toward a Learning Society or Towards Learningfare?', *Social Policy Review* 9: 50–68.

Albeda, W. (1984) *De crisis van de werkgelegenheid en de verzorgingsstaat* (Kampen: J.H. Kok).

Albert, M. (1993) *Capitalism against Capitalism* (London: Whurr).

Albert, Michel and Rauf Gonenc (1997) 'The Future of Rhenish Capitalism', *The Political Quarterly* 67: 184–193.

Albo, G. (1994) '"Competitive Austerity" and the Impasse of Capitalist Employment Policy' *The Socialist Register 1994* (London: Merlin Press).

—— (1997) 'A World Market of Opportunities. Capitalist Obstacles and Left Economic Policy' *The Socialist Register 1997* (London: Merlin Press).

Altvater, Elmar and Birgit Mahnkopf (1996) *Grenzen der Globalisierung. Ökonomie, Ökologie und Politik in der Weltgesellschaft* (Münster: Westfälisches Dampfboot).

Ambrosius, Gerold (1996) *Wirtschaftsraum Europa. Vom Ende der Nationalökonomien* (Frankfurt/Main: Fischer).

Amin, A. (ed.) (1994a) *Post Fordism: A Reader* (Oxford: Blackwell).

—— (1994b) 'Post-Fordism: Models, Fantasies, and Phantoms of Transition', in A. Amin (ed.) *Post Fordism: A Reader* (Oxford: Blackwell).

Amin, A. and A. Malmberg (1994) 'Competing Structural and Institutional Influences on the Geography of Production in Europe', in A. Amin (ed.) *Post Fordism: A Reader* (Oxford: Blackwell).

Anderson, Perry (1994) 'Introduction', in Perry Anderson and Patrick Camiller (eds) *Mapping the West European Left* (London and New York: Verso).

—— (1997) 'The Europe to Come', in Peter Gowan and Perry Anderson (eds) *The Question of Europe* (London and New York: Verso).

Andersson, T. (1993) 'Utlandsinvesteringar och policy-implikationer', *Industrins utredningsinstitut. Working Paper* 371, Stockholm.

Andeweg, R.B. and G.A. Irwin (1993) *Dutch Politics and Government*, Houndmills: Macmillan.

Artis, M. (1998) 'The Unemployment Problem', *Oxford Review of Economic Policy* 14(3): 98–109.

Artis, M. and Cobham, D. (eds) (1991) *Labour's Economic Policies, 1974–79* (Manchester: Manchester University Press).

Artis, M. and B. Winkler (1997) 'The Stability Pact: Safeguarding the Credibility of the European Central Bank', *CEPR Discussion Paper* No.1688.

Astudillo, J. (1998) *Los Recursos del Socialismo: las Cambiantes Relaciones entre el PSOE y la UGT (1982–1993)* Madrid: Centro de Estudios Avanzados en Ciencias Sociales.

Bahnmüller, R. (1996) 'Konsens perdu? Gruppenarbeit zwischen Euphorie und Ernüchterung', in R. Bahnmüller and R. Salm (eds) *Intelligenter, nicht härter arbeiten? Gruppenarbeit und betriebliche Gestaltungspolitik* (Hamburg: VSA-Verlag).

Bailey, P., A. Parisotto and G. Renshaw (eds) (1993) *Multinationals and Employment. The Global Economy of the 1990s* (Geneva: International Labour Office).

Bakker, Isabella (ed.) (1994) *The Strategic Silence* (London: Zed Books).

—— (1999) 'Neoliberal Governance and the New Gender Order', *Working Papers in Local Governance and Democracy* 99/1: 49–59.

Barber, Benjamin R. (1996) *Jihad vs. McWorld. How Globalism and Tribalism are Reshaping the World* (New York: Ballantine Books).

Barry, A., R. Osborne and N. Rose (eds) (1996) *Foucault and Political Reason: Liberalism, Neo-Liberalism and Rationalities of Government* (London: UCL Press).

Becker, Gary S. (1974) 'A Theory of Marriage: Part II', *Journal of Political Economy* 82(2) (March/April): 11–26.

Becker, U. (2000) 'Welfare State Development and Employment in the Netherlands in Comparative Perspective', *Journal of European Social Policy* 10(3): 219–39.

—— (2001) 'A Dutch Model? Employment Growth by Corporatist Consensus and Wage Restraint?', *New Political Economy* 6(1).

Bellah, Robert N., Richard Madsen, William M. Sullivan, Ann Swidler and Steven M. Tipton (1985) *Habits of the Heart. Individualism and Commitment in American Life* (Berkeley, CA: University of California Press).

—— (1992) *The Good Society* (New York: Vintage Books).

Benería, Lourdes 1999: Globalization, Gender and the Davos Man, *Feminist Economics* 5(3): 61–83.

Benington, J. and D. Donnison (1999) 'New Labour and Social Exclusion: the Search for a Third Way – or Just Gilding the Ghetto Again?', in H. Dean and R. Woods (eds) *Social Policy Review 11* (London: Social Policy Association).

Bentolila, S. and J. Dolado (1993) 'La contratación Temporal y Sus Efectos Sobre la Competitividad', *Papeles de Economía* 56:112–27.

—— (1994) 'Spanish Labour Market', *Economic Policy* 18: 55–99.

Bentolila, S. and G. Saint-Paul (1992) 'The Macroeconomic Impact of Flexible Labor Contracts , with an Application to Spain', *European Economic Review* 36: 113–47.

Berggren, C. (1993) 'The Volvo Uddevalla Plant: Why the Decision to Close is Mistaken', *Journal of Industry Studies* 1(1): 75–87.

Bergström, V. (1993) 'Kursomläggningen', in V. Bergström (ed.) *Varför överge den svenska modellen?* (Stockholm: Tiden).

Berié, Hermann (1993) 'Europäische Sozialpolitik. Von Messina bis Maastricht', in Gerhard Kleinhenz (ed.) *Soziale Integration in Europa I. Schriften des Vereins für Sozialpolitik*, vol. 222, 1 (Berlin: Duncker & Humblot).

Bermeo, Nancy (ed.) (2001) *Unemployment in the New Europe* (Cambridge: Cambridge University Press).

Bieler, Andreas (2000) *Globalisation and Enlargement of the EU: Austrian and Swedish Social Forces in the Struggle over Membership* (London: Routledge).

Bieler, Andreas and A.D. Morton (eds) (2001) *Social Forces in the Making of the New Europe. The Restructuring of European Social Relations in the Global Political Economy* (Houndmills: Palgrave).

Bieling, Hans-Jürgen (1993) *Nationalstaat und Migration im Postfordismus – Gerwerkschaften vor der Zerreißprobe*, Forschungsgruppe Europäische Gemeinschaften FEG-Studie Nr. 2 (Marburg).

—— (2000a) *Dynamiken sozialer Spaltung und Ausgrenzung. Gesellschaftstheorien und Zeitdiagnosen* (Münster: Westfälisches Dampfboot).

—— (2000b) *Sozialdemokratische Wirtschafts- und Beschäftigungspolitik in der neoliberalen Konstellation*, FEG-Arbeitspapier Nr. 20 (Marburg).

Bieling, Hans-Jürgen and Frank Deppe (eds) (1997) *Arbeitslosigkeit und Wohlfahrtsstaat in Westeuropa. Neun Länder im Vergleich* (Opladen: Leske & Budrich).

Bieling, Hans-Jürgen and Jochen Steinhilber (2000) *Die Konfiguration Europas. Dimensionen einer kritischen Integrationstheorie* (Münster: Westfälisches Dampfboot).

Biernacki, R. (1995) *The Fabrication of Labour: Germany and Britain, 1640–1914* (Berkeley, CA: University of California Press).

Bispinck, R. and T. Schulten (2000) 'Alliance for Jobs – is Germany following the Path of "Competitive Corporatism"?', in G. Fajertag and P. Pochet (eds) *Social Pacts in Europe – New Dynamics* (Brussels: European Trade Union Institute).

Blackburn, Robin (1997) 'Reflections on Blair's Velvet Revolution', *New Left Review* 223: 3–16.

Blair, Tony (1997) *New Britain: My Vision of a Young Country* (Oxford: Westview Press).

Blair, Tony and Gerhard Schröder (1999) *Europe: The Third Way/Die Neue Mitte*, available at http://www.labour.org.uk/views/items/00000053.html.

Blanchard, O.J. (1998) 'Discussion to "Regional Non-adjustment and Fiscal Policy" ', *Economic Policy* 26 (April): 249.

Blancke, Susanne, Christian Roth and Josef Schmid (1999) *Employability als Herausforderung für Politik, Wirtschaft und Individuum. Konzept- und Literaturstudie*, available at http://www.uni-tuebingen.de/uni/spi/schemp.htm.

Bochel, C. and H. Bochel (1998) 'The Governance of Social Policy', *Social Policy Review* 10: 57–74.

Böhl, H. de Liagre (1999) 'Consensus en polarisatie. Spanningen in de verzorgingsstaat', in R. Aerts, H. de Liagre Böhl, P. de Rooy and H. te Velde, *Land van kleine gebaren. Een politieke geschiedenis van Nederland 1780–1990* (Nijmegen: SUN).

Boltho, A. (1982) 'Growth', in A. Boltho (ed.) *The European Economy: Growth and Crisis* (Oxford: Oxford University Press).

Bonder, M., B. Röttger and G. Ziebura (1992) *Deutschland in einer neuen Weltära. Die unbewältigte Herausforderung* (Opladen, Leske & Budrich).

Bourdieu, P., C. Debons, D. Hensche and B. Lutz (eds) (1997) *Perspektiven des Protests. Initiativen für einen europäischen Wohlfahrtsstaat* (Hamburg: VSA-Verlag).

Bowring, Finn (1997) 'Communitarianism and Morality: In Search of the Subject', in *New Left Review* 222: 93–113.

Boyer, Robert (1989) *Regulation Theory: A Critical Introduction* (New York: Columbia University Press).

—— (1990) 'The Impact of the Single Market on Labour and Employment: A Discussion of Macro-Economic Approaches in the Light of Research in Labour Economics', *Labour and Society* 15(2): 109–42.

—— (1991) 'The Eighties: The Search for Alternatives to Fordism', in B. Jessop, H. Kastendiek and K. Nielsen (eds) *The Politics of Flexibility* (Aldershot: Edward Elgar).

—— (1995) 'Capital–Labour Relations in OECD Countries: From the Fordist Golden Age to Contrasted National Trajectories', J. Schor and J. Il You (eds) *Capital, the State and Labour: A Global Perspective* (Aldershot: Edward Elgar).
—— (1997) 'French Statism at the Crossroads', in C. Crouch and W. Streeck (eds) *Political Economy of Modern Capitalism* (London: Sage).
Boyer, R. and P. Petit (1991) 'Technical Change, Cumulative Causation and Growth', *Technology and Productivity: The Challenge of Economic Policy*, OECD Technology and Productivity Programme (Paris: OECD).
Brandt Report (1980) *North–South: A Programme for Survival* (London: Pan Books).
Brenner, R. (2000) 'The Boom and the Bubble', *New Left Review* 6: 5–44.
Brochmann, G. (1993) '"Fortress Europe" – a European Immigration Regime in the Making?', in *Migration. The Politics of Contemporary Population Movements*, papers presented at Sampol konferansen 1993, Department of Comparative Politics, University of Bergen (Norway).
Brown, Phillip and Rosemary Compton (eds) (1994) *A New Europe? Economic Restructuring and Social Exclusion* (London: UCL Press).
Buchele, R. and J.Christiansen (1999) 'Labor Relations and Productivity Growth in Advanced Capitalist Economies', *Review of Radical Political Economics* 31(1): 87–110.
Bussemaker, J. and K. van Kersbergen (1994) 'Gender and Welfare States: Some Theoretical Reflections', in D. Sainsbury (ed.) *Gendering Wefare States* (London: Sage).
Buti, M., D. Franco and H. Ongena (1997) 'Budgetary Policies during Recessions: Retrospective Application of the Stability and Growth Pact to the Post-war Period', *Economic Paper* No. 121 (Brussels: European Commission).
Cafruny, Alan W. and Magnus Ryner (eds) (2003) *A Ruined Fortress? Neoliberal Hegemony and Transformation in Europe* (Lanham, MD: Rowman & Littlefield).
Cameron, D. (1984) 'Social Democracy, Corporatism, Labour Quiescence and the Representation of Economic Interest in Advanced Capitalist Society', in J.J. Goldthorpe (ed.) *Order and Conflict in Contemporary Capitalism* (Oxford: Garamond Press).
Cameron, David R. (1997) 'Economic and Monetary Union: Underlying Imperatives and Third Stage Dilemmas', *Journal of European Public Policy* 4: 455–85.
—— (1998) 'EMU After 1999: The Implications and Dilemmas of the Third Stage', *Columbia Journal of European Law* 4: 425–46.
—— (1999) 'Unemployment in the New Europe: The Contours of the Problem' (Florence: European University Institute), EUI working papers, Robert Schumann Centre, no. 99/35.
—— (2000) *The Europeanization of Employment Policy*, paper prepared for presentation at the Max Planck Institute for the Study of Societies, Cologne, 30 May.
—— (2001) 'Unemployment, Job Creation and Economic and Monetary Union', in N. Bermeo (ed.) *Unemployment in the New Europe* (Cambridge: Cambridge University Press).
Castells, M. (1996) *The Rise of the Network Society* (Oxford: Blackwell).
Castillo, J. (1994) '¿Nuevas Formas de Trabajo o Precarización del Empleo?', in F. Valdés Dal-Ré (eds) *Sindicalismo y Cambios Sociales* (Madrid: CES Colección Estudios).
CEC (Commission of the European Communities) (1988) *Research on the Cost of Non-Europe* (Luxembourg: Office for Official Publications of the European Communities).
—— (1993) *Growth, Competitiveness, Employment: The Challenges and Ways Forward into the 21st Century*, White Paper (Luxembourg: Office for Official Publications).
—— (1994) *European Social Policy*, White Paper (Luxembourg: Office for Official Publications).
—— (1996) *For Employment in Europe. A Pact of Confidence*, CSE (96), 1 endg. (Brussels).

—— (1998) *Guidelines for Employment Measures of the Member States in 1998* (Brussels).

—— (2000) 'The EU Economy 2000 Review, *European Economy*, No. 71 (Luxembourg: Office for Official Publications).

Cecchini, P. (1985) *Europa '92 – Der Vorteil des Binnenmarktes* (Baden-Baden: Nomos).

—— (1988) *The European Challenge – 1992: The Benefits of a Single Market* (Aldershot: Wildwood House).

Centraal Planbureau (2000) *Macro Economische Verkenning 2001* (The Hague: Sdu Uitgevers).

Cerny, P. (1990) *The Changing Architecture of Politics: Structure, Agency and the Future of the State* (London: Sage).

CGG (Commission on Global Governance) (1995) *Our Global Neighborhood* (Oxford: Oxford University Press).

Chanda, N. (2000) 'The Tug of War for Asia's Best Brains', *Far Eastern Economic Review*, 9 November: 38; available at http://www.feer.com/—0011—09/p038innov.html.

Checkel, Jeffrey T. (1999) 'Social Construction and Integration', *Journal of European Public Policy* 6(4) (Special Issue): 545–60.

Chesnais, F. (1986) 'Science, Technology and Competitiveness', *STI Review* 1: 86–129.

Christiansen, Thomas, Knud Erik Jørgensen and Antje Wiener (1999) 'The Social Construction of Europe', *Journal of European Public Policy* 6(4) (Special Issue): 528–44.

Clarke, Simon (1988) *Keynesianism, Monetarism and the Crisis of the State* (Aldershot: Edward Elgar).

Clarke, S.E. and G.L. Gaile (1998) *The Work of Cities* (Minneapolis: University of Minnesota Press).

Clayton, R and J. Pontusson (1998) 'Welfare State Retrenchment Revisited', *World Politics* 51(1): 67–98.

Coates, K. and S. Holland (1995) *Full Employment for Europe. The Commission, the Council and the Debate on Employment in the European Parliament 1994–95* (Nottingham: Spokesman).

Cochrane, A. (1999) 'New Labour, New Urban Policy?', in H. Dean and R. Woods (eds) *Social Policy Review 11* (London: Social Policy Association).

Cohen, D. (1998) *The Wealth of the World and the Poverty of Nations* (Cambridge, MA/London: MIT Press).

Cohen, R. (1987) *The New Helots. Migrants in the International Division of Labour* (Oxford: Oxford Publishing Services).

Cohen, R. and F. M. Deng (1998) *Masses in Flight. The Global Crisis of Internal Displacement* (Washington, DC: Brookings Institution).

Collinge, C. (1996) *Spatial Articulation of the State: Reworking Social Relations and Social Regulation Theory* (Birmingham: Centre for Urban and Regional Studies).

Compston, Hugh (ed.) (1997) *The New Politics of Unemployment* (London: Routledge).

Cook, Joanne (1998) 'Flexible Employment: Implications for Gender and Citizenship in the European Union', *New Political Economy* 3(2): 261–77.

Cook, J., M. Roche, C.C. Williams and J. Windebank (2001) 'The Evolution of Active Welfare Policies as a Solution to Social Exclusion in Britain', *Journal of European Area Studies* 9(1): 13–26.

Corpelijn, A.W.F. (1992) 'De kwaliteit van nieuwe werkgelegenheid', *Economisch- Statistische Berichten*, 5 February: 133–5.

Council of the EU (1999) *Council Resolution on the 1999 Employment Guidelines*, available at http://europa.eu.int/comm/employment—social/empl&esf/empl99/guide—en.htm (accessed 10 December 2001).

Cowles, M.G. (1995) 'Setting the Agenda for a New Europe: The ERT and EC 1992', *Journal of Common Market Studies* 33(4): 501–26.

Cox, K.R. (1995) 'Globalization, Competition and the Politics of Local Economic Development', *Urban Studies* 32(2): 213–24.

Cox, R.H. (1998) 'The Consequences of Welfare Reform: How Conceptions of Social Rights are Changing', *West European Politics* 27(1): 1–16.

Cox, Robert W. (1981) 'Social Forces, States and World Orders: Beyond International Relations Theory', *Millenium: Journal of International Studies* 10(2): 126–55.

—— (1983) 'Gramsci, Hegemony and International Relations: An Essay in Method', *Millenium: Journal of International Studies* 12(2): 162–75.

—— (1987) *Production, Power, and World Order. Social Forces in the Making of History* (New York: Columbia University Press).

—— (1993) 'Structural Issues of Global Governance: Implications for Europe', in S. Gill (ed.) *Gramsci, Historical Materialism and International Relations* (Cambridge: Cambridge University Press).

Crone, F. (1984) 'Arbeidstijdverkorting: 25 uur met behoud van loon', *Tijdschrift voor politieke ekonomie* 8(1): 42–58.

Crouch, C. (1993) *Industrial Relations and European State Traditions* (Oxford: Oxford University Press).

—— (1998) 'The Social Contract and the Problem of the Firm', in Martin Rhodes and Yves Mény (eds) *The Future of European Welfare: A New Social Contract?* (Houndmills: Macmillan).

—— (2000) *After the Euro* (Oxford: Oxford University Press).

Cutler, A.C., V. Haufler and T. Porter (eds) (1999) *Private Authority and International Affairs* (Albany, NY: State University of New York Press).

Daalder, H. (1974) *Leiding en lijdelijkheid in de Nederlandse politiek* (Assen: Van Gorcum).

Dahrendorf, R. (1990) *Reflections on the Revolution in Europe* (London: Chatto & Windus)

Daly, M. (1994) 'Comparing Welfare States: Towards a Gender Friendly Approach', in D. Sainsbury (ed.) *Gendering Welfare States* (London: Sage).

Davis, M. (1984) 'The Political Economy of Late Imperial America', *New Left Review* 143: 4–38.

de Brunhoff, S. (1968) *The State, Capital and Economic Policy* (London: Pluto Press).

De Geer, H. (1989) *I vänstervind och högevag* (Stockholm: Allmäna förlaget).

de Grauwe, Paul (1997) *The Economics of Monetary Integration*, 3rd rev. edn (Oxford: Oxford University Press).

de Swaan, A. (1992) 'Perspectives for Transnational Social Policy', *Government and Opposition* 27.1: 33–51.

—— (ed.) (1994) *Social Policy Beyond Borders* (Amsterdam: Amsterdam University Press).

Deacon, B. (1995) 'The Globalisation of Social Policy and the Socialisation of Global Politics', *Social Policy Review* 7: 55–76.

—— (with M. Hulse and P. Stubbs) (1997) *Global Social Policy: International Organizations and the Future of Welfare* (London: Sage).

Deacon, B. and M. Hulse (1997) 'The Making of Post-Communist Social Policy: The Role of International Agencies', *Journal of Social Policy* 26(1): 43–62.

Deakin, N. and J. Edwards (1993) *The Enterprise Culture and the Inner City* (London: Routledge).

Deakin, N. and R. Parry (2000) *The Treasury and Social Policy: The Contest for Control of Welfare Strategy* (Basingstoke: Macmillan).

Delors, J. (1992) *Our Europe*, 2nd edn (London: Verso); first edition 1988.

Delsen, L. (2000) *Exit poldermodel. Sociaal-economische ontwikkelingen in Nederland* (Assen: Van Gorcum).

Deppe, F. (1979) *Autonomie und Integration. Materialien zur Gewerkschaftsanalyse* (Marburg: VAG-Verlag).

Deppe, F. and M. Felder (1993) 'Zur Post-Maastricht-Krise der Europäischen Gemeinschaft', *FEG-Arbeitspapier No. 10* (Marburg).

Deppe, F. and K.-W. Weiner (eds) (1991) *Binnenmarkt '92. Zur Entwicklung der Arbeitsbeziehungen in Europa* (Hamburg: VSA-Verlag).

Deppe, F., M. Felder and S. Tidow (2000) *Structuring the State – the Case of European Employment Policy*, paper presented at the International Conference 'Linking EU and National Governance', Mannheim, 1–3 June.

Deubner, C., U. Rehfeld and F. Schlupp (1992) 'Franco-German Relations within the International Division of Labour: Interdependence, Divergence or Structural Dominance?', in W. Graf (ed.) *The Internationalization of the German Political Economy: Evolution of a Hegemonic Project* (New York: St Martin's Press).

DfEE (Department for Education and Employment) (1998) *Learning is the Key to Prosperity* (London: DfEE).

DGB (Deutsche Gewerkschafts Bund) (2000) *Arbeit 2000 – Beschäftigungspolitische Vorschläge des DGB für das Jahr 2000*, February (Berlin: DGB).

Dickens, R., P. Gregg and J. Wadsworth (2000) 'New Labour and the Labour Market', *Oxford Review of Economic Policy* 16(1): 95–113.

Dolado, F and S. Bentolila (1992) *Who are the Insiders? Wage Setting in Spanish Manufacturing Firms*, Banco de España, Servicio de Estudios, working paper 9229.

Dolowitz, D.P. (1997) 'Reflections on the UK Workfare System', *Review of Policy Issues* 3(1): 3–15.

Dolowitz, D. and D. Marsh (1996) 'Who Learns What from Whom? A Review of the Policy Transfer Literature', *Political Studies* 44(2): 343–57.

Dölvik, J.E. (1997) *Redrawing Boundaries of Solidarity? ETUC, Social Dialogue and the Europeanisation of Trade Unions in the 1990s*, ARENA Report No. 5, Fafo Report No. 238 (Oslo).

Dölvik, J.E. and A. Martin (2000) 'A Spanner in the Works and Oil on Troubled Waters: The Divergent Fates of Social Pacts in Sweden and Norway', in G. Fajertag and P. Pochet (eds) *Social Pacts in Europe – New Dynamics* (Brussels: European Trade Union Institute).

Dörre, Klaus (1999) 'Global Players, Local Heroes. Internationalisierung und regionale Industriepolitik', *Soziale Welt* 50(2): 187–206.

—— (2000) 'Arbeit, Partizipation und Solidarität im Aktionärskapitalismus', *Widerspruch* 20(1): 28–40.

Dräger, K. and F.O. Wolf (1999) 'Beschäftigungsglamour', *Blätter für deutsche und internationale Politik* 7/1999: 782–7.

Drainville, André (1994) 'International Political Economy in the Age of Open Marxism', *Review of International Political Economy* 1(1): 105–32.

DTI (Department of Trade and Industry) (1998) *Our Competitive Edge: Building the Knowledge-Driven Economy*, available at http://www2.dti.gov.uk/comp/competitive/main.htm (accessed 10 January 1999).

Duff, A. (1997) *The Treaty of Amsterdam* (London: Sweet & Maxwell).

Dunsire, A. (1996) 'Tipping the Balance: Autopoiesis and Governance', *Administration and Society* 28(3): 299–334.

Dyson, K. and K. Featherstone (1999) *The Road to Maastricht* (Oxford: Oxford University Press).

Ebbinghaus, B. and P. Manow (eds) (2001) 'Introduction', in *Comparing Welfare Capitalisms. Social Policy and Political Economy in Europe, Japan and the USA* (London: Routledge).

EC (European Commission) (1993) *Growth, Competitiveness, Employment: The Challenges and Ways Forward into the 21st Century – White Paper*, COM(93) 700, December 1993; available at http://europa.eu.int/en/record/white/c93700/ch8—1.html.

—— (1995a) *A European Strategy for Encouraging Local Development and Employment Initiatives*, COM 273 (95) Final (Brussels).

—— (1995b) *Teaching and Learning: Towards the Learning Society (White Paper on Education and Training)*, Com (95) 590 final, 29 November (Brussels).

—— (1996a) *Action for Employment in Europe: A Confidence Pact*, CSE (96) 1 Final (Brussels).

—— (1996b) *Benchmarking the Competitiveness of European Industry*, Com (96) 436 final, 9 October (Brussels).

—— (1997a) *The Competitiveness of European Industry* (based on the working document of Commission services) (Luxembourg: Office for Official Publications of the European Communities).

—— (1997b) *Benchmarking: Implementation of an Instrument Available to Economic Actors and Public Authorities*, Com (97) 153/2 final, 16 April (Brussels).

—— (1997c) *Employment Report in Europe 1997: An Employment Agenda for the Year 2000* (Brussels: European Commission).

—— (1998a) *Employment Policies in the EU and in the Member States*, Joint Report (Luxembourg).

—— (1998b) *Eurobarometer 48* (Luxemburg: Office for Official Publications of the European Communities).

—— (1999a) *Community Policies in Support of Employment*, Communication of the Commission, available at http://europa.eu.int/comm/employment—social/empl&esf/news/127—en.htm (accessed 9 December 2001).

—— (1999b) 'Report on the Economic and Structural Reform in the European Union', in *European Economy*, Supplement A. Economic trends, No. 1 (January) (Luxembourg: Office for Official Publications of the EC).

—— (1999c) *The European Employment Strategy. Investing in People* (Luxembourg: Office for the Official Publications of the European Communities European Commission).

—— (2000a) *Recommendation for a Council Recommendation on the Implementation of Member States' Employment Policies*, Com (2000) (Brussels); available at http://www.europa.eu.int/comm/employment—social/empl&esf/news/recommend00—en.htm (accessed 12 February 2001).

—— (2000b) *Joint Employment Report 2000*, available at http://www.europa.eu.int/comm/employment—social/empl&esf/ees—en.htm (accessed 17 September 2001).

—— (2000c) *Guidelines for Member States' Employment Policies for the Year 2000 & Council Recommendation on the Implementation of Member States' Employment Policies* (Brussels).

—— (2000d) *Industrial Relations in Europe 2000* (Luxembourg).

—— (2000e) *Employment in Europe* (Brussels: European Commission).

—— (2001) *Employment in Europe: Autumn Update* (Brussels: European Commission).

Economist (2000) 'Survey Globalisation and Taxes', supplement to the edition of 29 January.

Edquist, C. and B.A. Lundvall (1993) 'Comparing the Swedish and Danish Systems of Innovation', in R.R. Nelson (ed.) *National Innovation Systems: A Comparative Analysis* (Oxford: Oxford University Press).

EGB (Europäische Gewerkschaftsbund) (1996) *EGB-Beschäftigungsmanifest* (Brussels).

Eichengreen, B. and Jeffry Frieden (1998) *Forging an Integrated Europe* (Ann Arbor, MI: University of Michigan Press).

Eichengreen, B. and C. Wyplosz (1998) 'The Stability Pact: More than a Minor Nuisance?', *Economic Policy* 26 (April): 65–113.

Ekengreen, M. (1997) 'The Temporality of European Governance', in K.E. Jorgensen (ed.) *Reflective Approaches to European Governance* (Basingstoke: Macmillan).

Eklund, I. (1999) 'Kraven i arbetslivet', *Statistics Sweden. Välfärdsbulletinen* 4.

Elfring, T. and R.C. Kloosterman (1989) 'De Nederlandse "job machine" ', *Economisch-Statistische Berichten*, 2 August: 736–40.

Elman, Amy (ed.) (1996) *Sexual Politics and the European Union* (Oxford: Berghahn Books).

Elson, Diane (ed.) (1995) *Male Bias in the Development Process* (Manchester: Manchester University Press).

—— (2000) *Progress of the World's Women 2000*, United Nations Development Fund for Women, Biennal Report (New York).

Elson, Diane and Nilufer Cagatay (1999) *Engendering Macroeconomic Policy and Budgets for Sustainable Development*, paper presented at the First Global Forum on Human Development, 29–31 July, UN Headquarters, New York; available at http://www.undp.org/hydro/HDFCagatayElson.htm.

—— (2000) 'The Social Content of Macroeconomic Policies', *World Development Report* 28(7) (July): 1,347–64.

Emmerij, L. (1994) 'A Transnational Policy for a Global Labour Market', in Z. Suda (ed.) *The Globalization of Labor Markets. A Challenge to the Social Contract* (Prague: European Institute of Education and Social Policy).

Empter, S. and A. Esche (eds) (1997) *Eigenverantwortung und Solidarität. Neue Wege in der Sozial- und Tarifpolitik* (Gütersloh: Bertelsmann).

Erixon, L. (1989) 'Den tredje vägen – inlåsning eller förnyelse?', *Ekonomisk debatt* 3.

—— (1994) 'Rehn-Meidnermodellen. En tredje väg i den ekonomiska politiken', *Arbetslivscentrum. Research Report* 4 (Stockholm).

ERT (European Roundtable of Industrialists) (1983) *Foundations for the Future of European Industry*, Memorandum to EC Commissioner Davignon, 10 June (Paris).

—— (1986) *Making Europe Work* (Paris).

—— (1990) *European Labour Markets: Employment Policies in Europe for the 1990s* (Brussels: European Roundtable of Industrialists).

—— (1992) *Lifelong Learning* (Brussels: European Roundtable of Industrialists).

—— (1993a) *European Labour Markets. An Update on Perspectives and Requirements for Job Generation in the Second Half of the 1990s* (Brussels: European Roundtable of Industrialists).

—— (1993b) *Beating the Crisis: A Charter for Europe's Industrial Future* (Brussels: European Roundtable of Industrialists).

—— (1994) *European Competitiveness: The Way to Growth and Jobs* (Brussels: European Roundtable of Industrialists).

—— (1995) *Moving Towards a Learning Society* (Brussels: European Roundtable of Industrialists).

—— (1996) *Benchmarking for Policy-Makers: The Way to Competitiveness, Growth and Job Creation* (Brussels: European Roundtable of Industrialists).

—— (1997) *A Stimulus to Job Creation* (Brussels: European Roundtable of Industrialists).

—— (1998) *Job Creation and Competitiveness through Innovation* (Brussels: European Roundtable of Industrialists).

Esping-Andersen, G. (1985) *Politics Against Markets* (Princeton, NJ: Princeton University Press).

—— (1987) 'Institutional Accommodation to Full Employment: A Comparison of Policy Régimes', in H. Keman (ed.) *Coping with the Economic Crisis* (London: Sage).
—— (1990) *The Three Worlds of Welfare Capitalism* (Cambridge: Polity).
—— (1994) 'Equality and Work in the Post-Industrial Life Cycle', in D. Miliband (ed.) *Reinventing the Left* (Cambridge: Polity).
—— (ed.) (1996) *Welfare States in Transition* (London: SAGE/UNRISD).
—— (1999) *Social Foundations of Post-Industrial Economies* (Oxford: Oxford University Press).
Etzioni, Amitai (1988) *The Moral Dimension. Towards a New Economics* (New York: Free Press).
—— (1993) *The Spirit of Community. Rights, Responsibilities, and the Communitarian Agenda* (New York: Crown Books).
—— (1996) *The New Golden Rule: Community and Morality in a Democratic Society* (New York: Basic Books).
European Council (1996) *Presidency Conclusions, Florence European Council 21–22 June 1996*, available at http://europa.eu.int/en/record/florence/flore-en.htm.
—— (1997a) *Presidency Conclusions*, available at http://ue.eu.int/de/Info/eurocouncil/index.htm.
—— (1997b) *Extraordinary Meeting on Employment, Presidency Conclusions*, 20–1 November, available at http://ue.eu.int/de/Info/eurocouncil/index.htm.
European Council (1999) *'Resolution of the European Council on the European Employment Pact', Presidency Conclusions*, 3 and 4 June, SN 150/99 EN Annexes (Cologne).
European Council in Cardiff (1998) *Presidency Conclusions*, 15–16 June, available at http://ue.eu.int/de/Info/eurocouncil/index.htm.
European Council in Essen (1994) *Presidency Conclusions*, 9–10 December, available at http://ue.eu.int/de/Info/eurocouncil/index.htm.
European Council in Lisbon (2000) *Presidency Conclusions*, 23–24 March, available at http://ue.eu.int/de/Info/eurocouncil/index.htm.
European Parliament (1997) *Employment*, CONF 3884/97, 21 April (Brussels).
Eurostat (1997) *Demographic Statistics* (Luxembourg: Eurostat).
Fajertag, G. and P. Pochet (eds) (2000) *Social Pacts in Europe – New Dynamics* (Brussels: European Trade Union Institute).
Fairclough, N. (2000) *New Labour, New Language?* (London: Routledge).
Falkner, Gerda (1998) *EU Social Policy in the 1990s. Towards a Corporatist Policy Community* (London and New York: Routledge).
Felder, M. (2001) *Die Transformation von Staatlichkeit. Europäisierung und Bürokratisierung in der Organisationsgesellschaft* (Opladen: Westdeutscher Verlag).
Ferner, Anthony and Richard Hyman (eds) (1998) *Changing Industrial Relations in Europe* (Oxford: Blackwell Publishers).
Finer, C.J. (1997) 'The New Social Policy in Britain', *Social Policy & Administration* 31(5): 154–70.
Flassbeck, Heiner (1999) 'Markt und Gerechtigkeit', *Blätter für deutsche und internationale Politik* 12/1999: 1450–9.
Flecker, J. and T. Schulten (1999) 'The End of Institutional Stability: What Future for the "German Model"?', *Economic and Industrial Democracy* 20(1): 81–115.
Flórez, I. (1994) *La contratación laboral como medida de política de empleo en España* (Madrid: CES).
FNV (Federatie Nederlandse Vakverenigingen) (1983) *Jaarverslag FNV 1982* (Amsterdam: Federatie Nederlandse Vakverenigingen).
—— (1984) *Jaarverslag FNV 1983* (Amsterdam: Federatie Nederlandse Vakverenigingen).
—— (1985) *Jaarverslag FNV 1984* (Amsterdam: Federatie Nederlandse Vakverenigingen).

—— (1986) *Jaarverslag FNV 1985* (Amsterdam: Federatie Nederlandse Vakverenigingen).
—— (1987) *Jaarverslag FNV 1986* (Amsterdam: Federatie Nederlandse Vakverenigingen).
—— (1988) *Jaarverslag FNV 1987* (Amsterdam: Federatie Nederlandse Vakverenigingen).
—— (1989) *Jaarverslag FNV 1988* (Amsterdam: Federatie Nederlandse Vakverenigingen).
—— (1990) *Jaarverslag FNV 1989* (Amsterdam: Federatie Nederlandse Vakverenigingen).
—— (1991) *Jaarverslag FNV 1990* (Amsterdam: Federatie Nederlandse Vakverenigingen).
—— (1992) *Jaarverslag FNV 1991* (Amsterdam: Federatie Nederlandse Vakverenigingen).
—— (1993) *Jaarverslag FNV 1992* (Amsterdam: Federatie Nederlandse Vakverenigingen).
—— (1994) *Jaarverslag FNV 1993* (Amsterdam: Federatie Nederlandse Vakverenigingen).
—— (1995) *Jaarverslag FNV 1994* (Amsterdam: Federatie Nederlandse Vakverenigingen).
—— (1996) *Jaarverslag FNV 1995* (Amsterdam: Federatie Nederlandse Vakverenigingen).
—— (1997) *Jaarverslag FNV 1996* (Amsterdam: Federatie Nederlandse Vakverenigingen).
—— (1998) *Jaarverslag FNV 1997* (Amsterdam: Federatie Nederlandse Vakverenigingen).
—— (1999) *Jaarverslag FNV 1998* (Amsterdam: Federatie Nederlandse Vakverenigingen).

Forrester, Viviane (1998) *Der Terror der Ökonomie* (Munich: Goldmann).

Frank, A.G. (1975) *On Capitalist Underdevelopment* (Bombay: Oxford University Press).

—— (1998) *ReORIENT: Global Economy in the Asian Age* (Berkeley, CA: University of California Press).

Frank, A.G. and B.K. Gills (eds) (1993) *The World System. Five Hundred Years or Five Thousand?* (London: Routledge).

Fraser, Nancy (1989) *Unruly Practices: Power, Discourse and Gender in Contemporary Social Theory* (Minneapolis: University of Minnesota Press).

Freyssenet, M. (1998) 'Reflective Production: An Alternative to Mass Production and Lean Production', *Economic and Industrial Democracy* 19(1): 91–114.

Frieden, J., D. Gros and E. Jones (eds) (1998) *The New Political Economy of EMU* (Lanham, MD: Rowman & Littlefield).

Friedman, M. and R. Friedman (1980) *Free to Choose* (London: Secker & Warburg).

Fröbel, F., J. Heinrichs and O. Kreye (1980) *The New International Division of Labour. Structural Unemployment in Industrialised Countries and Industrialisation in Developing Countries* (Cambridge: Cambridge University Press).

Fuentes Quintana, E. (1988) 'Tres Decenios de la Economía Española en Perspectiva', in J.L. García Delgado (eds) *España. Economía* (Madrid: Espasa-Calpe).

Gabaglio, E. (1999) Der Euro erfordert eine neue europäische Tarifordnung', *Gewerkschaftliche Monatshefte* 5/1999: 257–62.

Gamble, A. and A. Payne (1996) *Regionalism and World Order* (Houndmills and London: Macmillan).

Gardner, J.N. (1991) *Effective Lobbying in the European Community* (Deventer: Kluwer).

Gazier, Bernard (ed.) (1999) *Employability: Concepts and Policies. Report 1998*, Employment Observatory RESEARCH Network (Berlin: IAS).

George, V. (1998) 'Political Ideology, Globalisation, and the Welfare Futures in Europe', *Journal of Social Policy* 27(1): 17–36.

Geyer, R. (1993) 'Socialism and the EC After Maastricht: From Classic to New-Model European Social Democracy', in A.W. Cafruny and G.G. Rosenthal (eds) *The State of the European Community*, vol. 2 (Boulder, CO.: Lynne Rienner Publishers).

Giddens, Anthony (1995) *Beyond Left and Right. The Future of Radical Politics* (Cambridge: Polity Press).

—— (1998) *The Third Way. The Renewal of Social Democracy* (Cambridge: Polity Press).

Gilbert, E. and E. Helleiner (eds) (1999) *Nation-States and Money. The Past, Present and Future of National Currencies* (London and New York: Routledge).

Gill, Stephen (1992) 'The Emerging World Order and European Change: The Political Economy of European Union', *The Socialist Register* (London: Merlin Press).

—— (1995) 'Globalisation, Market Civilization and Disciplinary Neoliberalism', *Millenium: Journal of International Studies* 24(3): 299–423.

—— (1998) 'European Governance and New Constitutionalism: Economic and Monetary Union and Alternatives to Disciplinary Neo-Liberalism in Europe', *New Political Economy* 3(1): 5–26.

—— (2000a) 'Theoretische Grundlagen einer neo-gramscianischen Analyse der europäischen Integration', in Hans-Jürgen Bieling and Jochen Steinhilber (eds) *Die Konfiguration Europas. Dimensionen einer kritischen Integrationstheorie* (Münster: Westfälisches Dampfboot).

—— (2000b) 'Toward a Postmodern Prince? The Battle in Seattle as a Moment in the New Politics of Globalisation', *Millenium* 26(1): 131–41.

—— (2001) 'Constitutionalising Capital: EMU and Disciplinary Neo-Liberalism', in A. Bieling and A.D. Morton (eds) *Social Forces in the Making of the New Europe* (Basingstoke: Macmillan).

Gill, S and D. Law (1993) 'Global Hegemony and the Structural Power of Capital', in S. Gill (ed.) *Gramsci, Historical Materialism and International Relations* (Cambridge: Cambridge University Press).

Giovanoli, Mario (2000) *International Monetary Law. Issues for the New Millenium* (Oxford: Oxford University Press).

Giugni, G. (1981) 'The Italian System of Industrial Relations', in P.B. Doeringer (eds) *Industrial Relations in International Perspective: Essays on Research and Policy* (London: Macmillan).

Glyn, A. (1995) 'Social Democracy and Full Employment', *New Left Review* 211 (May–June): 33–55.

Glyn, A. and S. Wood (2001) 'New Labour's Economic Policy: How Social-Democratic is the Blair Government?', in A. Glyn (ed.) *Social Democracy in Neoliberal Times* (Oxford: Oxford University Press).

Goetschy, Janine (1999) 'The European Employment Strategy: Genesis and Development', *European Journal of Industrial Relations* 5(2): 117–37.

Gottfried, H. (1995) 'Developing Neo-Fordism: A Comparative Perspective', *Critical Sociology* 21(3): 39–70.

Gourevitch, P., P. Lange and A. Martin (1981) 'Industrial Relations and Politics: Some Reflections', in P.B. Doeringer (eds) *Industrial Relations in International Perspective: Essays on Research and Policy* (London: Macmillan).

Grahl, J. and P. Teague (1990) *The Big Market. The Future of the European Community* (London: Lawrence & Wishart).

Gramsci, Antonio (1971) *Selections from Prison Notebooks*, translated and edited by Q. Hoare and G. Nowell Smith (London: Lawrence & Wishart; New York: International Publishers).

—— (1991) *Gefängnishefte* (Hamburg: Argument).

Gray, A. (1998) 'New Labour – New Labour Discipline', *Capital and Class* 65: 1–8.

Greenwood, J. (1997) *Representing Interests in the European Union* (London: Macmillan).

Gros, D. and N. Thygesen (1998) *European Monetary Integration* (London: Longman).

Grote, J.R. and P.C. Schmitter (1999) 'The Renaissance of National Corporatism: Unintended Side-effect of European Economic and Monetary Union or Calculated Response to the Absence of European Social Policy?', *Transfer: Quarterly of the European Trade Union Institute* 5(1–2): 34–63.

Grover, C. and J. Stewart (1999) '"Market Workfare": Social Security and Competitiveness in the 1990s', *Journal of Social Policy* 28(1): 73–96.

—— (2000) 'Modernizing Social Security? Labour and its Welfare-to-Work Strategy', *Social Policy and Administration* 34(3): 235–52.

Gualmini, E. (1998) 'Italy', in H. Compston (ed.) *The New Politics of Unemployment* (London: Routledge).

Guttmann, Robert (2000a) *Reform des internationalen Währungssystems*, paper for the Enquete-Commission of the German Parliament, Globalization of the World Economy – Challenges and Answers, Working Group: Financial Markets, 14/26.

—— (2000b) *Investment- und Pensionsfonds*, paper for the Enquete-Commission of the German Parliament, Globalization of the World Economy – Challenges and Answers, Working Group: Financial Markets, 14/25.

Haffner, M. (1998) 'Woningbelastingen in Europa', *Economisch-Statistische Berichten*, 27 February: 171.

Hall, P.A. (1993) 'Policy Paradigms, Social Learning and the State: The Case of Economic Policymaking in Britain', *Comparative Politics* 25(3): 275–96.

—— (1998) *Organized Market Economies and Unemployment in Europe: Is it Finally Time to Accept Liberal Orthodoxy?*, paper presented at the 11th International Conference of Europeanists, Baltimore, Maryland, 26–28 February.

Hall, P.A. and D. Soskice (2001) 'An Introduction to Varieties of Capitalism', in P.A. Hall and D. Soskice (eds) *Varieties of Capitalism: The Institutional Foundations of Comparative Advantage* (Oxford: Oxford University Press).

Hall, R.B. and Th.J. Biersteker (eds) (2002) *The Emergence of Private Authority in Global Governance* (Cambridge: Cambridge University Press).

Hantrais, L. (1995) *Social Policy in the European Union* (London: Macmillan).

Harris, N. (1995) *The New Untouchables. Immigration and the New World Worker* (London: Penguin Books).

Harvey, D. (1989) *The Condition of Postmodernity: An Enquiry into the Origins of Cultural Change* (Cambridge, MA, and Oxford: Blackwell Publishers).

Hassel, Anke (1998) 'Soziale Pakte in Europa', *Gewerkschaftliche Monatshefte* 10/1998: 626–37.

—— (1999) *Bündnisse für Arbeit: Nationale Wettbewerbsfähigkeit im europäischen Regimewettbewerb*, Max Planck Institut für Gesellshaftsforschung. Discussion Paper 99/5 (Cologne).

Haughton, G., M. Jones, J. Peck, A. Tickell and A. While (2000) 'Labour Market Policy as Flexible Welfare: Prototype Employment Zones and the New Workfarism', *Regional Studies* 34(7): 669–80.

Hay, C. (1999) *The Political Economy of New Labour. Labouring under False Pretences?* (Manchester: Manchester University Press).

Hay, Colin and Matthew Watson (1998) *Rendering the Contingent Necessary: New Labour's Neo-Liberal Conversion and the Discourse of Globalization*, paper presented at the American Political Science Association Conference, Boston, 3–6 September.

Headey, B., R.E. Goodin, R. Muffels and H.-J. Dirven (1997) 'Welfare over Time: Three Worlds of Welfare Capitalism in Panel Perspective', *Journal of Public Policy* 17(3): 329–59.

Hedborg, A. and R. Meidner (1984) *Folkhemsmodellen* (Stockholm: Rabén & Sjögren).

Hein, Eckhard (2000) 'Zentralbankpolitik, Arbeitsmarktinstitutionen und Makroökonomische Resultate', *WSI-Mitteilungen* 2/2000: 107–17.

Heinelt, Hubert (ed.) (1996) *Politiknetzwerke und europäische Strukturfondsförderung. Ein Vergleich zwischen EU-Mitgliedstaaten* (Opladen: Leske & Budrich).

Helleiner, Eric (1994) *States and the Reemergence of Global Finance. From Bretton Woods to the 1990s* (Ithaca, NY, and London: Cornell University Press).

—— (1995) 'Explaining the Globalization of Financial Markets: Bringing States Back In', *Review of International Political Economy* 2(2): 315–42.

Hemerijck, A.C. (1995) 'Corporatist Immobility in the Netherlands', in C. Crouch and F. Traxler (eds) *Organized Industrial Relations in Europe: What Future?* (Aldershot: Avebury Ashgate).

Hemerijck, A., M. van den Meer and J. Visser (2000) 'Innovation through Co-ordination – Two Decades of Social Pacts in the Netherlands', in G. Fajertag and P. Pochet (eds) *Social Pacts in Europe – New Dynamics* (Brussels: European Trade Union Institute).

Hewson, M. and T.J. Sinclair (eds) (1999) *Approaches to Global Governance Theory* (Albany, NY: State University of New York Press).

Higgins, W. (1985) 'Political Unionism and the Corporatism Thesis', *Economic and Industrial Democracy* 6(3): 349–81.

Higgott, R., G. Underhill and A. Bieler (eds) (1999) *Non-State Actors and Authority in the Global System* (London: Routledge).

High Level Group on Benchmarking (1999) 'First Report by the High Level Group on Benchmarking', *Benchmarking Papers* No. 2 (Brussels: European Commission, Directorate-General III).

Hirsch, Joachim (1995a) *Der nationale Wettbewerbsstaat. Staat, Demokratie und Politik im globalen Kapitalismus* (Berlin: VSA).

Hirsch, Joachim (1995b) 'Nation-state, International Regulation and the Question of Democracy', *Review of International Political Economy* 2(2): 267–84.

Hirst, P. and G. Thompson (1996) *Globalization in Question. The International Economy and the Possibilities of Governance* (Oxford: Polity Press).

Hix, S. (1994) 'The Study of the European Community: The Challenge to Comparative Politics', *West European Politics* 17(1): 1–30.

—— (1999) *The Political System of the European Union* (London: Macmillan).

Hoffman, J. and R. Hoffman (1997) *Globalization. Risks and Opportunities for Labour Policy in Europe*, DWP 97.04.01 E (Brussels: European Trade Union Institute).

Holman, O. (1992) 'Transnational Class Strategy and the New Europe', *International Journal of Political Economy* 22(1): 3–22.

—— (1996) *Integrating Southern Europe: EC Expansion and the Transnationalisation of Spain* (London: Routledge).

Holman, O. and K. van der Pijl (1996) 'The Capitalist Class in the European Union', in G. Kourvetaris and A. Moschonas (eds) *The Impact of European Integration. Political, Sociological and Economic Changes* (London).

Holman, O., H. Overbeek and M. Ryner (eds) (1998) 'Neoliberal Hegemony and the Political Economy of European Restructuring' (2 vols), *International Journal of Political Economy* 28(1) (spring):1–99; and 28(2) (summer): 1–123.

Holmes, M.R. (1985) *The Labour Government, 1974–79: Political Aims and Economic Reality* (Basingstoke: Macmillan).

Hoskyns, Catherine (1996) *Integrating Gender: Women, Law and Politics in the European Union* (London: Verso).

Huber, E. and J.D. Stephens (1998) 'Internationalization and the Social Democratic Model', *Comparative Political Studies* 31(3): 353–97.

—— (1999) *Welfare State and Production Regimes in the Era of Retrenchment*, Occasional Paper One (Princeton, NJ: School of Social Sciences, Institute for Advanced Study).

—— (2001) *Development and Crisis of the Welfare State: Parties and Politics in Global Markets* (Chicago: University of Chicago Press).

Huffschmid, Jörg (1999) *Politische Ökonomie der Finanzmärkte* (Hamburg: VSA).

Hümer, Gerhard, Michael Mesch and Franz Traxler (eds) (1999) *The Role of Employer Associations and Labour Unions in the EMU: Institutional Requirements for European Economic Policies* (Aldershot: Ashgate Publishing).

Huntington, S.P. (1991) 'Transnational Organizations in World Politics', in R. Little and M. Smith (eds) *Perspectives on World Politics*, 2nd edn (London: Routledge); first published 1973.

Hyde, M., J. Dixon and M. Joyner (1999) ' "Work for Those That Can, Security for Those That Cannot": The United Kingdom's New Social Security Reform Agenda', *International Social Security Review* 52(4): 69–86.

Immervoll, H., L. Mitton, C. O'Donoghue and H. Sutherland (1999) 'Budgeting for Fairness? The Distributional Effects of Three Labour Budgets' (Cambridge: Cambridge University Department of Applied Economics); available at http://www.econ.cam.ac.uk/dae/ mu/cathal/32.htm (accessed 10 April 2001).

Irish Presidency (1996) *Die Europäische Union heute und morgen. Anpassung der Europäischen Union zum Nutzen ihrer Bürger und Vorbereitung der Europäischen Union auf die Zukunft. Allgemeiner Rahmen für einen Entwurf zur Revision der Verträge* (Dublin II), CONF 2500/96 (Brussels).

Iriso Napal, P. (1993) *Sistemas de Negociación Colectiva y Acción Sindical. Sindicatos y Trabajadores en la Empresa* (Madrid: Centro de Estudios Avanzados en Ciencias Sociales).

Iversen, T. and A.Wren (1998) 'Equality, Employment, and Budgetary Restraint. The Trilemma of the Service Economy', *World Politics* 50: 507–46.

Iversen, T., J. Pontusson and D. Soskice (eds) (2000) *Unions, Employers and Central Banks. Macroeconomic Coordination and Institutional Change in Social Market Economies* (Cambridge: Cambridge University Press).

Jacquemin, A. and L.R. Pench (eds) (1997) *Europe Competing in the Global Economy*, Reports of the Competitiveness Advisory Group (Aldershot: Edward Elgar).

Jessop, Bob (1990) *State Theory: Putting the Capitalist State in its Place* (Cambridge: Polity).

—— (1993) 'Towards a Schumpeterian Workfare State? Preliminary Remarks on Post-Fordist Political Economy', *Studies in Political Economy* 40(1): 7–39.

—— (1994) 'Post-Fordism and the State', in A. Amin (ed.) *Post Fordism: A Reader* (Oxford: Blackwell).

—— (1995) 'Die Zukunft des Nationalstaats: Erosion oder Reorganisation? Grundsätzliche Überlegungen zu Westeuropa', in *Europäische Integration und politische Regulierung – Aspekte, Dimensionen, Perspektiven*, FEG-Studie Nr. 5 (Marburg).

—— (1998a) 'The Rise of Governance and the Risks of Failure: The Case of Economic Development', *International Social Science Journal* 155: 29–46.

—— (1998b) 'Die Erfahrungen mit New Labour – eine Politik für den Post-fordismus?', in C. Görg and R. Roth (eds) *Kein Staat zu machen. Zur kritischen Sozialwissenschaft* (Münster: Westfälisches Dampfboot).

—— (1999) 'Narrating the Future of the National Economy and the National State? Remarks on Re-mapping Regulation and Re-inventing Governance', in G. Steinmetz (ed.) *STATE/CULTURE: State Formation after the Cultural Turn* (Ithaca, NY: Cornell University Press).

—— (2000a) 'The State and the Contradictions of the Knowledge-Driven Economy', in J.R. Bryson, P.W. Daniels, N.D. Henry and J. Pollard (eds) *Knowledge, Space, Economy* (London: Routledge).

—— (2000b) 'The Crisis of the National Spatio-Temporal Fix and the Ecological Dominance of Globalizing Capitalism', *International Journal of Urban and Regional Studies* 24(2): 273–310.

—— (2000c) 'From Keynesianism to Workfarism', in Gayle Lewis (ed.) *Rethinking Welfare Policy* (London: Sage).

Jessop, B., K. Bonnett and S. Bromley (1990) 'Farewell to Thatcherism? Neo-Liberalism vs New Times', *New Left Review* 179: 81–102.

Jessop, B., K. Bonnett, S. Bromley and T. Ling (1988) *Thatcherism: A Tale of Two Nations* (Cambridge: Polity).

Jimeno, J. and L. Toharia (1992) 'Productivity and Wage Effects of Fixed-term Contracts', Working Paper No. 9211, FEDEA (Fundación de Estudios de Economia Aplicada).

Johansson, Karl Magnus (1999) 'Tracing the Employment Title in the Amsterdam Treaty: Uncovering Transnational Coalitions', *Journal of European Public Policy* 6(1): 85–101.

Jones, M. (1999) *New Institutional Spaces: TECs and the Remaking of Economic Governance* (London: Jessica Kingsley).

Jones, M. and A. Gray (2001) 'Social Capital, or Local Workfarism? Reflections on Employment Zones', *Local Economy* 16(1): 2–10.

Jopp, M. and O. Schmuck (eds) (1996) *Die Reform der Europäischen Union. Analysen Positionen – Dokumente zur Regierungskonferenz 1996/97* (Bonn: Europa Union Verlag).

Jordana, J. (1994) 'Sindicatos y políticas en España: la influencia de las condiciones organizativas en las estrategias sindicales', *Revista Internacional de Sociología* 8–9: 137–86.

Jørgensen, Knud Erik (1999) 'The Social Construction of the Acquis Communautaire: A Cornerstone of the European Edifice', *European Integration Online Papers* 6(5).

Kalecki, M. (1990) 'Political Aspects of Full Employment', in *Collected Works of Michael Kalecki, Volume 1: Capitalism: Business Cycles and Full Employment* (Oxford: Clarendon Press); first published in 1943.

Kaluza, Hildegard (1998) *Der Europäische Sozialfonds. Seine Entwicklung und Funktion im europäischen Integrationsprozeß mit einem Exkurs zu seiner Bedeutung für die bundesdeutsche Arbeitsförderung* (Baden-Baden: Nomos).

Kaplinsky, R. (1984) *Automation: New Technology and Society* (Geneva: ILO).

Keller, Berndt (1999) 'Aktuelle Entwicklungen "europäischer" Beschäftigungspolitik: Vom Weißbuch zum Beschäftigungskapitel', *Sozialer Fortschritt* 6/1999: 141–50.

Keller, B. and B. Sörries (1998) 'Der neue Sozialdialog auf europäischer Ebene: Erfahrungen und Perspektiven', *Mitteilungen aus der Arbeitsmarkt- und Berufsforschung* 31(4): 715–25.

—— (1999) 'Der sektorale soziale Dialog und Europäische Sozialpolitik – erste Empirie und Entwicklungsperspektiven', *Mitteilungen aus der Arbeitsmarkt- und Berufsforschung* 32(1): 118–27.

Keynes, John Maynard (1997) *The General Theory of Employment, Interest, and Money* (New York: Prometheus Books).

Klamer, A. (1990) *Verzuilde dromen. 40 jaar SER* (Amsterdam: Balans).

Kleinknecht, A. (1998) 'Is Labour Market Flexibility Harmful to Innovation?', *Cambridge Journal of Economics* 22: 387–96.

Kloosterman, R. (1994) 'Three Worlds of Welfare Capitalism? The Welfare State and the Post-Industrial Trajectory in the Netherlands after 1980', *West European Politics* 17(4): 166–89.

Kofman, E. (1995) 'Citizenship for Some but not for Others: Spaces of Citizenship in Contemporary Europe', *Political Geography* 14(2): 121–38.

Köhler, Gernot (1999) 'Global Keynesianism and Beyond', *Journal of World-Systems Research* V(2): 253–74.

Kohler-Koch, Beate and Rainer Eising (eds) (1999) *The Transformation of Governance in the European Union* (London and New York: Routledge).

Kok, W. (1985) 'Een maakbare samenleving', *Tijdschrift voor politieke ekonomie* 9(2): 24–34.

König, Heinz (ed.) (1994) *Bringt die EU-Beschäftigungsoffensive den Aufschwung? Die deutsche Wirtschaftsforschung nimmt Stellung zum Delors-Weißbuch*, ZEW Sonderband (Mannheim: ZEW).

Kool, C.J.M., A.P. van Veen, C.G. Koedijk and A. van Witteloostuijn (1998) 'Nederland investeert! Of toch niet?', *Economisch-Statistische Berichten*, 17 April: 318–20.

Knill, Christoph and Dirk Lehmkuhl (1999) 'How Europe Matters: Different Mechanisms of Europeanization', *European Integration Online Papers (EioP)*, vol. 3, no. 7; available at http://www.eiop.or.at/eiop/texte/1999-007a.htm.

Krätke, M. (1997) 'Standortkonkurrenz – Realität und Rhetorik', in: Loccumer Intitiative kritischer Wissenschaftlerinnen und Wissenschaftler, *Ökonomie ohne Arbeit – Arbeit ohne Ökonomie? Entwicklungstendenzen des Kapitalismus und politische Interventionen* (Hannover: Offizin Verlag).

Kratochwil, Friedrich and John Gerard Ruggie (1986) 'International Organization: A State of the Art on an Art of the State', *International Organization* 40: 753–75.

Krieger, H. and D. Fröhlich (1998) 'Gibt es bei den neuen Formen der Arbeitsorganisation in Deutschland eine Modernisierungslücke?', *WSI-Mitteilungen* 51(3): 153–64.

Kuhnle, Stein (1999) 'Survival of the European Welfare State', *Arena Working Paper* 99/19 (Oslo).

Laclau, E. (1977) *Politics and Ideology in Marxist Theory. Capitalism, Fascism, Populism* (London: New Left Books).

Lafontaine, O. (1999) *Das Herz schlägt links* (Munich: Econ-Verlag).

Lafontaine, O. and D. Strauss-Kahn (1999) 'Making the Best of the Euro', available at http://www.germany-info.org/EU/eu-st—01—14—99.htm.

Lange, Peter Michael (1987) *Stato e regolazione sociale: nuove prospettive sul caso italiano*, ed. Peter Lange and Marino Regini (Bologna: Il Mulino).

Lange, Peter and Marino Regini (eds) (1989) *State, Market and Social Regulation: New Perspectives on Italy* (Cambridge : Cambridge University Press).

Lange, P., G. Ross and M. Vannicelli (1982) *Unions, Change and Crisis: French and Italian Union Strategy and the Political Economy* (London: Allen & Unwin).

Lankowski, C. (1982) ' Modell Deutschland and the International Regionalization of the West German State in the 1970s', in A. Markowits (ed.) *The Political Economy of West Germany: Modell Deutschland* (New York: Praeger).

Lasch, Christopher (1996) *The Revolt of the Elites and the Betrayal of Democracy* (New York and London: W.W. Norton).

Lash, S. and L. Urry (1987) *The End of Organised Capitalism* (Cambridge: Polity Press).

Layard, R. (1998) *Tackling Unemployment* (Basingstoke: Macmillan).

Layard, R., S. Nickell and R. Jackman (1991) *Unemployment: Macroeconomic Performance and the Labour Market* (Oxford: Oxford University Press).

Lazonick, W. and M. O'Sullivan (2000) 'Maximizing Shareholder Value: A New Ideology for Corporate Governance', *Economy and Society* 29(1): 13–35.

Leborgne, D. and A. Lipietz (1988) 'New Technology, New Modes of Regulation: Some Spatial Implications', *Environment and Planning D: Society and Space* 6: 263–80.

Leibfried, S. (1993) 'Toward a European Welfare State', in C. Jones (ed.) *New Perspectives on the Welfare State in Europe* (London: Routledge).

Leibfried, S. and P. Pierson (2000) 'Social Policy', in H. Wallace and W. Wallace (eds) *Policy-making in the European Union* (Oxford: Oxford University Press).

Leslie, D., D. Blackaby, S. Drinkwater and P. Murphy (1997) 'Unemployment, Ethnic Minorities and Discrimination', *EUI Working Papers*, RSC No. 97/26.

Levy, J.D. (1999) 'Vice into Virtue? Progressive Politics and Welfare Reform in Continental Europe', *Politics and Society* 27(2): 239–73.

Lewis, G. (1998) ' "Coming Apart at the Seams": The Crises of the Welfare State', in G. Hughes and G. Lewis (eds) *Unsettling Welfare: The Reconstruction of Social Policy* (London: Routledge).

Leys, C. (1989) *Politics in Britain: From Labourism to Thatcherism* (London: Verso).

Lindblom, Charles E. (1975) 'Inkrementalismus: die Lehre vom "Sich-Durchwursteln" ', in W.-D. Narr and C. Offe (eds) *Wohlfahrtsstaat und Massenloyalität* (Cologne: Kiepenheuer & Witsch).

Lipietz, Alain (1985) *Mirages and Miracles* (London: Verso).

—— (1989) 'The Debt Problem, European Integration, and the New Phase of World Crisis', *New Left Review* 178: 37–50.

—— (1996) 'Social Europe: The Post-Maastricht Challenge', *Review of International Political Economy* 3(3): 369–79.

Ljunggren, S. (1993) 'Myt och verklighet i den ekonomiska krisen', *Zenit* 120/121: 12–21.

LO (Landsorganisationen i Sverige) (1997a) *En solidarisk väg* (Stockholm: Landsorganisationen).

—— (1997b) 'Bilaga och mötesmateriel om lönebildning', *LO Tidningen*, 7 February.

—— (1997c) 'LOs yttrande över betänkandet "Sverige och EMU" ', Sweden. Ministry of Finance, *Remissyttranden över betänkandet 'Sverige och EMU' (SOU 1996: 158)*, Ds. 1997, 22.

—— (1997d) *Att tänka Europeiskt – allianser för sysselsättning* (Stockholm: Landsorganisationen).

Loescher, G. (1993) *Beyond Charity. International Cooperation and the Global Refugee Crisis* (Oxford: Oxford University Press).

Lonnroth, J. (1994) 'Global Employment Issues in the Year 2000', *Monthly Labor Review* 117(9): 5–15; available at http://ebsco.pica.nl:8080/cgi-bin/ebsco/afo—9403.sgm/181244044.

Lönnroth, Karl-Johan (1998) 'Die neuesten Entwicklungen in der Europäischen Beschäftigungsstrategie', in *ESF InforRevue* 6/1998: 31–3.

Lund, G. (1996) 'Achieving a High Level of Employment: A Common Task for the European Union', *The Future of the European Union* (Brussels: ETUI).

Lutz, Burkard (1984) *Der kurze Traum immerwährender Prosperität. Eine Neuinterpretation der industriell-kapitalistischen Entwicklung im Europa des 20. Jahrhunderts* (Frankfurt/Main and New York: Campus).

McNamara, Kathleen R. (1998) *The Currency of Ideas. Monetary Politics in the European Union* (Ithaca, NY, and London: Cornell University Press).

Majone, G. (1993) 'The European Community between Social Policy and Social Regulation', *Journal of Common Market Studies* 31(2): 153–70.

Malo de Molina, J. (1987) 'Política de Empleo y Mercado de Trabajo', in *El Debate sobre la Flexibilidad del Mercado de Trabajo* (Madrid: Estudios de la Fundación Fondo para la Investigación Económica y Social).

Mandel, E. (1972) *Der Spätkapitalismus* (Frankfurt: Suhrkamp).

Mandelson, P. (1997) 'Extract from a Speech by the Minister without Portfolio', on 14 August, at the Fabian Society, available at http://www.cabinet-office.gov.uk/seu/index/more.html (accessed 4 March 1998).

Maravall, J.M. (1995) *Los Resultados de la Democracia* (Madrid: Alianza Editorial).

Maravall, J.M. and M. Fraile (1998) 'The Politics of Unemployment. The Spanish Experience in Comparative Perspective', *Centro de Estudios Avanzados en Ciencias Sociales, Estudio/working paper 1998/124*.

Marglin, Stephen and Juliet B. Schor (eds) (1990) *The Golden Age of Capitalism. Reinterpreting the Post-war Experience* (Oxford: Clarendon Press).

Markovits, A. and C. Allen (1984) 'Trade Unions and the Economic Crisis: The West German Case', in P. Gourevitch, A. Markovits, A. Martin and G. Ross *Unions and Economic Crisis* (London: George Allen & Unwin).

Marks, Gary, Liesbet Hooghe and Kermit Blank (1996) 'European Integration from the 1980s: State-Centric v. Multi-level Governance', *Journal of Common Market Studies* 31(4): 473–524.

Martin, A. (1986) 'The Politics of Employment and Welfare: National Policies and International Interdependence', in K. Banting (ed.) *The State and Economic Interests* (Toronto, University of Toronto Press).

—— (2000) 'Social Pacts, Unemployment, and EMU Macroeconomic Policy', European University Institute, EUI–RSC Working Paper 2000/32.

Martin, A and G. Ross (1999) 'In the Line of the Fire: The Europeanization of Labor Representation', in A. Martin and G. Ross (eds) *The Brave New World of European Labor. European Trade Unions at the Millennium* (New York and Oxford: Berghahn Books).

Martín, C. (1997) 'El mercado de trabajo español en perspectiva europea: un panorama', *Papeles de Economía* 72: 2–21.

Martin, C.J. (1995) 'Nature or Nurture? Sources of Firm Preference for National Health Reform', *American Political Science Review* 43(4): 898–915.

Marx, Karl (1953) *Grundrisse der Kritik der Politischen Ökonomie* (Berlin).

Mazier, J. (1982) 'Growth and Crisis: A Marxist Interpretation', in A. Boltho (ed.) *The European Economy: Growth and Crisis* (Oxford: Oxford University Press).

Merkel, W. (1987) *Prima e dopo Craxi: le trasformazioni del PSI* (Padua: Liviana Editrice).

Mesch, M. (1984) 'Einkommenspolitik in Westeuropa 1945–80', *Wirtschaft und Gesellschaft* 10(2): 237–69.

Messner, D. (1997) *The Network Society: Economic Development and International Competitiveness as Problems of Social Governance* (London: Frank Cass).

Meyer, Thomas (1999) 'The Third Way at the Crossroads', *Internationale Politik und Gesellschaft* 3: 294–304.

Michalet, C.A. (1991) 'Global Competition and its Implication for Firms', OECD Technology and Productivity Programme, *Technology and Productivity: The Challenge of Economic Policy* (Paris: OECD).

Michelsen, K. (1997) *Die gescheiterte Transformation des schwedischen Modells*, FEG-Studie Nr. 9 (Marburg).

Michie, Jonathan (1995) 'Unemployment in Europe', in Ash Amin and John Tomaney (eds) *Behind the Myth of European Union. Prospect for Cohesion* (London and New York: Routledge).

Mishra, R. (1999) *Globalisation and the Welfare State* (Cheltenham: Edward Elgar).

Mittelman, J.H. (ed.) (1996) *Globalization: Critical Reflections*, International Political Economy Yearbook vol. 9 (Boulder, CO: Lynne Rienner).

Mjöset, L. (1987) 'Nordic Economic Policies in the 1970s and the 1980s', *International Organization* 41(3): 403–56.

Moravcsik, A. and K. Nicolaïdis (1999) 'Explaining the Treaty of Amsterdam: Interests, Influence, Institutions', *Journal of Common Market Studies* 1/1999: 59–85.

Mossler, K., J. Torége and A. Öström (1999) '120 000 barn berörs av langvarigt socialbidrag', *Statistics Sweden. Välfärdsbulletinen* 2.

Mueller, Frank (1996) 'National Stakeholders in the Global Contest for Corporate Investment', *European Journal of Industrial Relations* 2(3): 345–68.

Murray, R. (1971) 'Internationalization of Capital and the Nation State', *New Left Review* 67: 84–108.

Myles, J. (1994) 'Decline or Impasse? The Current State of the Welfare State', in W. Clement and R. Mahon (eds) *Swedish Social Democracy: A Model in Transition* (Toronto: Canadian Scholars' Press).

Navarro, V. (1998) 'Neoliberalism, "Globalization", Unemployment, Inequalities, and the Welfare State', *International Journal of Health Services* 28(4): 607–82.

Nelson, Barbara (1990) 'The Origins of the Two-Channel Welfare State: Workmen's Compensation and Mothers' Aid', in Linda Gordon (ed.) *Women, the State, and Welfare* (Wisconsin: University of Wisconsin Press).

Nickell, S. (1997) 'Unemployment and Labour Market Rigidities: Europe versus North America', *Journal of Economic Perspectives* 11(3): 55–74.

Notermans, T. (1993) 'The Abdication of Policy Autonomy: Why the Macroeconomic Policy Regime Has Become So Unfavourable to Labor', *Politics & Society* 21: 133–67.

O'Reilly, J. and S .Bothfeld (1996) 'Labour Market Transitions and Part-time Work', *Employment Observatory, Policies*, no. 54: 21–6 (Berlin: European Commission, MISEP).

Obradović, Daniela (1996) 'Policy Legitimacy and the European Union', *Journal of Common Market Studies* 34(2): 191–221.

Obstfeld, M. and G. Peri (1998) 'Regional Non-adjustment and Fiscal Policy', *Economic Policy* 26 (April): 202–57.

OECD (1988) *New Technology in the 1990s: A Socio-Economic Strategy* (Paris: OECD).

—— (1991–9) *OECD Economic Surveys: Germany* (Paris: OECD)

—— (1994) *The OECD Jobs Study* (Paris: OECD)

—— (1995) *The OECD Jobs Study: Implementing the Strategy* (Paris: OECD)

—— (1996a) *Economic Outlook* (December) (Paris: OECD).

—— (1996b) *Employment Outlook 1996* (Paris: OECD).

—— (1997) *Employment Outlook 1997* (Paris: OECD).

—— (1999) *Employment Outlook 1999* (Paris: OECD).

—— (2000a) *Employment Outlook 2000* (Paris: OECD).

—— (2000b) *Economic Outlook 67* (Paris: OECD).

Ohmae, Kenichi (1993) 'The Rise of the Region State', *Foreign Affairs* 72 (spring): 78–87.

Österreich (1997) *Beschäftigungsgipfel. Österreichisches Positionspapier*, 14 November (n.p.).

Ostner, Ilona and Jane Lewis (1995) 'Gender and the Evolution of European Social Policies', in Stephan Leibfried and Paul Pierson (eds) *European Social Policy: Between Fragmentation and Integration* (Washington, DC: Brookings Institution).

Overbeek, H.W. (1990) *Global Capitalism and National Decline: The Thatcher Decade in Perspective* (London: Unwin & Hyman).

—— (ed.) (1993) *Restructuring Hegemony in the Global Political Economy: The Rise of Transnational Neo-liberalism in the 1980s* (London: Routledge).

—— (1998) 'Global Restructuring and Neoliberal Labor-Market Regulation in Europe', in O. Holman, H.W. Overbeek and M. Ryner (eds) 'Neoliberal Hegemony and the Political Economy of European Restructuring', vol. 1, *International Journal of Political Economy* 28(1) (spring): 54–99.

—— (2000) 'Transnational Historical Materialism: Theories of Transnational Class Formation and World Order', in R.P. Palan (ed.) *Global Political Economy. Contemporary Theories* (London: Routledge).

Overbeek, H.W. and K. van der Pijl (1993) 'Restructuring Capital and Restructuring Hegemony: Neo-liberalism and the Unmaking of the Post-war Order', in H.W. Overbeek (ed.) *Restructuring Hegemony in the Global Political Economy: The Rise of Transnational Neo-liberalism in the 1980s* (London: Routledge).

Palan, R. and J. Abbott (with P. Deans) (1996) *State Strategies in the Global Political Economy* (London: Pinter).

Panitch, L. (1979) 'Corporatism in Liberal Democracies', in G. Lehmbruch and P. Schmitter (eds) *Trends Towards Corporatist Intermediation* (London: Sage).

—— (1996) 'Rethinking the Role of the State', in J. Mittelman (ed.) *Globalization: Critical Reflections*, International Political Economy Yearbook vol. 9 (Boulder, CO: Lynne Rienner).

Panitch, L. and C. Leys (1997) *The End of Parliamentary Socialism: From New Left to New Labour* (London: Verso).

Papademetriou, D.G. (1994) 'At a Crossroads: Europe and Migration', in K.A. Hamilton (ed.) *Migration and the New Europe* (Washington, DC: Center for Strategic and International Studies).

Pearce, J. and J. Sutton (1986) *Protection and Industrial Policy in Europe* (London: Routledge & Kegan Paul).

Peck, J. and N. Theodore (2000) 'Beyond "Employability"', *Cambridge Journal of Economics* 24(4): 729–49.

—— (2001) 'Exporting Workfare/Importing Welfare-to-Work: Exploring the Politics of Third Way Policy Transfer', *Political Geography* 20(5): 427–60.

Pellerin, H. and H.W. Overbeek (2001) 'Neo-Liberal Regionalism and the Management of People's Mobility', in Andreas Bieler and A.D. Morton (eds) *Social Forces in the Making of the New Europe. The Restructuring of European Social Relations in the Global Political Economy* (Houndmills: Palgrave).

Pfau-Effinger, Birgit (2000) 'Gender Culture and Social Change in the European Context', in Simon S. Duncan and Birgit Pfau-Effinger (eds) *Gender Work and Culture in the European Union* (London: Routledge).

Philpott, J. (1999) 'Improving Employability and Welfare to Work Policies: A U.K. Perspective', in Bernard Gazier (ed.) *Employability: Concepts and Policies. Report 1998*, Employment Observatory RESEARCH Network (Berlin: IAS).

Pierson, P. (1995) *Dismantling the Welfare State? Reagan, Thatcher and the Politics of Retrenchment* (Cambridge: Cambridge University Press).

Pitruzello, S. (1999) *Decommodification and the Worlds of Welfare Capitalism. A Cluster Analysis* (Florence: European Forum), European University Institute, Seminar Paper WS/90.

Platzer, Hans-Wolfgang (1999) 'Die EU-Sozial- und Beschäftigungspolitik nach Amsterdam: Koordinierte und verhandelte Europäisierung?', *Integration* 22(3): 176–90.

Polanyi, K. (1957) *The Great Transformation: The Economic and Political Origins of Our Time* (Boston, MA: Beacon Press).

Polavieja, J. (1998) 'The Dualisation of Unemployment Risks Class and Insider/Outsider Patterns in the Spanish Labour Market', *Centro de Estudios Avanzados en Ciencias Sociales*, Estudio/working Paper 1998/128.

Polavieja, J. and A. Richards (1997) 'Trade Unions, Unemployment and Working Class Fragmentation in Spain', *Centro de Estudios Avanzados en Ciencias Sociales*, Estudio/working Paper 199/112.

Pollack, M.A. (1998) 'Beyond Left and Right. Neo-liberalism and Regulated Capitalism in the Treaty of Amsterdam, *Working Paper Series in European Studies*, 2/1998, available at http://polyglot.lss.wisc.edu/eur/.

Pontusson, J. (1992a) *The Limits of Social Democracy: Investment Politics in Sweden* (Ithaca, NY: Cornell University Press).

—— (1992b) 'Unions, New Technology and Job Redesign at Volvo and British Leyland', in M. Golden and J. Pontusson (eds) *Bargaining for Change* (Ithaca, NY: Cornell University Press).

Portuguese Presidency (2000) *Employment, Economic Reform and Social Cohesion – Towards a Europe Based on Innovation and Knowledge* Council document 5256/00 (Lisbon).

Poulantzas, N. (1973) *Political Power and Social Classes* (London: New Left Books).

—— (1974) *Les Classes sociales dans le capitalisme aujourd'hui* (Paris: Editions du Seuil).

—— (1978) *State, Power, Socialism* (London: Verso).

Putzhammer, H. (1999) 'Aspekte einer europäischen Beschäftigungspolitik', *Gewerkschaftliche Monatshefte* 50(5): 263–9.

Raisons d'Agir (2000) *Proposals for a Charter for the European Social Movement*, available at www.zeg.org/raison/Charteang.doc.

Ramsay, R. (1998) *Prawn Cocktail Party: The Hidden Power behind New Labour* (London: Vision Books).

Recio, A. (1991) 'La segmentación del mercado de trabajo en España', in F. Miguélez and C. Prieto (eds) *Las Relaciones Laborales en España* (Madrid: Siglo XXI).

Reflexionsgruppe (1995a) *Zwischenbericht des Vorsitzenden der Reflexionsgruppe zur Regierungskonferenz 1996*, SN 509/95 (Reflex 10), 24 August.

—— (1995b) *Bericht der Reflexionsgruppe*, SN 520/1/95 REV 1 (Reflex 21), Brussels, 5 December.

Regini, M. (1981) *I dilemmi del sindacato* (Bologna: Il Mulino).

—— (1995) *Uncertain Boundaries: Construction of European Economies* (Cambridge: Cambridge University Press).

—— (2000) 'Between Deregulation and Social Pacts: The Responses of European Economies to Globalization', *Politics and Society* 28(1): 5–33.

Regini, M. and I. Regalia (1997) 'Employers, Unions and the State: The Resurgence of Concertation in Italy', *West European Politics* 25(1): 210–30.

Reich, R. (1992) *The Work of Nations: Preparing Ourselves for 21st-Century Capitalism* (New York: Random House).

Reuten, G. (1998) 'Loonmatiging levert geen werk op', *Zeggenschap* 4: 8–11.

Rhodes, M. (1997) 'Globalisation, Labour Markets and Welfare States: A Future of "Competitive Corporatism"?', *EUI Working Papers*, No. 97/36.

—— (1998) 'Globalization, Labour Markets and Welfare States: A Future of "Competitive Corporatism"?', in Martin Rhodes and Yves Mény (eds) *The Future of European Welfare: A New Social Contract?* (Houndmills: Macmillan).

—— (2001) 'The Political Economy of Social Pacts: "Competitive Corporatism" and European Welfare Reform', in P. Pierson (ed.) *The New Politics of the Welfare State* (Oxford: Oxford University Press).

Riemer, J. (1982) 'Alterations in the Design of Model Germany: Critical Innovations in the Policy Machinery for Economic Steering', in A. Markovits (ed.) *The Political Economy of West Germany: Modell Deutschland* (New York: Praeger),

Rifkin, Jeremy (1995) *The End of Work. The Decline of the Global Labor Force and the Dawn of the PostMarket Era* (New York: Putnam Publishing).

Robinson, P. (2000) 'Active Labour-Market Policies: A Case of Evidence-Based Policy-Making?', *Oxford Economic Policy Review* 16(1): 13–26.

Rojo, L.A. (1987) 'La Crisis de la Economía Española, 1973–1984', in J. Nadal *et al. La Economía Española en el Siglo XX. Una Perspectiva Histórica* (Barcelona: Ariel).

Rokkan, S. (1978) 'Dimensions of State Formation and Nation-Building: A Possible Paradigm for Research on Variations within Europe', in C. Tilly (ed.) *The Formation of National States in Western Europe* (Princeton, NJ: Princeton University Press).

—— (1999) *State Formation, Nation-Building and Mass Politics in Europe: The Theory of Stein Rokkan* (Oxford: Oxford University Press).

Rosamond, Ben (1999) 'Discourses of Globalization and the Social Construction of European Identities', *Journal of European Public Policy* 6(4): 652–68.

Ross, George (1995a) 'Assessing of the Delors Era and Social Policy', in Stephan Leibfried and Paul Pierson (eds) *European Social Policy. Between Fragmentation and Integration* (Washington, DC: Brookings Institution).

—— (1995b) *Jacques Delors and European Integration* (Cambridge: Polity Press).

Rossilli, Mariagrazia (1997) 'The European Community's Policy on the Equality of Women: From the Treaty of Rome to the Present', *European Journal of Women's Studies* 4(1): 63–82.

Roth, Christian (1998) 'Beschäftigung', in J. Bergmann and C. Lenz (eds) *Der Amsterdamer Vertrag. Eine Kommentierung der Neuerungen des EU- und EG-Vertrags* (Cologne: Omnia).

Roth, Christian and Josef Schmid (2000) *Multi-level Governance in the European Employment and Labour Market Policy. A Conceptual Outline and Some Empirical Evidence*, Working Paper, *German Policy Sudies* 1/2000; available at http://www.uni-tuebingen.de/uni/spi/schromlg.htm (accessed 16 June 2002).

Rothstein, B. (1986) *Den socialdemokratiska staten* (Lund: Arkiv).

Rubery, Jill (1998) *Equity and Employment: Complementary or Competitive Objectives of European Policy?*, paper presented to the IAFFE Conference, University of Amsterdam, 2–5 June.

Rubery, Jill, Mark Smith, Colette Fagan and Damian Grimshaw (1998) *Women and European Employment* (New York and London: Routledge).

Ruggie, J.G. (1982) 'International Regimes, Transactions, and Change: Embedded Liberalism in the Postwar Economic Order', *International Organization* 36(2): 379–415.

—— (1998) *Constructing the World Polity: Essays on International Institutionalization* (New York: Routledge).

Ruigrok, W. and R. van Tulder (1995) *The Logic of International Restructuring* (London and New York: Routledge).

—— (1996) 'The Price of Diversity: Rival Concepts of Control as a Barrier to an EU Industrial Strategy', in P. Devine, Y. Katsoulacos and R. Sugden (eds) *Competitiveness, Subsidiarity, and Industrial Policy* (London: Routledge).

Rustin, M. (1998) 'The New Labour Project', *Soundings* 8: 7–14.

Ryner, M. (1999) 'Neoliberal Globalization and the Crisis of Swedish Social Democracy', *Economic and Industrial Democracy* 20(1): 39–79.

—— (2000) 'Der neue Diskurs über den "Dritten Weg": Zur Dynamik des sozialdemokratischen Neoliberalismus', in Hans-Jürgen Bieling and Jochen Steinhilber (eds) *Die Konfiguration Europas. Dimensionen einer kritischen Integrationstheorie* (Münster: Westfälisches Dampfboot).

—— (2002) *Capitalist Restructuring, Globalisation and the Third Way: Lessons from the Swedish Model* (London: Routledge).

Sabatier, Paul A.(1993) 'Advocacy-Koalitionen, Policy-Wandel und Policy-Lernen: Eine Alternative zur Phasenheuristik', in A. Heritiér (ed.) *Policy-Analyse. Kritik und Neuorientierung*, PVS-Sonderheft 24 (Opladen: Westdeutscher Verlag).

Salvati, M. (1984) *Economia e politica in Italia dal dopoguerra ad oggi* (Milan: Garzanti).

Salverda, W. (1999) 'Polderblijheid, polderblindheid', *Economisch-Statistische Berichten*, 26 March: 224–9.

Sandberg, A. (1994) ' "Volvoism" at the End of the Road?', *Studies in Political Economy* 45: 160–80.

Sandberg, A., A.G. Broms, A. Grip, L. Sundström and J. Steen (1992) *Technological Change and Co-Determination in Sweden* (Philadelphia: Temple University Press).

Sandholtz, W. (1993) 'Choosing Union: Monetary Politics and Maastricht', *International Organization* 47(1): 1–39.

Sandholtz, W. and A. Stone Sweet (1998) *European Integration and Supranational Governance* (Oxford: Oxford University Press).

Sandholtz, Wayne and John Zysman (1989) '1992: Recasting the European Bargain', *World Politics* 42: 95–128.

Sassen, S. (1991) *The Global City: New York, London and Tokyo* (Princeton, NJ: Princeton University Press).

—— (1996) *Transnational Economies and National Migration Policies* (Amsterdam: IMES).

—— (1998a) 'Zur Einbettung des Globalisierungsprozesses: Der Nationalstaat vor neuen Aufgaben', *Berliner Journal für Soziologie* 3/1998: 345–57.

—— (1998b) *Globalization and Its Discontents* (New York: New Press).

Sassoon, Donald (1996) *One Hundred Years of Socialism. The West European Left in the Twentieth Century* (New York: New Press).

Sayer, A. (1992) *Method in Social Science*, 2nd edn (London: Routledge).

Sbragia, A. (2000) ' The European Union as Coxswain: Governance by Steering', in J. Pierre (ed.) *Debating Governance: Authority, Steering, and Democracy* (Oxford: Oxford University Press).

Scharpf, F.W. (1999) *Governing in Europe: Effective and Democratic?* (Oxford: Oxford University Press).

Schmid, G. (1997) 'Beschäftigungswunder Niederlande?', *Leviathan* 25(3): 302–37.

—— (1998) *Transitional Labour Markets: A New European Employment Strategy* (Berlin: Wissenschaftszentrum Berlin), Working Paper FS I 98–206.

Schmidt, E. (1971) *Ordnungsfaktor oder Gegenmacht. Die politische Rolle der Gewerkschaften* (Frankfurt/Main: Suhrkamp).

Schmitter, P. (1991) The European Community as an Emergent and Novel Form of Political Domination, *Estudio / Working Paper* 1991/26, CEACS (Madrid: Fundacion Juan March).

Schmitter, P.C. and J.R.Grohe (1997) 'Der korporatistische Sisyphus: Vergangenheit, Gegenwart und Zukunft', *Politische Vierteljahresschrift* 38(3): 530–54.

Schröder, Gerhard and Tony Blair (1999) *Der Weg nach vorn für Europas Sozialdemokraten*, available at http://spd.de.

Schröder, Wolfgang (1994) 'Wege aus der Beschäftigungskrise. Beschäftigungspolitische Ansätze in der EU', *WSI-Mitteilungen* 6/1994: S. 390–400.

Schulten, Thorsten (1996) *'European Works Councils' – New Forms of European Labour Relations Regulation*, FEG-Arbeitspapier No. 14 (Marburg).

—— (1998) 'Perspektiven nationaler Kollektivvertragsbeziehungen im integrierten Europa', in Beate Kohler-Koch (ed.) *Regieren in entgrenzten Räumen*, PVS-Sonderheft 29 (Opladen: Westdeutscher Verlag).

—— (1999a) 'New Forms of Work Organisation in Germany', *EIROnline*, March, available at www.eiro.eurofound.ie/1999/03/Features/de9903288f.html.

—— (1999b) 'Lohnzurückhaltung – Grundlage für eine solidarische Lohn- und Beschäftigungspolitik in Europa? Erfahrungen aus Deutschland und den Niederlanden im Vergleich', *Sozialismus* 10: 38–41.

Schulten, T. and R. Bispinck (eds) (1999) *Tarifpolitik unter dem Euro* (Hamburg: VSA-Verlag).

Schulten, T. and A. Stückler (2000) 'Lohnpolitik in Europa', *WSI Informationen zur Tarifpolitik*, October (Düsseldorf).

Schumann, M. (1998) 'Frißt die Shareholder Value- Ökonomie die Modernisierung der Arbeit?', in H. Hirsch-Kreinsen and H. Wolf (eds) *Arbeit, Gesellschaft , Kritik – Orientierungen wider den Zeitgeist* (Berlin: Sigma).

Schwartz, H. (2001) 'The Danish "Miracle": Luck, Pluck or Stuck?', *Comparative Political Studies* 34(2): 131–55.

SCP (Sociaal Cultureel Planbureau) (1996) *Sociale en Culturele Verkenningen 1995* (Rijswijk: Sociaal en Cultureel Planbureau).

—— (1998) *Sociaal en Cultureel Rapport 1998* (Rijswijk: Sociaal en Cultureel Planbureau).

—— (1999) *Sociale en Culturele Verkenningen 1998* (Rijswijk: Sociaal en Cultureel Planbureau).

—— (2000) *Sociaal en Cultureel Rapport 2000. Nederland in Europa* (Rijswijk: Sociaal en Cultureel Planbureau).

Seeleib-Kaiser, M (n.d.) 'Globalization and the Re-commodification of the workforce', in Forschungsgruppe Europäische Gemeinschaften (FEG), Studie Nr. 10, *Labour Markets and Employment Policy in the European Union* (Marburg: Philipps-Universitaet Marburg).

Segura, J., F. Durán, L. Toharia and S. Bentolila (1991) *Análisis de la contratación temporal en España*. (Madrid: Ministerio de Trabajo y Seguridad Social).

Senker, P. (1989) 'Technical Change, Work Organization and Training', *New Technology, Work and Employment* 4 (1): 46–53.

SER (Sociaal Economische Raad) (1998) *Socio-economic Policy 1998–2002* (The Hague: Social and Economic Council).

Shaw, Jo (1999) 'Constitutional Settlements and the Citizen after the Treaty of Amsterdam', in Karlheinz Neunreither and Antje Wiener (eds) *European Integration After Amsterdam* (Oxford: Oxford University Press).

Shepley, S. and J. Wilmont (1995) 'Core vs. Periphery', in A. Amin and J. Tomaney (eds) *Behind the Myth of European Union* (London: Routledge).

Shonfield, A. (1965) *Modern Capitalism* (Oxford: Oxford University Press).

Simai, M. (ed.) (1995a) *Global Employment. An International Investigation into the Future of Work*, 2 vols (London and Tokyo: Zed Books and United Nations University Press).

—— (1995b) 'Employment and the Internationalization of the Labour Markets', in M. Simai (ed.) *Global Employment. An International Investigation into the Future of Work*, vol. 1 (London and Tokyo: Zed Books and United Nations University Press).

Singer, J.D. (1961) 'The Level of Analysis Problem', *World Politics* 14(1): 77–92.

Smith, Joan (1997) 'The Ideology of "Family and Community": New Labour Abandons the Welfare State, *The Socialist Register 1997* (London: Merlin Press).

Smith, W. Rand (1998) *The Left's Dirty Job. The Politics of Industrial Restructuring in France and Spain* (Pittsburgh: University of Pittsburgh Press).

Smulders, P. and J. Klein Hesselink (1997) 'Nederland lang geen koploper flexibilisering', *Economisch-Statistische Berichten*, 19 November: 888–90.

Soskice, D. (1999a) 'Divergent Production Regimes: Coordinated and Uncoordinated Market Economies in the 1980s and 1990s', in H. Kitschelt, P. Lange, G. Marks and J.D. Stephens (eds) *Continuity and Change in Contemporary Capitalism* (Cambridge: Cambridge University Press).

—— (1999b) *The Political Economy of EMU. Rethinking the Effects of Monetary Integration on Europe*, Discussion Paper, Wissenschaftszentrum Berlin (WZB), FS I 99–302.

—— (2000) 'Macroeconomic Analysis and the Political Economy of Unemployment', in T. Iversen, J. Pontusson and D. Soskice (eds) *Unions, Employers, and Central Banks. Macroeconomic Coordination and Institutional Change in Social Market Economies* (Cambridge: Cambridge University Press).

SPE-ECOFIN-Gruppe (1998) 'Der neue europäische Weg. Die Wirtschaftsreform im Rahmen der Wirtschafts- und Währungsunion', October.

Stalker, P. (2000) *Workers Without Frontiers. The Impact of Globalization on International Migration* (Boulder, CO: Lynne Rienner).

Standing, G. (1988) *Unemployment and Labour Market Flexibility: Sweden* (Geneva: ILO).

—— (1999) *Global Labour Flexibility. Seeking Distributive Justice* (London: Macmillan).

Statistics Sweden (1998) 'Ökade inkomster och ojämnare fördelning 1996', *Pressmeddelande fran SCB* 1998: 100.

—— (2000) 'Arbetsinkomst för helårs- och heltidsanställda individer'; available at www.scb.se/befolvalfard/inkomster/hink/hinktab2.asp.

Steinhilber, Jochen (2000) *Die 'Grande Nation' und das 'Haus Europa'. Frankreichs widersprüchlicher Entwicklungsweg* (Hamburg: VSA).

Stella, D. (2000) 'Globalization, Think Tanks and Policy Transfer', in D. Stone (ed.) *Banking on Knowledge: The Genesis of the Global Development Network* (London: Routledge).

Stichting van de Arbeid (1993) *A New Course. Agenda for the 1994 Negotiations on Collective Labour Agreements in a Medium-term Perspective* (The Hague: Stichting van de Arbeid).

Strange, S. (1989) *Casino Capitalism*, 2nd edn (Oxford: Basil Blackwell).

Streeck, W. (1989) 'Skills and the Limits of Neo-Liberalism: The Enterprise of the Future as a Place of Learning', *Work, Employment and Society* 3(1): 89–104 (Cologne).

—— (1994) 'Pay Restraint without Incomes Policy: Institutionalized Monetarism and Industrial Unionism in Germany', in R. Boyer and R. Dore (eds) *The Return to Incomes Policy* (London: Pinter).

—— (1995a) From Market Making to State Building? Reflections on the Political Economy of European Social Policy', in S. Leibfried and P. Pierson (eds) *European Social Policy: Between Fragmentation and Integration* (Washington, DC: Brookings Institution).

—— (1995b) 'Politikverflechtung und Entscheidungslücke: Zum Verhältnis von zwischenstaatlichen Beziehungen und sozialen Interessen im Europäischen Binnenmarkt', in Karlheinz Benetele, Bernd Reissert and Ronald Schettkat (eds) *Die Reformfähigkeit von Industriegesellschaften* (Frankfurt/Main and New York: Campus).

—— (1995c) *German Capitalism: Does it Exist? Can it Survive*, Max Planck Institut für Gesellschaftsforschung. Discussion Paper 1995(5).

—— (1998a) 'Vom Binnenmarkt zum Bundesstaat?, Überlegungen zur politischen Ökonomie der europäischen Sozialpolitik', in Stephan Leibfried and Paul Pierson (eds) *Standort Europa, Sozialpolitik zwischen Nationalstaat und Europäischer Integration* (Frankfurt/Main: Suhrkamp).

—— (1998b) *The Internationalization of Industrial Relations in Europe: Prospects and Problems*, MPIfG Discussion Paper 98/2 (Cologne: Max Planck Institute for the Study of Societies).

—— (1999) *Competitive Solidarity: Rethinking the 'European Social Model'*, MPIfG Working Paper 99/8 (Cologne: Max Planck Institute for the Study of Societies).

—— (2000) 'Competitive Solidarity: Rethinking the "European Social Model" ', in Karl Hinrichs, Herbert Kitschelt and Helmut Wiesenthal (eds) *Kontingenz und Krise. Institutionenpolitik in kapitalistischen Gesellschaften. Claus Offe zu seinem 60. Geburtstag* (Frankfurt and New York: Campus).

Stuurman, S. (ed.) *Socialisten in No Nonsense tijd* (Nijmegen: SUN).

Summers, L. (1990) *Understanding Unemployment* (Cambridge, MA: MIT Press).

Sweden (1995) *Strengthening the Fight Against Unemployment – an Issue for the Intergovernmental Conference* 1 (September).

Sweden, Ministry of Foreign Affairs (1997) *Berättelse om verksamheten i den Europeiska unionen under 1996* Skr. 1996/97: 80.

Swenson, P. (1989) *Fair Shares: Unions, Pay and Politics in Sweden and West Germany* (Ithaca, NY: Cornell University Press.)

Suda, Z. (ed.) (1994) *The Globalization of Labor Markets. A Challenge to the Social Contract* (Prague: European Institute of Education and Social Policy).

Symes, Valerie (1997) 'Unemployment in Europe: A Continuing Crisis', in Valerie Symes, Carl Levy and Jane Littlewood (eds) *The Future of Europe. Problems and Issues for the Twenty-First Century* (London: Macmillan Press).

Tabaksblat, M. (2000) *How to Achieve What is Set Out in Lisbon*, Speech at the European Business Summit, Brussels, 10 June, available at http://www.ert.be/pd/pdc/endc03thml (accessed 13 January 2001).

Talani, L.S. (2000) *Betting for and Against EMU* (London: Ashgate).

Teague, Paul (1994) 'Between New Neynesianism and Deregulation: Employment Policy in the European Union', *Journal of European Public Policy* 1(3): 315–45.

—— (1998) 'Monetary Union and Social Europe', *Journal of European Social Policy* 8(2): 117–37

—— (1999a) 'Reshaping Employment Regimes in Europe: Policy Shifts Alongside Boundary Change', *Journal of Public Policy* 1: 33–62.

—— (1999b) *Economic Citizenship in the European Union. Employment Relations in the New Europe* (London and New York: Routledge).

Teeple, G. (1995) *Globalization and the Decline of Social Reform* (Toronto: Garamont Press).

Theobald, Hildegard (1999) *Geschlecht, Qualifikation und Wohlfahrtsstaat. Deutschland und Schweden im Vergleich* (Berlin: Sigma).

Theodore, N. and J. Peck (1999) 'Welfare-to-Work: National Problems, Local Solutions?', *Critical Social Policy* 19 (4): 485–510.

Therborn, G. (1986) *Why Some Peoples are More Unemployed Than Others. The Strange Paradox of Growth and Unemployment* (London: Verso).

Therborn, G. and W. Koole (1989) 'De Casablanca-solution voorbij. De merkwaardige dood van het keynesianisme en de relatieve verpaupering van Nederland', in P. Fortuijn and S. Stuurman *Socialisten in no nonsense-tijd* (Nijmegen: SUN).

Tidow, Stefan (1996) *Zur Krise des 'Modell Österreich'. Korporatistische Regulierung im Umbruch*, FEG-Studie Nr. 8 (Universität Marburg).

—— (1998) *Europäische Beschäftigungspolitik. Die Entstehung eines neuen Politikfeldes: Ursachen, Hintergründe und Verlauf des politischen Prozesses*, FEG-Arbeitspapier Nr. 18 (Marburg).

—— (1999) 'Benchmarking als Leitidee. Zum Verlust des Politischen in der europäischen Perspektive', *Blätter für deutsche und internationale Politik* 3: 301–9.

—— (2000) 'Europäische Beschäftigungspolitik im Wandel der Integrationsprojekte', in Hans-Wolfgang Platzer (ed.) *Arbeitsmarkt- und Beschäftigungspolitik in der EU. Nationale und europäische Perspektiven* (Baden-Baden: Nomos).

Tietmeyer, Hans (1996) *Die europäische Wirtschaft zwischen globalen Märkten und Internen Herausforderungen*, Jean Monnet Lecture, European University Institute, 28 November, available at http://www.iue.it/ANN/tietspeechDE.html.

Tomlinson, J. (1985) *British Macroeconomic Policy since 1940* (London: Croom Helm).

Tömmel, I. (1994) 'Interessenartikulation und transnationale Politikkooperation im Rahmen der EU', in V. Eichener and H. Voelkoz (eds) *Europäische Integration und verbändliche Regulierung* (Marburg: Metropolis).

—— (1995) 'Die Europäische Integration: ökonomische Regulierung und Politikgestaltung zwischen Staat und Markt', in Bob Jessop, Ingeborg Tömmel, Bernd Röttger, Anja Bultemeijer, Frank Deppe, Thorsten Schulte, Nikos Kotzias, Hans-Jürgen Bieling *Europäische Integration und politische Regulierung – Aspekte, Dimensionen, Perspektiven*, FEG-Studie No. 5 (Marburg).

—— (1998) 'Transformation of Governance: the European Commission's Strategy for Creating a "Europe of the Regions" ', *Regional and Federal Studies* 8(2): 52–80.

—— (2000) 'Jenseits von regulativ und distributiv', in Edgar Grande and Markus Jachtenfuchs (eds) *Wie problemlösungsfähig ist die EU?* (Baden-Baden: Nomos).

Traxler, Franz (1995) 'Vom Nachfrage- zum Angebotskorporatismus? Sozialpartnerschaftliche Stabilitätsbedingungen im Wandel', in Emmerich Tálos (ed.) *Sozialpartnerschaft. Kontinuität und Wandel* (Vienna: Verlag für Gesellschaftskritik).

—— (2000) 'National Pacts and Wage Regulation in Europe', in G. Fajertag and P. Pochet (eds) *Social Pacts in Europe – New Dynamics* (Brussels: European Trade Union Institute).

Tronti, Leonello (ed.) (1998) *Benchmarking Employment Performance and Labour Market Policies. Final Report 1997*, European Commission, Employment Observatory – RESEARCH Network (Berlin: IAS Berlin).

Tsoukalis, Loukas (1997) *The New European Economy Revisited* (Oxford: Oxford University Press).

Turner, L. (1996) 'The Europeanization of Labour: Structure before Action', *European Journal of Industrial Relations* 2(2): 325–44.

UNCTAD (1994) *Transnational Corporations, Employment and the Workplace. An Executive Summary* (New York and Geneva: United Nations).

—— (1993) *World Investment Report* (Geneva: United Nations).

—— (1997) *World Investment Report* (Geneva: United Nations).

—— (1998) *World Investment Report* (Geneva: United Nations).

—— (2001) *World Investment Report* (Geneva: United Nations).

—— (2002) *World Investment Report* (Geneva: United Nations).

Unger, Frank, Andreas Wehr and Karen Schönwälder (1998) *New Democrats, New Labour, Neue Sozialdemokraten* (Berlin: Elefanten Press).

UNHCR (1997) *The State of the World's Refugees. A Humanitarian Agenda* (Oxford: Oxford University Press).

Uterwedde, Henrik (2000) 'Frankreichs Beschäftigungspolitik: alte und neue Antworten', in Hans-Wolfgang Platzer (ed.) *Arbeitsmarkt- und Beschäftigungspolitik in der EU* (Baden-Baden: Nomos).

Valdés Dal-Ré, F. (1985) 'Flexibilidad en el mercado de trabajo y ordenamiento laboral', *Papeles de Economía Española* 22: 302–15.

van Apeldoorn, B. (1998) 'Transnationalization and the Restructuring of Europe's Socio-economic Order', *International Journal of Political Economy* 28(1): 12–53.

—— (2000) 'Transnational Class Agency and European Governance: The Case of the European Round Table of Industrialists', *New Political Economy* 5(2): 157–81.

—— (2001) *Globalisation, European Integration, and the Transformation of European Corporate Governance: The Rise of a European Shareholder Capitalism*, paper presented at the Annual Convention of the European Community Studies Association (ECSA), Madison, Wisconsin, 31 May–2 June.

—— (2002) *Transnational Capitalism and the Struggle over European Integration* (London and New York: Routledge).

van Apeldoorn, B., H. Overbeek and M. Ryner (2003) 'Theories of European Integration: A Critique', in A. Cafruny and M. Ryner (eds) *A Ruined Fortress? Neoliberal Hegemony and Transformation in Europe* (Lanham, MD: Rowman & Littlefield).

van der Horst, H. (1994) *The Low Sky. Understanding the Dutch* (Amsterdam: Scriptum).

van der Pijl, K. (1984) *The Making of an Atlantic Ruling Class* (London: Verso).

—— (1989) 'Ruling Classes, Hegemony, and the State System: Theoretical and Historical Considerations', in K. van der Pijl (ed.) *Transnational Relations and Class Strategy*, *International Journal of Political Economy* 19(3) (fall): 7–35.

—— (1998) *Transnational Classes and International Relations* (London and New York: Routledge).

van der Ploeg, F. (1997) 'The Political Economy of a Consensus Society: Experience from Behind the Dykes', *Economic and Social Review* 28(4): 307–32.

van der Wurff, R. (1993) 'Neo-liberalism in Germany? The "Wende" in Perspective', in H.W. Overbeek (ed.) *Restructuring Hegemony in the Global Political Economy: The Rise of Transnational Neo-liberalism in the 1980s* (London: Routledge).

van Empel, F. (1997) *The Dutch Model. The Power of Consultation in the Netherlands* (The Hague: Stichting van de Arbeid).

van Witteloostuijn, A. (2000) 'Nieuwe Economie en oude wetten', *De Academische Boekengids* 21: 12–16.

Vannicelli, M. (1984) *A Labor Movement in Search of a Role: The Evolution of the Strategy of the Italian Unions since 1943*, Harvard University, PhD thesis.

Vendrik, K. (1995) 'De kunst van het publieke debat', in K. van Kersbergen and I.M.A.M. Pröpper (eds) *Politiek debat en democratie* (The Hague: SDU).

Visser, J. (2000) 'From Keynesianism to the Third Way: Labour Relations and Social Policy in Postwar Western Europe', *Economic and Industrial Democracy* 21(4): 421–56.

Visser, J. and A. Hemerijck (1997) *'A Dutch Miracle'. Job Growth, Welfare Reform and Corporatism in the Netherlands* (Amsterdam: Amsterdam University Press).

Vobruba, G. (1995) 'Social Policy on Tomorrow's Euro-Corporatist Stage', *Journal of European Social Policy* 5(4): 303–15.

von Hayek, F.A. (1991a) '1980s Unemployment and the Unions', in F.A. von Hayek *Economic Freedom* (Oxford and Cambridge, MA.: Basil Blackwell).

—— (1991b) 'Full Employment at Any Price?', in F.A. von Hayek *Economic Freedom* (Oxford and Cambridge, MA: Basil Blackwell).

Vos, C.J. (1990) 'Keertijd of continuiteit? De Nederlandse arbeidsverhoudingen in de jaren tachtig', *Tijdschrift voor arbeidsvraagstukken* 6(4): 60–71.

Wacquant, L. (1997) 'Vom Wohltätigen Staat zum strafenden Staat: Über den politischen Umgang mit dem Elend in Amerika', *Leviathan* 1: 50–66.

Walby, Sylvia (1997) *Gender Transformations* (London and New York: Routledge).

—— (1999) 'Changes in Women's Employment in the United Kingdom', *New Political Economy* 4(2): 195–213.

Wallace, H. (2000) 'The Institutional Setting: Five Variations on a Theme', in H. Wallace and W. Wallace (eds) *Policy-making in the European Union* (Oxford: Oxford University Press).

Wallerstein, I. (1974) *The Modern World-System I. Capitalist Agriculture and the Origins of the European World-Economy in the Sixteenth Century* (New York: Academic Press).

—— (1983) *Historical Capitalism* (London: Verso Books).

—— (1993) 'World Systems Versus World-Systems. A Critique', in A.G. Frank and B.K. Gills (eds) *The World System. Five Hundred Years or Five Thousand?* (London: Routledge).

Watson, Gregory H. (1993) *Benchmarking: Vom Besten lernen* (Landsberg/Lech: Verlag Moderne Industrie).

Weidenfeld, Werner (ed.) (1998) *Amsterdam in der Analyse. Strategien für Europa* (Gütersloh: Verlag Bertelsmann Stiftung).

Weiler, J.H.H. (1997) 'The Reformation of European Constitutionalism', *Journal of Common Market Studies* 35(1): 97–131.

Welzmüller, R. (1999) 'Europäische Währungsunion und Beschäftigungspolitik', in T. Schulten and R. Bispinck (eds) *Tarifpolitik unter dem Euro* (Hamburg: VSA-Verlag).

Wendt, Alexander (1992) 'Anarchy is What States Make of It: The Social Construction of Power Politics', *International Organization* 46: 391–407.

—— (1998) 'On Constitution and Causation in International Relations', in Tim Dunne, Michael Cox and Ken Booth (eds) *The Eighty Years' Crisis: International Relations 1919–1999* (Cambridge: Cambridge University Press).

Wilding, P. (1997) 'Globalization, Regionalization and Social Policy', *Social Policy and Administration* 31 (4): 410–28.

Willke, H. (1992) *Ironie des Staates. Grundlinien einer Staatstheorie ployzentrischer Gesellschaften* (Frankfurt: Suhrkamp).

—— (1996) *Ironie des Staates* (Frankfurt: Suhrkamp).

Wilthagen, Tom (1998) 'Flexicurity: A New Paradigm for Labour Market Policy Reform?' (Berlin: Wissenschaftszentrum Berlin), Working Paper FS I 98–202.

Wolinetz, S. (1989) 'Socio-Economic Bargaining in the Netherlands: Redefining the Post-War Policy Coalition', *West European Politics* 12(1): 79–98.

World Bank (1997) *World Development Report* (Washington, DC: World Bank).

—— (2002) *World Development Report* (Washington, DC: World Bank).

Wright Mills, C. (1971) *The New Men of Power* (New York: Kelley).

Young, Brigitte (2000) 'Disciplinary Neoliberalism in the European Union and Gender Politics', *New Political Economy* 5(1): 77–98.

—— (2001a) 'The "Mistress" and the "Maid" in the Globalized Economy', in *The Socialist Register 2001* (London: Merlin Press).

—— (2001b) 'Globalization and Gender: A European Perspective', in Rita Mae Kelly, Jane Bayes, Mary Hawkesworth and Brigitte Young (eds) *Gender, Globalization and Democratization* (Lanham, MD: Rowman & Littlefield Publishers).

Ziebura, Gilbert (1992) 'Nationalstaat, Nationalismus, supranationale Integration: Der Fall Frankreich', *Leviathan* 4: 467–89.

Ziltener, P. (2000) 'EC Social Policy: The Defeat of the Delorist Project', in V. Bornschier (ed.) *State-building in Europe: The Revitalization of Western European Integration* (Cambridge: Cambridge University Press).

Zolberg, A.R., A. Suhrke and S. Aguayo (1989) *Escape from Violence. Conflict and the Refugee Crisis in the Developing World* (Oxford: Oxford University Press).

Zysman, J. (1983) *Governments, Markets and Growth* (Ithaca, NY: Cornell University Press).

Index

Note: Where a page number is followed by an '*n*' the reference is to a footnote; where followed by an '*f*' it indicates a figure; and where followed by a '*t*' it indicates a table.